Foundations of Mac OS X Leopard Security

Charles S. Edge, Jr., William Barker, and Zack Smith

Apress®

FOUNDATIONS OF MAC OS X LEOPARD SECURITY

Copyright © 2008 by Charles S. Edge, Jr., William Barker

ISBN-13 (pbk): 978-1-59059-989-1

ISBN-10 (pbk): 1-59059-989-6

ISBN-13 (electronic): 978-1-4302-0646-0

ISBN-10 (electronic): 1-4302-0646-2

Printed and bound in the United States of America 9 8 7 6 5 4 3 2 1

Trademarked names may appear in this book. Rather than use a trademark symbol with every occurrence of a trademarked name, we use the names only in an editorial fashion and to the benefit of the trademark owner, with no intention of infringement of the trademark.

Lead Editor: Jeffrey Pepper
Technical Reviewers: Mike Lee, Frank Pohlmann
Editorial Board: Clay Andres, Steve Anglin, Ewan Buckingham, Tony Campbell, Gary Cornell, Jonathan Gennick, Matthew Moodie, Joseph Ottinger, Jeffrey Pepper, Frank Pohlmann, Ben Renow-Clarke, Dominic Shakeshaft, Matt Wade, Tom Welsh
Project Manager: Candace English
Copy Editor: Kim Wimpsett
Associate Production Director: Kari Brooks-Copony
Senior Production Editor: Laura Cheu
Compositor: Susan Glinert Stevens
Proofreader: Nancy Bell
Indexer: Julie Grady
Cover Designer: Kurt Krames
Manufacturing Director: Tom Debolski

Distributed to the book trade worldwide by Springer-Verlag New York, Inc., 233 Spring Street, 6th Floor, New York, NY 10013. Phone 1-800-SPRINGER, fax 201-348-4505, e-mail orders-ny@springer-sbm.com, or visit http://www.springeronline.com.

For information on translations, please contact Apress directly at 2855 Telegraph Avenue, Suite 600, Berkeley, CA 94705. Phone 510-549-5930, fax 510-549-5939, e-mail info@apress.com, or visit http://www.apress.com.

Apress and friends of ED books may be purchased in bulk for academic, corporate, or promotional use. eBook versions and licenses are also available for most titles. For more information, reference our Special Bulk Sales–eBook Licensing web page at http://www.apress.com/info/bulksales.

This book is dedicated to my loving wife, Lisa.
—*Charles*

To my family and friends, who incessantly inspire me to follow my dreams.
—*William*

Contents at a Glance

PART 1 ▪▪▪ The Big Picture

PART 2 ▪▪▪ Security Essentials

PART 3 ▪▪▪ Network Security

PART 4 ▪▪▪ Sharing

PART 5 ▪▪▪ Workplace Security

Contents

PART 1 ▪▪▪ The Big Picture

PART 2 ▪▪▪ Security Essentials

PART 3 ■■■ Network Security

PART 5 ■■■ Workplace Security

About the Authors

CHARLES EDGE has been working with Apple products since he was a child. Professionally, Charles started with the Mac OS and Apple server offerings in 1999 after years of working with various flavors of Unix. Charles began his consulting career working with Support Technologies and Andersen Consulting. In 2000, he found a new home at 318, a consulting firm in Santa Monica, California, which is now the largest Mac consultancy in the country. At 318, Charles leads a team of more than 40 engineers and has worked with network architecture, security, and storage for various vertical and horizontal markets. Charles has spoken at a variety of conferences including DefCon, Black Hat, LinuxWorld, Macworld, and the WorldWide Developers Conference. Charles' first book, *Mac Tiger Server Little Black Book*, can be purchased through Paraglyph Press. Charles recently hung up his surfboard and moved to Minneapolis, Minnesota, with his wife, Lisa. Charles can be contacted at `krypted@mac.com`.

WILLIAM BARKER is a technical consultant at 318 and a freelance writer. He has a penchant for all things Web 2.0 related and is eagerly anticipating the day he can wash his dishes and take out the trash online. His web site, `techiestravel.com`, is a hobby haven for two of his passions, technology and travel. He also wears a musician hat from time to time, making music: DJing, playing guitar, playing piano, and mixing CDs for friends. He lives in Venice, California, with his trusty automobile, Lucille.

ZACK SMITH has been working as an IT consultant his entire adult life. He has consulted for insurance companies, entertainment companies, medical organizations, and governmental agencies. Zack is an Apple Certified Trainer and has taught at Apple and various market centers in Boston, Virginia, Los Angeles, and Cupertino. As a certified instructor, Zack has taught Apple's Security Best Practices class, as well as many other system administrator–level classes (such as Mac OS X Deployment and Mac OS X Directory Services). Zack has been a speaker at Macworld San Francisco as well as many other smaller venues such as IT user groups. Zack is also the author of a set of open source IT administration software and scripts and has long-term plans of being a full-time Objective C developer. When not attending IT and security conferences or traveling for work at 318, Zack can be found in Portland, Oregon, with his partner in crime, Anna, and dog, Watson.

About the Technical Reviewer

MIKE LEE, the world's toughest programmer, has been bending computers to his will since the mid-90s. Having recently retired as majordomo of Delicious Monster Software, he's now working at United Lemur, a charity-driven software company dedicated to raising money and awareness for Madagascar and the world's few remaining lemurs. Mike and his wife are originally from Honolulu but currently live in Seattle, where they are raising two cats. Mike's hobbies include weightlifting, single malts, and fire. Mike can be contacted at mike@unitedlemur.org.

Acknowledgments

I'd like to thank all the folks at Apple for the hard work they have put into the various flavors of OS X and into educating the Mac community on their fantastic product, in particular, Joel Rennich, Schoun Regan, Josh Wisenbaker, Greg Smith, JD Mankovsky, David Winter, Stale Bjorndal, Eric Senf, Cawan Starks, Martin Libich, and a short list of others who have helped me through the years! This includes the late Michael Bartosh, who is sorely missed on many fronts.

Thanks are also in order to the crew at 318 for their hard work, especially Kevin Klein. Without you guys I never would have been able to take the time to complete this book: David, Tim, Thomas, Beau, Zack, Kevin, Kevin, William, Joel, Robert, Jordan, Susie, Dan, Phil, Max, Daniel, Adrian, John, John, Jon, Marc, Monica, Karl, Chris, Cade, Christian, Eli, Drake, Erin, Ehren, Kennon, Theresa, Tony, and everyone else.

Also thanks to the fine staff at Apress for turning this book into something to be proud of: Jeffrey Pepper, Candace English, Kim Wimpsett, Tina Nielsen, Steve Anglin, and the myriad of others whose hard work went into this title. Thanks also to the technical reviewer, Mike Lee, and to my coauthors, Zack and William.

I also have to thank the organizers of SANS, DefCon, BlackHat, LayerOne, and the other security conferences and those in the white/gray hat and InfoSec communities for bringing to light many vulnerabilities before they are discovered by others with a flair for exploitation. Finally, a huge thanks goes out to the open source community. It is on the shoulders of these giants that we all sit!

Charles S. Edge, Jr.

Many thanks are in order for making this dream a reality. I'd be remiss if I didn't thank my coauthor Charles Edge who brought me into this crazy experience in the first place. Thank you to everyone at Apress (Candace, Laura, Mike, Kim, and all the others) for their tireless work and dedication to this book. The development team at Apple should be acknowledged for their constant desire to improve and reinvent a product that continues to amaze novices and experts alike. My parents deserve a huge thank you for introducing me to the wonders of reading and computer technology at a very early age. A heartfelt thanks goes to my good friend Adam, who took a chance at giving me my first paid writing job and is a constant inspiration to my craft. Last but certainly not least, this book is inspired by the technical writers of the world. It is an unsung art to write technically, and the attention to detail that those who write books covering technical materials must provide is truly staggering. Because of their experimentation, we learn how to make our lives easier and more enjoyable.

William Barker

Introduction

A common misconception in the Mac community is that the Mac is more secure than any other operating system on the market. Although this might be true in most side-by-side analyses of security features right out of the box, what this isn't taking into account is that security tends to get overlooked once the machine starts to be configured for its true purposes. For example, when sharing is enabled or remote control applications are installed, then a variety of security threats are often established—no matter what the platform is.

In the security sector, the *principle of least privilege* is a philosophy that security professionals abide by when determining security policies. This principle states that if you want to be secure, you need to give every component of your network the absolute minimum permissions required to do its job. But what are those permissions? What are the factors that need to be determined when making that decision? No two networks are the same; therefore, it's certainly not a decision that can be made for you. It's something you will need to decide for yourself based on what kinds of policies are implemented to deal with information technology security.

Security Beginnings: Policies

Security in a larger organization starts with a security policy. When looking to develop security policies, it is important that the higher-level decision makers in the organization work hand in hand with the IT team to develop their policies and security policy frameworks. A security policy, at a minimum, should define the tools used on a network for security, the appropriate behavior of employees and network users, the procedures for dealing with incidents, and the trust levels within the network.

The reason policies become such an integral part of establishing security in a larger environment is that you must be secure but also be practical about how you approach security in an organization. Security can be an impediment to productivity, both for support and for nonsupport personnel. People may have different views about levels of security and how to enforce it. A comprehensive security policy makes sure everyone is on the same page and that the cost vs. protection paradigm that IT departments follow are in line with the business logic of the organization.

On small networks, such as your network at home, you may have a loose security policy that states you will occasionally run security updates and follow a few of the safeguards outlined in this book. The smaller a network environment, the less likely security is going to be taken seriously. However, for larger environments with much more valuable data to protect, the concern for security should not be so flippant. For example, the Health Insurance Portability and Accountability Act (HIPAA) authorizes criminal penalties of up to $250,000 and/or 10 years imprisonment per violation of security standards for patient health information. The Gramm-Leach-Bliley Act establishes financial institution standards for safeguarding customer information and imposes penalties of up to $100,000 per violation.

Everyone in an organization should be concerned about security policies because everyone is affected to some extent. Users are often affected the most, because policies often consist of a set of rules that regulate their behavior, sometimes making it more difficult for them to accomplish their tasks throughout their day. The IT staff should also be consulted and brought into the decision-making process since they will be required to implement and comply with these policies, while making sure that the policies are realistic given the budget available. In addition, you must notify people in advance of the development of the policy. You should contact members of the IT, management, and legal departments as well as a random sampling of users in your environment. The size of your policy development will be determined by the scope of the policy and the size of your organization. Larger policies may require many people to be involved in the policy development. Smaller policies may require participation by only one or two people within the organization.

As an example, a restrictive policy that requires all wireless users to use a RADIUS server would incur IT costs not only from the initial install but also with the installs and configurations necessary to set up the RADIUS clients on each of the workstations. A more secure RADIUS server would also cause additional labor over other less secure protocols such as WEP. You also need to consider IT budgeting and staffing downtime.

When developing your actual policy, keep the scope limited to what is technically enforceable and easy to understand, while protecting the productivity of your users. Policies should also contain the reasons a policy is needed and cover the contacts and responsibilities of each user. When writing your policy, discuss how policy violations will be handled and why each item in the policy is required. Allow for changes in the policies as things evolve in the organization.

Keep the culture of your organization in mind when writing your security policy. Overly restrictive policies may cause users to be more likely to ignore them. Staff and management alike must commit to the policies. You can often find examples of acceptable use policies in prepackaged policies on the Internet and then customize them to fulfill your organization's needs.

A Word About Network Images

Whether you are a home user or a corporate network administrator, the overall security policy of your network will definitely be broken down into how your computers will be set up on the network. For smaller environments, this means setting up your pilot system exactly the way you want it and then making an image of the setup. If anything were to happen to a machine on your network (intrusion or virus activity, for example), you wouldn't need to redo everything from scratch. If you're in a larger, more corporate environment, then you'll create an image and deploy it to hundreds or thousands of systems using NetInstall, Casper Suite, LanDESK, or a variety of other tools that you may or may not have experience with.

Risk Management

By the end of this book, we hope you will realize that if a computer is plugged into a network, it cannot be absolutely guaranteed secure. In a networked world, it is not likely that you will be able to remove all of the possible threats from any networked computing environment. To compile an appropriate risk strategy, you must first understand the risks applicable in your specific environment. Risk management involves making decisions about whether assessed risks are sufficient enough to present a concern and the appropriate means for controlling a significant risk to your environment. From there, it is important to evaluate and select alternative responses to these risks. The selection process requires you to consider the severity of the threat.

For example, a home user would likely not be concerned with security threats and bugs available for the Open Directory services of Mac OS X Server. However, in larger environments running Open Directory, it would be important to consider these risks.

Risk management not only involves external security threats but also includes fault tolerance and backup. Accidentally deleting files from systems is a common and real threat to a networked environment.

For larger environments with a multitude of systems requiring risk management, a risk management framework may be needed. The risk management framework is a description of streams of accountability and reporting that will support the risk management process for the overall environment, extending beyond information technology assets and into other areas of the organization. If you are managing various systems for a large organization, it is likely there is a risk management framework and that the architecture and computer policies you implement are in accordance with the framework.

All too often, when looking at examples of risk management policies that have been implemented in enterprise environments, many Mac administrators will cite specific items in the policies as "not pertaining" to their environment. This is typically not the case, because best practices are best practices. There is a reason that organizations practice good security, and as the popularity of Mac based network environments grows, it is important that administrators learn from others who have managed these enterprise-class environments.

As mentioned earlier, managing IT risk is a key component of governmental regulations. Organizations that fall under the requirements of Sarbanes-Oxley, HIPPA, or the Gramm-Leach-Bliley Act need to remain in compliance or risk large fines and/or imprisonment. Auditing for compliance should be performed on a regular basis, with compliance documentation ready and available to auditors.

Defining what is an acceptable risk is not something that we, the authors of this book, can decide. Many factors determine what is an acceptable risk. It is really up to you, the network administrator, to be informed about what those risks are so that you can make an informed decision. We will discuss options and settings for building out secure systems and a secure networked environment for your system. However, many of the settings we encourage you to use might impact your network or system in ways that are not acceptable to your workflow. When this happens, a choice must be made between usability and performance. Stay as close to the principle of least privilege as much as possible, keeping in mind that you still need to be able to do your job.

How This Book Is Organized

The first goal of this book is to help you build a secure image, be it at home or in the office, and then secure the environment in which the image will be used. This will involve the various options with various security ramifications, but it will also involve the network, the sharing aspects of the system, servers, and finally, if something drastic were to happen, the forensic analysis that would need to occur.

Another goal of this book is to provide you with the things to tell users not to do. Adding items to enforce your policy and security measures will help you make your network, Mac, or server like a castle, with various levels of security, developed in a thoughtful manner. To help with this tiered approach, we've broken the book down into five parts.

Part 1: The Big Picture

First, an introduction to the world of security on the Mac comprises Part 1:

Chapter 1, "Security Quick-Start": If you have time to read only one chapter, this is the chapter for you. In this chapter, we cover using the GUI tools provided by Apple to provide a more secure environment and the best practices for deploying them. We give recommendations and explain how to use these various features and when they should be used. We also outline the risks and strategies in many of their deployments.

Chapter 2, "Security Fundamentals": In this chapter, we define many of the common risks to users and computers. We then focus on many of the common security principles used when securing an operating system and the network environment. This chapter is a birds'-eye view into the complex world of information security.

Chapter 3, "Securing User Accounts": Mac OS X is a multiuser operating system. One of the most important security measures is to understand the accounts on your system and when you are escalating privileges for accounts. This chapter explains how to properly secure these users and groups.

Part 2: Security Essentials

Part 2 gets down to some of the essential elements of security on a Mac:

Chapter 4, "Malware Security: Combating Viruses, Worms, and Root Kits": Viruses, spyware, and root kits are at the top of the list of security concerns for Windows users. However, Mac users are not immune. In this chapter, we go into the various methods that can be used to protect Mac systems against these and other forms of malware.

Chapter 5, "Securing Web Browsers and E-mail": Safari, Firefox, Internet Explorer, Mail.app, and Entourage—with all these programs to manage, how do you lock them all down appropriately? In this chapter, we discuss cookies, Internet history, and browser preferences and when you should customize these settings. We also give some tips for third-party solutions for protecting your privacy. In addition, this chapter provides readers with best security practices for the mail clients that they likely spend much of their time using.

Chapter 6, "Reviewing Logs and Monitoring": What good are logs if they aren't reviewed? In this chapter, we discuss what logs should be reviewed and what is stored in each file. We then move on to various monitoring techniques and applications and the most secure ways to deploy them in typical environments.

Part 3: Network Security

Part 3 describes how you secure a Mac network:

Chapter 7, "Securing Network Traffic": As useful as securing the operating system is, securing the network backbone is a large component of the overall security picture. In this chapter, we explore some of the techniques and concepts behind securing the network infrastructure. This includes the common switches, hubs, and firewalls used in Mac environments and the features you may have noticed but never thought to tinker with. We also cover how to stop some of the annoying issues that pop up on networks because of unauthorized (and often accidental) user behavior.

Chapter 8, "Setting Up the Mac OS X Firewall": The firewall option in Mac OS X is just a collection of check boxes. Or is it? We discuss using and securing the Mac OS X software firewall, and we go into further detail on configuring this option from the command line. We also discuss some of the other commands that, rather than block traffic, allow an administrator to actually shape the traffic, implementing rules for how traffic is handled, and mitigate the effects that DoS attacks can have on the operating system.

Chapter 9, "Securing a Wireless Network": Wireless networking is perhaps one of the most insecure things that users tend to implement themselves. In this chapter, we cover securing wireless networks, and then, to emphasize how critical wireless security is (and how easy it is to subvert it if done improperly), we move on to some of the methods used to exploit wireless networks.

Part 4: Sharing

File Sharing needs a section all to itself. Files are what hackers are after, and securing them should be a top priority in any environment. Part 4 covers the following:

Chapter 10, "File Services": What is a permission model, and why do you need to know what it is, when all you want to do is allow people access to some of the files on my computer? Knowing the strategies involved in assigning file permissions is one of the most intrinsic security aspects of a shared storage environment. It is also important to understand the specific security risks and how to mitigate them for each protocol used, including AFP, FTP, NFS, and SMB, which are all covered in this chapter.

Chapter 11, "Web Site Security": Apache is quite possibly the most common web server running on the *nix platform. Entire books are dedicated to explaining how to lock down this critical service. In this chapter, we focus on the most important ways to lock down the service and some Apple-centric items of Apache not usually found in discussions about Apache on the *nix platform. We also provide you with other resources to look to if you require further security for your web server.

Chapter 12, "Remote Connectivity": One of the most dangerous aspects of administration is the exposure of the very tools you use to access systems remotely. Many of these programs do not always need to be running and can be further secured from their default settings. In this chapter, we cover many of the methods for protecting these services and some of the ways that vendors should change their default settings to make them more secure. We also cover some of the ways you can secure these tools, and we help administrators make choices about how to best implement remote administration utilities to counteract these shortcomings.

Chapter 13, "Server Security": Mac OS X Server is very much like Mac OS X Client, without many of the bells and whistles and with a more optimized system for sharing resources. This is true with many server-based operating systems. Because a Mac OS X server fills a different role in a networked environment, it should be treated differently from Mac OS X Client. For this reason, we cover many of the security options that are available as well as those that are crucial to securing Mac OS X Server. We also cover many of the security options from Mac OS X that should specifically not be used in Mac OS X Server.

Included with server security is directory services, which are critical to expanding technology infrastructures. By interconnecting all the hosts of a network, you are able to better control the settings and accounts on systems. In this chapter, we also focus on the ways to securely deploy Mac OS X clients to various directory services and point out the items to ask for (if you are in a larger network infrastructure) or to set up in order to help make the directory service environment as secure as possible.

Part 5: Workplace Security

How secure is your work environment's network? This part explores security as it pertains to environments with multiple Mac computers connected on a network:

Chapter 14, "Network Scanning, Intrusion Detection, and Intrusion Prevention Tools": Host-based intrusion detection systems (IDS) are quickly becoming a standard for offering signature-based and anomaly-based detection of attacks. Some of these tools allow for augmenting the operating system settings to further secure the hosts on which they run. In this chapter, we provide a best practices discussion for deploying and using IDSs. We also cover the various attacks that have been developed over the past few years against IDS systems and explore add-ons for IDSs that provide rich aggregated data about the systems.

Chapter 15, "Backup and Fault Tolerance": If you don't have a backup plan now, then you will after you read this chapter. Backups are the last line of defense in a security environment. Backups are critical and should be provided in tiers. In this chapter, we describe some of the strategies for going about implementing a backup plan, from choosing the right software package to properly implementing it. We also cover some of the more common techniques for providing fault-tolerant services and the security risks that can be introduced by doing so.

Chapter 16, "Forensics": What do you do when your systems are compromised? What happens after the attack? In this chapter, we cover the basics of computer forensics and how a user can be their own digital sleuth. The goal is not to have you testifying in court on large-scale network attacks but instead to help first responders get comfortable with safely imaging Mac systems for investigations without contaminating evidence.

Appendixes

The following are the appendixes:

Appendix A, "Xsan Security": Here we provide tips on securing your Xsan.

Appendix B, "Acceptable Use Policy": This appendix contains an acceptable use policy from the SANS Institute that has been reprinted here with their consent.

Appendix C, "Secure Development": Here we give a brief rundown of Apple's development architecture.

Appendix D, "Introduction to Cryptography": In this appendix, we give a brief history of cryptography and look at some of the protocols used today and how they came about.

## PART 1

The Big Picture

CHAPTER 1

■■■

Security Quick-Start

If you are looking for a quick-and-dirty start to securing your Mac, this is the chapter for you. This chapter is meant as a quick-start, written for the "I need to get my Mac secured right away" readers. For the quick-and-dirty basics of getting your Mac secured, follow the instructions in this chapter. From Chapter 2 on, you'll be introduced to all the other intricacies surrounding securing the Mac OS, and we'll explain why we suggest the quick-start steps in more detail. Keep in mind that Chapter 1 gives just the basics, and although it will leave you with a fairly secure system, it's not as comprehensive as the subsequent chapters, where we delve deeper into the specifics of most settings. To get a more thorough understanding of Mac OS X security and the tools you can use to secure your Mac, we urge you to keep reading beyond the basics.

Securing the Mac OS X Defaults

Mac OS X, because it is built on a Unix architecture, is a fairly secure and stable operating system right out of the box. There is a commonly held belief that the Mac can be further secured only through the Unix command line and that the graphical user interface (GUI) does not need to be tinkered with to make it more secure. This could not be further from the truth. There are many ways in which Mac OS X can and should be made more secure without dipping into the Unix command line.

In fact, there are many security holes built into the Mac OS intentionally. Why is that? The answer lies in the relationship between ease of use and security. Generally, in the world of operating systems, the easier an operating system becomes to use, the less secure it is. When the engineers at Apple redesigned their OS from 9 to X, with the most advanced operating system architecture out there, they considered security very heavily, but they also considered usability. To ensure the most secure operating system possible without sacrificing ease of use, many security features are disabled by default, giving you, the user, the choice of whether to practice good security by enabling or disabling the features.

Having said that, many features of Mac OS X are already fairly secure without changing anything out of the box, with little—or no—trade-off to functionality. In fact, certain features should not be changed unless changing them is absolutely required; for example, you should not enable the root account unless you need to run a process that requires it, as is the case with programs such as Carbon Copy Cloner. Remember that when defaults are temporarily changed to complete certain tasks, you will need to go back and undo the changes after you have completed the tasks that required the change. Many security breaches occur because users forget to put security settings back the way they were.

Customizing System Preferences

The default settings for Mac OS X's System Preferences are fairly secure but can be further optimized to provide a higher level of protection. Seemingly innocuous settings can be used to exploit some of the Mac's core features. Therefore, to reduce the likelihood that this will occur, you should go through the options listed throughout the next few pages and disable any that aren't being used. You can then enable any security features that will not conflict with your needs along the way.

One of the most important concepts to understand with OS X security is that your computer is a multiuser operating system. Every machine has at least one user account and one local administrative account (sometimes referred to as the *root* account), which has access to take ownership of all the files on the system. There will always be more than one account on the machine and thus the potential for multiple breaches in security. In the next section, we will be getting a little more familiar with account settings and the ways in which you can secure users in the Accounts preference pane.

Accounts Preferences

In this section, we will tackle the most important topic: passwords. Your system is only as secure as your passwords. The stronger a password, the longer it will take to break. In Mac OS X, Apple has developed the Password Assistant to assist with password security. To set a password, open the Accounts preference pane, and click your account. This opens a window with your name, short name, and an option to change your password (see Figure 1-1). The name is typically your full name or the full name you may have entered when the account was created. The short name is a shortened version of the name (the first letter of the first word and the full second word by default).

Note We'll discuss users and groups in detail in Chapter 3. We will touch on a few of the important points in this section: disabling login items, setting account types, and basic user security.

Notice that there is no password; there is only an option to change a password. Apple carefully designed this pane so that a user could not easily view another user's password; with administrator access, they would only be able to change it. This is becoming a fairly standard practice with password handling industry-wide. When you click the Change Password button on the Accounts preference pane, a smaller window will pop up asking you to type the old password and then the new password (see Figure 1-2). You must enter the new password twice to ensure accuracy.

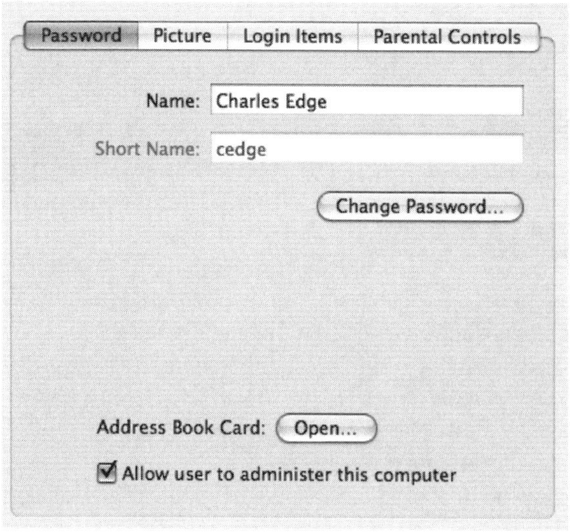

Figure 1-1. *Account settings*

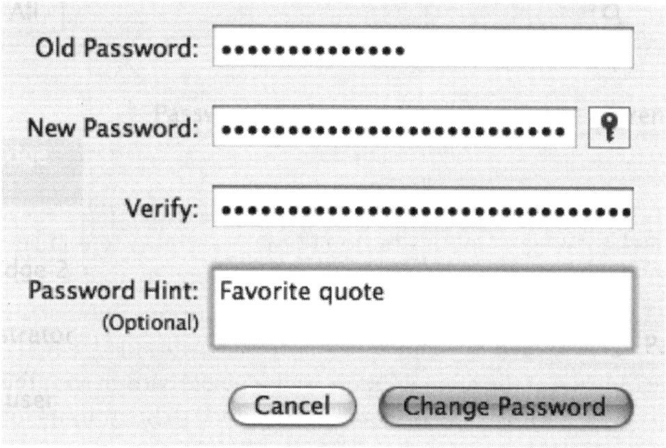

Figure 1-2. *Changing a password*

Clicking the key icon in the Change Password window opens the Password Assistant (see Figure 1-3). The Password Assistant is a random password generator that can be used to help create a more secure password. It's a great utility if you need suggestions for more complex passwords. All too often users will use passwords such as *password* and *god*. This tool was created to counteract this alarming trend.

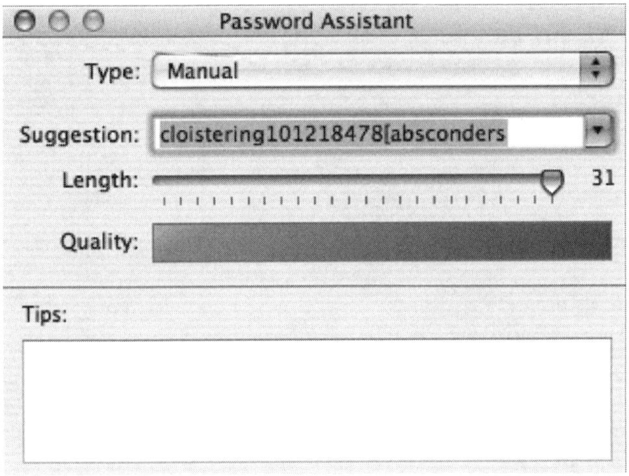

Figure 1-3. *Password Assistant*

■Note When setting passwords, you should include numbers, letters, and special characters, such as !, @, #, or $. Using various sets of characters yields very secure passwords.

Login Options

To make the login screen more secure, you should alter the default settings of the Login Options tab in the Accounts preference pane. Click the Login Options button of the Accounts preference pane. (You may need to click the little padlock icon at the bottom of the screen to access this screen as an administrator.) The Show the Restart, Sleep, and Shut Down Buttons option of the Login Options window (see Figure 1-4) is enabled by default. If this option is disabled, when the machine boots, it will hide these buttons at the login window so that users cannot shut the system down at the login screen. Any systems that provide services that need to be running for other users should have this option disabled.

The Show Password Hints option can be helpful if you need a hint to remind you of your password in case you forget it. However, this can also give someone trying to guess your password valuable insight into what the password may be. For example, it is common to have a hint something along the lines of "My dog's name." This would require very little effort on the part of someone attempting to break into your system to guess your password. All too often, we find that users enter the actual password into the password hint field. Obviously, this is not best practice in any situation unless it is merely impossible for you to memorize your password.

■Tip If you do need help remembering your password, using password hints are better than writing passwords down.

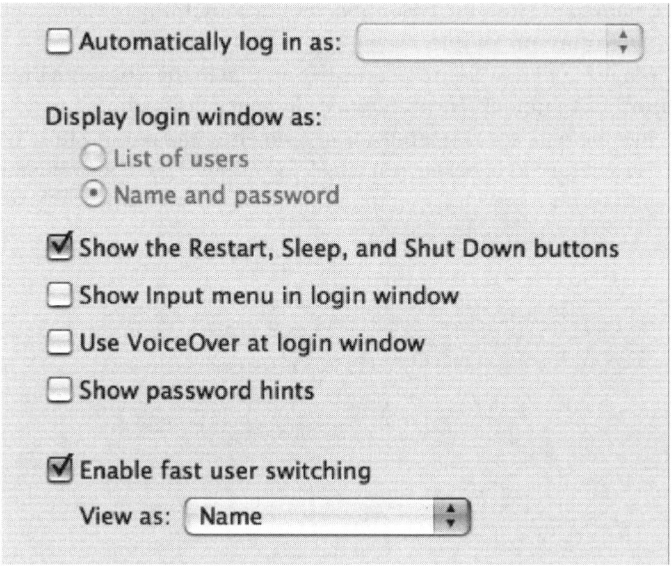

Figure 1-4. *Login options*

The Enable Fast User Switching option is a way to allow multiple users to log into the computer concurrently. This allows users to stay logged in while accessing other accounts. It poses a security risk, though, because it is possible to access or alter processes being run by other users. To limit what each user can do to access another user's processes, make sure that all nonadministrative users are not allowed administrative access to the system. Better yet, if this is a feature that you are not likely to use, disable it by unchecking the Enable Fast User Switching option. If you do enable it, you will see the message in Figure 1-5 warning you that this is a security risk.

Figure 1-5. *Fast user switching warning*

The administrative user should be logged in only when administrative tasks (changing passwords, configuring network settings, and so on) are necessary, not for everyday work. This is a key component of Unix system administration and a good way to keep from harming the system by accident or accidentally allowing a rogue process to harm the system. Running a second account also gives you a path to get into the computer should something render your regular, nonadministrative login account inoperable.

To create a second account to use, open System Preferences, and go to the Accounts preference pane. From here, click the lock to unlock the preference, and click the + symbol to add the account (see Figure 1-6). Leave the type set to User Account, and enter the name, short name, and password you want the account to have. Do not check the Allow User to Administer This Computer box if this is the nonadministrative account for regular use of your system. Now click Create Account.

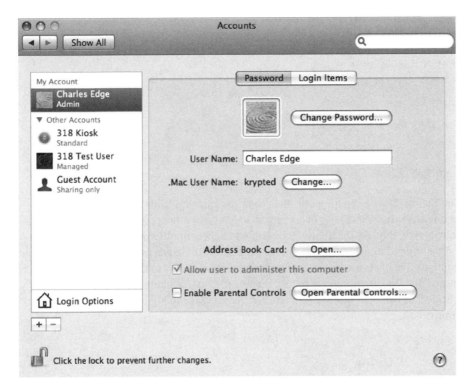

Figure 1-6. *Creating an account*

Once you have created the new account, log out of the administrative account and log in as your nonadministrative account. Remember, you can always copy your documents, music, and other data out of your administrative account and, if need be, log in as the administrative user to access anything that won't copy using the regular user. Migrating your user profile to a nonadministrative user creates a much more secure computing environment.

Security Preferences

Another place to change the default settings for security purposes is in the Security preference panel (see Figure 1-7). Here, you will find options (that we explain in the rest of this section) for enabling many of the miscellaneous security features that Apple has developed that do not fit into any other System Preferences panel. There are other items that allow for heightened security, but these are typically located within the applications or operating system features they were designed to protect. Some of these basic security features we will review later in this chapter. Others will be reviewed throughout the remainder of the book.

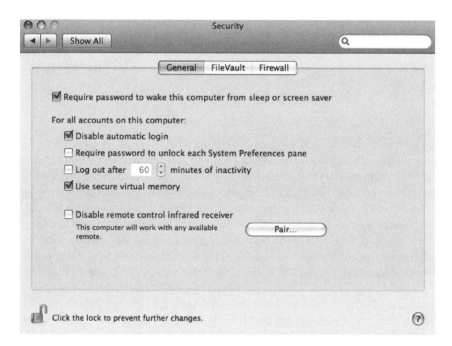

Figure 1-7. *Security preference pane, General tab*

The first and most important of these options is the automatic login, which allows anyone with physical access to your computer to restart the computer and, if the password is remembered, not be required to enter a password in order to get your data. Automatic login is enabled by default. This is one of the first things you should change because it gives people the ability to log into your system and access your data. With automatic login enabled, few of the other options to secure your computer are relevant because they already have access to your computer.

You can use the option called Require Password to Wake This Computer from Sleep or Screen Saver on the General tab of the Security preference pane to force your computer to require a password to wake it up after it has gone to sleep or after the screen saver has been activated. This is critical and is not enabled by default. The Require Password to Wake This Computer from Sleep option makes it easy to lock your system, whether in a timed or manual way. Using the Exposé application to assign a key or *hot corner* (moving the cursor to a corner of the screen to activate the display) to put a system to sleep allows you to put your machine to sleep when you are finished using it. Later in this chapter we will review setting up automatic sleep, Exposé, and screen saver options.

The option Logout When Inactive allows users to have their systems logged out whenever they are left inactive for a period of time. This setting supersedes any settings for putting a system to sleep or activating a screen saver. The automatic logoff option will log users out of their accounts when they are inactive. This can be a dangerous feature because it is possible for users to lose data they were working on if the machine automatically logs them out.

Virtual memory is a means of using hard drive space as temporary memory in order to allow the computer to perform more work than the computer has available memory for. Virtual memory creates virtual chunks of memory in files called *swap files* on your hard drive. When this transitory memory is no longer needed, the swap files are deleted (which doesn't always happen immediately). Valuable information can be gleaned from a system by viewing the virtual memory swap files and reconstructing user operations. The option to secure virtual memory encrypts the swap files, preventing others from using them to gather private data. This is an important feature to enable.

FileVault

Let's face it. We're human, and we forget passwords all the time. What happens when you forget the password for your computer and you are the only one with an account on the machine? On the Web, there is a system that web sites use when users forget their passwords. It's called a *self-service password reset* whereby they can reset the password on their own (usually by answering a secret question on a web prompt and then receiving a new temporary password via e-mail). For a machine with many users, this would certainly be a handy feature to have and would significantly reduce the volume of calls to the help desk. Apple supplied Mac owners with this feature via the password reset utility included on the Mac OS X CD. You can boot a computer to the CD and reset the password at any time by rebooting the computer and holding down the C key.

But what if you want to limit someone's ability to access your data if they were able to reset the password? Many of us travel with laptops that, if stolen and the password were to be reset, would give users access to data they shouldn't be able to access. For example, students would have access to tests, children would have access to our web site viewing habits, employees would have access to confidential data about other employees—all if they were able to get physical access to our computers while we were away. The ability to easily reset a password introduces you to a feature of the Mac OS X security preferences that protects data, even if the password is reset using the CD: FileVault. FileVault removes the ability to access data in a user's folder, even if the password is reset, by encrypting the contents of a user's home folder into a secured disk image.

■**Note** The FileVault feature is only as strong as the password protecting the home folder.

FileVault is not for everyone. It can cause some inconveniences. By enabling FileVault, Windows file sharing and printer sharing are disabled. By enabling FileVault, you will break these connections if another user is relying on them, so be cautious. It will sometimes slow down the logout process because it encrypts the data in the logout process. FileVault can also have complications with certain applications, such as Adobe Illustrator. If you suspect that FileVault is causing an application to be problematic, then turn it off to see whether that fixes the issue. Even with these inconveniences, FileVault is an excellent way to secure the data on your machine.

To use FileVault, you will need to set it up in the Security preference pane. Open System Preferences, and click Security (see Figure 1-8). Then click the FileVault tab. Next, click Turn On FileVault. At this point, you will need to give the system a master password. The master password can unlock any FileVault on a computer, so it needs to be a strong one. To enable the master password, click the Set Master Password button, and type the password you want to use twice. Then, enter a hint to help you if you forget it at a later date (do not enter the password itself!), as shown in Figure 1-9.

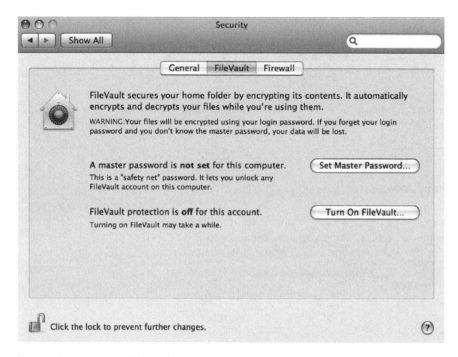

Figure 1-8. *Setting up FileVault*

Note If you suspect that others will enable FileVault to encrypt their home folders, such as students, children, or employees, then setting up a master password before they can enable FileVault will help ensure that you will always be able to log into any FileVault disk images that are created by other users on the system.

At this point, you will be prompted for the password of the account you are currently logged into. You can stop the process of encrypting the user's home folder and just enable a master password by clicking Cancel (see Figure 1-10), or you can encrypt the user's home folder by entering the password for the user and clicking OK. Keep in mind that the amount of time the encryption takes depends on how large the home folder is. It can take a while, so be patient. Interrupting the process can cause corruption or cause you to have to start the process all over again.

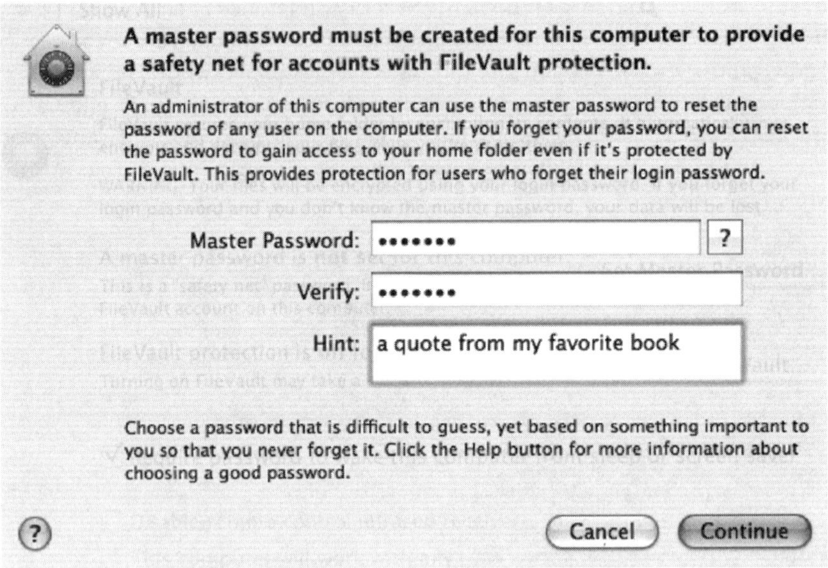

Figure 1-9. *Setting the master password*

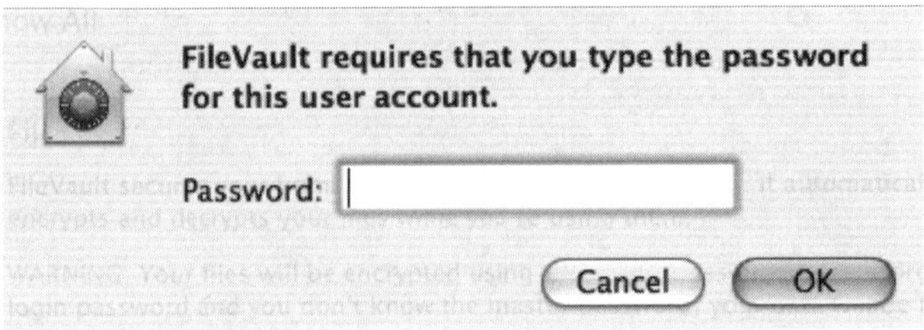

Figure 1-10. *Authenticating to an account*

If you want to change FileVault settings later, you can do so by returning to the Security preference pane (see Figure 1-10). You can change the master FileVault password or turn off FileVault completely (if the home folder is large, be prepared to wait a while for it to decrypt).

Infrared Controls in Security Preferences

Apple is now shipping infrared remote controls with many of its new computers, including MacBooks, MacBook Pros, and iMacs. As of this book's publication, there is little that can be done to damage systems with the infrared remote controls; however, theoretically it does allow someone to walk by the machine and launch menu options by use of a remote, which can be rather annoying. (If you do not have an infrared receiver, then you will not have this option in your Security Preferences.) Once the technology is more thoroughly utilized, there is also the theoretical chance that it could be used to exploit the system. This is a new concern since the release of the wifi exploit at DefCon 2006 by David Maynor that we cover further in Chapter 9.

Noticing this as a possibility, Apple introduced the ability to enable and disable the remote control infrared receiver in the Security preferences. If you still want to use an infrared receiver, you can pair the receiver to your system, which disables all receivers other than the one used to pair with the computer. To pair your infrared remote control with your computer, hold the fast-forward and menu buttons down on the remote for five seconds. If you will not be using an infrared receiver, then you should disable the ability to do so. To turn off the ability to use an infrared receiver, click the Security pane in System Preferences, and select Disable Remote Control Infrared Receiver (see Figure 1-11). You may also want to unpair the remote (because you have a new remote or lost your old one). To do this, simply click on the Unpair button in this window (Pair turns into Unpair when the remote is paired with the machine).

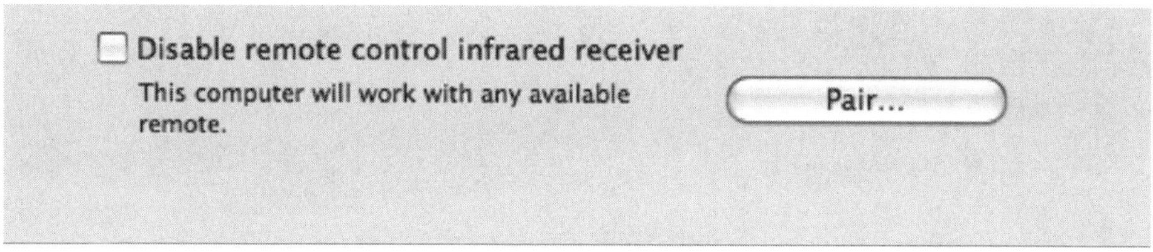

Figure 1-11. *Disabling the remote control infrared receiver*

Other System Preferences

The security features built into the Network preference pane include the ability to configure your client system to work with a proxy server and other advanced networking features. These advanced networking techniques will be covered in depth in subsequent chapters. Suffice it to say that networking options are aplenty here.

The Mac OS X firewall is a software-based application firewall built into the operating system designed to block unwanted network traffic. It is disabled by default, and you should usually enable it. To do this, open the Security preference pane, and click the Firewall tab. Then, select the Allow Only Essential Services option (see Figure 1-12).

■**Note** We discuss the firewall in further detail in Chapter 8.

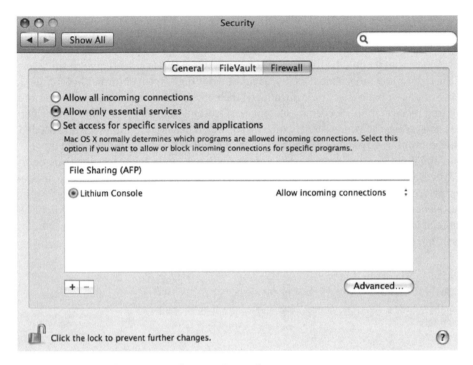

Figure 1-12. *Firewall options in the Security preference pane*

Software Update

You can use the Software Update preference pane to keep your system updated with the latest Apple updates and security patches (see Figure 1-13).

By default the Software Update feature is turned on, which means that the system will automatically search for updates on a weekly basis. There are rare situations where you will not want to run certain software updates because they can cause conflicts with other installed software, as has been the case with Apple QuickTime updates and the Final Cut software on multiple occasions. But for most users Software Update is one of the best ways to keep the latest and greatest security patches on their system, so it should be enabled. Before running any software updates on mission-critical systems, you should test them in a lab environment. Typically, security updates will not cause issues with other applications, but it is still wise to test them in a lab environment before installing them on mission-critical machines.

■Note To manually run the Software Update feature, open the Software Update preference pane, and then click the Check Now button on the Update Software tab.

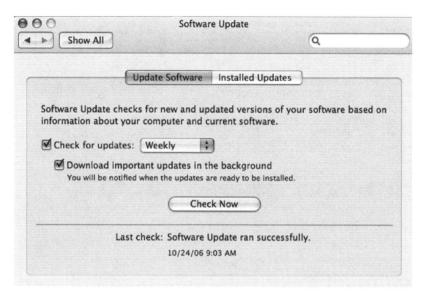

Figure 1-13. *Software Update preference pane*

For many, using the Mac OS X Software Update preference pane will be adequate to keep their computer updated. However, if you have multiple systems on your network that need updating, you can quickly bottleneck your Internet pipe if multiple users are downloading updates all at the same time. You will most likely want to deploy a solution to help you conserve your bandwidth by managing these updates. The Software Update Server feature in Mac OS X Server is a great solution for controlling Apple software updates. However, this is not going to be the right solution for everyone because it requires an OS X Server to use.

■**Note** There are ways to run the Software Update Server feature without having it run on a Mac, but it is best to run it on Mac OS X Server for simplicity's sake.

Security updates should always be taken seriously and run when possible (see Figure 1-14). One unique aspect of the Apple Software Update preference pane is that security updates are always deployed independently from other updates. Security updates rarely force a restart of the computer and almost invariably contain a comprehensive description explaining what they fix and why they were written.

Occasionally a software update will fail. When this occurs, it is possible for the update to become stuck in the software update cache. To clear these out or retrieve them, browse to the /Library/Caches/com.apple.softwareupdate/swcdn.apple.com folder, and find the update on your system. The update will be located in the folder with the corresponding month and date (see Figure 1-15). You can delete the update or run it again from this location. If the update is not located in these folders, then you should be able to run the Software Update feature and have it install again after a restart. You can also utilize this technique to save the update and burn it to optical media or a network drive for future installations.

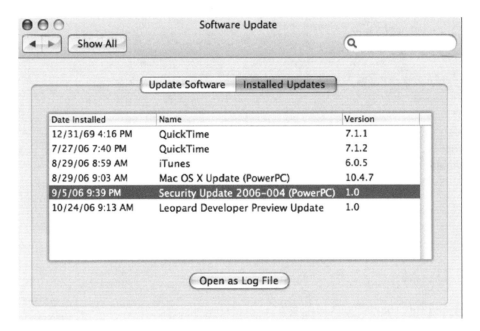

Figure 1-14. *List of security updates in Software Update*

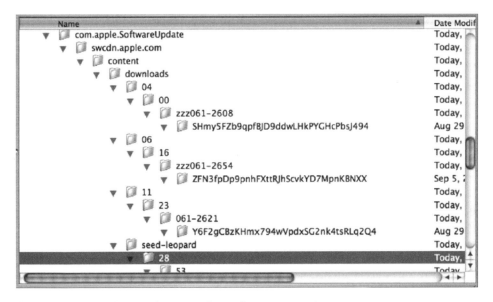

Figure 1-15. *Navigating to where security updates are stored*

Bluetooth Security

Bluetooth is a globally unlicensed short-range radio frequency for wireless networks, also known as IEEE 802.15.1. In other words, Bluetooth is a wireless technology that provides a way to connect and exchange information between devices such as personal digital assistants (PDAs), mobile phones, laptops, PCs, printers, and digital cameras. The Apple Bluetooth keyboard and mouse are popular Bluetooth devices in Apple environments.

Bluetooth works by pairing two devices. Once two devices are paired, they are able to freely exchange data while paired. To pair a device with an Apple computer, you will need your computer to be *discoverable*, or awaiting a pairing. You are also required to accept the pairing in most cases. However, there are a variety of attacks that can force a pairing if your system is set to be discoverable without using a password. This creates a security vulnerability that can be prevented by not having Bluetooth enabled unless you are actively using a device via Bluetooth.

Bluetooth is enabled and discoverable by default. If you do not want to use Bluetooth on your system, then open System Preferences and select the Bluetooth preference pane. Once you have this pane open, then click the Turn Bluetooth Off button to disable Bluetooth on your system (see Figure 1-16). If you want to use Bluetooth but do not want your system to be discoverable, then you can disable discoverability by unchecking the Discoverable box on this pane.

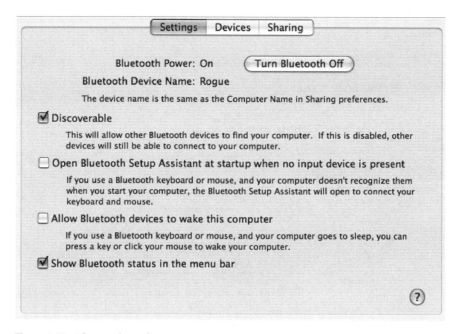

Figure 1-16. *Bluetooth preference pane*

The Devices tab of the Bluetooth preference pane offers a way to view devices that have been paired with Mac OS X computers (see Figure 1-17). Here, you will see any devices previously paired and be able to configure each device with its appropriate settings.

The Sharing tab of the Bluetooth preference pane allows more granularity when configuring exactly what options are available for various types of Bluetooth connectivity (see Figure 1-18). Here, it's possible to allow for file transfer, file exchange, and synchronization between the device and the computer. If you are not using these features, then disable them because this is a prime target for attacks.

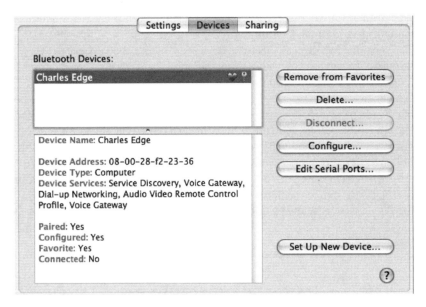

Figure 1-17. *Configuring Bluetooth devices*

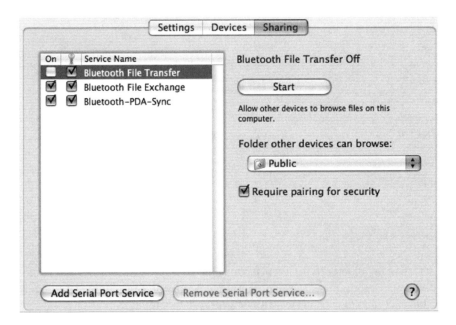

Figure 1-18. *Bluetooth sharing*

Bluetooth-PDA-Sync allows administrators to perform PDA synchronization using Bluetooth. Serial ports are often used to synchronize Palm Pilots, Blackberrys, and other devices. Bluetooth can operate as a wireless serial port. Here, it is possible to disable the Bluetooth-PDA-Sync feature by clicking the Edit Serial Ports button and clicking the Stop Serial Port button on the Edit Serial Port screen. If you do want to use Bluetooth as a serial port, you should leave the

Require Pairing for Security box checked because this will force a more secure pairing of the device.

Printer Security

In the move from Tiger to Leopard, Apple removed the Printer Setup utility. All controls for printing have now been moved into the Print & Fax preference pane in System Preferences. The Print & Fax preference pane offers few options for configuring access to shared printers and faxes. When sharing printers, only the printers that the user needs should be configured. Allowing a user to print to a printer that they shouldn't be using can cause confidentiality issues if the documents they are printing land in the wrong hands. To disable printers not in use, uncheck each printer on the Sharing tab (see Figure 1-19).

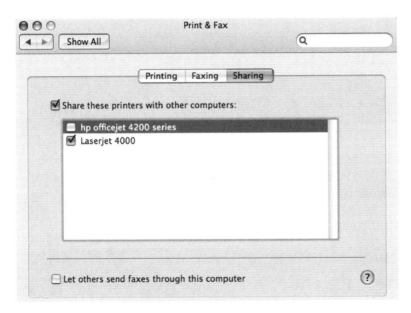

Figure 1-19. *Printer sharing*

You can get more control over printer sharing by using Terminal or the Common Unix Printing System (CUPS) web interface to configure the CUPS. CUPS uses the Internet Printing Protocol (IPP) to provide printing services to users. The CUPS daemon is controllable through a variety of mechanisms such as configuration files and web interfaces, which is convenient but also not entirely secure. If you do not need to allow access to printers installed on your computer, it is best to leave printer sharing disabled.

If, however, you do need to give access to printers on the computer but you want to limit this access, CUPS via the web interface can be helpful. CUPS uses HTTP as its transport protocol and has a built-in web interface to allow configuration of the service. To access the web interface, type the address **http://127.0.0.1:631** into your web browser (see Figure 1-20). The CUPS server has a configuration file that is editable from within the CUPS web interface. Security settings that can be altered by editing this file include the following:

- MaxCopies

- Port

- BrowseAllow

- BrowseAddress

- SystemGroup

- The Location's directive's Allow option

■**Note** The Location directive has an Allow option that can be used to dictate which addresses are allowed to access shared printing and remote administration.

- AuthType

- AuthClass

- The Limit directive's Require User option

■**Note** The Limit directive has a Require User option that dictates what access various users have. You should limit users' access on an "as-needed" basis.

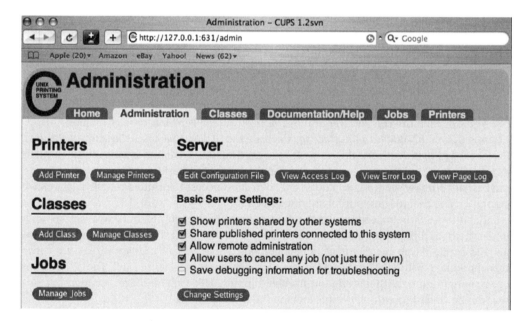

Figure 1-20. *CUPS web interface*

Sharing Services

If you are not sharing any resources on your computer, disable any sharing services that might be running. To do this, open the Sharing preference pane, and review the items on the Services tab that are being used to share resources (see Figure 1-21).

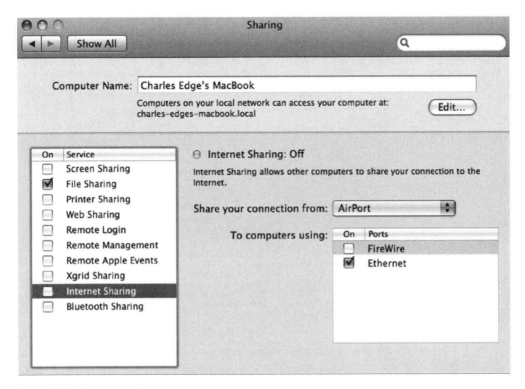

Figure 1-21. *Sharing preferences*

■**Tip** Disable all services that are not needed by the user you are configuring access for. These services are more comprehensively discussed in Chapter 10, Chapter 11, and Chapter 12.

Securely Erasing Disks

When you delete a file from a hard drive, the file is marked for deletion but is often kept by the file system until the system needs to free up space for new files. When you format a hard drive, something similar occurs. To ensure that data isn't accessed by malicious users, always securely erase a disk before disposing of it or repurposing the drive.

To securely erase a disk, open Disk Utility, and click the drive in the left column. Next, click the Erase tab, and then click the Security Options button (see Figure 1-22).

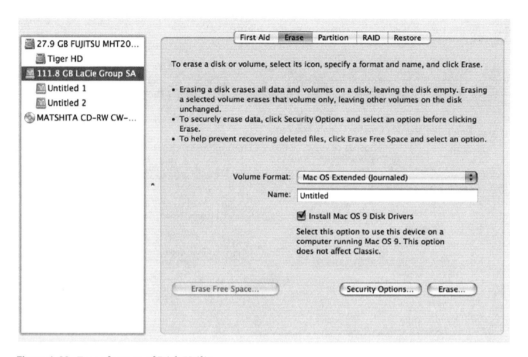

Figure 1-22. *Erase feature of Disk Utility*

This will display a list of secure erase options (see Figure 1-23). The Zero Out Data option will write zeroes over the entire hard drive. This can take minutes to hours depending on the size of the drive. For those needing a more secure erase option, Mac OS X also has a 7- or 35-pass erase available. These options will write data onto every sector of the drive in the number of passes selected. This can take tens of hours for larger drives but will yield a more secure removal of your data, rendering it virtually impossible to extract data from the drive if it were sent to drive recovery.

■**Note** Make sure you no longer need the data before performing any erase options. Once you have erased it, the cost of retrieving the data will be great, if it is even possible.

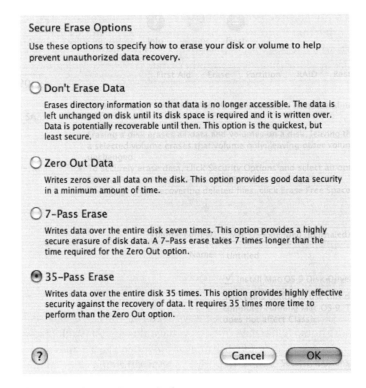

Figure 1-23. *Secure Erase window*

Using the Secure Empty Trash Feature

The Secure Empty Trash feature works much the same way as the Secure Erase feature. This is more secure than simply emptying the trash in that it also overwrites the location of the hard drive where the data in the trash was stored with random data. This will cause the data to be much harder to recover if it were to fall into the wrong hands. To securely empty the trash, click Finder ➤ Secure Empty Trash (see Figure 1-24).

Figure 1-24. *Secure Empty Trash menu item*

In Finder, click the Secure Empty Trash screen, and then click the OK button to make the files unrecoverable. It is worth noting that there are a variety of popular applications to help undelete files. As Figure 1-25 states, by clicking the OK button to securely erase your trash, you will not be able to recover the files at a later date, even with these data recovery applications.

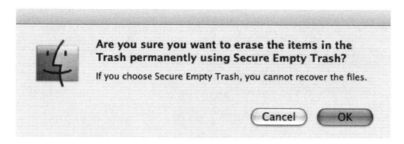

Figure 1-25. *Secure Empty Trash confirmation*

Using Encrypted Disk Images

Encrypted disk images offer you a place to keep files in an encrypted form. You can use these if you do not want to keep your entire home folder encrypted as you would with FileVault (likely because of speed or compatibility issues). Encrypted disk images are much like ZIP files that compress a bunch of files into one file, but anyone attempting to access the data within them will need a password to do so.

To create an encrypted disk image, open Disk Utility, and click New Image in the toolbar. The following screen (Figure 1-26) will have a wide variety of options. The Volume Size and Encryption settings are the most important to consider when creating the disk image. The volume size determines the size limit of the disk image. The encryption type can be 128-bit or (for more security) 256-bit; 256-bit images are harder to crack, but they are slower to create and to open when created. They will also take up more disk space than 128-bit. It's important to consider whether 256-bit encryption is worth the performance hit and disk space increase you will experience from using it.

Note If you are unsure what the size of your disk image should be and are not worried about limiting its size, choose Sparse Disk Image from the Image Format options, and the image will automatically grow as it requires more space (such as when you add files to it).

When you click the Create button, you will be asked for a password. Next you will click the Create button, and OS X will create a file using the encryption algorithm you have selected. Once you have created an encrypted disk image, you will need the password anytime you need to access that image.

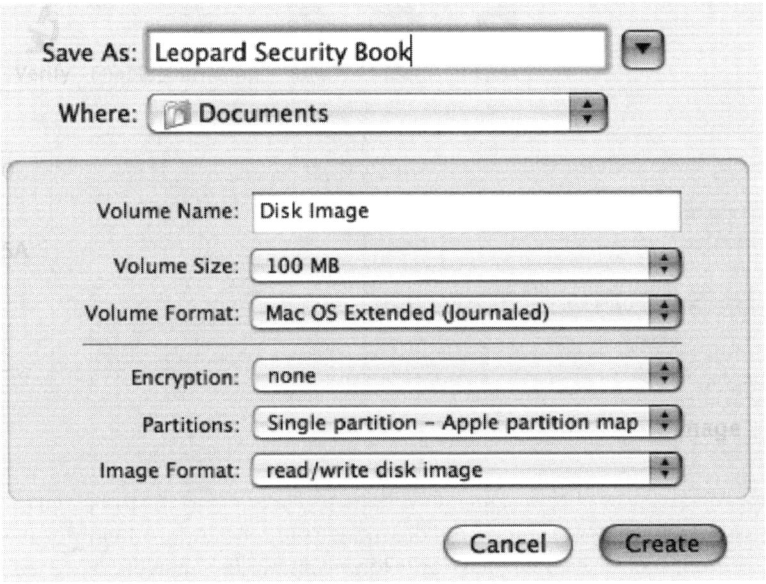

Save As: | Leopard Security Book|

Where: 📁 Documents ⬍

Volume Name: | Disk Image |

Volume Size: | 100 MB | ⬍

Volume Format: | Mac OS Extended (Journaled) | ⬍

Encryption: | none | ⬍

Partitions: | Single partition – Apple partition map | ⬍

Image Format: | read/write disk image | ⬍

(Cancel)   (Create)

Figure 1-26. *Encrypted Disk Image options*

Securing Your Keychains

Mac OS X uses encrypted keychains to keep track of commonly used passwords and certificates that are accessed regularly. It is meant to make your life easier by automating the manual reentry of this information every time you need to access it. One keychain password can be used to unlock a number of passwords, allowing your computer to keep track of credentials, saving you time, and allowing you to not have to keep track of them yourself. This is also helpful in that it allows a single service to maintain a centralized database of passwords, rather than having each application ask for passwords. This provides a substantially secure way of caching passwords for future use. But it's secure only if used correctly. When setting the keychain password, make sure to use a difficult password to crack that is unique from all the other passwords on the machine.

■**Note** You can use the Keychain Access Utility to view and manage keychains.

It is possible to have multiple keychains, and each user will begin with their default keychain stored at /Applications/Utilities/Keychain Access. When you open the Keychain Access Utility, you will see four panels. The first, labeled Keychains, lists all the keychains on the system known to the Keychain Access Utility. From here you can lock and unlock keychains by clicking them and clicking the lock icon at the top of the screen (see Figure 1-27).

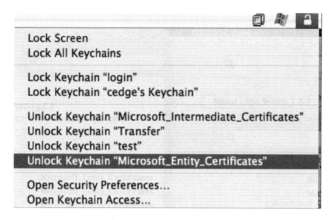

Figure 1-27. *Keychain Access options*

You can create new keychains by clicking Open Keychain Access and clicking the + sign on the next screen. This essentially creates an encrypted disk image file containing other information that needs to be secured, such as cached passwords to web sites. The password assigned to each keychain will open the disk image, thereby unlocking the keychain. Each keychain can and should have a different password.

Best Practices

To wrap this chapter, here is a "cheat sheet" of some of the most important practices you should employ in keeping your Mac secure. Some of these will be covered in later chapters:

- Install antivirus software (see Chapter 4).

- Always install Apple's security updates.

- Open files only from known sources (see Chapter 10).

- Use a standard account for everyday work (see Chapter 3).

- Disable automatic login, and assign a password for every user (see Chapter 3).

- Lock your screen when you step away, and require a password to unlock it.

- Give your keychain its own password, and lock it when it is not in use.

- Use a firewall (see Chapter 8).

- Encrypt important files.

- Protect your wireless network with WPA, and use VPNs when using public wireless (see Chapter 9).

- Protect sensitive e-mail from prying eyes using encryption (see Chapter 5).

- Practice private surfing (see Chapter 5).

- Encrypt your chat sessions (see Chapter 5).

CHAPTER 2

■ ■ ■

Security Fundamentals

You just bought your first Mac. Or maybe you've been buying Macs for years. You might even be part of the Mac cult phenomenon that is rapidly afflicting the world, spanning generations of Macophiles before you. Perhaps you've inherited the responsibility of overseeing a network with Mac computers. What made you buy a Mac? Perhaps it was the ease of use or the creative software bundled with it, or perhaps you just really related to the Mac guy more than the PC guy on the television commercials. Whatever the case may be, congratulations. You will now be working with one of the most advanced, most innovative, and most powerful operating systems on the market today.

Presumably you or the person who purchased the computer bought into the security hype surrounding Macs. "Viruses don't infect Macs," as Apple's web site boasts. Although much has been done by the Mac community to make this statement true, in the past few years security holes have been cropping up all over the place in the Mac community. A Mac is far from being 100 percent secure. In fact, Apple has been releasing security patches on a regular basis to address these security holes. Apple even admits on its web site that a Mac running with factory settings will protect you from viruses much better than a PC, but it's a good idea to run extra virus and security software.

In Chapter 1, we gave you a quick-and-dirty way to secure your Mac. In this chapter, we start to break down the fundamentals of security on a Mac. We explore what hackers are hunting for and the various security risks inherent with owning a Mac, including discussing the different forms security can take on. We'll begin to explore the command line and the various commands you'll be using throughout the book to harness the power of the Unix shell.

■**Tip** The command line is a powerful security tool that we use consistently in our discussion of Mac security fundamentals. However, like most of the security tools discussed throughout this book, a more thorough understanding of the tool is required, independent of this book. Some tools, like the command line, are simply too complicated to cover within the confines of one chapter in a book. In fact, many of the most useful tools have entire books dedicated to their use. We encourage you to expand your knowledge of Mac security beyond the confines of this book. For an excellent introduction to the command line, we highly recommend *The Mac OS X Command Line: Unix Under the Hood*, by Kirk McElhern (Sybex, 2005).

Note There is more to security best practices than running security updates. Good security design is a process of reviewing the risks and determining which vulnerabilities are acceptable vs. what it would cost to remedy the problem. In fact, some security measures can be rather expensive. If you are trying to maintain a secure home network or you are in charge of administering your organization's security, whether it's your home office or a networked environment of 100,000 computers, it is most important to define how important your data is to you and how much it would mean if it fell into the wrong hands or was somehow lost.

What Can Be Targeted?

In this ultraconnected world, everyone and everything can be attacked. Home users are just as vulnerable as users in larger networked environments. Elements such as cookies, insecure forms on web sites, computer logs, phishing scams (such as that suspicious e-mail that "assists" you in resetting your PayPal password while secretly directing you to a rogue web server), e-mail, and banking records are often the easiest targets.

Platforms with low market shares, such as the Mac, are less likely to get attacked than those with high market shares, as evidenced by the thousands of exposed vulnerabilities on Windows. Hacking, packet sniffing, exposing passwords, and other more specific attacks are statistically rarer on a Mac, but they still occur and are not as difficult to perpetrate on a Mac as one might think. For example, running a high-end packet sniffer such as Ethereal on a network can start exposing passwords in minutes on a network that is submitting information over insecure channels, whether it's on a Mac or a PC. And as the Mac continues to increase its market share (currently at 3.2 percent; Apple sold 34 percent more Macs in 2007 than in 2006[1]), you will start to see the number of attacks increasing.

Worms are also a weakness on the Mac. (People tend to call them *viruses*, but technically this is incorrect; you'll learn more about worms and viruses in Chapter 4.) Most of the worm threats are based on insecure Microsoft Office code, causing an infection on the computer and in many cases causing documents to be destroyed or lost. Several antivirus packages deal with these, but sadly they are not nearly as feature rich or powerful as the antivirus applications available for Windows computers.

Many attacks that can affect a Mac do not specifically target Apple's operating system. Most of the services that are at the core of OS X users are rooted in Unix and have been in use for more than 30 years. They have become more secure over time but unfortunately still have flaws in their original architecture. Packages such as Apache (the built-in web server), Samba (the built-in file and printer sharing server), and CUPS (the default printing software) are vulnerable to well-known attacks if left unsecured.

The Accidental Mac Administrator

What makes the Mac community unique is that many of the Mac system administrators are often not techies. A good portion of their job is often rooted in other disciplines, such as teaching, running a library or media lab, or editing film. Unfortunately, administrators in Mac environments

---

1. According to www.systemshootouts.org/mac_sales.html, 2007

tend to spend less time securing their networks and more energy on the creative side of using a Mac. Additionally, because security is often not the primary responsibility of many Mac administrators, they are generally not as educated in security best practices as others.

Ironically, some in the Mac community consider security precautions pointless, citing that Mac OS X is perfectly secure out of the box, and many administrators buy into that idea. This is an alarmingly inappropriate position to take with any operating system considering today's connected world. If proper security precautions are not taken, any computer can be hacked, no matter what operating system it's running. And although it is true that a properly secured Mac-based environment has fewer risks than a Windows-based environment, steps must be taken to properly implement a secure Mac-based network.

Conversely, there are also those in the IT world, the Chicken Littles, if you will, who constantly see the sky falling when it comes to computer security. Adopting an overly alarmist position about security can also have dire effects on your budget. Some administrators go overboard, exhibiting what we call *alarmism*. Alarmism is generally only a good idea when those who work around you blatantly refuse to practice even the most basic of security precautions (such as using a word like *password* as the server password—don't laugh, we've seen it).

Kinds of Attacks

In the military, an *attack* is classified as an aggressive attempt to conquer and destroy an enemy, sometimes by denying them access to resources. Computer attacks are no different. Many computer attacks involve trying to steal or destroy data; others involve blocking access to network resources. The following is a list of computer security attacks that are commonly discovered when investigating hacked systems:

Brute-force attacks: This is an attack that attempts to try every possible combination of a password or cipher key (discussed in more detail in Appendix E) in order to gain unauthorized access to resources.

Buffer overflows: Also known as a *buffer overrun*, buffer overflows are attacks that cause a program or computer to crash or act in some way that it was not designed to. Programming errors allowing certain memory exceptions typically cause buffer overflows.

Spoofing attacks: These include attacks where one person or program impersonates another person or program in order to gain access using false credentials. Spoofing attacks include man-in-the-middle attacks, phishing attacks, and referrer spoofing (see Chapter 11 for more information on referrer spoofing).

Viruses and malware: Discussed in detail in Chapter 7, these are software programs that are installed on your computer for the express purpose of causing it harm. (*Malware* is short for "malicious software.")

War driving: This means looking for wireless networks built using no or poor security and exploiting them. War driving is covered further in Chapter 9.

OS 9 vs. OS X

In the days of OS 9 obscurity, fewer vulnerabilities were available for the Mac. Since the introduction of OS X, the Mac has gained a tremendous amount of notoriety, garnering more and more attention from the computing community, and hackers have taken notice. In fact, hackers have started to use OS X as a hacking tool, discovering vulnerabilities within the operating system and exploiting them. DefCon, a hacker conference held annually in Las Vegas, is a good example of how the Mac OS X adoption has taken the hacker community by storm. In 2000, one of the authors of this book attended with what he thinks was the only Mac in the building. His 540c was the laughing stock of the conference and was unhackable because it was relatively obscure. Over the past seven years, as Mac OS X has been more widely adopted, there have been an increasing number of Mac laptops in the DefCon audience. Now you can see those glowing apples all over the floor. Why?

In many ways, the MacBook is the perfect hacking computer. It has a nice graphical user interface (GUI) that people can use to do their regular work. They can still run Windows or Linux using Boot Camp or Parallels. They can use a Terminal shell to do their bidding, the tool of choice for most hackers because of its complexity. In short, this powerful tool has been harnessed to do hackers' bidding. But if you think that hackers aren't exploring ways to attack other hackers, think again. They've discovered exploits, and they use them with increasing frequency as the market share numbers rise.

Mac OS 9 applications can run in some versions of OS X and are known to OS X as *classic* applications. OS 9, or classic mode, was designed to allow for a smoother transition to OS X but is no longer officially supported (termed a *dead product*). Leopard does not support the use of Mac OS 9 applications, which do not run on the Intel chipset now used in all newly manufactured Mac systems. These dead products are a security risk because they are no longer protected from the increasing number of threats. On computers that have been migrated from OS 9, there are often folders that should be archived and removed if they still exist. These folders, which live in the root of the hard drive, include the following:

Applications (OS 9): This is the location of applications during the migration to OS 9.

System folder: This is the old operating system for OS 9.

Desktop (OS 9): This allowed access to the OS 9 Desktop folder during the transition to OS X but is only a shortcut.

Documents: This folder might contain user data, although it is likely that the data is old and duplicates data in the Documents folder of a user's hard drive.

If they must remain on the machine, they should be limited to only the applications that are needed. Sensitive documents should be kept in the documents folder in OS X and preferably stored using FileVault, covered further in Chapter 1.

Darwin vs. Aqua

Aqua is the commonly used name of the Graphical User Interface, or GUI, built on top of the core operating system in Mac OS X. Mac OS X is arguably one of the most beautiful operating systems to date. When we think of Aqua, we think of rich graphics, flashy screens, and animations that help us save files and navigate around the system. What we don't think about is that many of these screens are actually working with preference files and editing configuration files within the Unix underpinnings of the system.

Beneath the interface of Mac OS X is another layer called Darwin, a Unix-based foundation based on FreeBSD, Apache, and other open source programs. Darwin is a complete operating system, comparable to a different operating system altogether. Darwin, released by Apple Computer in 2000, provides the kernel, libraries, networking support, and command-line environment that comprise the Unix-based components of the operating system.

Why is it important that we familiarize you with these layers of the operating system when discussing security? Essentially, to secure a Mac, you must be familiar with both of these layers because there are tools that are better to use with one or the other. Many of the topics that we will cover throughout this book involve using tools that Apple has placed in System Preferences or applications. But these will not fully secure a system. We will also point to tools that are available only in the command line. It is necessary for you to use both command-line tools and GUI tools if you are attempting to secure your Mac in a comprehensive way.

There are also a variety of hybrid tools developed in XCode. Many of these are based on command-line tools but have a graphical interface, rendering them easier to use. These include applications like batchmod (for managing permissions), lingon (for controlling services) and Carbon Copy Cloner (for cloning drives).

Unix Security

Unix comes with its own security model, independent of anything that Apple might have done to make its operating system easier to use and more pleasant to work with.

Understanding the command line will give you a better understanding of Unix. This understanding extends past the command line and into system internals. This allows administrators to know how firmware, bootloaders, kernel components, the I/O Kit driver framework, user libraries, and other core pieces of software work underneath the operating system. If you understand how these pieces interact, where they originated, and how they evolved, then you will be armed to properly protect against security threats.

A solid understanding of system internals is useful in programming and troubleshooting systems. Programmers can use this knowledge to construct more secure systems software with applications that interact with the system in a more secure way. Armed with this knowledge, system administrators and power users can harness the power of the rich environment offered by Mac OS X to keep it secure. Knowledge of Mac-specific system internals allows Linux, Unix, Windows, and other Unix administrators to compare and contrast Mac OS X with their specific types of systems, which benefits administrators by providing them with a deeper understanding of how each system runs.

■**Tip** If you are interested in learning as much as possible about the internal system and the underpinnings of OS X, read *Mac OS X Internals: A Systems Approach* by Amit Singh (Addison-Wesley, 2006).

When Apple built Mac OS X, it left many of the advanced Unix tools out of the standard version, allowing users to still access them by installing the Developer Tools. The Developer

Tools are provided by Apple with all copies of Mac OS X and are required for installing many of the command-line-oriented tools mentioned in this book.

To install the Developer Tools, follow these steps:

1. Insert the Developer Tools CD for your operating system into your computer.

2. Open the installer.

3. Click Continue to run the installer.

4. Click Agree to agree to the licensing agreement.

5. Click Custom for a custom installation.

6. Select the components you want to install.

7. Click Install to complete your installation of the Apple Developer Tools.

In the Beginning...the Command Line

One of the most complicated parts of Mac OS X is the command line. For novice Mac users, the command line is a scary world that doesn't use animations or wizards to tell them what to do. It is a powerful tool that allows *you* to tell the computer what you want it to do. If you are to perform any kind of upper-level security work on the Mac, you will need to fire up the command line, so you should have at least a modicum of comfort with it. To help ease with this transition, the following is a quick-and-dirty listing of the most common commands you'll need to know. You can then use the man command followed by any of these commands to learn more about them. We might introduce other commands over the course of the rest of this book, but these make up the core toolset that most Mac users will require:

awk: Finds and replaces text using a built-in language or regular expressions

bash: The default command interpreter (or *shell*) for 10.3 and newer

bless: Sets volume boot options such as the start-up disk

cat: Displays the contents of a file

cd: Changes the current working directory

chflags: Changes a file or folder's flags, such as the Finder's locked bit

chmod: Changes file/folder permissions for owner and group

chown: Changes file/folder owner and group

chroot: Runs a command with a different root directory

cksum: Prints checksum and byte counts (data transmission errors)

clear: Clears the Terminal screen (Ctrl+L)

cmp: Compares two files

comm: Compares two sorted files line by line

cp: Copies one or more files to another location

crontab: Schedules a command to run at a later date/time

cut: Divides a file into several parts

date: Displays or changes the date and time

dd: Converts and copies data such as a forensic file system copy

df: Displays free disk space

diff: Displays the differences between two files

diff3: Shows differences among three files

dig: The standard DNS lookup

diskutil: Provides disk utilities, such as Format, Verify, Repair, and Repair Permissions

dscl: Provides a directory service command-line utility

du: Estimates file space usage

echo: Displays a message on the screen with a newline character

exit: Exits the current shell

fdisk: The partition table manipulator for Darwin UFS/HFS/DOS

find: Searches for files that meet a desired criteria

fsck: Performs a file system consistency check and repair

fsaclctl: Performs a file system enable/disable ACL

fs_usage: Performs file system usage

sftp: A secure file transfer program, part of the OpenSSH suite

GetFileInfo: Retrieves file system attributes of Mac OS Extended (HFS+) volumes

grep: Searches file(s) for lines that match a given pattern

groups: Prints group names a user belongs to

gzip: Compresses or decompresses files

head: Displays the first lines of a file

hdiutil: Manipulates the disk image framework

history: The command history for the bash shell

hostname: Displays the current boot hostname

id: Displays the unique ID

`installer`: Installs standard Mac OS X `.pkg` and `.mpkg` installers

`kill`: Sends a terminate signal to a running process number

`kinit`: Obtains a ticket from a Kerberos Key Distribution Center server

`kdestroy`: Removes Kerberos tickets from the credential cache

`less`: Displays output one screen or page at a time

`ln`: Makes hard or soft links between files

`locate`: Finds files using a prebuilt index

`ls`: Lists information about files or directories

`lsbom`: Lists a bill of materials file from a Mac OS X Package Installer

`lsof`: Lists open files for a running process

`man`: Displays the help manual

`md5`: Displays the MD5 fingerprint for a file

`mkdir`: Creates new folder(s)

`mount`: Mounts a local or remote file system

`mv`: Moves or renames files or directories

`nice`: Sets the processor usage priority of a command

`nohup`: Runs a command immune to hang-ups

`open`: Opens a file/folder/URL/application

`osascript`: Interacts or executes an AppleScript

`passwd`: Modifies a user password

`paste`: Merges lines of files

`pico`: An elementary text editor

`ping`: Tests network addresses

`pmset`: Manipulates power management settings

`ps`: Displays static process listings

`pwd`: Prints current working directory

`quota`: Displays disk usage and limits

`rm`: Removes files

`rmdir`: Removes folder(s)

`rsync`: A remote file copy, sync file tree

say: Converts text to audible speech

screencapture: Captures screen image to file or disk

scutil: Manages system configuration

sdiff: Merges two files interactively

security: Manages keychains, keys, and certificates

sed: Displays the Stream Editor

serveradmin: Manages Mac OS X Server settings

declare: Sets a bash shell variable to a value

setenv: Sets an environment variable to a value

setfile: Sets attributes of Mac OS Extended (HFS+) file systems

shutdown: Shuts down or restarts OS X

sleep: Delays for a specified time before running another command

softwareupdate: A system software update tool

sort: Sorts text files based on different criteria

split: Splits a file into fixed-size pieces

srm: Securely removes a file, overwriting multiple times

su: Substitutes a user identity

sudo: Executes a command as another user, obtaining a root shell with sudo -s

tail: Outputs the last lines of a text file

tar: Displays the tape archiver

top: Displays an interactive process listing with CPU, RAM displays, and processes

touch: Changes file timestamps

traceroute: Performs a trace route to a host

umask: Invokes a user's file creation mask

umount: Unmounts a device from the system

uname: Prints system information

unset: Removes variable or function names

unsetenv: Removes environment variable

users: Prints login names of users currently logged in

vi: Displays an advanced text editor

wc: Obtains byte, word, and line counts

where: Reports all known instances of a command

who: Prints all usernames currently logged on

whoami: Prints the current username

xargs: Displays the execution utility, useful with the find command

Physical Security

Theft is one of the biggest threats to the security of your data. Apple takes physical security very seriously, and you should also. Since the days of OS 9, a slot for a physical locking mechanism (see Figure 2-1) has been provided with each Apple computer and monitor sold. Locks are usually available at the Apple store or online and often cost less than $50. These locks typically involve locking the computer to a desk in order to make it more difficult to steal.

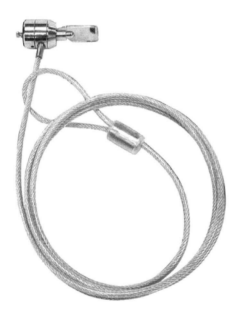

Figure 2-1. *Apple security locks*

Using a locking mechanism to lock the machine isn't going to deter a thief 100 percent of the time, but it will work in a large percentage of situations. Most thieves will not try to break the lock or move furniture to get to a locked laptop. Having said that, try not to lock a laptop to a corner of a table that can be lifted. If possible, lock your devices to an immobile surface.

Many of the vendors of security locks guarantee that if your laptop or desktop is stolen while it is locked in place, they will replace it for free.

■**Note** Some vendors that provide security locks include Kensington, Tryten, and Targus.

A good way to deter computer thieves is to put freestanding servers or client computers in a server rack. Fully enclosed server racks have walls and doors on them. The front and back doors are locked to limit access into the racks themselves. We have heard of only one situation where a thief actually stole a computer rack, and that rack was on casters (wheels).

Here are some suggestions for purchasing secure racks:

- The APC NetShelter racks are common and usually come with keyed access to the metal or glass doors. APC also develops NetBotz, a family of network-accessible appliances that detect and produce various types of alarms based on environmental factors that can threaten the availability of network-critical physical infrastructure such as heat, humidity, and other physical threats to your computing assets. One nice feature of the NetBotz is that it can detect movement and record it using a video camera.

- Belkin also builds and distributes full-sized racks and rack-optimized hardware.

- The XRackPro2 by GizMac is a rack-mounted enclosure cabinet specifically designed for noise reduction and security. The XrackPro2 is available in a variety of sizes including 4U, 12U, and 25U.

- Acousti Products builds full-sized and soundproofed cabinets that can be purchased for a variety of purposes.

Equipment Disposal

No matter how much you may love your Mac, there will come a time when it will be old and no longer appropriate for use. At that point, it is important to make sure that the computer is disposed of properly.

Some people buy old hardware (such as that found on eBay) just to mine information out of it or test their forensic abilities. If data is compromised in this way, then this poses the risk that your data could be stolen. A variety of services will dispose of computers properly. However, before sending a computer to a disposal facility, it is important to erase all of the data from the hard drive or remove the drive entirely. Mac OS X has some nice built-in hard drive–erasing features that can securely erase data (as described in Chapter 1).

■Note Performing a 35-pass erase of data is the most time-consuming, but the most secure way to erase the data (covered further in Chapter 1).

In addition to the security implications of getting rid of old hardware, think of the environmental implications as well. In much the same way that old engine oil contains dangerous chemicals to the environment, computers do as well. Computers should be disposed of in as appropriate a manner as you might dispose of oil.

Computer disposal requirements are different for homes than they are for businesses. Under the Resource Conservation and Recovery Act (RCRA), computers disposed of by a household are not considered hazardous waste, while computers disposed of by a business are. Computers donated or sold to scrap dealers and recyclers may end up being improperly disposed. To minimize the risk of liability, businesses need to ensure that their computers are disposed of properly.

Some disposal services include the following:

- For home users, Apple offers a free recycling program for your old computers and monitors when you buy a new Mac, as well as a free iPod recycling program through Apple's retail stores that gets you a 10 percent discount on new iPods.

- For companies, Apple has a trade-in program for educational and business customers in the United States. You can talk to your local representative in the Mac Business Unit for more information on this.

- For switchers, Apple accepts all electronics free of charge, regardless of the manufacturer of the computer.

- eWaste Center is a company that can dispose of a wide variety of equipment nationally. You can find eWaste Center at `http://www.ewastecenter.com`.

- Also check your local municipalities' web sites for city disposal sites. Some cities will allow you to dispose computers for free up to a certain pound limit.

No matter how you choose to dispose of hardware, it is important to make sure that the drives are erased or removed before disposing. Inadvertently putting your sensitive data into the wrong hands can be catastrophic.

Physical Devices and Optical Media

Removable media such as USB drives, FireWire drives, USB and FireWire jump drives, and CDs/DVDs can be how viruses find their way onto your network and how confidential data finds its way out of your environment, no matter how secure the environment may be.

Setting up limited accounts on OS X will not restrict users' ability to work with external optical media on systems. Guest accounts still have access to removable media in much the same way that a standard account or an administrative account would have.

One way to restrict the use of removable media is to use permissions in the operating system to do so. The disk arbitration daemon is the service responsible for mounting disks that are inserted into your computer. Through each iteration of Mac OS X, it has been possible to kill the disk arbitration daemon. To do so, just move the disk arbitration `plistfile` from the `/System/Library/LaunchDaemons` folder, and restart your computer.

Another way to lock removable media from being accessible is to use Open Directory policies. Open Directory and using it to enforce policies on computers in networked environments is discussed in more detail in Chapter 13.

Firmware and Firmware Password Protection

Open Firmware and EFI are the two faces of firmware.

Open Firmware

Open Firmware is hardware-independent firmware developed by Sun Microsystems. It was primarily used in PowerPC-based Apple Macintosh computers, as well as some Sun SPARC-based workstations and servers. It supported an interactive command-line interface mode accessed by holding the Cmd+Opt+O+F key combination at boot.

EFI

EFI is the next generation of firmware now being used with modern Apple hardware, introduced on the new Intel Mac hardware. This new system retains much of its configuration options such as modifier keys (T and C as mentioned earlier) and firmware password support. Apple has made an obvious effort to allow backward compatibility with the procedures used in setting up a firmware password and other firmware-related operations. Currently there is a firmware prompt like Open Firmware had, but this will most likely change over time because of the extensibility of this new system and the current development examples available.

Firmware Protection

No discussion of physical security would be complete without discussing firmware password protection. Firmware is the software integrated into the hardware, sometimes referred to as the *logic board* or *motherboard* of the machine. It is the "brain" behind how the hardware talks to the rest of the system and can be a first point of entry in taking over a computer. Protecting the firmware with a password has many benefits.

Since the introduction of G3 computers, Apple has given you, the user, the ability to restrict access to a computer's firmware configuration via a password. This security mode comes in two flavors. The first and default *command* mode restricts access to special configuration keyboard selections that are checked at boot time. These keys, known as *snag* or *modifiers*, temporarily alter the configuration parameters such as the start-up disk or boot mode. For example, pressing T for Target Disk mode boots you into Target Disk mode, and pressing C allows you to boot off the CD. The second security mode, known as *full*, works in conjunction with legacy Open Firmware systems to prompt for a password at every boot, no matter what.

▪**Note** Standard x86 PCs have a similar technology known as a *BIOS password*.

Here are the models that support firmware password protection:

- Slot loading iMac and newer iMac G3s

- Flat-panel iMac and iMac G5

- All iBooks

- All eMacs

- Power Mac G4 AGP graphics card and newer models

- Power Mac G4 Cube

- Power Mac G5

- PowerBook G3 (with FireWire)

- PowerBook G4

- Any Intel-based Mac

Enabling firmware password protection has the following effects on Mac computers:

- Blocks the ability to use boot modifier keys such as the C, N, and T keys to boot from CD, DVD, NetBoot, and Target Disk modes, respectively

- Blocks modifier keys to boot in verbose mode and single-user mode

- Blocks resetting PRAM

- Requires a password to use Startup Manager (the Opt key)

- Requires a password to enter commands into Open Firmware on Power PC computers

To enable firmware password protection, follow these steps:

1. Copy the Firmware Password application from the `Applications/Utilities/` folder on the software installation discs that came with your computer.

2. Open the Firmware Password application.

3. Click the Change button to authenticate. Enter the administrator username and password when prompted, and click the Change button (see Figure 2-2).

■**Note** Keep in mind that it is possible and relativity easy to recover a password that is stored in firmware with System Administrator (root) access, and thus a password should be chosen that is not used elsewhere on other systems or services. You can find an example script that decodes this password at `http://www.wallcity.org/books/sec/decodeofpw.sh`.

---

4. Select the Require Password to Change Firmware Settings check box (see Figure 2-3).

5. Type your password in the Password and Verify fields, and click the OK button.

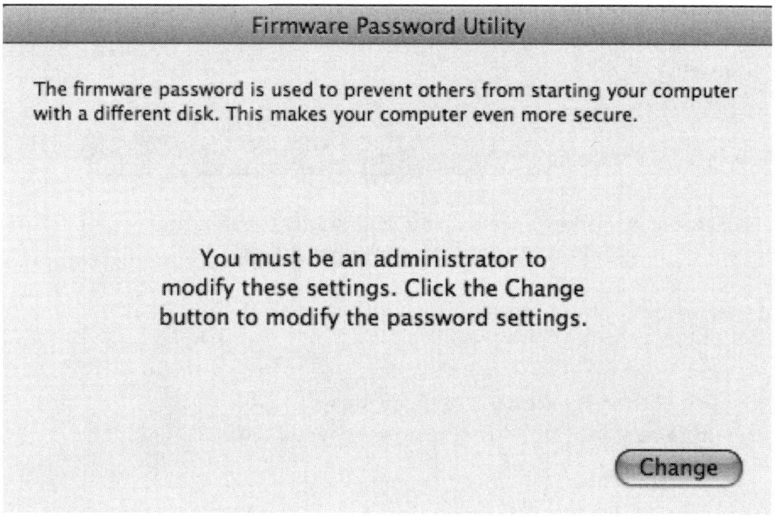

Firmware Password Utility

The firmware password is used to prevent others from starting your computer with a different disk. This makes your computer even more secure.

You must be an administrator to modify these settings. Click the Change button to modify the password settings.

Change

Figure 2-2. *Firmware password warning*

Firmware Password Utility

The firmware password is used to prevent others from starting your computer with a different disk. This makes your computer even more secure.

☑ Require password to change firmware settings

Password: ●●●●●●●●

Type a password or phrase

Verify: ●●●●●●●●

Retype the password or phrase

Cancel   OK

Figure 2-3. *Firmware password entry*

6. If you see the screen shown in Figure 2-4, then the settings change was successful, and your computer will be protected by the Open Firmware Password application until the setting is reset.

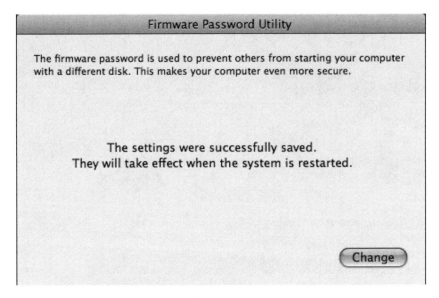

Figure 2-4. *Firmware password confirmation*

If you want to automate this process during imaging, you can download a free closed-source tool from Mac Enterprise called OFPW. Once you have installed this tool, you can use OFPW to set the firmware password by using the following commands:

```
sudo /usr/local/bin/OFPW -pass desiredpassword
sudo /usr/local/bin/OFPW -mode1
```

From time to time, you may want to troubleshoot the machine at the firmware level, for instance, by resetting the PRAM. These lower-level troubleshooting techniques require access to the firmware.

To disable Open Firmware password protection on Power PC Macs, follow these steps:

1. Start Open Firmware by pressing and holding the Cmd+Opt+O+F key combination during start-up.

2. At the Open Firmware prompt, type **reset-nvram**, and press Return.

3. When prompted for your password, enter it, and press the Return key.

4. When the system responds with OK, type **reset-all**, and press Return.

5. When the computer restarts, Open Firmware password protection will be disabled.

To disable firmware password protection on Intel Macs, follow these steps:

1. Open the Firmware Password application.

2. Click Change, and uncheck the Require Password to Change Firmware Settings box.

3. Click OK and authenticate as an administrator.

■Note Also consider that the Casper Suite by JAMF Software allows you to push out EFI/Open Firmware settings en masse.

On 10.2 and 10.3 systems, you can also require the entry of the root password during single-user boot Open Firmware systems. To do this, the `console` and `ttys` settings need to be marked with the comment `insecure` in the `/etc/ttys` file. The system then requires a root password, which is optionally encrypted in the `/etc/master.passwd` file. If no password is specified in this file, the single-user access is effectively disabled. (This procedure is deprecated on modern operating system versions.) To require the root password during a single-user boot, follow these steps:

1. Log in as an administrator.

2. Open the Terminal application from `/Application/Utilities`, and start a root shell:

   ```
   sudo -s
   ```

3. Create a backup of the `/etc/ttys` file using this:

   ```
   cp /etc/ttys /etc/ttys.bkp
   ```

4. Using a text editor, find the word `secure` on all noncommented lines, and replace it with the word `insecure`. Alternatively, you can use the following command to do this automatically:

   ```
   sed s/secure/insecure/g /etc/ttys.bkp >/etc/ttys
   ```

5. Reboot the system, and attempt to boot into single-user mode by holding Cmd+S during start-up.

■Note To comment a command line, use a command-line editor such as pico or vi to find and edit the line by entering a # in front of the line you want to edit and then save the changes. Be careful when editing command-line files with standard word processing programs such as Microsoft Word or TextEdit because these programs will try to save these files as rich-text files, which can possibly render them unusable.

On 10.4 and 10.5 systems, you can force single-user mode to reboot before dropping into a root shell by using the following line in the .profile for the root user. This method uses the process ID number to determine whether this root login is occurring in single-user mode. The variable $$ holds this numeric value, which is usually 2 for 10.4 and 3 for 10.5. The script checks that this current value is less than or equal to 3 and triggers a reboot (or another command).

1. Obtain a root shell by typing **sudo -s** as an administrator.

2. Type the following , noting the use of single quotes:

   ```
   echo '[ $$ -le 3 ] && reboot' >>~root/.profile
   ```

3. Alternatively, you can change the reboot command to lock or halt (research the man pages for these options). This method is not foolproof because a clever attacker with good timing could press Ctrl+C to bypass the start-up script, causing it to stop running before is executed. But because it is a nonstandard configuration anyway, overall it should slow down any potential attack and more than likely stop one.

There are ways to potentially bypass firmware password protection. Any user with administrative access to a computer can disable it by running the Firmware Password Utility. On some hardware, this can also be accomplished by changing the physical amount of RAM on the computer and resetting the parameter RAM (PRAM) three times. Additionally, if a legacy computer is capable of booting into OS 9, then Open Firmware can easily be bypassed. However, all these techniques require physical access to the machine.

Although these relatively complex subversions might cause you to doubt firmware protection and consider it a relatively weak security feature, let's not underestimate its importance. Without the firmware password, any user sitting at a workstation with a small window of time could reboot the computer and boot into a full-screen command-line mode known as *single-user mode* (Cmd+S at start-up). They would then be granted full system administrator (root) privileges to all files/folders on the system. This means in a scenario where an attacker had a period of 30 seconds to a minute alone with a machine, they could conceivably enable a remote access configuration and user account (such as root) that would allow them to obtain administrative rights to subsequent boots of the graphical operating system either locally or remotely.

Multifactor Authentication

When addressing physical security in a network, you should also consider multifactor authentication. Multifactor authentication is the act of requiring multiple sources of identification to authenticate a user. This can be the combination of a smart card and a password or biometrics and a password.

Smart cards are digital identification cards and can be used for the authentication of a user's identity. The most common example is in conjunction with a Public Key Infrastructure (PKI) on a network. The smart card stores an encrypted digital certificate issued from the PKI along with any other relevant or needed information about the cardholder. Many companies use smart cards as their primary method of access control, mainly because they are a privacy-enhancing technology. Most people carry incriminating information around themselves in their wallet or purse. By employing contactless smart cards that can be read without having to remove the card from the wallet or even the garment it is in, one can add even more authentication value to the human carrier of the cards and increase the anonymity of those who use the network.

Biometrics is the science and technology of authentication (that is, establishing the identity of an individual) by measuring the subject person's physiological or behavioral features. Just like something out of a James Bond movie, a user places their hand on a finger print scanner or aligns their eye with a retinal scanner. If the image matches the information in the user database, the user is authenticated. Since a fingerprint, blood vessel print, or retinal image is unique, the only way the system can authenticate is if the proper user is there.

▪Note UPEK has a fingerprint scanner on the market. For more information about it, refer to `http://upek.com/mac`. In our testing, the device works effectively. It can be used in a multifactor environment and can bypass password use altogether (but is not recommended). The UPEK ties into the existing Mac OS X authorization framework. Prior to the release of the UPEK, the SonyPuppy was the last fingerprint scanner with a solid Mac client.

The only way an unauthorized user can get access is by physically kidnapping the authorized user and forcing them through the system. For this reason, biometrics are the strongest (and the costliest) form of authentication. One should never rely solely on biometrics because many of the biometric mechanisms are not as secure as they are made out to be and because there are ways to bypass or trick them in most situations. However, biometrics offers increasingly reliable mechanisms for authentication and can do well in two-factor authentication scenarios where both username/password combinations and biometric tokens are used.

These technologies are becoming more reliable, and they will become widely used over the next few years. Implementations have been limited mainly because of the high cost associated with these technologies. However, when strong username and password requirements are combined with biometrics and smart cards, a *multifactor authentication* scenario is employed, creating a very strong authentication environment.

Keeping Current: The Cat-and-Mouse Game

Enforcing security is like a cat-and-mouse game. New technology breeds new developments that create new flaws that run rampant in the operating system. This means more mice for the cats to find. The cat will eventually find them, and security updates will be released; it's just a matter of when and at what cost to the security fabric.

Some security flaws result in code developed by the community that is used to further protect resources. This is how software firewalls, proxy servers, and other security features not typically included in operating systems by default have developed over time. This community development leads to a more secure environment and better-protected resources.

Software developers are not always quick to release updates or even admit the possibility of exploits. The best way to keep updated on ways to protect your system are to keep up-to-date on the various exploits that have been released in the security community and the countermeasures that are found to combat them. Keeping current on the security community allows you to know more than what the developers are admitting to and be able to stay best protected. To keep current, consider reading the release notes for security patches and visiting web sites such as `http://www.afp548.com` and `http://www.macenterprise.org`.

The NSA and the Mac

In 2004, the National Security Agency (NSA) developed a document, referred to as the *NSA Whitepaper*, that offers a solid foundation of security principles as they pertain to Mac OS X. The document has since been updated, and many in the government sector use it as a guideline for implementing security on the Mac platform. These guidelines have been adopted by the Mac community as the standard for securing Mac systems across the board, nongovernment and home systems alike. We cover most of what is in this document in this book, but we highly recommended it as a supplement to this book.

The items covered in the guide are meant for non–Open Directory environments. If you are running Open Directory, the guide will offer a framework, but many of the items will need custom policies implemented if there are not already managed preferences in place. For more on Open Directory environments, see Chapter 11.

In addition, the Apple Security Configuration Guide will step users through a secure installation of Mac OS X and give specific settings to be used for optimal security. Because of the outdated nature of the document, there will be items that are no longer available during both the installation and post-installation configuration of your system(s). However, the settings are rather similar, and the gist is the same.

Another tenet of the Security Configuration Guide is to set up your computer while disconnected from the Internet and connect the computer to the Internet only when all the updates and security settings have been applied. The idea behind this is that if your computer gets attacked during the setup, it will not have all of the appropriate security settings and may become compromised before it is even finished being set up. This is a basic tenet of security and true across all operating systems.

A Word About Parallels and Boot Camp

With the introduction of the Intel-based Mac, the ability to install Windows using Parallels, VMware, or Boot Camp on a Mac has now been fully realized. However, with this cross-platform ability comes all the security headaches that can plague a Windows machine. Although the extent of security measures to be implemented in a Windows environment exceeds the breadth of this book, suffice it to say that security concerns in a Windows environment on a Mac still apply and should be taken. A proper firewall, antivirus software, and file-sharing precautions are mandatory (at a minimum) for a properly secured Windows environment on a Mac.

Caution Virtual machines increase the surface space of attacks on the Mac. You will need to secure the Windows systems independently from the Mac.

CHAPTER 3

■■■

Securing User Accounts

Work has been done over the years to harden OS X by strengthening its user security. *Hardening* describes the strengthening of an element of security in an operating system to make it more secure. User accounts can be hardened in OS X by limiting the resources users can access. You can accomplish this two ways: by using the built-in GUI tools or by using the command line. In this chapter, we will go deeper into securing the Mac by focusing first on restricting user access and then on more advanced command-line security that can be used to harden user accounts.

Introducing Authentication, Authorization, and Identification

Authentication is an operating system's attempt to verify the digital identity of someone or something attempting to communicate with the computer, such as a request to log into the system. The sender attempting to be authenticated might be an actual person using a computer, a computer itself attempting to authenticate, or a computer program looking to run software on the machine. For example, if you were attempting to install software, authentication is the act of your Mac asking for your username and password and verifying that you are who you say you are.

Note Because authentication is the act of establishing or confirming something as authentic, a key component of authentication is protecting authentication attempts such as passwords or key pairs in transit.

Authorization is how the system, once you are identified, determines whether you have access to a given resource. Most modern multiuser operating systems include an authorization process. This gives the operating system the ability to identify users and then verify whether they have the appropriate credentials to use a resource. Permissions are generally defined by a system administrator, either on the computer itself or in a networked environment.

On Mac OS X, the authorization process starts with the /etc/authorization file, which contains rules used when authorizing users. Authorization is extensible using pluggable authentication modules (PAMs), which were initially developed by Sun Microsystems. A PAM allows multiple authentication schemes to be integrated with new software, which allows programs that rely on authentication to be written independently of the underlying authentication scheme.

To distinguish authentication from authorization, the shorthand notations A1 (authentication) and A2 (authorization) are occasionally used.

Verifying that the person sending you information is really who they say they are is obviously desirable all the time. Authentication, however, is time-consuming and can inconvenience users while resulting in overhead on the authentication services. To make situations like this more convenient and efficient, many systems use a method of *identification* that verifies that the person or entity is the same one you communicated with when you last authenticated. The means of identification can be established through the use of a ticket or token issued when authentication is done. This saves the user from being required to authenticate on each communication with the server.

WHEN IS SECURE TOO SECURE?

One example of where security and usability often collide is in the deployment of one-time passwords. A one-time password is a password that must be changed each time you log into your computer. This effectively makes any intercepted password good for only the brief interval of time before the legitimate user logs in the next time. This way, if someone intercepts a password, it would probably already be expired or be on the verge of expiration within a matter of hours.

For nearly every situation, this is too much security and impacts the ability of users to remember passwords. In our experience, when one-time passwords are deployed, it typically means users are writing passwords down. Anytime your password policy causes users to have to write down their passwords, it is a good idea to review whether you are being too strict with password policies.

Managing User Accounts

Mac OS X is a multiuser operating system. Every file on the system is owned by a user, and every process is run by a user. One great way to analyze the processes in use on your system, along with the name of the users running them, is to view them using the Activity Monitor, accessible via the Utilities folder on the machine. As you can see in Figure 3-1, a variety of accounts are listed in the User column, each running separate processes. The process has permissions to only those resources to which the accounts can access. Therefore, processes are restricted from accessing data they should not be able to access. This security extends to files and other system resources on your computer.

Key to being able to secure an operating system is understanding what each of the user accounts are capable of performing on the operating system. Next, we will discuss varying types of accounts within Mac OS X.

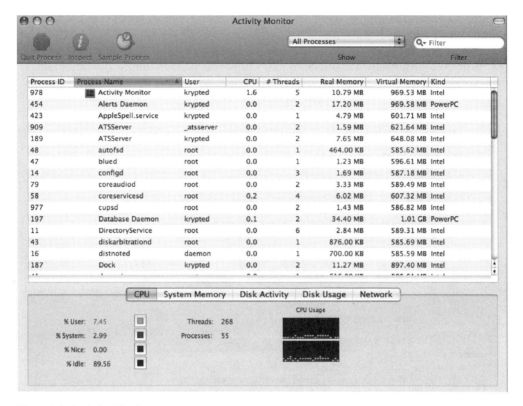

Figure 3-1. *Activity Monitor*

Introducing the Account Types

Limiting the capabilities of users in a standard operating environment is one of the first and most important steps in securing a system or a network, no matter which operating system you are using. Traditionally, Mac OS X has had only three user account types: administrator, standard, and root (superuser). In Leopard, Apple has expanded that number to six: standard, managed, administrative, sharing, guest, and root.

The first and default user of a system is an administrative user; this user has almost unlimited access to the system. Administrative users can use many of the configuration utilities and change permissions of files to gain access to other users' folders if need be.

With all the power that an administrative user has, it is easy to accidentally damage the operating system. Best practices for operating in a secure environment dictate that once a Mac is set up, the administrative account should not be used for everyday use, and the standard account should be used instead. When the system needs more privileges than what a standard account allows, you will be prompted to authenticate as an administrator.

When using your computer, it is best to use a standard user account, even if you are a seasoned administrator. Standard users can operate basic applications, access their own files, and change some of their settings. They cannot make global configuration changes or changes to other accounts. The reasoning behind this is that it is easy to accidentally perform inappropriate actions on the system as an administrator without asking for authentication to confirm the action. As a standard user, the likelihood of viral activity and misconfiguration on the system is almost nonexistent.

Sharing accounts were added so that you can give other users access to log into shared resources over the network on your computer without giving them physical access to the machine locally.

To set up a sharing account, follow these steps:

1. Open System Preferences from the Apple menu.

2. Click Accounts to open the Accounts preference pane, and authenticate if needed by clicking the lock icon.

3. Click the plus sign on the lower-left side of the pane.

4. Select Sharing Only in the Type field (see Figure 3-2).

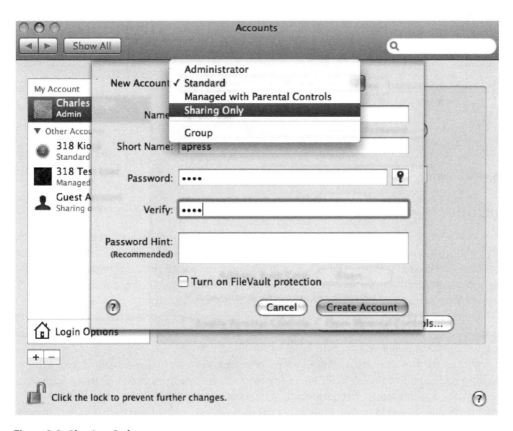

Figure 3-2. *Sharing Only account*

5. Enter a name for the account in the Name field. This is the full name of the user who will be logging in.

6. Enter a short name for the account in the Short Name field (keep in mind that this will be difficult to change at a later date).

7. Enter a password for the account.

8. Enter the password again in the Verify field.

9. Enter a hint for a password reminder.

10. Click the Create Account button.

Adding Users to Groups

You can grant access to resources based on group memberships. In Leopard, Apple has introduced a new account type to the GUI of Mac OS X called a *group*. Groups contain users who are created on the Accounts preference pane. To create a group, follow these steps:

1. Open System Preferences from the Apple menu.

2. Open the Accounts preference pane by double-clicking Accounts.

3. Click the plus sign on the lower-left side of the Accounts preference pane.

4. Change the account type to Group.

5. Give the group a name (see Figure 3-3).

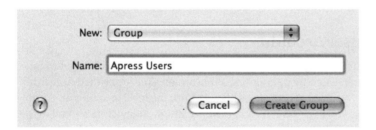

Figure 3-3. *Creating a group*

6. Add users to the group by selecting the check boxes for each user you want to include as a member of the group (Figure 3-4).

7. Close the window to save the group settings.

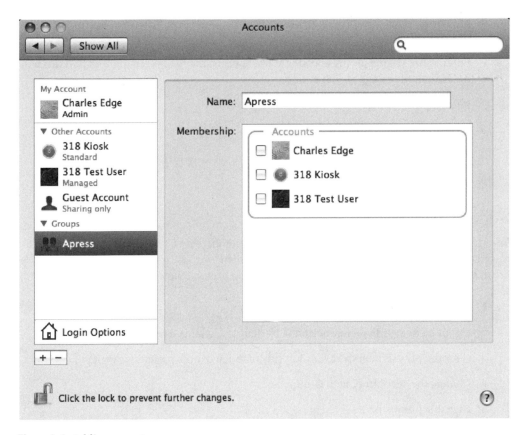

Figure 3-4. *Adding users to groups*

Enabling the Superuser Account

Some items in this book will require the superuser, often referred to as the *root user*, to be enabled. The root account is disabled by default (for a reason) and has unbridled access to everything on the computer. This level of access is different from the level of access an administrative user has. For example, you can erase most of the operating system while booted to the operating system as a root user. If you enable root, disable it when you are finished with the task at hand.

To enable the root account, follow these steps:

1. Open the Directory Utility from the /Applications/Utilities folder.

2. Click the lock icon to authenticate as an administrator.

3. Click the Edit menu, and select Enable Root User from the menu (see Figure 3-5).

4. Save the settings by closing the Directory Utility.

Edit	Window	Help	
Undo			⌘Z
Redo			⇧⌘Z
Cut			⌘X
Copy			⌘C
Paste			⌘V
Clear			
Select All			⌘A
Change Root Password...			
Enable Root User			
Search For Mac OS X Servers			
Special Characters...			⌥⌘T

Figure 3-5. *Enabling root*

Be very careful when enabling root. It is rarely required as a permanently accessible user account. Unless you are using the root account for specific tasks, such as running Carbon Copy Cloner, disable it for the majority of the time. To disable the root account, follow these steps:

1. Open Directory Utility from the /Applications/Utilities folder.

2. Click the lock icon to authenticate as an administrator.

3. Click the Edit menu, and select Disable Root User in the menu (see Figure 3-6).

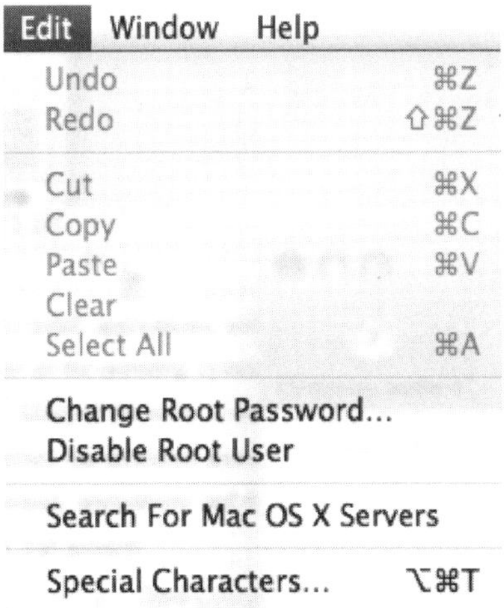

Edit	Window	Help	
Undo			⌘Z
Redo			⇧⌘Z
Cut			⌘X
Copy			⌘C
Paste			⌘V
Clear			
Select All			⌘A
Change Root Password...			
Disable Root User			
Search For Mac OS X Servers			
Special Characters...			⌥⌘T

Figure 3-6. *Disabling the root account*

4. Save the settings by closing the Directory Utility.

Setting Up Parental Controls

Parental Controls is a new System Preferences pane introduced in Leopard. Parental Controls existed in Tiger but did not use the same techniques for management, such as a dedicated preference pane and the command sandbox. Parental Controls now give you the ability to lock certain features down on a Mac. Using the new Parental Controls preference pane, you can configure controls for any user with the account type of Managed and have control over what they can do with Mail.app, iChat, and web browsing with Safari.

■**Note** Tiger used MCX for policy management, which Leopard also supports.

To use Parental Controls, open Mac OS X's System Preferences, and click the Parental Controls preference pane. Click the account you want to control, and then click the Enable Parental Controls button (see Figure 3-7). If the account is not in the list, then go to the Accounts preference pane, and verify that either the Enable Parental Controls check box is checked or the account is not an administrative account. If you are setting up an account initially, you can simply create the account as a managed account with a Parental Controls account.

Figure 3-7. *Enabling the Parental Controls feature*

Once you have enabled Parental Controls, you can control whether the user is forced to use Simple Finder (a limited way of interacting with the Finder where most of the command keys are disabled and many Finder options are also disabled), control which applications a user is able to access, control whether they can burn CDs and DVDs, place limits on how long they can be on the computer, limit access to whom the user is able to converse with over iChat and Mail, restrict access to web sites they can navigate to, and even review logs of attempted violations of these rules from another computer.

To specifically restrict access to applications a user is allowed to access, open the Parental Controls preference pane, open the user you want to control access for, click the System tab, and choose the Only Allow Selected Applications (see Figure 3-8). Then go through the list of applications, and place a check mark next to the application the user should be able to access. Other settings, such as enabling Simple Finder, disabling the user's ability to manage printers, disabling the user's ability to change their password, and disabling a user's ability to change the contents of their dock are all configured when using Parental Controls.

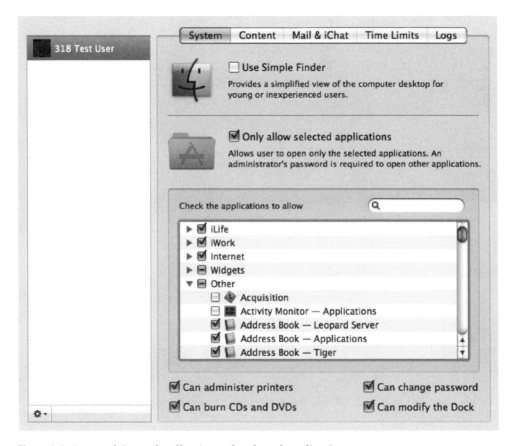

Figure 3-8. *Parental Controls, allowing only selected applications*

You can also block web sites or dictionary items that have specific words in their names. The Hide Profanity in Dictionary option (see Figure 3-9) sets restrictions on the words in the dictionary that users can look up.

■**Note** There is no graphical control beyond the Hide profanity option to customize the words that users are allowed to look up in the dictionary.

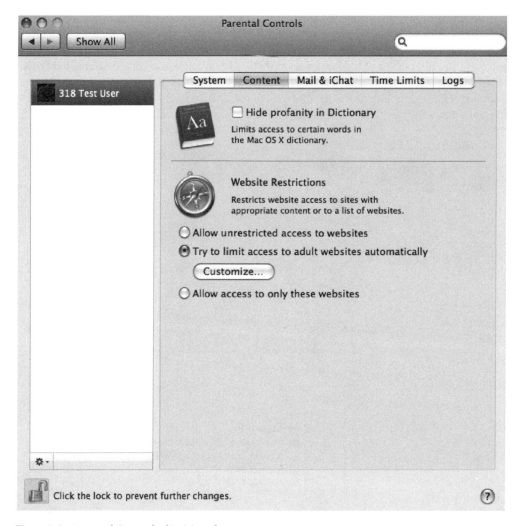

Figure 3-9. *Parental Controls, limiting the content*

Limiting access to certain web sites is a very nice feature. Traditionally, operating systems rely on external devices such as firewalls with content filtration to block adult web content. Now you can do it within Leopard using predefined filters from Apple's servers. To limit access to web sites prefiltered by Apple, click the Content tab of the Parental Controls preference pane, and then click Try to Limit Access of Adult Websites. This will automatically enable a filter of sites that Apple has chosen as inappropriate due to adult content.

You can also set up an opt-in list of web sites that the user is allowed to visit. Access the list by using the Content tab on the Parental Controls preference panel to allow sites (see Figure 3-10) in the Website Restrictions section. If this is enabled, even though the prebuilt list of sites has restricted access, the sites listed in the Always Allow These Sites section will still be accessible.

If a user with this control enabled attempts to go to a site not in the list of allowed sites, then the user will have to enter an administrative password to be allowed to visit the site. If a site is listed in the Never Allow These Sites section, an administrator password will not be requested, and access to the sites in this list will be denied whether or not they are allowed by the adult content filter.

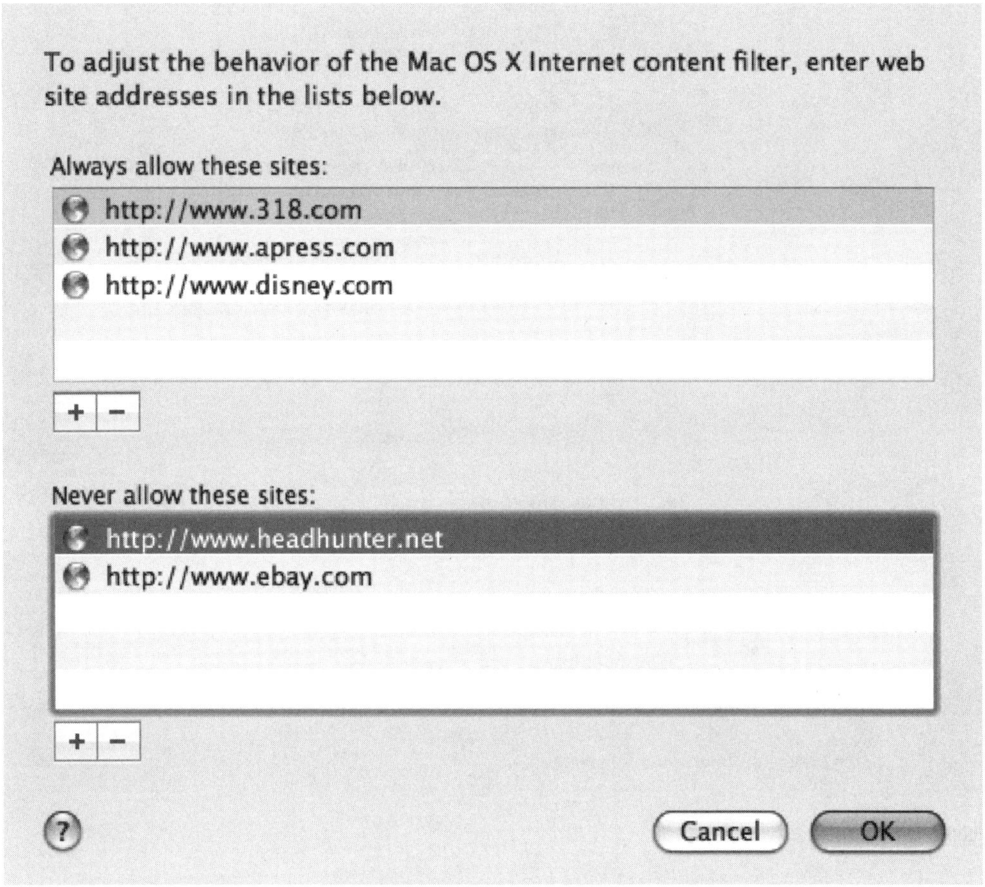

To adjust the behavior of the Mac OS X Internet content filter, enter web site addresses in the lists below.

Always allow these sites:

 🌐 http://www.318.com
 🌐 http://www.apress.com
 🌐 http://www.disney.com

＋ －

Never allow these sites:

 🌐 http://www.headhunter.net
 🌐 http://www.ebay.com

＋ －

?   (Cancel) (OK)

Figure 3-10. *Allowed and disabled web sites*

The Parental Controls feature can also limit who can be communicated with via Apple Mail and iChat. Keep in mind that if you choose to use Parental Controls to manage iChat and Mail, then you will need to build a list of all of the users that the managed user will be able to communicate with. To limit access to Mail, open the Parental Controls preference pane, click the managed user, and check the Limit Mail box (see Figure 3-11). To limit access to iChat in the same manner, check the Limit iChat box.

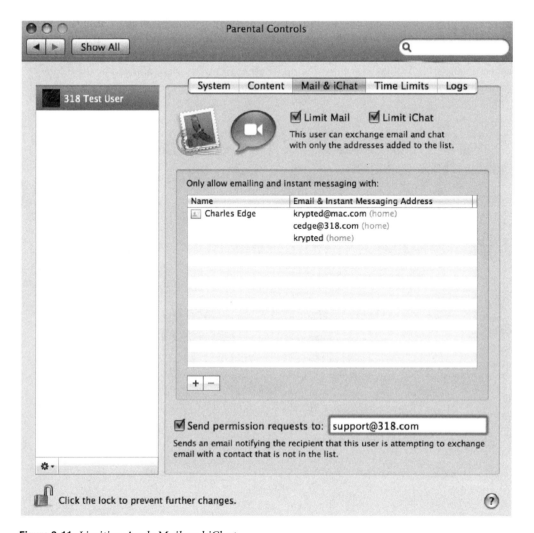

Figure 3-11. *Limiting Apple Mail and iChat*

Once you have set the managed user to limit mail and/or iChat access, then you'll want to build a list of people the user is allowed to communicate with. By clicking the + box, the users included in the Add Users screen (see Figure 3-12) will automatically be added to the user's list of people you have deemed safe for them to instant message and communicate with via email.

You can also set up permission requests so that when communication is attempted by users not in the accepted list, an email is sent to the address indicated in the Send Permission Requests To field (shown earlier in Figure 3-11). This allows you to know when changes need to be implemented in the list.

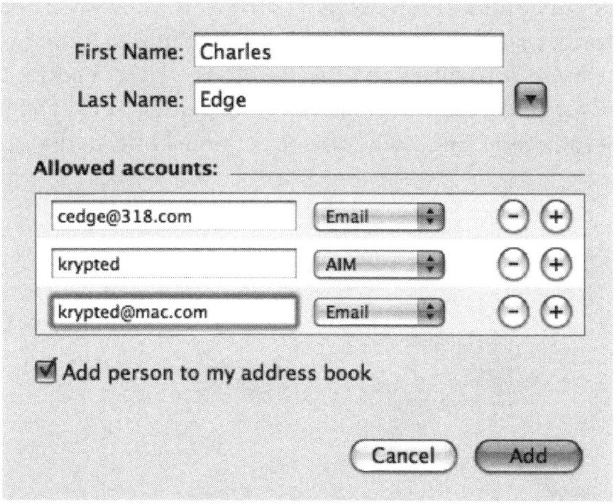

Figure 3-12. *Manually adding users*

You can also add users to the screen based on their entry in your Address Book. To do this, click the disclosure button to the right of the Last Name menu (see Figure 3-13), and browse to the user you want to add. Select multiple people by holding down the Cmd key while selecting each person or by holding the Shift key down when selecting a group of people. Once you are satisfied with all of the users in the list, then click the Add button, and the new entries will populate the list.

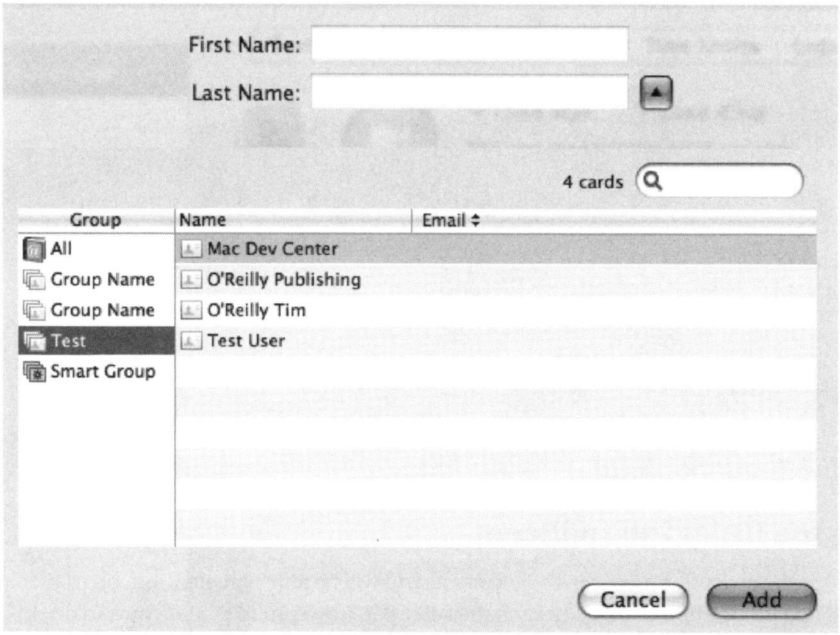

Figure 3-13. *Adding addresses from Address Book*

Once you have configured your Parental Controls for messaging protocols, you can set time limits. Time limits allow you to restrict access to the computer at specific times or limit the total amount of time the computer can be used. You will also be able to set a period for bedtime or times when the computer cannot be used. To access time limits, click the Time Limits tab of the Parental Controls preference panel. From here, you will be able to set time limits in hours for weekdays as well as weekend days (see Figure 3-14).

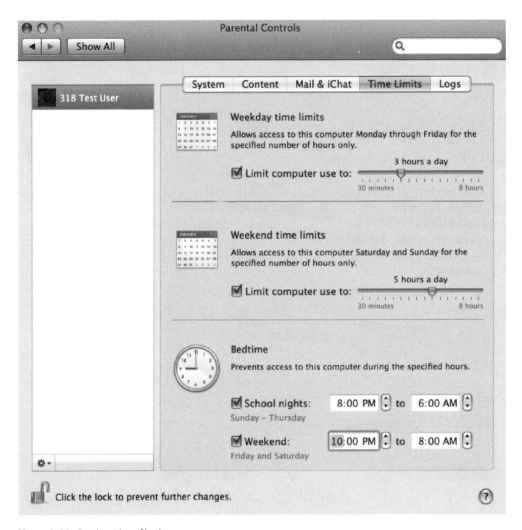

Figure 3-14. *Setting time limits*

Managing the Rules Put in Place

Once you have set the controls for your managed users, you will be able to review logs on traffic, allowing you to find users attempting to breach the rules you have put in place. You can do this using the Logs tab of the Parental Controls preference pane.

You can also copy Parental Controls settings from one user to another. This makes it easy to set up multiple accounts on a system and quickly assign the same settings to new accounts. To do this, click the account with the settings you would like to copy, click the cogwheel icon at the bottom left of the screen, and choose the Copy Settings for "<Username> Test User" option (see Figure 3-15).

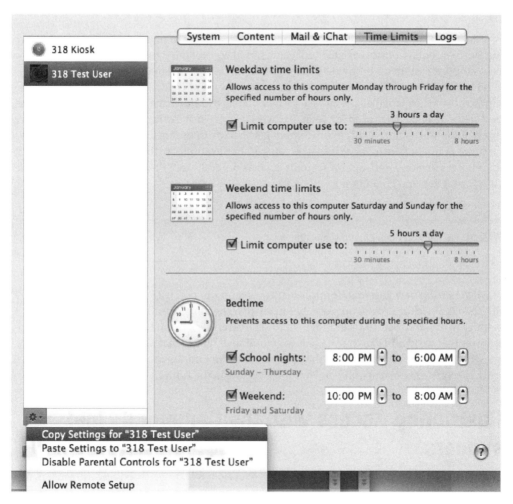

Figure 3-15. *Copying settings for one user*

To copy managed user settings from one user to another user, click the user with the settings you want to copy, select the Paste Settings for the Target Account option, and verify that the settings have been applied (see Figure 3-16).

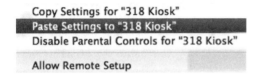

Figure 3-16. *Pasting settings to another user*

Parental Controls is not just for parents to control access to resources for their children. Although Parental Controls existed in Tiger, it has been expanded to include the options in the new sandbox system and provide a more granular control of managed settings in Leopard. Sandbox represents a giant step forward from the options in Tiger, and as such, it's a powerful new feature in Leopard that can be used in the workplace to limit what managed users can access, be it web sites or contacts used for iChat. It can even limit when a computer can be accessed, and in a manner that is not easily circumvented. It's also worth noting that Open Directory allows far more granular control of access to resources. For example, with Open Directory, you can limit access to global settings on systems such as other System Preferences, Bluetooth, Fast User Switching, and Login Items.

■**Note** For more on Open Directory, see Chapter 13.

Overall, the new Parental Controls feature, in conjunction with Open Directory, is useful for schools as well as in the workplace, because Open Directory can also push Parental Controls settings to hundreds or thousands of systems concurrently. Parental Controls is missing some features that we would like to see, such as an online database that is updated with acceptable sites, but overall it is a great step in the right direction for limiting access to local resources. You can expect that Apple will build on Parental Controls in the future.

Restricting Access with the Command Line: sudoers

You can use Parental Controls to restrict access to certain resources. By editing the sudoers file, you can take a much more granular approach to securing users' access to resources. *Sudo* stands for "su do," and *su* stands for "substitute user." sudo is a command-line utility in Unix, Linux, and Mac OS X that allows users to run programs as though they were another, more powerful user. By default, sudo will run as a system's superuser, or root account (although this can be changed using the runas_default setting in the sudoers file). As stated earlier, by default, the root, or superuser, account is disabled in Mac OS X but can be enabled using Directory Utility. In Mac OS X Server (as opposed to Client), the root account is enabled by default and automatically given the password of the first administrative user who is created during installation.

The syntax sudo will run one command as another user. su will run all commands that follow it as the administrative user who is invoked. su and sudo are useful but also very powerful and can be used to accomplish almost anything once invoked, so take precautions. You should use su and sudo in as limited a fashion as possible. In fact, you should use su with even more caution than sudo because it maintains the elevated permissions for the duration of a Terminal session, and its use is generally not recommended.

Note By default, any administrative user can use the sudo command.

The sudoers file is located at /private/etc/sudoers. Editing the sudoers file is a direct way of adding or removing the ability for users and groups to run certain commands and do certain tasks from the system without having to use the GUI. Before editing the sudoers file, you should always back up the file. The following code is the default content of the sudoers file on a system (the lines that start with # are inactive):

```
# sudoers file.
#
# This file MUST be edited with the 'visudo' command as root.
#
# See the sudoers man page for the details on how to write a sudoers file.
#

# Host alias specification

# User alias specification

# Cmnd alias specification

# Defaults specification
Defaults    env_reset
Defaults    env_keep += "BLOCKSIZE"
Defaults    env_keep += "COLORFGBG COLORTERM"
Defaults    env_keep += "__CF_USER_TEXT_ENCODING"
Defaults    env_keep += "CHARSET LANG LANGUAGE LC_ALL LC_COLLATE LC_CTYPE"
Defaults    env_keep += "LC_MESSAGES LC_MONETARY LC_NUMERIC LC_TIME"
Defaults    env_keep += "LINES COLUMNS"
Defaults    env_keep += "LSCOLORS"
Defaults    env_keep += "SSH_AUTH_SOCK"
Defaults    env_keep += "TZ"
Defaults    env_keep += "DISPLAY XAUTHORIZATION XAUTHORITY"
Defaults    env_keep += "EDITOR VISUAL"

# Runas alias specification

# User privilege specification
root    ALL=(ALL) ALL
%admin    ALL=(ALL) ALL
```

```
# Uncomment to allow people in group wheel to run all commands
# %wheel     ALL=(ALL)     ALL

# Same thing without a password
# %wheel     ALL=(ALL)     NOPASSWD: ALL

# Samples
# %users  ALL=/sbin/mount /cdrom,/sbin/umount /cdrom
# %users  localhost=/sbin/shutdown -h now
```

In the following lines (part of the original file), root and users in the admin group are given access to a Host_Alias of ALL to Runas_Alias for all users and run Cmnd_Alias of ALL. This is unlimited access to the system, and it is what makes root the powerful account that it is. If you want to reduce the access that administrative users (users defined as administrators in the Accounts preference pane) are given, you can edit this setting. Let's take a look at the following two lines that are in the default sudoers file:

```
root    ALL=(ALL) ALL
%admin  ALL=(ALL) ALL
```

■**Note** In a Unix file, anytime you see an item with % in front of it, you are typically looking at a variable. Thus, %admin is the administrators group. If you create a new group called pirates on the Accounts preference pane, then you would refer to it as %pirates here.

Table 3-1 lists some of the flags that you can use to define privileges in the sudoers file.

Table 3-1. *sudoers Flags*

Flag	Description
mail_always	Sends mail to the mailto user for every sudo event.
mail_badpass	Sends mail to the mailto user if the password is entered incorrectly.
mail_no_user	Sends mail to the mailto user if the user is not in the sudoers file.
mail_no_host	Sends mail to the mailto user if the host disallows the user.
mail_no_perms	Sends mail to the mailto user if a disabled command is run.
tty_tickets	Users must authenticate per shell instance.
authenticate	Users must authenticate before running commands.
root_sudo	Disables users from invoking a shell using sudo.
log_host	Adds the hostname to logs.
log_year	Adds the year to logs.
set_home	Sets the HOME variable (~) to the target user's home.

Table 3-1. *sudoers Flags*

Flag	Description
always_set_home	Always sets the HOME variable (~) to the target user's home.
path_info	Disables prompts that a command is not in a user's path.
fqdn	Puts fully qualified hostnames in the sudoers file.
insults	Insults users when they enter incorrect passwords.
requiretty	Disables running visudo unless a Terminal session is present.
env_editor	Allows other text editors for editing sudoers file. This is useful if limiting to pico or vi.
rootpw	Prompts for root password instead of invoking a user's password.
runaspw	Prompts for the password of the user defined by runas_default.
targetpw	Prompts for the password of the user specified when using -u.
set_logname	Logs sudo events using the invoking user's name.
stay_setuid	Runs sudo as the real UID of the invoking user (same as set_logname).

To edit the sudoers file, you will be using the visudo command. This command will lock the file so that it can not be written to by multiple programs. It will also verify that the file is complete with all its necessary parts and will check the file for syntax errors before allowing you to save it. Because the visudo command uses the vi text editor to edit the sudoers file, you will likely want to become familiar with vi before editing your sudoers file.

■**Note** Before editing the file, it is also a good idea to read the man (manual) page for visudo by entering man visudo at the command line. This will go into full detail on the uses and syntax for the program.

If the file is not edited properly, it should not allow you to save it when you are finished editing. You can use the -c option with visudo to run a check of the file's syntax and ensure it is able to parse properly. The -c stands for check mode. You can run the command by entering the following:

```
visudo -c
```

This should return with the following line provided that the file parses correctly:

```
/private/etc/sudoers file parsed OK
```

Now that you know how to check the file, let's take a look at the -f option, which is used to specify an alternate sudoers file location, leaving the live sudoers file untouched. There are a variety of reasons you might want to work in a separate location, such as if you were going to take the file to another system or don't want it to go live for a few days. For example, you can use the following command to create a temporary sudoers file called sudoers.inprogress:

```
visudo -f /etc/sudoers.inprogress
```

You can use aliases in the sudoers file to indicate a variable that contains a user, multiple users, a group, or multiple groups. When working with multiple users on a system, it is always a good idea to create aliases on the system. If you need to apply the same access rights to a group of users, you can do this by using an alias membership rather than by applying permissions for each user individually. When referencing an alias or group of users in sudoers, you will notice that % will be placed in front of the group name. To be clear, the % character is not used to signify the name of a new group but is used to reference groups. For example, by adding the following line to the sudoers file, you could create an alias called powerusers that contains members of a group called admin, the user called cedge, and a user called MyCompany. We will also create an entry that simply lists those who the webmasters are:

```
User_Alias        powerusers = %admin, cedge,  MyCompany
User_Alias        websusers = mark, joel, michael
```

Setting up a Runas_Alias for a user or group will define the user or system daemon that a user or alias can run as when using the sudo command. In the following line, we will tell the system that the webusers defined previously are able to run commands as the apache system user:

```
Runas_Alias       webusers = apache
```

The Host_Alias allows you to define a group of computers, also called *hosts*. You can reference hosts by name, by IP, or by a range of either. When defining a range, it is often easiest to use wildcards, which are used as catchalls. Wildcards that can be used are similar to those available in shell scripting, as shown in Table 3-2.

■**Note** When using wildcards, you will not be granting access to commands in subfolders of those you define. You will need to specify those separately.

Table 3-2. *Wildcards*

Wildcard	Description
?	Matches a single character
*	Matches multiple characters
[...]	Matches a character in a range
[!...]	Matches a character that is not in the range
\x	Escapes characters, similar to regular expressions

For example, if you want to create an alias list of all your servers, which are named afpserver1, afpserver2, odserver1, odserver2, adserver1, and adserver2, then you could use *server? for the Host_Alias. Additionally, you can use specific IP addresses or IP addresses with a subnet defined. The Host_Alias comes in handy when you are pushing out a sudoers file to a large number of machines and want to have different options for different hosts. An example of a Host_Alias configuration might include the following:

```
Host_Alias    Servers = *server?, 10.0.1.0/255.255.255.0
Host_Alias    Workstations = 10.0.2.0/255.255.255.0
```

The next portion of the sudoers file defines the commands that aliases or users can access. Cmnd_Alias is used to set them. For example, if you want to give a user access to run all the commands in the /usr/sbin directory and all the commands located in the /usr/bin folder, you would use the following line:

```
Cmnd_Alias = /usr/sbin/*, /usr/bin/*
```

The final portion of the sudoers file is where access to resources is granted to users or aliases. In previous sections of the sudoers file, we defined lists of groups, computers, and commands. Now you can take all of this and put it together by listing the group of users that has access to run specified commands on specified machines. The basic syntax of the sudoers file would read like this:

```
<User_Alias>    <Host_Alias> = (<Runas_Alias>) <Cmnd_Alias>
```

To put this into a real-world example, you can look at allowing the web scripters who were defined earlier to access the /private/etc/httpd program on servers. Here you will also introduce NOPASSWD and PASSWD into the sudoers file. This tells the system whether to prompt a user for a password when they are attempting to sudo the command that is being called. Keep in mind when using the NOPASSWD tag, you will not be prompted for a password. Once you've written in a section and you're committing a password to authenticate, it's a good idea to give it a once-over to catch any errors with the line before submitting the password to the system.

The section of the sudoers file for webscripters is as follows:

```
User_Alias    webscripters = mark, joel, michael
Runas_Alias   webscripters = apache
Host_Alias    Servers = *server?, 10.0.1.0/255.255.255.0
Cmnd_Alias    web = /private/etc/httpd
Webscripters  Servers = (webscripters) NOPASSWD: web
```

Once you have written a good sudoers file, you can push it to other users. You can do this through a variety of ways, such as ARD, radmind, the Casper Suite, or SSH. These are a bit beyond the scope of this book, but it's worth researching. You can find more information on ARD at http://www.apple.com/remotedesktop. You can find more information on radmind at http://rsug.itd.umich.edu/software/radmind. You can find more information on the Casper Suite at http://www.jamfsoftware.com/products/casper5.php.

Note If rules in sudoers conflict, the last rule applied will be activated.

Securing Mount Points

Navigating the file system through the Finder or through Terminal on a mounted drive is one of the most common tasks a user will do on their computer. It is also one of the most common things an attacker who is actually looking for information will do. You never want your system to be compromised, but when it does happen, you want to limit the access that an unauthorized user will have. Restricting access to disks, volumes, and RAIDs using mount options is one way to accomplish this.

Note Each disk in a computer has a collection of disks that are mounted. This can be seen and controlled easily in the Disk Utility application. However, you will often need more granular controls, such as mounting a volume in verbose mode.

Once a disk is mounted, it is typically considered a *volume*. Running a df command will show you all the volumes mounted and is exclusively for viewing mounted disks. The mount command will also display mounted disks but can also be used to mount disks with different options, giving administrators a higher level of control over those disks. Until a disk is mounted, it will be listed in /dev/diskname (disks are often listed sequentially, as disk0s2, disk0s3, and so on). The mount command will be active only until the first reboot.

Common options for the mount command include the following:

- -t specifies the file system type.

- -r mounts the file system as read-only.

- -f forces the file system into a read-only state.

- -a mounts all the file systems available in the fstab file.

- -d uses all the options in a dry run.

- -v uses verbose mode with the mount command.

Administrators can mount drives that have disabled the ability to write to them or enabled other access options by mounting a disk using the -o flag in the command. The proper syntax for this command is to put the option in front of the o, such as -fo or -do. One example of using the option with the mount command is using the -ro command to make a disk read-only (or more specifically revoke-write access), often used when forensics are being performed on a system.

It is also possible to stop Mac OS X from automatically registering and mounting drives that are inserted into it by disabling diskarbitrationd, the system process that polls for new disks. There are multiple methods for doing this, which will force users to use the mount command in order to register a new disk with the operating system. One way is to kill the process and then remove the /usr/sbin/diskarbitrationd file, completely removing the daemon. Another is to move the /System/Library/LaunchDaemons/com.apple.diskarbitrationd.plist file to another location, such as the Desktop. Renaming the property list (plist) file is typically the best choice. You can also control the mounting and unmounting of disks using Disk Utility or the Terminal diskutil framework.

■**Note** Disk Arbitration is covered in further detail in Chapter 16.

SUID Applications: Getting into the Nitty-Gritty

There are a variety of applications running on your system, and not all run as your user. When you open Activity Monitor from /Applications/Utilities and change the filter option to Administrator Processes, you will see all the processes running on the system as root. Applications that are running as root often have the SUID bit set, causing them to be run as the owner of the file, which for many of these applications is root. To view whether a file has the SUID bit set, you can run an ls -l command in a given directory to look for any file with a listing that has an s listed rather than an execute bit in the permissions line for owners of the file. For example:

```
-r-s--x--x    1 root  root 19809 Jan 14 14:05 ps
```

Binary files (executables) that are not written well can cause SUID bits to allow for privilege escalation. Although you might not want to allow SUID files on your system, it's not realistic to remove the SUID bit from all files because some applications will require certain files to be SUID, such as login. Most SUID applications exist to specifically let users perform privileged operations or gain access to resources that require root privileges when they are not logged in as the root user. Therefore, the root user owns most SUID applications.

Many applications that are not written specifically to allow manual privilege escalation actually provide a way to execute a command. Vi allows users to run commands from within the interactive text editor. Many other commands, such as less and more, allow commands to be executed by pressing the ! key while viewing a file that takes up more than one page of content. Knowing whether each SUID application is dangerous requires knowing the details of using each of these applications and whether a shell command can be run from within the command or some binary file can be invoked receiving root access. To find all SUID applications, use the following command for a listing of all SUID or SGID files:

```
sudo find / -type f \( -perm -04000 -or -perm 02000 \) -ls
```

■**Note** Mac OS X allowed SUID shell scripts until the 10.3.9 software update, so if you are running an operating system prior to Tiger 10.4, consider SUID shell scripts while auditing your system.

To fix the SUID scenario, set the UID for a user. In our example, the user will be test. If the file is executed, it will now run with the rights of the user invoking the file and not with the rights of the user who runs it:

```
chmod u+s test
```

If you are in a SGID scenario rather than a SUID scenario, set the GID for test. If executed, the file will now run with the rights of the group of the file and not with the rights of the group that runs it:

```
chmod g+s test
```

If an SGID (group SUIDs) is set on a directory, all new created files inside this folder won't get the main group ID of the creator. Instead, they will be created with the group ID of the folder. For example, the SGID is set for the test folder folder1, and it has the group ID for www. Now, if the root user creates a file inside folder1, the group ID for this file will not be root but www. SUID and SGID can be set at the same time.

Creating Files with Permissions

By default, when creating a new file, the default permissions of that file are determined by the umask variable. You can work with the umask to edit the default permissions of new files. You can configure the umask setting by using the umask command.

First, run the command umask from a Terminal screen by typing umask at a command prompt. When you do this, you will get a number as your response. The umask variable is subtracted from the total number possible for securing Unix files, 777. This leads to a umask of 0022 creating new files on a hard drive with permissions of 755.

■**Note** For more information on POSIX permissions, see Chapter 10.

If you enter umask 0002 at the command line, then you will be telling the system to create new files with permissions of 775. However, if you use a umask of 077, then you will cause all new files to be readable only by the user who creates and subsequently owns the files.

Using the umask command to set default file permissions applies to the umask setting only for your session. This means the next time you restart your system, this setting will be lost. To permanently reset the permissions for new files, you will need to edit the globalpreferences. plist file on a per-user basis by inserting an NSUmask override setting in the file ~/Library/ Preferences/.GlobalPreferences.plist. Insert these lines using your favorite plist file editor (as shown in Figure 3-17) or using the defaults command:

```
<key>NSUmask</key>
<integer>0</integer>
```

Replace the 0 with the decimal conversion of the octal umask you want to set. A decimal NSumask of 0 gives the octal umask value of 000 we require.

S

Figure 3-17. *Editing a plist using Plist Editor Pro*

■**Note** To edit this globally, insert the same setting into the file /Library/Preferences/
.GlobalPreferences.plist.

PART 2

■ ■ ■

Security Essentials

CHAPTER 4

■ ■ ■

Malware Security: Combating Viruses, Worms, and Root Kits

In this chapter, we will discuss malware. *Malware* is a term used by security professionals to reference any software that is designed to infiltrate or damage computer systems without the owner's informed consent. "Informed" is the key word here. A user might consent by clicking an Accept dialog box to allow a software package to install but might not be fully informed of the vulnerabilities that can potentially be exploited by that software package. Beta versions of new software can sometimes have potentially damaging effects on an operating system but would not be considered malware because their intent to do harm is consented to (however unwelcomed) by the user installing the software. What we will explore in this chapter are the ill effects that can arise from unintentionally installed software on a Mac and how to safeguard your machine from them.

Note *Malware* is the term used by many security professionals as a blanket reference to a variety of threats in much the same way that most average users consider *viruses* to mean all threats. However, malware is just one kind of threat to an operating system, and a virus is merely one type of malware.

Classifying Threats

When discussing how to combat malware threats, it's important to break down the different kinds of threats that can exist on a Mac. As mentioned, to most users, a virus is something that threatens productivity on a machine, and the term is frequently used to classify all malware. But we should to make the distinction between viruses and malware. *Malware* is the over-arching term for certain kinds of threats to the operating system, while a *virus* is just one form of malware. What distinguishes a virus from other forms of malware is its ability to replicate itself and spread to other files on a computer, thereby infecting them. However, a virus will infect files on only a single computer; it will not automatically copy its code and spread itself to other computers on a network. This is what distinguishes a virus from a worm.

Worms are not classified as viruses. Worms spread themselves through network connections by automatically copying themselves onto other computers using the security flaws of the target computers. There are no known viruses that can cause damage on a Mac, much like they can on a Windows machine, which leads to the misconception that Macs cannot be harmed by malware. However, there are indeed worms and other forms of malware that can and do affect Macs. In February 2006, OSX.Leap.A, a Mac worm, spread across the Internet over iChat and infected client computers. The distribution of OSX.Leap.A, like many malware threats for OS X, was relatively low. But for those who were infected, the cleanup was a disaster because many applications on the infected systems were hopelessly corrupted, along with their user-specific preferences files.

■Note Most worm threats have a *payload*, the malicious code or program carried out by the worm. If this payload is written in a language that a Mac cannot speak, then the payload will not be able to run, and the worm will not infect the computer. Some threats have a payload that will lie dormant until something triggers its release.

A *Trojan horse* is malicious code embedded within a self-contained application that becomes destructive only when an infected application is opened. Trojans closely resemble viruses because both can cause damage when a file is infected. However, a virus is added to an application after the application is written, whereas Trojan horses are written, created, and distributed as a single application for the sole purpose of infecting computers. Trojan horses can be used to erase files, get passwords, and send e-mail to other users. Back Orifice is one such example. The threat to Macs here is low, since most Trojan horses will not run on Mac systems. But Mac systems can still be carriers.

A *logic bomb* is a virus threat resembling a Trojan horse, but it's architected to initiate when a specific event occurs. Logic bombs are brought into the operating system on the coattails of a virus or a worm, containing the payload that will be launched when the trigger event occurs. It is a ticking time bomb ready to go off on a scheduled date or after being resident in the operating system for a certain period of time. In some cases, programmers have been known to (and indicted for) deploying logic bombs into their own code in order to make more work for their clients and to change the stock prices for their companies.

A *trapdoor* is an exploitable opening within an application's code. Trapdoors are usually designed for the purpose of program debugging by programmers. They're similar to logic bombs; however, they're meant to troubleshoot bugs in programming code rather than intentionally inflict harm on a machine. Typically, they are merely forgotten entryways accidentally included with the software's final release. Usually, there is no way to combat these vulnerabilities, except to continually update the software with any updates available from the software manufacturer.

A *zombie* is a system that has been remotely triggered to perform a task. Often the tasks zombies perform allow an attacker to originate their attacks from another system undetected. An attacker can also build a virtual army of zombies to attack a target. Zombies, also referred to as *drones*, are often used to perpetrate Denial of Service (DoS) attacks and Distributed Denial of Service (DDoS) attacks. Trinoo and Tribe Flood Network are examples of DDoS attacks created for Unix variants and Windows computers.

A *retrovirus* is designed to attack a machine's backup topology. It will wait until all your backup media is infected with the virus before it performs any actions that can cause damage. This makes it impossible to restore the system to an uninfected state once the computer has been infected. Retroviruses are designed to avoid detection by antivirus software. Many of the virus types described in this chapter are available for the Mac, but we have yet to see a retrovirus for Retrospect, BakBone, or any other application used to back up a Mac. However, a few specific attacks against Retrospect have been reported, usually exploiting weak passwords.

■**Note** Retroviruses are not named after Retrospect, the popular backup application from EMC.

A *macro virus* is a virus attack designed to exploit applications that have the ability to create mini-programs, called *macros*, within documents. Microsoft Word and Microsoft Excel are examples of software that can create these dangerous documents. Thus, most of the known macro viruses in existence are designed for Microsoft Office. And these macro viruses are cross-platform, found on both Macs and PCs. However, their damaging effects are felt only on Windows machines.

Table 4-1 summarizes the types of threats discussed in this section.

Table 4-1. *Threat Breakdown*

Threat	Description	Vulnerability for a Mac
Virus	Program that can copy itself and infect a computer without the permission or knowledge of the end user	None in the wild yet
Worm	Self-replicating computer program, often used to distribute malicious content	Common
Trojan horse (Trojan)	Code inserted into an application that causes a program to perform destructive actions not intended in the original code	Very rare
Logic bomb	Malicious code triggered by a specific event such as a specific date and time	Rare
Trapdoor	Forgotten debugging routines that can be exploited	Rare
Zombie	Remotely triggered applications running in the background of a system used to remotely execute code	Rare
Retrovirus	Attacks against backup systems	None yet
Macro virus	A virus written using the macro feature of Microsoft Office and then deployed using Microsoft Office documents	Common

The Real Threat of Malware on the Mac

A program called Elk Cloner is credited with being the first computer virus to spread to other computers outside of the lab in which it was created. Since then, viruses have become increasingly rampant on the Internet in both commercial and residential home networks and have caused billions of dollars in lost productivity. The MyDoom virus alone was estimated by mi2g, a global risk specialist, to have cost $43.9 billion in damages worldwide. This is equivalent to the total revenue earned by GM in the first quarter of 2007.

In March 1999, an e-mail worm named Melissa wreaked havoc across the Internet, so much so that companies unplugged their mail servers from their networks for days because of the flood of e-mail messages Melissa generated. In 2001, two more worms—Code Red and Nimda—generated so much traffic that administrators completely shut down their networks' connections to the Internet. In January 2003, a worm called, very simply, *worm*, imposed so much network traffic that it even sent ATM machines offline. Even Apple had a rather embarrassing incident where it shipped a batch of iPods that had been infected by RavMonE.exe, a virus that came from a Windows computer located within Apple's corporate network.

Viruses are very real threats. And contrary to popular belief, the Mac is not immune to them. Don't believe the media hype. Yes, it is far more likely that you will suffer from file corruption from a virus attack while working on a Windows machine, but the Mac is still prone to infection.

Macs typically are "silent" carriers of viruses. Most of the time, these come in the form of macro viruses. Many Mac users won't discover that they have a macro virus until a PC user complains they sent them one. These viruses are typically written to exploit security holes in Microsoft application software and operating systems. Because Macs at their core are fundamentally different from Windows machines, these viruses won't have the same effect on the Mac and may go unnoticed for a while. But they will attach themselves to outgoing emails sent by the e-mail program and infect files sent to friends, colleagues, clients, and family. For example, many viruses are written to specifically attack Microsoft Office for Windows. When an infected file is moved from a Mac to Windows, because of the lack of some security features of Office in the Mac environment, the Mac user may "carry" the virus within the infected file and not even know it until it is passed to a Windows machine. Most commonly, the virus may infect Microsoft Word's `normal.dot` file, which all new Word documents are based on. This will cause all new Word files created by the infected computer to be infected with the macro virus. The virus may not affect the computer in any other way. This is the case with the most common virus seen on the Mac for almost a decade, the W97M virus, which is a strain of the original Melissa virus from 1997.

There are ways to spot a macro virus. For example, if you open a Word document with macros enabled, you will usually receive an alert letting you know the file is corrupted. If you receive a macro alert, stop and check that document out a little more intensely. In fact, check it for viruses. Word will even allow you to view the macro to see what it does before opening the document. This will help you keep macros that can damage Word and Excel on your computer at bay and keep your office installation at an optimal performance level.

The most disturbing threat to the Mac platform of a virus or worm is that although it is possible to get infected, few systems run any antivirus software that is capable of detecting infections. This lack of concern places the Mac OS in a fairly susceptible position.

■**Tip** If your machine detects the W97M virus, immediately delete the `normal.dot` file to keep future new documents from becoming infected when created.

Script Virus Attacks

For now, Automator is probably the most underutilized and underappreciated gem of the Mac OS X operating system. It is Mac OS X's personal robot, designed to eliminate some of the repetitive tasks that we all must perform while working on our Macs by essentially "automating" them. It is a major time-saver. It can also be a huge viral headache. Automator relies heavily on workflows that are built with *scripts*, automatic functions that tell your computer what to do. You can probably deduce that viruses work the same way—they are scripts that tell your computer what to do. For this reason, Automator workflows are huge security risks and should be treated with caution. E-mailing workflows as attachments should be avoided at all costs, simply because the potential for disastrous results from a user accidentally opening a dangerous workflow is way too high. Automator is equally underappreciated by the virus-writing community because it is underutilized by Mac users as a whole. However, it is important to be conscious of what workflows can do. Before opening a workflow, understand exactly what it will do to the system before running it.

The same is true for AppleScript and shell scripts. Like Visual Basic in Microsoft Office, these two methods of scripting offer powerful functions that can be used to perform a variety of actions such as erasing drives, deleting files, and corrupting operating systems—dangerous operations that viruses are famous for performing. With just one dangerous line of code, shell scripts can erase your hard drive while the operating system is running. Or an AppleScript might run a complicated find operation across the entire hard drive, deleting all files of a certain type. This can be catastrophic because there is no undo command in the Terminal (which is where shell scripts originate) and because Terminal commands don't put files in the trash, when they're deleted, they're gone, headed for disk recovery.

Socially Engineered Viruses

Gullibility and the good intentions of less-than-savvy users are the chief enablers of socially engineered viruses. These threats are completely based in social interaction. In other words, they do not spread without direct action from a user. E-mail hoaxes are prime examples of socially engineered viruses. Typically, an e-mail hoax will contain a message instructing the user to perform an action on their computer, such as deleting certain key system files, which can seriously damage an operating system installation under the guise of making the computer run better. Also, users are often instructed to forward the message to others, allowing the virus to spread to other computers and to negatively impact the bandwidth demand on a network.

Here is an example of an e-mail hoax:

TO: cedge@318.com

Subject: !!!

Merry Christmas everyone! Be careful out there. There is a new virus on America Online being sent by E-Mail. If you get anything called "Good Times", DON'T read it or download it. It is a virus that will erase your entire hard drive. Forward this to all your friends. It may help them a lot.

Combating e-mail hoaxes is not a no-win situation. There are excellent web sites such as About.com, the McAfee Virus Hoax page, or the Symantec Latest Threats page that will generally dispel the usefulness of the e-mail right away. Also, Googling the Internet with the exact words from the e-mail in quotes should be all that is required to determine whether a specific e-mail is a hoax.

Using Antivirus Software

Antivirus software has one primary function: to examine a system or a network for viruses and either attempt to fix the files infected or remove the virus-infected file from the system or network. Most antivirus packages include an autoupdate feature that enables them to update their definitions for new threats as soon as they are discovered. But not all antivirus software deals with viruses in the same way. A wide variety of software packages are available for scanning, repairing, and thwarting virus threats on the Mac. In the following sections, we will talk about the general state of antivirus packages for the Mac, touch on a few of the antivirus packages out there, and discuss the pros and cons of how they deal with viral threats.

Antivirus Software Woes

Because viruses on Macs are not as chronic as they are in the Windows environment, fewer antivirus products are available for the Mac than for the PC. In addition, those that do exist for the Mac are not as comprehensive, which can be disconcerting. In fact, most of the antivirus applications for the Mac will not even clean a file infected with a virus; they will instead just quarantine the file with no other choice left but to delete it. That is definitely not a desirable effect when the file infected is valuable. Some programs will not even scan e-mail on a Mac, even though Mac users can carry viruses in their e-mail just like everyone else. This can be disconcerting because e-mail is the method most used by viruses to infect computers.

Virus definitions are files that tell the antivirus software what a virus will look like, how to clean the infected file when it's found (if the application allows for cleaning of the file), and how to remove the virus from the machine. An antivirus software package often cannot clean a virus unless it knows the signature of the virus within its definition. Only viruses that have been found by the vendor of the application can be cleaned. Therefore, virus definitions for many of the Mac antivirus packages are frequently out-of-date and are generally updated far less frequently than in antivirus software made for Windows machines. Nonetheless, you should still regularly check for updates to your Mac antivirus packages.

■**Note** If you think your machine might have a virus, connect the Mac to a clean Windows box with the latest antivirus software updates, and run a scan.

Norton AntiVirus

Symantec has been cleaning up viruses for a long time. The company leads the way in virus research and mitigation. When new viruses spring up, the first place most savvy network engineers consult, no matter the platform, is the Symantec Latest Threats web site. Symantec's

Norton AntiVirus, available through most computer retailers for less than $50 USD, will scan e-mail, automatically update virus definitions, scan files as they are accessed, and scan files on demand. This makes Norton AntiVirus the most feature-rich product for virus scanning available on the Mac platform today. Symantec's Norton AntiVirus for the Mac also has the most frequently updated virus definition files for the Mac. For example, OSX.Leap.A, a zero-day exploit, was discovered on February 16, 2006, and added to the Norton AntiVirus definitions that same day. Symantec's antivirus products are also fairly straightforward and common.

■**Note** *Zero-day exploits* are released before, or on the same day as, the vulnerability—and, sometimes, the vendor patch—is released to the public. The term derives from the number of days between the public advisory and the release of the exploit.

Let's dive into an antivirus package that may not be as well known but definitely has some powerful features. And did we mention that it was free?

ClamXav

ClamXav is a free antivirus application for the Mac written by Mark Allen. It is available at `http://www.markallan.co.uk/clamXav/index.php?page=dl` in a variety of languages, including Spanish, English, Danish, French, Japanese, and Korean. Although ClamXav lacks many of the features available in some of the commercial packages available, it is a great freeware application that should be used as a first-line-of-defense warning system against viruses. Although the graphical user interface (GUI) was written by Allen, the underlying code is actually developed and distributed by the open source community as part of the ClamAV project; Allen is commendable for not charging for its use. As freeware, it can be distributed to large numbers of users to help administrators discover virus outbreaks and perform quarantine measures on infected files.

ClamXav will not clean files; it only scans and quarantines them, which can be helpful on a machine with limited infection. However, on a system where a virus or worm has been self-propagating itself for days, weeks, and even years, this could mean that every single file that the user has ends up getting quarantined. This can cause hours of lost time in rebuilding a file structure to its original hierarchy. ClamXav also does not provide scanning for incoming e-mail, which, as previously discussed, is the primary method for distributing viruses on any computer platform.

■**Note** ClamXav should not be run on Mac OS X Server.

ClamXav is built on open source technology. At the core, it is a command-line utility, with a GUI built on top of it, allowing administrators to control it easily. You can also configure ClamAV, the back-end package of ClamXav, from the command line.

Installing ClamXav 1.0.8 on Mac OS X is fairly straightforward:

1. Download the installer from Allan's web site at `http://www.clamxav.com`.

2. Once you've downloaded the installer, double-click it to open the disk image. Drag the icon from this window to the Applications folder.

3. Double-clicking the ClamXav icon in your Applications folder will open a screen containing a message from Allan asking for a donation. Bypass this message by clicking the Maybe Later button if you are not yet convinced that ClamXav is for you (but we suggest donating if you do continue to use the application).

4. Click Yes in the next dialog box that asks to install the ClamAV engine. Once the installer is finished, ClamXav is ready to run.

The main ClamXav screen (shown in Figure 4-1) allows you to select items to scan, to start and stop scans, to review logs, and to set preferences for ClamXav. The Choose What to Scan button allows you to select a location to scan with the option to run an instant scan or an instant update to the software.

■**Note** ClamXav 1.0.8 was used for this walk-through. ClamXav does not officially support Leopard but does work and will likely have a support version by the time this book is published.

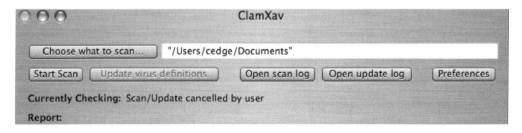

Figure 4-1. *ClamXav virus scanner*

To automate virus scanning, follow these steps:

1. Click the Preferences button, and then click the Schedule tab of the Preferences screen.

2. From here, click the Scan subtab (shown in Figure 4-2), which opens an authentication screen.

3. Click the padlock, and enter the password for an administrative account of the computer.

4. To schedule scans, place check marks in the days you want the computer to be scanned for viruses and the time that scans should be run. If you want to see whether any infected files were found at the end of each scan, you can check the Open Scan Log Automatically After Scheduled Scan box.

5. Clicking the Save Schedule Settings button will commit these changes the next time a scan or update is run.

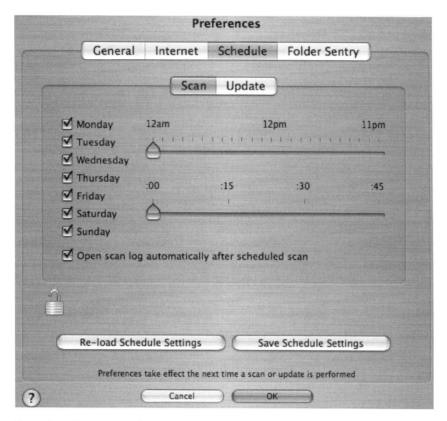

Figure 4-2. *ClamXav preferences pane (Scheduler)*

To automate scanning for viruses and checking for virus updates, use the Update subtab of the Schedule tab, and place a check beside each day that you want the virus update check to occur. Once you've set the days, click the Scan subtab and place the sliders to the appropriate time to perform the check. Click the OK button to commit the changes.

The Folder Sentry is a nice feature that allows administrators to specify that when files are created in certain watch folders, they will automatically be scanned. You can turn on the Folder Sentry feature by using the Folder Sentry tab in the ClamXav preferences (see Figure 4-3). The Folder Sentry application runs in the background and activates only when one of the watch folders has been edited. To add a watch folder, drag the folder from a Finder window into the Folders Being Watched field. The Scan Inserted Disks option will scan all disks that are attached or mounted on the system. The Launch ClamXav Sentry When You Log In to This Computer option will add ClamXavSentry to your users' Login Items. The Delete Infected Files option will delete files that are infected automatically when they are detected. Use this option with caution because it is fairly dangerous to automatically delete files without knowing which files are being deleted. Most often, this option is best left unchecked. It's better to review your logs regularly, manually fixing files if they become infected.

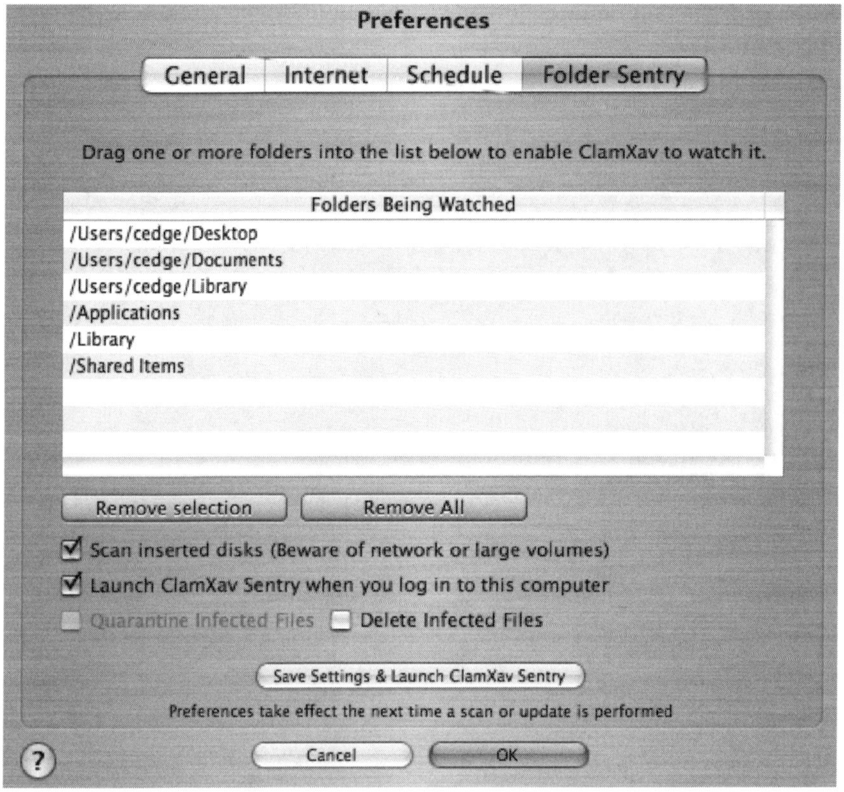

Figure 4-3. *ClamXav preferences page (Folder configuration)*

Allen has a Donate button on the ClamXav web site, and if you like the software, then we greatly encourage that you send him a donation through PayPal. With support from the Mac community, ClamXav will likely become a better application as time goes on.

Sophos Anti-Virus

Sophos Anti-Virus for Mac OS X is a very popular and well-designed antivirus application that can be purchased for the Mac. Sophos Anti-Virus maintains very current virus definitions, quarantines infected files, and has an automatic updater for virus definitions. Sophos Anti-Virus for the Mac is able to plug into the Sophos Enterprise Console (which requires a Windows computer) for the centralized management of client systems. Sophos Anti-Virus is available at `http://www.sophos.com/products/es/endpoint/sav-mac.html` along with a white paper on why viruses aren't just a Windows problem.

Sophos Anti-Virus is a manual virus scanner and does not run in the background to check files. Sophos also does not fix or clean files but instead quarantines them to a location of your choosing.

Installing Sophos Anti-Virus is fairly straightforward:

1. Download the trial from http://www.sophos.com, or insert a Sophos CD and launch the installer.

2. Click Continue at the Welcome screen and the Important Information screen.

3. At the Select a Destination screen, choose the hard drive where Sophos Anti-Virus will be installed, and click the Continue button again.

4. Then click Install, and wait for the installer to complete.

Running the Sophos program couldn't be easier. Once Sophos Anti-Virus has been installed, launch the Sophos Anti-Virus application from the Applications folder on your hard drive. At Sophos Anti-Virus's initial screen (see Figure 4-4), click the green Play button to start a scan and the red Stop button to stop a scan process. If there are multiple volumes on the computer, use the button to the left of the disk icon to select and unselect volumes for scanning.

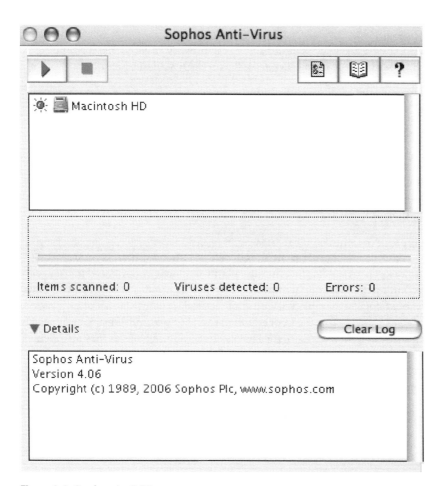

Figure 4-4. *Sophos Anti-Virus scanner*

You can configure preferences for the application by choosing Preferences from the Sophos Anti-Virus menu at the top of the screen. Preferences include the following:

- Archive Files scans the contents of compressed files, archives, and mailboxes.

- Included Non-Macintosh Virus Detection scans for non-Mac viruses in files.

- Enable Disinfection enables actions on infected files.

- Confirm Disinfection confirms actions on infected files.

- Action On Infected Files allows the user to specify that a certain action be taken when infected files are found.

- Select Transfer Folder specifies the folder to which infected files are moved or copied.

- Enable Reporting builds reports when scanning is complete.

- Report Filename allows the user to specify the names of reports appropriately, which is especially useful when merging reports from multiple computers to a centralized repository.

- Enable Desktop Alerts gives the user the ability to configure whether alerts result in desktop prompts, what types of alerts are used, and the text of the alerts.

- Log File customizes the location and editor used in log files.

Sophos Anti-Virus is not as flexible as ClamXav, but if you already own licenses for the Windows platform, appropriating those licenses for a Mac is perfectly legal. If you do not currently own Sophos Anti-Virus, then you should look at a product capable of cleaning viruses rather than just quarantining them. Of course, quarantining infected files is better than sending them to your friends, family, clients, and co-workers.

McAfee VirusScan

VirusScan (originally Virex), found at `http://www.mcafee.com/us/enterprise/products/anti_virus/file_servers_desktops/virex.html`, is developed and maintained by McAfee, a popular antivirus software package for the Windows platform. It was once offered for free with .Mac subscriptions, but the free version definitions have since expired. Therefore, if you have this program, you should upgrade or replace it with another product to provide accurate protection. In general, VirusScan suffers from a lack of attention from McAfee and doesn't always catch viruses. It also does not scan e-mail or run in the background, scanning files as they are opened.

VirusScan does have some nice features, however. It has the ability to integrate with the McAfee ePolicy Orchestrator, a centralized policy configuration and enforcement framework developed by McAfee to allow large antivirus deployments to be managed effectively. Also, when VirusScan catches a virus, it is often able to clean it, which is a nice feature not available in many of its competitors. In that sense, it can be used as a secondary line of defense.

Best Practices for Combating Viruses

Viruses are made possible by our frequent use of the applications on our computers. It's the nature of the software industry that new versions of software are released regularly with new features. And with new innovative features come bugs, which in turn means new possibilities for exploitation by pesky code. But when systems are properly defended against these threats, compromises in system integrity can be mitigated.

Every Mac should have antivirus software installed on it, and you should run virus scans regularly to mitigate the damage that can be inflicted from an infection. Scheduled scans are also important to maintain the integrity of an antivirus solution. They often take a while, and it's sometimes very tempting to stop a scan while it's running, but without a regularly scheduled full system scan, you can never be 100 percent sure that a system or network is completely virus-free. Scanning for viruses and malware regularly, keeping the virus definitions up-to-date, and implementing the security updates regularly are all critical tasks for minimizing the likelihood of an infection.

You should also be wary of opening attachments such as Word documents, Excel spreadsheets, and even compiled applications without scanning them with antivirus software, mainly because these files have been known to contain viruses capable of damaging other computers. Resist opening e-mail attachments from people you do not know. If a file asks you to enter an administrative password, do not open the attachment. Macs are very good about limiting the damage that can be done by malware, but once software is allowed through the administrative password gateway, practically anything can happen to the computer.

It is also easy to fall into the "false sense of security" trap that every administrator falls into after running virus scans—coming up virus-free and assuming the system is in the clear. Virus software is software like any other. As such, it can be compromised or corrupted, and it's entirely possible that the virus scanner is not catching everything. Therefore, you should test your e-mail scanner on a regular basis. There are test virus files that have no ill effects on your computer that can be downloaded and run on the machine. Web sites such as Eicar.org have good tests for virus software integrity (http://www.eicar.org/anti_virus_test_file.htm).

A complete antivirus solution should not only include a scan and quarantine process but should also contain a cleaning/repairing component. For example, using ClamXav or Sophos Anti-Virus might yield 30 files in the quarantine, but you'll need another application to actually repair the files. At a minimum, using any of the virus utilities is a good idea because they offer an early warning system for viral infection.

Other Forms of Malware

Malware does not end with viruses and worms. Adware and spyware are other forms of malware that can range from mere annoyances to rather dangerous identity infiltration.

Adware

The term *adware* refers to any software that displays advertisements, whether or not it does so with the user's consent. Adware applications may display advertisements as an alternative to taking payment. These classify as adware in the sense of advertising-supported software, but not as spyware. For software to be classified as adware, it must not operate covertly or mislead the user, and it should provide the user with a specific product or service.

There is nothing unethical about adware. It is a common and valid business practice for companies to advertise via adware. However, when adware attempts to operate stealthily in the background, it becomes spyware.

Spyware

Spyware is classified as any software that covertly gathers information through an Internet connection without the user's knowledge, usually for advertising and marketing purposes. It is often bundled as a hidden component of free or shareware programs downloaded from the Internet. Once installed, spyware monitors Internet activity and transmits that information in the background to another party. Spyware is often fairly harmless to the operation of the host computer, but it can pose a security risk and most definitely poses a privacy concern because it can transmit a variety of data, including private information.

It is a common misconception that spyware incidents on the Mac are not possible. Although it is true that they are less common and do not install themselves automatically simply by browsing certain web sites, like they do on Windows machines, do not be mistaken. Spyware is a very real threat on any platform because it simply involves installing a program on the computer. Installation can take place using a variety of methods, most notably using files downloaded from web sites.

Spyware can allow an attacker to gain access to your personal data or track your Internet usage. It is usually covertly installed on computers and is often responsible for identity theft, password exposure, fraud, slow Internet activity, and sluggish computer performance. Because spyware attackers are rather skilled at what they do, as a community, operating system developers have been unable to completely eliminate spyware from ravaging systems. Practicing good browser security can help keep your system safe and secure. (We cover web browser security in more detail in Chapter 5.)

The most common application used to combat spyware on the Mac is MacScan. There are others, but they're not as widely distributed.

MacScan

MacScan by SecureMac is one example of a commercial program that can remove spyware and the data that spyware most commonly harvests on a Mac. MacScan checks for spyware in administrative applications running on a system and in web browser caches (see Figure 4-5), allowing the user to clean this data from the computer. MacScan is available at `http://macscan.securemac.com`.

It is important to point out that MacScan is a basic application, as are many of the spyware-oriented products for the Mac. The products available for the Windows platform such as Spybot Search & Destroy, Ad-Aware, and Spy Sweeper are far more advanced and feature rich. This is primarily because of the widespread nature of spyware in the Windows environment and the rarity of spyware within the OS X community.

Spyware on the Mac is rare, but it does happen, and staying proactive against this threat takes very little work to be effective. Regularly running an antispyware program such as MacScan can help keep spyware off your computer and provide due diligence for maintaining a spyware-free Mac.

Figure 4-5. *MacScan web files cleaner*

Root Kits

Root kits act like spyware but are typically much more dangerous. The difference between Rootkits and Spyware lies in the intent. Root kits are not meant to harvest data but to specifically allow an attacker to gain unauthorized access to a computer to compromise the integrity of the system. A root kit can be installed on a computer in a variety of ways and will provide unsavory characters with backdoors into the machine as a result. The primary objective of many root kits is to evade detection. As such, they often masquerade as other applications in order to hide themselves.

One example of a root kit threat for the Mac is SH.Renepo.B, released in October 2004. SH.Renepo.B deletes Unix commands, deletes various log files, edits the user's LimeWire configuration, modifies security preferences, launches a keystroke logger, installs software, changes the `hostconfig` file, scans the system for passwords, enables file sharing, creates an invisible folder named `canned.info` in each user's Public folder, and creates a process that spikes the processor of infected hosts. The payload for SH.Renepo.B is considerable, but the file size is only 46KB.

If a root kit does find its way onto your system, then a quick comparison of the date and times that a file were created and modified based on an originally known good set of the same files will often identify the presence of a root kit. Using check sums to calculate whether any changes have occurred is a better way of detecting a root kit. This process is discussed in further detail in Chapter 12.

Rootkit Hunter is a GPL-based terminal application that can scan for specific known root kits. However, many root kits are not known, or they're altered so they can't be discovered by root kit scanners. Rootkit Hunter will not find SH.Renepo.B, for example, but will find variants of the FreeBSD root kit that have been found in Mac OS X environments. SH.Renepo.B may be added to future releases of Rootkit Hunter, but it is not included at this time.

You can download Rootkit Hunter from `http://www.rootkit.nl`. To install Rootkit Hunter, follow these steps:

1. Download the gzipped tarball, extract it, and run the installation script.

2. Extract Rootkit Hunter using the command `tar zxf rkhunter-<version>.tar.gz`.

3. Run `./installer.sh` from inside the `rkhunter` directory.

4. Change directory (`cd`) into the `rkhunter` folder, and run the command `sudo./ rkhunter -checkall` to perform all the tests on the system.

Once you have Rootkit Hunter installed, you can invoke it using the following additional parameters:

`--configfile <filename>`: Uses a custom configuration file

`--createlogfile`: Creates a log at `/var/log/rkhunter.log`

`--cronjob`: Runs as cronjob

`--help`: Shows the Rootkit Hunter manual page

`--nocolors`: Doesn't use any colors in the output

`--report-mode`: Limits the contents of a report

`--skip-keypress`: Doesn't wait after every test (makes it noninteractive)

`--quick`: Performs quick scan

`--version`: Shows the version

Now we will create an example of a shell script (`rkexport.sh`) that will run `rkhunter` and append the output to a new `.txt` file that could be viewed from the Web provided that the `/admin` directory of your site is password-protected. Once you've run `rkhunter`, you can build on the previous section and run a ClamAV scan of the system and dump the results into the same file:

```
Date >> /opt/apache2/htdocs/admin
Whoami >> /opt/apache2/htdocs/admin
Rkhunter -version >> /opt/apache2/htdocs/admin
Rkhunter -checkall -skip-keypress -report-mode  >> /opt/apache2/htdocs/admin
Clamscan -V >> /opt/apache2/htdocs/admin
Clamscan / -r -i -move=/Quarantine >> /opt/apache2/htdocs/admin
```

This should provide you with output similar to the following:

```
Sun May  7 18:49:04 PDT 2006
Cedge
Rootkit Hunter 1.2.8
* MD5 scan
MD5 compared          : 0
Incorrect MD5 checksums : 0

* File scan
Scanned files: 342
Possible infected files: 0

* Rootkits
Possible rootkits:

Scanning took 110 seconds

*important*
Scan your system sometimes manually with full output enabled!
Some errors have been found while checking. Please perform a manual
check on this machine called Charles.local:

----------- SCAN SUMMARY -----------
Known viruses: 52427
Engine version: 0.88
Scanned directories: 1342
Scanned files: 60046
Infected files: 0
Data scanned: 14.93 GB
Time: 19.096 sec (0 m 9 s)
```

CHAPTER 5

■ ■ ■

Securing Web Browsers and E-mail

Identity theft is the fastest-growing crime in the world. It is the top concern of people contacting the Federal Trade Commission and has now passed drug trafficking as the number-one crime in the world, costing the United States more than 60 billion dollars over the years.

The most common ways we interact with the outside world from our computers is through the use of web browsers, instant messaging, and e-mail. Identity thieves use the Internet as their tool for stealing identities. Therefore, securing our messaging systems has become a high priority to protect us from identity theft.

When describing securing the web browser, we will be covering Safari and Firefox. You may be using another browser, such as Camino, but the majority of Mac users use Safari or Firefox (version 2.*x*) for their browsing. Likewise, you might be using one of many different e-mail programs. The two most common mail applications for the Mac are Entourage and Apple's Mail, so we will discuss these throughout the course of this chapter.

As we explain each of the security features of these messaging systems and what they do, you can apply the topics to other browsers, chat programs, and mail programs that you may be using and configure them for the same level of security. Although the actual terminology may change, the concepts remain constant across applications.

■**Note** We spend much of this chapter discussing how to tune your browser for security purposes, but this doesn't mean it's not possible for you to download and run software from questionable sources that could damage your computer. Downloading software from BitTorrent web sites, for example, is dangerous because there is often no way to know where this software came from or what this software will do when installed on your computer. Keep this in mind when downloading software from these unknown sources.

A Quick Note About Passwords

If you could take only one tip away from this book, take this one: *use good passwords*! This is a mantra that we will use repeatedly throughout this book. We cannot overstate its importance.

Your e-mail and online accounts are only as secure as the password you use to access them. And believe it or not, your e-mail account is valuable to a spammer. A resourceful spammer can make hundreds of dollars by using your e-mail account to send spam. Since most web servers are fairly locked down password-wise (you'd be surprised how many e-mail servers these days use weak passwords), the spammer needs your e-mail account's password to use it. And even if they do not access your messages, they might end up getting your e-mail account disabled by your provider because of the high level of garbage coming from your account.

The reason the complexity of the password becomes such an issue is that no matter how heavily you encrypt the password and its transport over wire, if the password is far too easy to guess, then you may as well not have encrypted it in the first place. When we refer to complex passwords, we are typically referring to passwords that consist of eight or more characters, contain a special character, and contain both letters and numbers.

Note Not all providers allow the use of special characters. The characters that provide the most problems tend to be those that Unix reserves, such as , , /, ?, and so on.

Securing Your Web Browser

A web browser is a tool used to view data that sits on a web server. The two most popular browsers in use on the Mac are Safari and Firefox. Both are based on the Gecko rendering engine, which is used by the Mozilla browser as well. They are similar in configuration when it comes to security, with the exception that Firefox has more granular security controls.

The primary concern with web browser security is privacy protection. This includes keeping prying eyes away from your online purchase information, away from your passwords for web merchants, and away from the history of web sites you have visited. When we look at securing a web browser, much of the security falls under keeping the browser from running cached scripts sitting on the web server against your local computer.

Securing Safari

Safari is on every Mac by default. The ever-prolific nature of Safari makes it particularly important to secure. Thankfully, most of this can be done using the dedicated Security preference tab in Safari. On this tab, you can disable features of Safari that you don't need, block pop-ups, view and configure cookies, and tell the browser to prompt you before sending insecure data over the Web. Out of the box, Safari disables pop-ups, but all of the other features are enabled; therefore, you should make a few minor adjustments to your Safari security configuration to maintain the highest level of security possible.

Setting the Safari Security Preferences

By default, Safari is set to block pop-up windows. Sometimes you may need to access features of sites that cause pop-ups, though, such as the address book feature of Hotmail. You can find the option to enable and disable pop-ups by clicking Safari ➤ Block Pop-Up Windows.

Note Many sites are savvy to the pop-up annoyance and now use Flash to present overlays.

A *cookie* is a small text file of information that certain web sites attach to a user's hard drive while the user is browsing the web site. A cookie can contain information that pertains to a specific web site such as the user ID, user preferences, shopping cart information, and any other setting that can be stored on a web site. For the longest time, cookies got a bad rap mainly because they were notorious for their security concerns. But most modern-day web sites no longer store clear-text passwords in the cookies, so they are at least manageable. The important thing to remember with cookies is that you should know where they come from. Some sneaky web sites will put cookies in your browser that come from other web sites. Apple has included a Show Cookies button that will show you the cookies on your machine. (See Figure 5-1.)

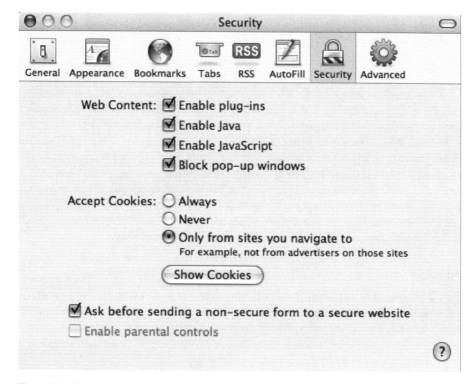

Figure 5-1. *Security preferences for Safari*

Tell your browser to accept cookies only from sites that you browse by clicking the Security icon on the Preferences tab and then choosing Only from Sites You Navigate To. By limiting cookies rather than disabling them, you will not run into many of the annoying compatibility issues with advanced web site browsing.

Web browser attacks on the Mac (such as home page hijacking, infiltrating your file system through a web browser, or installing applications onto the workstation) are even less likely than getting a virus on a Mac. However, good security dictates that if there are features included in browsers that you do not use, you should typically disable them. Some features, such as Java-based plug-ins, can reconfigure your operating system. Therefore, Apple has seen fit to give you the ability to disable Java plug-ins within your browser.

Windows has had a hard time with browser plug-ins. This is one place where your surfing can secm to come to a crippling halt in a Windows environment because of plug-ins that waste system resources. For debatable reasons, browser plug-ins have not been a huge concern on the Mac platform. You can see which browser plug-ins have been installed into Safari by selecting Help ➤ Plug-ins. If you take a look at the list that appears, you'll likely notice that nearly all the plug-ins are Apple-related (for example, related to QuickTime or iPhoto). If you see a browser plug-in that you do not want, then you can go to the /Library/Internet Plug-Ins folder and delete it.

Note Some older third party plug-ins, such as the Shockwave plug-in, have been integrated into Safari, meaning it is installed automatically on your machine.

Safari can also protect against the installation of unwanted software. When you download new software through Safari and go to run it for the first time or install the software, you will receive a message alerting you that the software was obtained through Safari. At the alert screen, you will be told that the software is an application downloaded from the Internet. You'll also be asked whether you're sure you want to open it. Here you will be able to click Show Web Page, which will open the site that the software was downloaded from so you can view the source. You can also click Cancel here, which will not open the software, or click Open if you do indeed want to open the software. One of the most dangerous things you can do on your computer is allow rogue software applications to be installed. This feature, which is available only in Leopard, will help you protect against unsolicited software being installed on your system.

Privacy and Safari

Clearing out all of the caches, history, downloads, and cookies on your system keeps prying eyes from finding them. However, this can be annoying because it may require you to reenter passwords for some sites, which, if you're like the rest of us, you may have forgotten. Clearing this information will also reset the history information, thus clearing out your autocomplete functionality for recently visited and nonbookmarked web sites.

You can reset Safari at any time by selecting the Reset Safari option in the Apple menu. On the Reset Safari screen, select which saved information you want to delete (see Figure 5-2). Clearing all this information is not necessary, though, so feel free to be selective with what you delete. We typically prefer to stick to the following for most systems:

- Clear History

- Empty the Cache

- Clear the Downloads Window

- Remove All Website Icons

- Clear Google Searches

- Close all Safari Windows

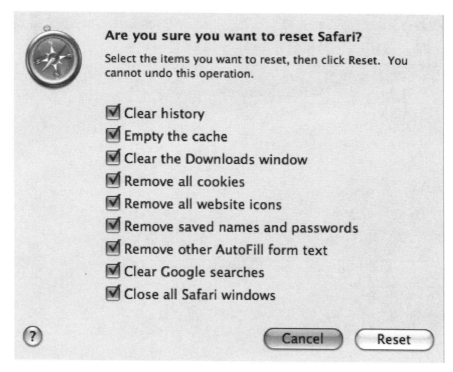

Figure 5-2. *Reset Safari warning*

Network Administrators

If you are a network administrator in charge of web browser security, there is a handy free utility called the Safari Toolkit (available at MacFixit.com among other download sites) that will allow you to not only customize the look and feel of Safari but also to secure the browser for individual users. If, in customizing the browser, you decide to remove any buttons that might affect security, consider setting the security options before removing those buttons. If, as a user, you see any differences between our web browser screens and your own, ask your organization or browser distributor whether any changes were made using the Safari Toolkit and check what settings are being used on your system image.

Securing Firefox

Firefox is a free, cross-platform, graphical web browser developed by the Mozilla Foundation with contributions from thousands of volunteers all over the world. Before its 1.0 release on November 9, 2004, Firefox had already garnered a great deal of acclaim from numerous media outlets, including *Forbes* and the *Wall Street Journal*. Now in version 2.0, Firefox has become more widely used than almost any other browser on the market, in large part because of the security features built into the browser (and because it isn't a hacker-targeted Microsoft product). For example, Figure 5-3 displays the rather powerful encryption features found in Firefox—features you're hard-pressed to find as easily configurable in other web browsers.

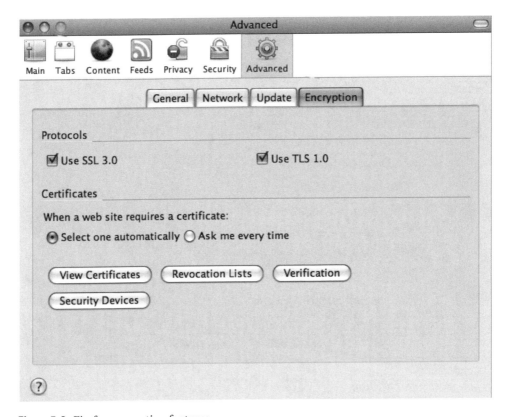

Figure 5-3. *Firefox encryption features*

Privacy and Firefox

One of the most compelling features of Firefox is the speed with which it is able to display pages. Luckily, the developers did not trade speed for security. This is made evident by reviewing the privacy features built into the web client (see Figure 5-4). Firefox gives users an impressive wide array of features, allowing users to get pretty granular about what they want their browser to do and not to do.

Clearing private data in Firefox is much like the Reset Safari feature with the exception that it enables you to select which items in the browser will be reset. Remember, though, if you choose to reset your private data, you risk losing the information stored in the browser such as passwords, preferences, and autocomplete entries from previously viewed web sites.

To clear private data in Firefox, click the Tools menu and select the Clear Private Data option. This option opens the Private Data screen (as shown in Figure 5-5). On the Private Data screen, you have more options than you had with Safari, and you can select exactly which of the options you want to reset.

Selecting the Cache check box doesn't remove all caches, and traces can still be found of images and pages visited. Visit `~/Library/Caches/Firefox/Profiles` in order to see whether there is any data left in your cache rather than assuming it was all cleared.

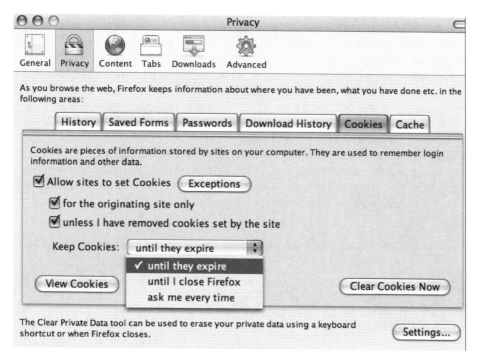

Figure 5-4. *Firefox privacy features*

Figure 5-5. *Firefox Private Data screen*

Dealing with Saved Passwords

If you allow Firefox to remember passwords, you should next set up a master password by clicking the Create Master Password button. This extra security layer will keep your password safe in the event that someone else uses your computer. A Firefox master password is not associated with any other program, which creates a secure environment within your Firefox experience to help you from having to reenter your password each time you visit certain sites. If your user account is in any way compromised, the damage to your overall security footprint will be minimal, and your saved passwords within Firefox will not be revealed.

To enable the Firefox master password, open the Firefox preferences, and click the Security tab. Here, you can enable remembered passwords by placing a check in the Remember Passwords box (don't you love it when they name buttons in a manner that makes sense?). On the Security tab, click Change Master Password (see Figure 5-6).

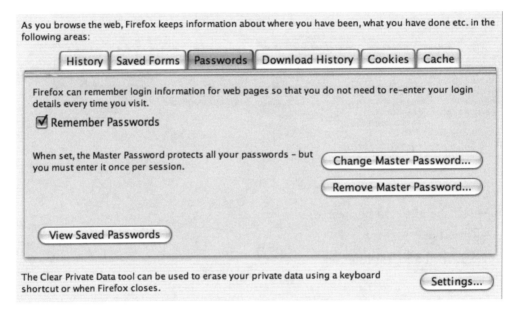

Figure 5-6. *Setting a master password*

The Change Master Password feature opens a screen with a blank password and the option to enter your new password and confirm the new password (as shown in Figure 5-7). Once you have set a password, you will be prompted for the password the first time your system attempts to access the passwords stored by Firefox. This is similar to the keychain concept in Mac OS X. This is an additional layer of security built into keychains. However, if you prefer using Firefox over using Safari, using a master password is suggested.

Note Notice the Password quality meter that is common with many applications on this screen; this gives you constant reminders to use good passwords.

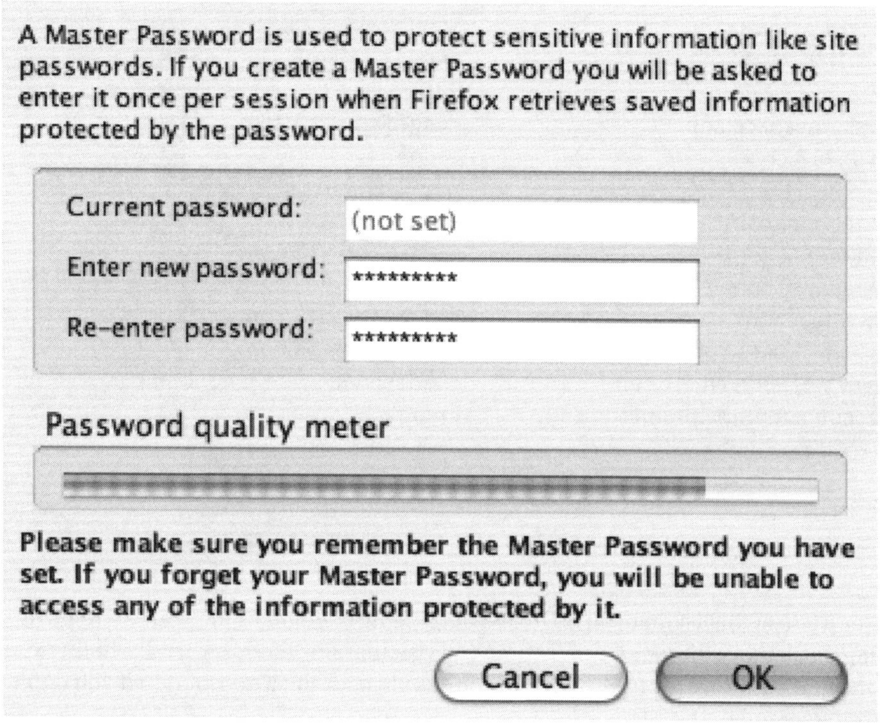

A Master Password is used to protect sensitive information like site passwords. If you create a Master Password you will be asked to enter it once per session when Firefox retrieves saved information protected by the password.

Current password: (not set)

Enter new password: ********

Re-enter password: ********

Password quality meter

Please make sure you remember the Master Password you have set. If you forget your Master Password, you will be unable to access any of the information protected by it.

Cancel   OK

Figure 5-7. *Firefox Master Password dialog box*

One of the dangers of Firefox is that on a system with stored passwords, if the master password is discovered or if the system is left unattended, then an attacker can come along, open Password Manager, click the server they want to see the password for, and then click the Show Passwords button. Once the master password has been entered, then you can open your Password Manager using the View Saved Passwords button (as shown in Figure 5-8) and view the cached information for web sites. If you click the Show Passwords button in the Password Manager, you will see a new column with the passwords.

Figure 5-8. *Firefox Password Manager window*

If you see a site in the list that you do not want to cache credentials for, you can remove this site using the Remove button. The next time you visit that site, Firefox will ask whether you want to cache that password for future access. You should click the Never button if you don't want Firefox to remember the password.

Once you are satisfied that the password security for your environment is adequate, it is time to move on to what features you want Firefox to allow. These features are addressed on the Content tab of the Firefox preferences (see Figure 5-9). These are similar to the ones in Safari. For example, the Block Popup Windows setting will cause pop-ups to be blocked, and the Java and JavaScript check boxes will disable Java and JavaScript on the sites being visited. One unique feature here is the ability to disable how Firefox handles images. You can uncheck the Load Images box to disable images from loading, or you can leave it checked and uncheck the box for the originating web site only, which will disable images located on different sites. As with most other features in Firefox, this can be applied to only certain sites using the Exceptions box.

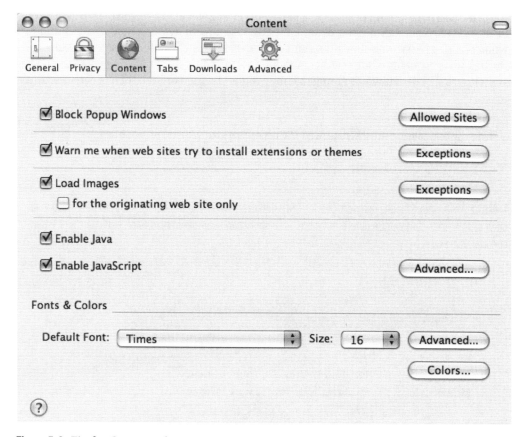

Figure 5-9. *Firefox Content tab*

Configuring Mail Securely

Different mail protocols have different levels of security. The default settings for most web hosts now include more secure protocols than the traditional POP and SMTP protocols. Mail.app has also been set up to allow for more protection of passwords in transit and more secure encryption protocols.

Using SSL

Secure Sockets Layer (SSL) is a protocol developed by Netscape for transmitting private documents via the Internet. SSL works by using a private key to encrypt data that's transferred while en route to another system. Both Safari and Firefox support SSL, and many web sites use SSL to secure confidential user information, such as credit card numbers for submissions over the Internet.

The most notable form of protecting passwords in transit is employing SSL. Transport Layer Security (TLS) is actually the successor of the SSL 3.0 protocol. These protocols are common when securing password submissions and other network traffic while the data is passing over the unknown elements of the Internet. Although SSL and TLS are similar and your system can support using both, it is worth noting that they cannot be used on web servers concurrently.

■**Note** By convention, URLs that require an SSL connection start with `https`, not `http`.

■**Note** Web sites typically use port 443 for SSL. However, when you are using SSL with other protocols such as IMAP, the port can be different. Figure 5-10 shows an example of how IMAP uses port 995 when secured using SSL.

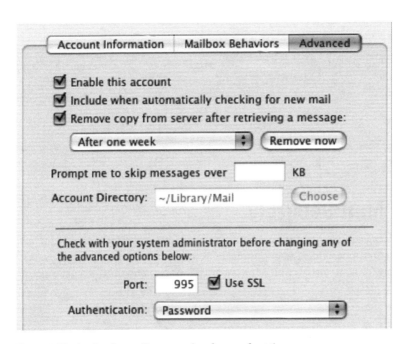

Figure 5-10. *An Apple mail account's advanced settings*

Sometimes with SSL you'll be asked to verify the authenticity of a server every time you open your e-mail client. This often has to do with the SSL certificate of your mail host being self-assigned. Self-assigned SSL certificates typically need to manually be trusted when you are visiting a site. If you choose not to trust a certificate, then SSL will not allow you to communicate over the secure channel to that host.

Note If you are required to accept the certificate every time you visit a site, then you can add the site as an x509 anchor in Safari by opening the Keychain Access utility and dragging the certificate into the X509 dialog box.

Now that your communications have been protected using SSL, let's look at how your password is actually sent over the wire. POP is a protocol used for downloading mail from a mail server. IMAP is a protocol used to synchronize mail between a mail client and a mail server.

POP and IMAP are merely protocols for accessing data; they do not tell a client how to actually authenticate into the remote host. For this, there are a variety of protocols including MD5, NTLM, KPOP, APOP, GSSAPI, Kerberos, and Password (PlainText). In the realm of layered security, the most important thing to know here is that you need to contact your mail provider and find out exactly what protocols are supported. If it does not support a protocol, you will not be able to use it.

Note Oftentimes the only way to get your Internet service provider to introduce support for a new protocol is to request it. When enough people speak up, the ISP will find a way to support what its users want.

The options for securing your mail password include the following:

MD5: Message Digest 5 (MD5) is a secure hashing function that converts an arbitrarily long data stream into a digest of fixed size. By breaking up messages and encrypting them, they are sent more securely.

NTLM: This is common in more Windows-oriented environments, such as with Microsoft Exchange.

Kerberized POP: POP is able to use Kerberos to access your servers. Kerberized POP can help more fully integrate your single sign-on environment. For more on Kerberos, please see Chapter 14.

Authenticated POP: An extension of the POP3 protocol, APOP encrypts both the username and the password.

Kerberos Version 5 (GSSAPI): This uses the latest version of Kerberos to encrypt e-mail and then authenticates the e-mail account against a directory server.

Kerberos Version 4: This is similar to Kerberos Version 5, but one version back.

Password: This is standard password authentication.

Some of these same authentication options are configurable in the SMTP settings, as shown in Figure 5-11. Keep in mind that if your username and password for SMTP are the same as your information for POP and you use SSL for SMTP and not POP, then you are still exposing your passwords.

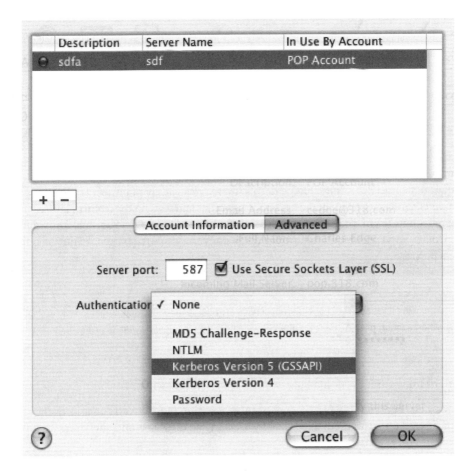

Figure 5-11. *Apple Mail's authentication settings*

Securing Entourage

You can configure Entourage to use SSL in much the same way as Mail. Open your accounts (listed under the Tools menu in Entourage), and choose the account you want to use SSL to secure. On the Account Settings screen, click the Click Here for Advanced Receiving Options button, and then select the This Incoming Service Requires a Secure Connection (SSL) box.

If your service provider runs IMAP or POP on customized ports, then select the Override Default IMAP option (or POP if you are using POP). You can always opt to use the Always Use Secure Password, which will force encryption on the password when you are checking e-mail (see Figure 5-12).

Once you have set SSL for your incoming mail, click the Click Here for Advanced Sending Options button. This opens a screen with similar options, including both options for using SSL and the default SMTP port (see Figure 5-13). Remember, both of these settings are specific to your Internet service provider's mail server settings and need to be verified with them before they can be applied.

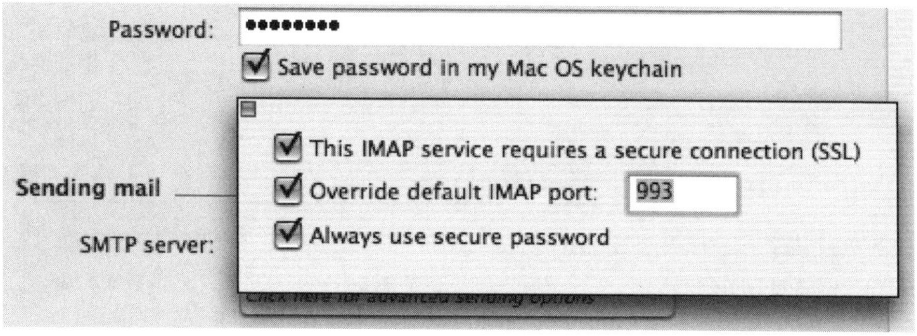

Figure 5-12. *Entourage advanced settings*

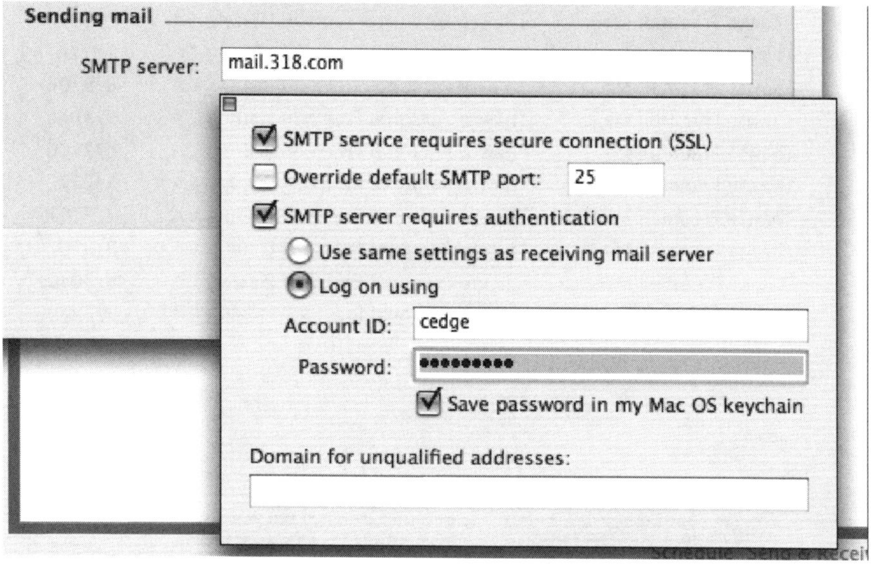

Figure 5-13. *Entourage's SMTP settings*

One unintended benefit to using SSL is that there are a large number of Internet service providers that are now blocking access to mail being sent over port 25, the default port for SMTP. Once you have set your computer to send mail over SMTP using SSL, you will often no longer run into issues with getting blocked when trying to send mail. One unintended annoyance is that you now may have to manage certificates for your mail, by accepting, denying, or importing certificates.

To add a different user's certificate to your cached certificates, open an e-mail that has been digitally signed, click the Info Bar, and click the View Details button. This opens a screen for viewing a user's certificate data.

You can open the Certificates screen (as shown in Figure 5-14), which shows all your user certificates. By clicking a certificate and hitting the button in the certificates toolbar, you will be able to click View to see more information about the certificate. You can also click Delete to delete the certificate.

Figure 5-14. *Entourage's Certificates screen*

■**Note** To view the certificates for a contact, go to Entourage's address book, double-click the person's name, and then click the Certificates tab.

The options in the Security preferences of Entourage (Figure 5-15) allow an administrator to tell Entourage to warn them when they are opening an attachment, warn them when an application other than Entourage attempts to access Entourage, and warn them when an application other than Entourage accesses the address book within Entourage. These help limit the ability for other applications to abuse Entourage if the system is infected with some form of malware.

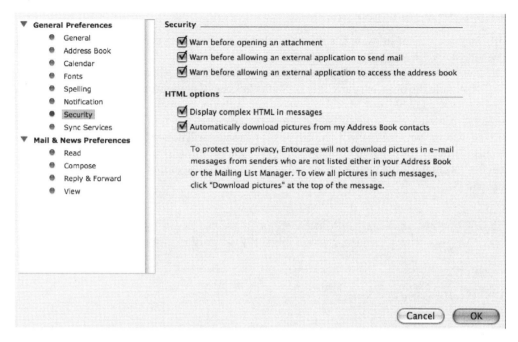

Figure 5-15. *Entourage Security preferences*

Fighting Spam

To quote Wikipedia, "Spamming is the abuse of electronic messaging systems to indiscriminately send unsolicited bulk messages." Spam often involves sending identical or nearly identical messages to hundreds, thousands, and even millions of recipients. Addresses of recipients are often harvested from chain e-mail letters or web pages, obtained from databases, or guessed by using common names and domains. Spam is not just an irritation; it costs the corporations, educational institutions, and governmental agencies that are forced to deal with it hundreds of millions of dollars.

Spam filters need to be trained. When a spam filter begins to filter spam, it may filter out e-mails that are not spam, called *false positives*. They are also likely to miss e-mails that might actually be spam. As you train your filter, you will be able to increase the intensity of the filter without increasing the number of false positives. A well-trained filter will minimize false positives while offering the best filtration available. Make sure to spend a little time with your filter to get it configured to maximize its potential. We'll cover more about how to train a spam filter later in this chapter.

Every e-mail message has a collection of headers associated with it. These include Sender, CC (Carbon Copy), To, Date, and X-Spam-Status. There are servers that perform spam filtration and assign X-Spam headers. This is meant to make it easier for mail clients to scan messages for spam quickly. The X-Spam-Status contains, among other information, a numerical score (from 0 to 10) that indicates the likelihood that a message is spam. E-mail programs that support the use of the X-Spam headers will compare this score against the score that has been determined as an acceptable risk. The headers are able to be accessed using the rule sets of Entourage and Mail.app.

Filtering Mail for Spam

An entire industry of software has risen up to help fight spam. On the Mac, the products are limited, and for desktop users we will primarily focus on the built-in spam prevention of the two most commonly used applications, Entourage and Apple's Mail.

To enable the built-in spam filter in Mail, click the Mail menu, and select Preferences. Then, click the Enable Junk Mail Filtering option, and choose what to do with spam using the When Junk Mail Arrives options (see Figure 5-16). Once you have configured what the client will do with the junk mail, select which types of messages will not be filtered. This is where you would configure the client to not flag as spam the mail coming from entries in your address book, mail coming from people on the previous recipients list, or mail that was sent using your full name.

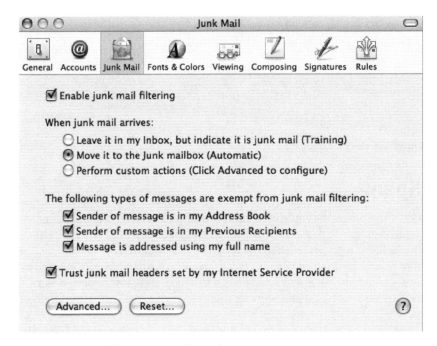

Figure 5-16. *Spam filtering in Apple Mail*

On the server side of things, the mail server will apply junk mail headers if the mail server is configured to scan mail for spam. On the client side, you have the ability to select whether to trust junk mail headers.

To teach Mail that a message is or is not spam, use the Reset button of the Junk Mail preference panel of Mail preferences to reset the junk mail filter. This will undo any other settings you've made to the filter.

Click the Advanced button to build custom rules (see Figure 5-17). This is a setting that allows you to access the X-Spam headers option by using the specific header criteria as part of a rule. You can also merge criteria to build very specific rule sets.

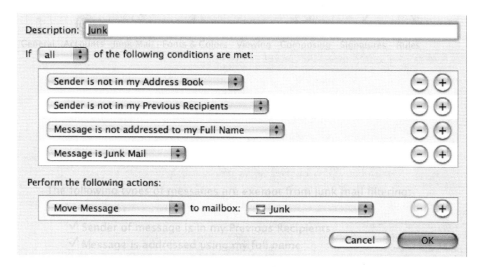

Figure 5-17. *Conditions and criteria in Entourage*

Filtering with Entourage

Entourage has a built-in spam filter. To enable and configure the spam filter in Entourage, follow these steps (see Figure 5-18):

1. Select Tools, and click Junk E-mail Protection.

2. At the Level screen, select the level of protection you want to use. Click OK.

Levels include the following:

None: Disables the Entourage spam filter.

Low: Filters out obvious junk mail but allows some spam to come through to the user.

High: Filters out as much junk as possible. This can cause some false positives, but for the false positives you should add those users to your address book in Entourage.

Exclusive: Allows incoming mail only from users who are listed in the Entourage contacts list or domains listed in the Mailing List Manager (accessible in the Tools menu).

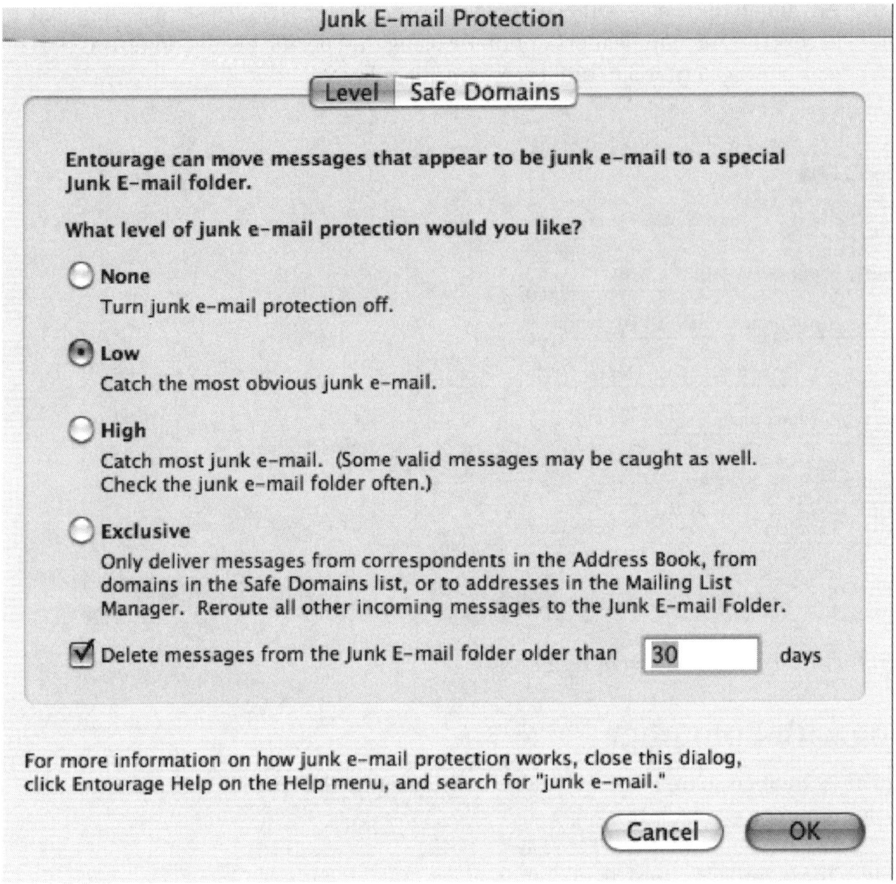

Figure 5-18. *Spam filter settings in Entourage*

Using White Listing in Entourage

The ability to establish white lists is a key to any antispam applications. A *white list*, also known as a *safe list*, is a list of addresses that will not be flagged as spam. This can be a list of e-mail addresses, domains, IP addresses, or server names. When the filter runs and attempts to identify spam, it will skip e-mail that is on a safe list.

To allow all mail from certain domains, you can click the Safe Domains tab of the Junk E-mail Protection screen and enter all the domains that you want to add to the white list. When doing so, separate each domain with a comma (,). When you white list a domain, none of the mail sent to you from that domain will be filtered using Entourage's spam filter. Rather than having to enter a lot of users on each or add entire domains worth of users into your address book, you can just enter a domain on the Safe Domains tab (Figure 5-19). For example, if you enter **apress.com**, then you will be able to receive e-mail from all users of the apress.com e-mail domain.

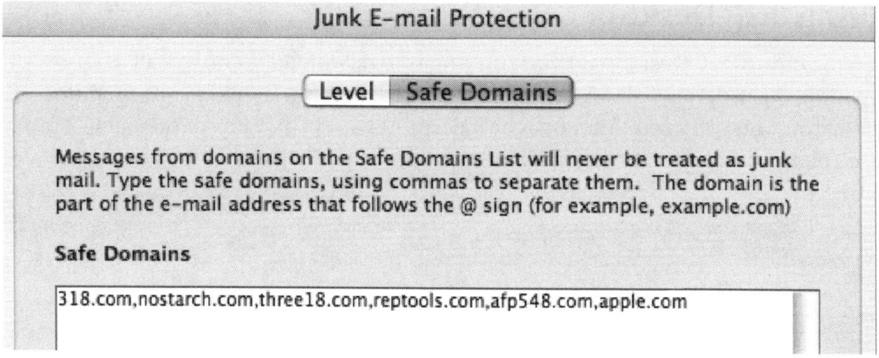

Junk E-mail Protection

[Level | Safe Domains]

Messages from domains on the Safe Domains List will never be treated as junk mail. Type the safe domains, using commas to separate them. The domain is the part of the e-mail address that follows the @ sign (for example, example.com)

Safe Domains

318.com,nostarch.com,three18.com,reptools.com,afp548.com,apple.com

Figure 5-19. *Safe domains in Entourage*

Once you receive messages that the Entourage filter considers spam, you will receive the Junk E-mail Found alert, as indicated in Figure 5-20. When you first start using the Entourage spam filter, you should click Open Folder on this screen and check whether the message was really spam. If you get messages that are mistakenly marked as spam, you can click the message, and Entourage will give a few different options for dealing with the message. One of them is to add the sender to your address book. (You can always undo this later by removing the user from your address book.)

Junk E-mail Found

Some messages from the account "Charles Edge" have been moved to the Junk E-mail folder. You should check the Junk E-mail folder regularly to ensure that you do not miss mail that you wish to receive.

☐ Don't show this message again

(Open Folder) (Junk E-mail Protection...) (OK)

Figure 5-20. *Junk Email Found alert*

Using PGP to Encrypt Mail Messages

PGP, developed by Phil Zimmerman, is an encryption suite (see Chapter 2 for more information on encryption) that will encrypt e-mail messages, files, and folders before they are sent. It can be downloaded and purchased at http://www.pgp.com for just under $300 (the license plus a one-year subscription). PGP can also be used to encrypt instant messaging traffic in iChat beyond what is available using iChat's default security options and can also encrypt full disks. Installing PGP Desktop will automatically encrypt iChat traffic. For the purpose of this chapter, we will focus on the mail encryption portion of the suite.

Configuring PGP Desktop

The first step to getting PGP Desktop up and running is to download it and install it. Once installed, opening the program will take you to the Setup Assistant. If this is your first time using PGP Desktop, you will need to set up a new account with PGP. Click in the field I Am a New User (see Figure 5-21), and then click Continue.

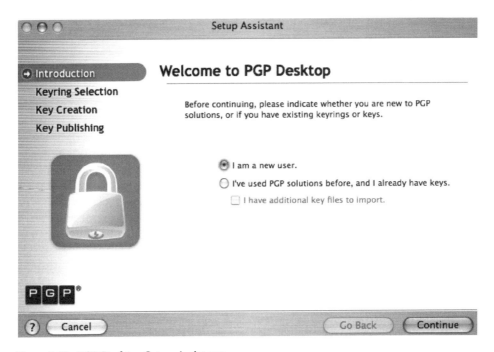

Figure 5-21. *PGP Desktop Setup Assistant*

The next screen displays the path of the encryption key files. This should say ~/Documents/PGP. Click Continue on this screen.

The next screen will allow you to enter Expert mode (see Figure 5-22), which gives you more granular control over the encryption options. Click Continue to move to the next screen.

Figure 5-22. *PGP Desktop PGP key generator*

Figure 5-23. *Setting contact information for PGP*

Next you will enter your passphrase (see Figure 5-24). This is the password that is used to unlock your account any time you reinstall PGP or use it to encrypt or decrypt data.

The next screen asks for your name and e-mail address (Figure 5-23). If you will be using your PGP account to encrypt mail for multiple accounts, click the More button, and enter each of the addresses you want to use. Once you have entered all your e-mail accounts, click the Continue button.

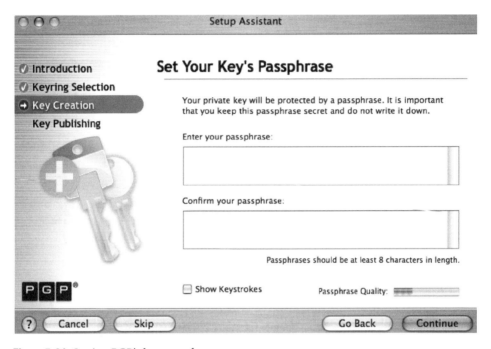

Figure 5-24. *Setting PGP's key passphrase*

Once you have entered the passphrase, click the Continue button. You will then see the PHP Key Creation Summary page. PGP will ask whether all the information is correct. If it is, click the Continue button. The system will now generate a key. When it is complete, click the Continue button. Next it is time to publish your key to the PGP Global Directory on the Internet. Click Continue, and the key will be published once it has been verified. When this process is complete, click the Finish button. You are now set up to have all your messages encrypted if both keys to both parties are known and trusted. All your outgoing messages will be digitally signed.

When the installer is complete, you will be placed into the PGP Desktop application (see Figure 5-25). From within PGP Desktop, click the Continue button to complete the Setup Assistant.

Once you have completed the Setup Assistant, it's time to teach your mail client how to use PGP. Getting started is as simple as opening the mail client, where you will be greeted by a message asking whether or not you want to secure the account (see Figure 5-26). If you want to use PGP with your mail client, click Yes, Secure This E-mail Account, and then click the Continue button. This message will come up for every e-mail account that you use on the machine. You do not need to encrypt every one of your e-mail accounts to use this encryption program.

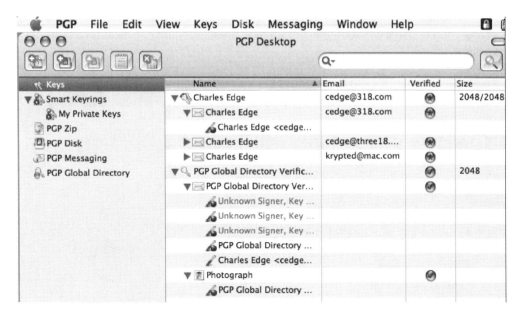

Figure 5-25. *PGP*

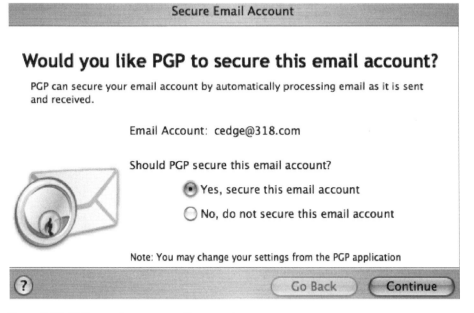

Figure 5-26. *PGP securing an e-mail account*

You will then be asked to associate a key for each account that you tell PGP to secure (see Figure 5-27). You can have a different key for each e-mail account or use one key to secure multiple accounts.

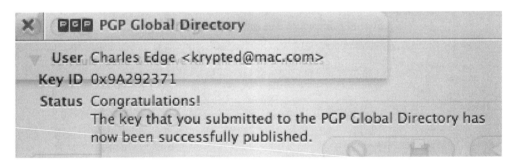

Figure 5-27. *Choosing the key to secure the e-mail account*

Once you click the Finish button, PGP will publish the new e-mail address that it has associated to your account to its global directory. You will receive a message telling you that the key for each account has been published (see Figure 5-28).

Figure 5-28. *Successfully published key*

Once you have chosen to secure an account, you will receive an e-mail to that account asking you to verify the association. Once verified, messages sent using PGP with your e-mail client will be encrypted by default (see Figure 5-29).

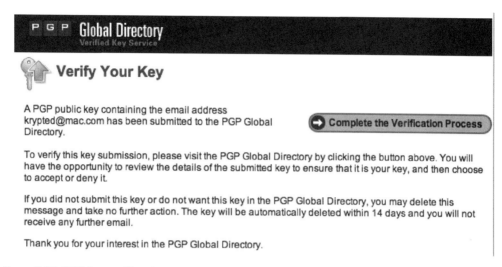

Figure 5-29. *PGP key verification*

GPG Tools

GPG (or GnuPG, downloadable at `http://www.gnupg.org`) is much like PGP; it allows users to encrypt files and e-mail. It is different in that GPG, and the suite of tools built around it, is open source. GPG is not as feature rich as PGP but does have some compelling features in that its use is more easily controlled with `Mail.app` and it is free.

To get started with GPG, you will first need to download GnuPG and install it. Once you've installed GnuPG, download and install GPGMail. The most recent releases of both are available through VersionTracker. Once you install them, you will see new fields in your `Mail.app` client when you are ready to send mail.

Using Mail Server–Based Solutions for Spam and Viruses

Many mail servers provide the ability to thwart spam and viruses when they enter the network via e-mail. The three most dominant products for mail servers on the Mac platform are Kerio MailServer, OS X Server Mail, and CommuniGate Pro. Each of these has their own strengths and weaknesses including virus and spam prevention capabilities. Each server platform offers ways to mitigate spam and viruses; however, they vary in implementation, terminology, and licensing structures.

Kerio

To configure the spam and virus filters on the Kerio MailServer, follow these steps:

1. Open the Kerio Administration Console.

2. Open the Configuration folder.

3. Open the Content Filter folder.

4. Click Spam Filter (see Figure 5-30).

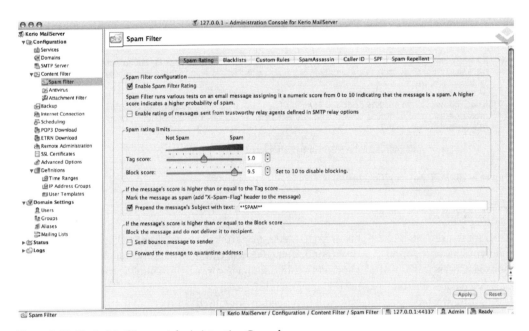

Figure 5-30. *Kerio MailServer Administrative Console*

5. Select the Enable Spam Filter Rating option. This will enable spam checking on incoming messages. Once a message has been scanned, it will be assigned a score. This is a rating based on the likelihood that the message is spam.

6. Rules offer Kerio administrators a way to provide more granular controls over filters. By using rules, it is possible to override the score assigned to messages with a score that will always flag those messages as spam. When creating custom rules, click the Custom Rules tab of the spam filter in Kerio. When you click Add, you will receive a screen similar to the one shown in Figure 5-31. The Description field of the rule allows administrators to keep track of what the rule is doing. The description has nothing to do with how the rule is processed.

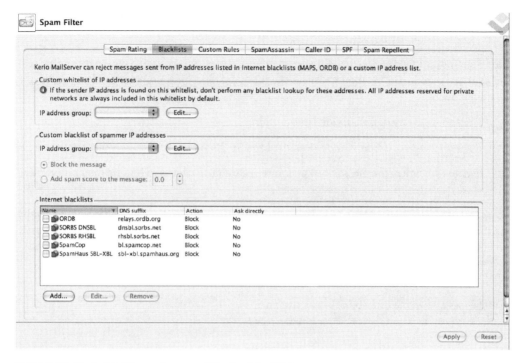

Figure 5-31. *Kerio MailServer's spam-filtering blacklists*

The If section can teach the filter to catch all mail that matches their filter. The three fields are Header, Type, and Content. The Header field allows administrators to choose which part of the message to match to the filter. The options here are as follows:

- From

- To

- Cc

- Subject

- Sender

- X-Envelope-To

- Received

The Type field allows the administrator to define what value type is present in the header field that is being matched. Types that are available include the following:

- Is Empty

- Is Missing

- Contains Address

- Contains Domain

- Contains substring

- Contains binary hex string

The Content field is not available for all types of rules. The content is the pattern that will be matched with incoming mail to trigger the rule's action. The action that is taken can be one of the following:

Treat the message as non-spam: Does nothing

Treat the message as spam and reject it: Allows the server to immediately discard the e-mail

Add spam score to the message: Allows you to configure clients to handle mail in a variety of ways using the X-Spam header

Once you are finished building out a rule, you can use the If the Message Was Rejected by a Custom Spam Rule area to determine how the message is handled. Here you can select whether to bounce the message (reject it and autoreply to the message), forward it into a quarantine e-mail address, or do both (see Figure 5-32).

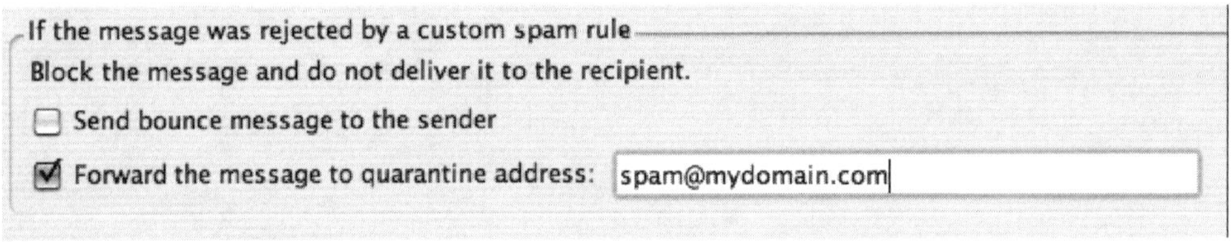

Figure 5-32. *Rejection action*

Mac OS X Server's Antispam Tools

Mac OS X Server has ClamAV and Spam Assassin installed by default. You can turn them on for the mail server using Server Admin, located in the /Applications/Server folder (see Figure 5-33). The GUI in Server Admin is easy to use and allows administrators to configure many of the most commonly used features of ClamAV and Spam Assassin. However, if you want to do anything not available in the GUI such as script new training events, then you will need to use the command line for either ClamAV or Spam Assassin to do so.

■**Note** Common add-ons for SpamAssassin include Vipul's Razor, Pyzor, and DCC. Vipul's Razor is a distributed, collaborative, spam detection and filtering network. Many of these applications use the reputation of a server, the reputation of the IP address block, and sometimes the reputation of the owner of the server or domain to further weigh spam to indicate the likelihood that a piece of mail is spam.

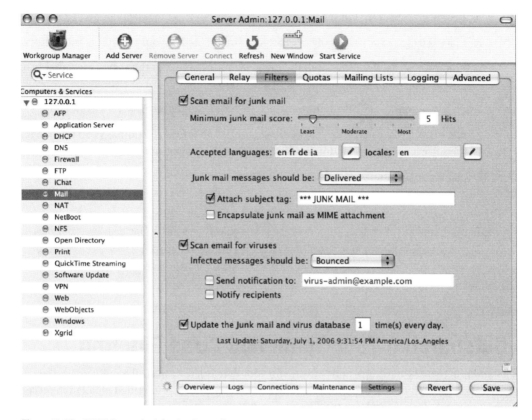

Figure 5-33. *OS X Server's Admin Console*

CommuniGate Pro

Stalker's CommnuniGate Pro also has the ability to scan for spam and viruses. However, these are not built-in spam and virus filtration services; they are plug-ins that can be purchased from Stalker at www.stalker.com. Most of these plug-ins are accessible through the use of rules on the server.

Antivirus filtration for CommuniGate can be provided using software from Kaspersky Labs, McAfee from Network Associates, and Sophos. Antispam filtration is provided using SpamCatcher from Mailshell.

It is also possible to use CGPSA, a package from TFF Enterprises at http://www. tffenterprises.com/cgpsa. CGPSA is free but does not come with support. CGPSA is difficult to configure, but once configured, it will give administrators the most bang for their buck. To install CGPSA in CommuniGate, follow these steps:

1. In your communigate directory, create a folder called cgpsa.

2. Download CGPSA from http://www.tffenterprises.com/cgpsa/cgpsa.tgz.

3. Download SpamAssassin at http://www.spamassassin.org.

4. Make sure Perl is installed on the server.

5. Install SpamAssassin on the server.

6. Place the `cgpsa` script into the `cgpsa` folder you created in your `communigate` directory.

7. Edit the `cgpsa` script to point to the Perl executable, and edit the `$cgp_base` variable to point to the CommuniGate installation on the system.

8. Place the `cgpsa.conf` file in the `Settings` folder of your `CommuniGate Pro` directory.

9. Place the `cgpsa.domainconf` file in the `Settings` folder for each domain you want to use the software with; by default this is `/var/CommuniGate/Domains/domain.com/Settings`.

10. Install the CommuniGate Pro CLI Perl Module, `CLI.pm`.

■**Note** As the number of mail threats on the Internet has grown, the variety of methods used to fight spam has also grown. One popular way to fight spam and viruses is to deploy a device on the network that intercepts traffic as it enters the network and scans it for mail threats. Examples of these devices include Barracuda, SonicWall, and Cisco.

Outsourcing Your Spam and Virus Filtering

In addition to using hardware and software on your network to scan mail for viruses and spam, you can also outsource spam and virus filtration. In fact, it is recommended for all mail servers because most of these services provide some kind of perimeter failover should your mail server go down.

Simply put, the outsourced mail filtering solution directs your MX record to the vendor's web site, and they then filter the mail for you. This reduces the bandwidth overhead coming into your network if you run your own mail server and helps with staffing overhead because it essentially eliminates the need for someone to spend the time trying to play catch-up with the spammers.

Outsourced filtration companies, such as Microsoft Exchange Hosted Solutions (EHS) and MX Logic, have gained wide adoption. This is because they require little maintenance, are inexpensive, and are easy to set up.

CHAPTER 6

■ ■ ■

Reviewing Logs and Monitoring

Hijackings and poor maintenance habits have the same consequences: disaster. It doesn't happen often, but when it does, it's tragic. Every once in a blue moon we'll hear about a commercial airplane that has crashed due to mechanical failure. Investigators immediately go to the crash site to get to work sifting through the wreckage looking for survivors but also for clues about why the tragedy occurred. Although the mystery of why the plane went down may or may not be solved, the real tragedy is that, statistically speaking, planes crash more often than not because of malfunctioning hardware, not because of poor maintenance habits. Airline maintenance crews who stick to a steadfast and detailed maintenance schedule rarely have this happen to them, mainly because they know precisely when the plane was maintained, at what time, and what maintenance was performed.

This is how many seasoned network administrators treat security. They proactively manage their systems, reviewing their logs regularly. They log when they perform maintenance on the machine and notice when peculiarities occur. Believe it or not, computers actually log more information than airlines do. Unfortunately, the logs often go unnoticed and unread. And yet they can be the single greatest insight into securing your systems. Even when security is compromised, many administrators don't think to check the logs to see what happened.

Why is this? It's simple. Logs can be pretty complicated to the untrained eye, and administrators just don't understand what the logs are telling them. In this chapter, we will show you where to look for log files on the Mac (and Windows machines as well, because they can tell you a lot about security with respect to a Mac) and show you what they mean. We hope that once you realize what kind of information is stored in logs, you'll start using them a lot more effectively.

What Exactly Gets Logged?

It can seem weird to think that much of what you do on your computer gets logged. Imagine if every move you made was written down, and you could review every step you made over the course of the day. Although we may never know whether the government (or Microsoft even) is actually recording our every move, logging every move on a computer is commonplace.

What gets logged is determined by the application or the operating system. This is different and can be configured manually for many programs. The act of escalating your privileges is typically logged, as are failures. The reason many items are logged is for later troubleshooting, but in reference to security, any item that elevates privileges, references a password entry, or indicates the occurrence of an application failure should be logged.

A log can be as simple as one line indicating the deletion of a file or as detailed as each file created during an installation or process. The following shows the output of the `install.log` file during the installation of DAVE, a software package used to integrate Mac and Windows environments (covered further in Chapter 10). The install log shows each file created during the process as well as the corresponding date, time, and system on which each was created (or touched).

```
Dec  7 20:56:53 charles-edges-macbook runner[7112]: Touched
'/./Applications/DAVE Browser.app'
Dec  7 20:56:53 charles-edges-macbook runner[7112]: Touched
'/./Applications'
Dec  7 20:56:53 charles-edges-macbook runner[7112]: Touched
'/./Library/Frameworks/Thursby.framework/Versions/
A/Resources/DAVENetworkLogin.app'
Dec  7 20:56:53 charles-edges-macbook runner[7112]: Touched
'/./Library/Frameworks/Thursby.framework/
Versions/A/Resources'
Dec  7 20:56:53 charles-edges-macbook runner[7112]: Touched
'/./Library/Application Support/DAVE/DAVE Tracing.app'
Dec  7 20:56:53 charles-edges-macbook runner[7112]: Touched
'/./Library/Application Support/DAVE'
Dec  7 20:56:53 charles-edges-macbook runner[7112]: Touched
'/./Applications/Utilities/DAVE Network Utility.app'
Dec  7 20:56:53 charles-edges-macbook runner[7112]: Touched
'/./Applications/Utilities'
Dec  7 20:56:53 charles-edges-macbook runner[7112]: Touched
'/./Library/Filesystems/DAVE/cifsd.app'
Dec  7 20:56:53 charles-edges-macbook runner[7112]: Touched
'/./Library/Filesystems/DAVE'
Dec  7 20:56:53 charles-edges-macbook runner[7112]: Touched
'/./Library/Filesystems/DAVE/tss_check_cifs.app'
Dec  7 20:56:53 charles-edges-macbook runner[7112]: Touched
'/./Library/Filesystems/DAVE'
Dec  7 20:56:53 charles-edges-macbook runner[7112]: Touched
'/./Library/Application Support/DAVE/Uninstall DAVE.app'
Dec  7 20:56:53 charles-edges-macbook runner[7112]: Touched
'/./Library/Application Support/DAVE'
Dec  7 20:56:53 charles-edges-macbook runner[7112]: Touched
'/./Library/Application Support/DAVE/DAVE Setup Assistant.app'
Dec  7 20:56:53 charles-edges-macbook runner[7112]: Touched
'/./Library/Application Support/DAVE'
```

Multiple instances of logging are possible because they take up such little processing speed. Logging software sends commands to log files while you're performing many of the common tasks you perform every day and when routine tasks are running on your system in the background. This may be some of those pesky items that cause the computer to run slowly at various times of the day, such as right around 3:15 a.m. (this is when the normal periodic unix scripts run).

When looking at logs, keep in mind that reading every line of every log file can become tedious. Rather than doing this, look for strange entries in the files. For example, if the previous log also had a line that indicated the installation of an application called keystrokelogger, that would be something to be concerned about.

Using Console

Trying to find and read all the system logs on a Mac used to be a daunting endeavor. With OS X, Apple has simplified this a bit by giving you a handy tool in the /Applications/Utilities folder called Console. We'll cover how to use Console to view and mark logs.

Viewing Logs

You can use Console to review logs quickly without having to open each file and read them independently. When you open Console, you are immediately viewing the Console log. Clicking the Logs button gives you a listing of all the logs that Console can show you. This list includes the most commonly used logs that savvy administrators review (see Figure 6-1).

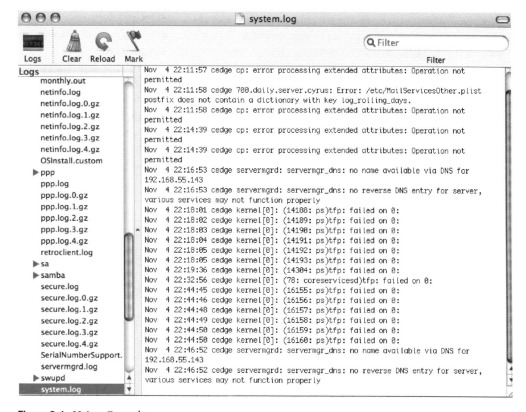

Figure 6-1. *Using Console*

Console was designed to give you an easy one-stop shop for reviewing system logs. Although this is helpful, Console doesn't show you all the logs on your computer. Each application stores log information a little bit differently, and it would be impossible to cover every aspect of every log file ever created. Luckily, many of the apps made for the Mac follow a fairly standard road map that Apple established with its own logs. We'll point out the ones to check for most security purposes. You can then apply this knowledge to other network-aware applications in order to check their logs for issues. Before we delve into what these logs can tell you, we'll discuss how you can interact with the logs.

Marking Logs

Much like using a sticky note or highlighter to highlight a passage in a book, it is possible in Console to do something similar, known as *marking logs*. When you mark logs, you select the log using the Logs window of Console and insert a line into the log using the Mark button so you can search for it later. The line appears in the log using five equal signs on either side, stamped with the time and location you inserted the mark. This makes it easier for you to refer to that event when you're interpreting the logs.

```
===== Saturday, November 4, 2006 11:13:36 PM America/Los_Angeles =====
```

Console also makes it easy to copy data out of the logs. When you click a log in Console, you can highlight text and copy it to TextEdit, Word, Excel, or any other program that supports pasting. To copy, you can either use the Cmd+C key or select Edit ➤ Copy. Notice that you cannot cut text. You can copy all the contents of a log and use the Clear button to erase the log files contents, but you cannot use the cut feature to remove highlighted text.

When you copy from a log and clear it, make sure you have copied all the data from the log file. *This is especially true if you are doing so in response to a security breach.* For performance and simplicity, when you first open a log file, it will show you only the first 128KB of data in the log. If you think there is more data in a log and want to see all of it, click the Reload button in Console while reviewing the log to check for more data. If there is any more data than what Console is showing you, it will display a prompt asking how much data you want to view (see Figure 6-2). Use the slider to tell Console how much data to display, and then click the Load button to see more entries in the log.

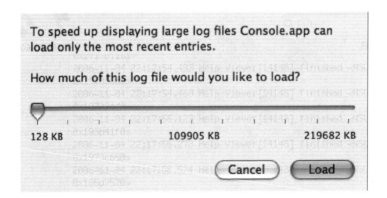

Figure 6-2. *Reloading a log*

▪ Note When you reload very large log files, such as `Console.log`, you might have to wait for a long time if the log size is bigger than a few megabytes.

Finding Logs

The /var/log directory is where OS X stores most of its important log files. This includes any log file that is stored in the /var/log directory. If you write an application or script that builds its own log file, then you can write these logs to /var/log, and they will automatically appear in Console under /var/log. Many developers put their logs here because the /var directory is used in most Unix distributions (flavors) to house most logs that are not user-specific. This includes logs for open source software that has been installed by Apple such as the firewall (ipfw), the Windows sharing component (Samba), the web server (Apache), and many other items.

The Finder is intentionally designed to not make these folders easily accessible. To get to the /var folder, you need to use the Terminal application and access it through the command line, or you can use the Cmd+Shift+G keystroke and type **/var** in the Go to the Folder field. This is a fairly standard way of accessing many of the logs we will be discussing in this chapter.

Generally you can configure third-party applications to log to wherever you want. For example, Rumpus, the popular FTP server, stores its logs in the /usr/local/Rumpus/Logs directory. However, you can customize this using the Log Folder field (as shown in Figure 6-3). Additionally, with third-party applications, you can usually customize the frequency that logs are trimmed and the amount of data that is written to the logs.

■**Note** To access the /usr/local folder, you need to use the Cmd+Shift+G keystroke and type **/usr/local**.

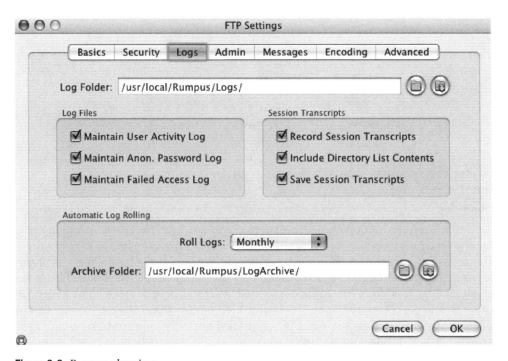

Figure 6-3. *Rumpus logging*

Reviewing User-Specific Logs

Many user-specific operating systems and third-party applications such as Carbon Copy Cloner, ClamXav, Squid, and Yasu log data into files in the user folder. These logs are stored in the ~/Library/Logs folder. By keeping these logs in each user's folder, the logs remain private to the user or to anyone who has access to their account. This is good for the privacy of each user but it can make it difficult to troubleshoot security issues.

■Note You can get around the multiuser issues with logs. Simply use the root account to view the logs for other users.

One log of note in the ~/Library/Logs folder is DiskUtility.log. This log file stores all the activities run by the Disk Utility application, including fixing permissions, fixing the disk, and reformatting. The Disk Utility logs do not get *rotated*, or cleared out on a routine basis, which makes them particularly useful if you are investigating suspicious behavior on the system. Let's say you suspect that the hard drive was reformatted. By reviewing DiskUtility.log for each user on a system, you will find who reformatted a hard drive as well as any settings that were customized during the reformat process. The following is a sample Disk Utility log:

```
**********
Jul 30 23:43:08: Disk Utility started.

Preparing to partition disk: "SWISSBIT Victorinox Media"
        Partition Scheme: Apple Partition Scheme
        Mac OS 9 Disk Drivers installed
        1 partitions will be created
        Partition 1
                    Name       : "Free Space"
                    Size       : 61.9 MB
                    Filesystem : Free Space
Creating Partition Map
Partition complete.
```

DiskUtility.log won't show whether someone ran a reformat or repair operation from the command line, though. For command-line information, it is often best to look into the command-line history for each user. This information is stored in the history file. The history file is different for each shell in which a user is operating. For example, the history file for the default shell, bash, is .bash_history and is located in the root of each user's home folder. The history files do not get rotated, but will overwrite themselves as there is a 150-command limit by default in Mac OS X. You can view history by using the history command (no arguments are needed), and you can clear the history by using history -c. Although the history file can be difficult to correlate events to, it is one of the most important items to review.

When you su a session, you are switching to the system's built-in administrative user. Any commands that are run as the root user would be available only in the root user's history. This means you need to log into each account in order to review the account's history.

Reviewing the history file can be fairly difficult if you are looking to correlate history events with other logs. Unfortunately, there are no date and time stamps available for the history file to indicate when commands were run, but you can see when items were run, and sometimes you can correlate this with system events from log files. To complicate matters even further, different users like to use different shells (a shell is just a different way to interface with the command line). Most use bash, but others use tcsh or ksh. Each shell has a different history file. So if you switch to the tcsh shell, you will be looking at yet another history. This gives you a lot of places to look for information if you have multiple shells running in Terminal. Luckily, bash is the most commonly used shell.

The last command will show a listing of the last users who logged into the computer and how long the login sessions were open. The format of the output of a last command is the username followed by the Terminal type, then the date logged in, and finally the start and stop time of the Terminal session. ttyp1 indicates the first Terminal window opened. If a second is opened, it is ttyp2, the third is ttyp3, and so on. This goes back to mainframe days when each terminal station had a unique identifier. This can give you a good log of recent login activity for a specific machine.

```
cedge     ttyp1          Sun Nov  5 11:39    still logged in
cedge     ttyp1          Sun Nov  5 11:39 - 11:39  (00:00)
cedge     ttyp3          Sat Nov  4 14:34    still logged in
cedge     ttyp3          Sat Nov  4 14:34 - 14:34  (00:00)
cedge     ttyp2          Sat Nov  4 14:34    still logged in
```

Another log of note is DiskRecording.log, which records whether any user has used the optical drive for CD burning. As you can see from the following log entries, the DiskRecording.log file does not indicate what data was burned, but it shows you what applications were used to burn to the optical media. This can be helpful if you are simply looking to correlate information between two different logs, such as finding instances in logs where large numbers of files were copied within a short span of burning a disc.

```
Disk Utility: Burn finished, Sat May 27 14:21:24 2006
Finder: Burn finished, Sun Aug 27 18:19:13 2006
iTunes: Burn finished, Fri Oct 27 09:18:28 2006
```

Showing the application and date stamp allows you to identify whether someone was burning a music CD or a DVD full of data files and when it was burned. The DiskRecording.log file is specific to each user and will not show you disc recording activity for other users. The DiskRecording.log file does not get archived or cleared unless it is manually deleted from the log. If you suspect that someone has tampered with it, you can look at the last entry in the log and compare that with the most recent modification date on the file.

launchd, the process that controls scheduled activities, also has the ability to log data. When you suspect a root kit (discussed further in Chapter 4) has infected your system as one user but isn't active for all users, take a look at the `launchd` logs for your user account to see whether any events are occurring that you should be concerned about, such as initiating services that are non-Apple or that are possibly damaging the system. The following command causes `launchd` to log to the specified /Users/cedge/Library/Logs/launchd.log file until you log out of the system:

```
launchctl stdout /Users/cedge/Library/Logs/launchd.log
```

Using the `launchctl` command in this manner will not cover logging after a restart. To get `launchd` to log data into a log file, add the following lines to your `launchd.conf` file:

```
 limit maxfiles 256 512<br>
stdout /Users/cedgejosh/Library/Logs/launchd.out
```

■**Note** The `stdout` command tells `launchd` to log information into the `launchd.out` file referenced in the `launchd.conf` file.

User logs can be helpful in determining what was done while logged into your account. When used in conjunction with the other logs mentioned, you can get a fairly specific idea of what was performed on the system recently.

Reviewing Library Logs

If you've ever helped a friend move and that friend was a fairly efficient mover, he probably assigned someone to stay in the moving truck to arrange everything so that the maximum amount of stuff could be fit into the truck. This lets everyone else maximize efficiency by going back and forth from the house to the truck with stuff. This idea can be translated into the ways in which software applications are programmed to work in an operating system. It often makes sense to use a shared library of items that many different applications can access. This allows less programming to write more features into applications and more efficient code, much like the guy in the truck allows the people moving furniture from the house to do so more efficiently.

Since the /Library folder keeps many shared application libraries (think of these as mini-applications), the types of logs stored here tend to be logs generated by libraries that are shared across multiple applications. This includes crash reporters that write application crash information into logs, web server logs, and directory service logs. Many application authors also choose their log destination as the /Library/Logs folder. For example, this would explain the random Timbuktu log you might notice in the /Library/Logs folder.

Many of the applications that provide shared libraries communicate using data that might not make much sense to the naked eye. In the crash logs you will typically see hexadecimal memory segments listed, followed by the library that wrote the alert and then the path to the library. For example:

```
0x96e15000 - 0x96e2ffff libPng.dylib
/System/Library/Frameworks/ApplicationServices.framework/
Versions/A/Frameworks/ImageIO.framework/Versions/
A/Resources/libPng.dylib
```

These hexadecimal sequences in the logs can help decipher why a crash occurred if foul play is suspected. Nine times out of ten, rather than confirm irregular activity, you will instead find that there is actually a technical problem that caused the crash.

secure.log: Security Information 101

The `secure.log` file can provide invaluable security information about your machine. This log file, found in the `/var/log` directory, tracks when passwords are entered on the computer and whether they are successful. When you turn your computer on, wake it from sleep, or enter a password to allow an installer to run, you should be required to enter a password (if you're following along with the tips in this book). The `secure.log` file can help you determine what exactly happened when you (or someone else) did this.

For example, the following are the logs of what the system reports when you are attempting to install software. There is a date and time stamp at the beginning, followed by the account ID of the user who has run the installer. Then, you can see the module attempting to perform security. When the system asks for a password, `com.apple.SecurityServer` is what is used. The first line states that `SecurityServer` was invoked, and the following lines detail what tasks were performed.

```
Nov  5 00:51:39 cedge com.apple.SecurityServer: authinternal authenticated user
cedge (uid 503).
Nov  5 00:51:39 cedge com.apple.SecurityServer: uid 503 succeeded authenticating
as user cedge (uid 503) for right system.privilege.admin.
Nov  5 00:51:39 cedge com.apple.SecurityServer: Succeeded authorizing right
system.privilege.admin by process /usr/libexec/security_authtrampoline for
authorization created by /Applications/Rumpus.app.
Nov  5 00:51:39 cedge com.apple.SecurityServer: Succeeded authorizing right
com.maxum.rumpustool by process
/Applications/Rumpus.app/Contents/Resources/rumpustool for authorization created
by /Applications/Rumpus.app.
```

There are two important security clues to look out for in `secure.log`. First, multiple bad password attempts can be a clear indicator of the need for heightened security on the machine, such as using a more complex password or restricting access to the services with the password attempts.

The second item to look out for is whether someone actually ran the programs being called up in the `Secure.log` file. For example, in the previous log snippets, you will see the string `cedge` in the field immediately following the date that something was run. This shows that the user with a short name of `cedge` ran this command.

ipfw.log

Contrary to popular belief, you can learn a lot from the Hollywood elite. Security guards who work at many of the residences of the rich and famous keep books of logs (or databases if they're technically savvy) of the comings and goings of people to their clients' estates. They often take photos or write down the names of people they turn away. This allows them to look for trends of certain people who they must constantly turn away and, if need be, obtain a restraining order against. For information about network traffic, it is best to look at the logs for your computers' security guard, the firewall, which has the job of allowing or turning away network traffic in much the same way. `ipfw` (short for IP firewall), the built-in firewall for OS X, has a feature-rich firewall that is capable of logging massive amounts of data.

`ipfwloggerd`, a process specifically designed for use with the firewall, logs `ipfw` events in an `ipfw.log` file. The `ipfw` log is by default located at `/private/var/log/ipfw.log`. By default the `ipfw.log` file logs only those events that `ipfw` determines are not acceptable. You can customize whether events get logged into the `ipfw.log` file by `ipfwloggerd` for each rule using the `/private/etc/ipfilter/ipfw.conf` file. This allows you to choose which patterns traffic should match in order to be logged. This file, explained further in Chapter 8, contains rules such as the following:

```
add 01000 allow all from any to any via en0
add 01010 deny all from any to 127.0.0.0/8
add 01020 deny ip from 224.0.0.0/4 to any in
add 01030 deny tcp from any to 224.0.0.0/4 in
```

To enable logging for each rule, add the word `log` following the `allow` or `deny` portion of the rule. An example of doing this would be to take the first line (allowing `any` to `any`) and make it look like the following:

```
add 01000 allow log all from any to any via en0
```

Adding `log` to this rule tells `ipfwloggerd` to start logging all traffic that touches the computer over the `en0` interface, which happens to be the primary Ethernet adapter in your computer. Once you enable logging, you will need to stop and restart `ipfw`, or simply reboot the computer to restart `ipfw`, before the new rules become active. Once the firewall is restarted, logs will begin to be gathered for network traffic. Logging firewall traffic can exponentially increase the contents of log files, so if you institute logging, consider rotating the logs more frequently. You can also write the logs off to a separate drive so as not to fill up your boot drive with firewall logs.

■**Note** If you have a computer with multiple Ethernet adapters, as all Mac Pros have, you will also want to log traffic on `en1`, the second adapter on your machine, if that adapter is connected to your network and you are interested in viewing these statistics.

The format of the previous log entries indicates information about the network traffic, or packet, that was processed by `ipfw`. Log entries include the date and time stamp (a common theme in the logs), the source of the packet (the IP address that the packet came from), and the destination of the packet (the IP address to which the packet is traveling). Log entries will also indicate the rule that was used to allow or deny access to your computer.

`ipfw.log` can help you get a handle on the comings and goings of network traffic on your computer but can be quite verbose. When scanning through the logs, your goal should not be to read every line but to look for any information that seems out of the ordinary, such as a large number of rejected traffic packets. You also want to look out for repeated attempts on ports that are out of the ordinary or do not have corresponding services attached to your system. As discussed further in Chapter 8, you can then choose to deny *any* access to the IP address in question. This way, if a potential attacker attempts to gain access into your system through other means, once they hit this critical IP security layer, their attempts will not be accepted even if their attempts are accepted elsewhere.

■Note If you enable logging for `ipfw`, be aware of the size to which log files can grow. If all instances of traffic to specified ports are logged, then the size of these files can fill a system.

Breaking Down Maintenance Logs

Chances are that you see your doctor at regular intervals. The dentist you'll see every six months, and the family physician you'll see every year. Just as your body needs to be maintained in regular intervals, so must your computer. Maintenance scripts run at scheduled times, and if one is missed, much like a doctor's appointment, it is usually scheduled for the next available appointment. Maintenance scripts need to be run because they log what devices were plugged into a system, they back up the user database, and they do much more. Machines can be left off at night, lids to laptops can get closed, and power outages can disable a system, helping to explain the disparity in time stamps you may see when viewing your maintenance scripts and why you may occasionally skip the execution of a maintenance script.

One thing that maintenance scripts do is rotate and archive log files. Log files can get really big. Try to imagine how large a log file would get if it logged every step, turn, and move you made. When archiving, the log files are usually archived into compressed files using the gz format, a compression technique commonly used to reduce the size of single files. Once archived, the file will be renamed and cleared and become ready to begin writing new data. Some people refer to archiving a log as *rotating it*.

■Note Console will uncompress files when they are accessed. This can be time-consuming on larger files, which is why Console will by default show you only the first 128K of a log file.

In addition to archiving logs, maintenance scripts also perform other functions. These include removing temporary files, performing backups, reviewing drive capacity, checking how long you've been logged into your computer, and checking network statistics.

Mac OS X uses three main maintenance scripts that log data into separate files. These are known as *periodic scripts*. They include daily, weekly, and monthly. You can manually run these periodic scripts by using the `periodic` command. For example, to run the daily `periodic` script, use the following command:

```
Sudo periodic daily
```

You can configure the periodic scripts to log more data than they do with the default settings. You can configure the manner with which `periodic` runs the daily scripts using the `periodic.conf` file located at `/etc/defaults`. You should make some minor adjustments to the `periodic.conf` file to increase the logging of events. These include the following:

- Change the NO in the lines for weekly_show_badconfig="NO" and monthly_show_badconfig= "NO" to YES to have a periodic report of when there is bad configuration data found by the monthly.out file.

- Change the NO in the line containing the daily_clean_logs_verbose="NO" option to YES to have periodic show the files as they are being deleted.

daily.out

The daily.out file is an output file created by the daily maintenance scripts that run on your system. Like many of the maintenance logs, daily.out begins with a time stamp to provide you with the context of when it ran. Next, the daily.out log shows what old logs were removed by the daily script. For example:

```
Sat Nov  4 22:11:41 PST 2006
Removing old log files:
Removing scratch and junk files:
Removing scratch fax files
Backing up NetInfo data
Checking subsystem status:
disks:
Filesystem    1K-blocks    Used    Avail Capacity  Mounted
/dev/disk0s2 116884912 36085140 80543772    31%    /

Last dump(s) done (Dump '>' file systems):
mail:Mail queue is empty

network:
Name  Mtu   Network     Address           Ipkts Ierrs  Opkts Oerrs  Coll
lo0   16384 <Link#1>                       54484     0  54484     0     0
lo0   16384 localhost    ::1               54484     -  54484     -     -
lo0   16384 127          localhost         54484     -  54484     -     -
en0   1500  <Link#4>     00:17:f2:2a:66:12 0         0      0     0     0
en1   1500  <Link#5>     00:17:f2:4a:31:33 51910 13491  39713     0     0
en1   1500  cedge-2.loc  fe80::217:f2ff:fe 51910     -  39713     -     -
en1   1500  (16)         00:00:6b:ff:d7    51910 13491  39713     0     0
en1   1500  192.168.55   192.168.55.143    51910     -      -     -     -

ruptime: no hosts in /var/rwho.
Rotating log files: system.log
```

The big thing to look out for here is that the Ipkts field is greater than the others. The Name field refers to the name of the interface that the MAC address and the other statistics will be relevant for. The Network field is similar to the Name field but states the network that the interface can run on. The MTU field is the maximum transmission unit, which means the largest "packet" size that can be transferred in one physical frame on a network. Ipkts refers to the incoming packets, and Opkts refers to outgoing packets. The Ipkts field should always be higher than the Opkts field. If anything here looks like it is out of the ordinary, such as the Opkts field being higher than the Ipkts field, it often means you need to reinstall the drivers for your network interface. Another item to look out for is high numbers of collisions (the Col column). If your collisions are more than 10 percent of the Ipkts field, then you might have issues with your network.

■**Note** If the same network interface is listed multiple times, it is nothing to be alarmed about.

The final action of the daily maintenance script is to rotate the system.log file. The system.log file is often the largest log file on the system. This is discussed in further detail later in this chapter. The daily script is supposed to run at 3:15 a.m. every day.

■**Note** People often ask whether they should leave their computers on at night. If they have a good battery backup system, we usually tell them to do so. This allows the daily script to run when it is supposed to run.

Yasu

Yasu is a nice little free application that will run maintenance scripts if they are missed because the computer was turned off during their regular schedules (see Figure 6-4). Not only is it important to run the periodic maintenance scripts in order to view their output logs for errors, but it is equally as important to run them in order to manage the size of the various log files that get archived with this script. To do this, simply open the Yasu program, make sure only the daily, monthly, and weekly cron script boxes are checked, and then click the OK button.

■**Caution** If you leave the check boxes at the bottom of the Yasu screen checked, then you will erase many of the log files that you might need to review!

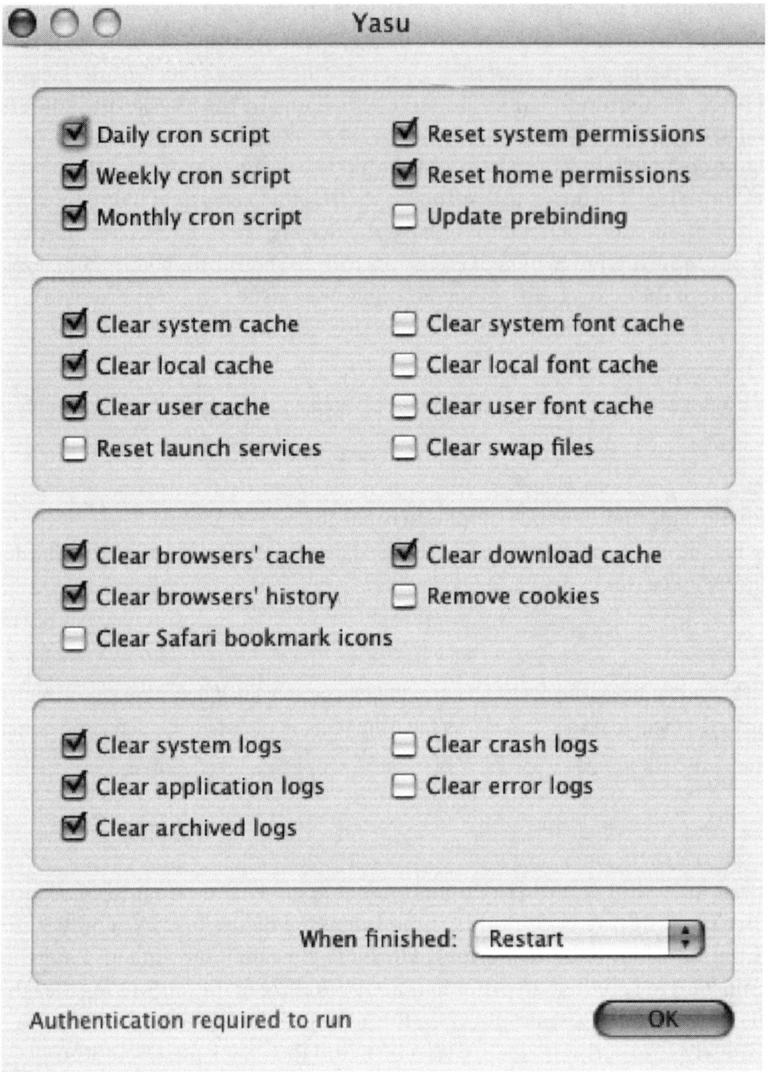

Figure 6-4. *Yasu*

weekly.out

The weekly `periodic` script runs at 3:15 a.m. on Saturdays. It updates the Whatis database (used for the `whatis` command, which searches through man pages for words you provide), updates the locate database (which searches through file names for words that you provide), and archives `ftp.log`, `lookupd.log`, `lpr.log`, `mail.log`, `netinfo.log`, `ipfw.log`, `ppp.log`, and `secure.log`. When it comes to rotating log files, this script is doing most of the heavy lifting in the background for you.

```
Sat Sep 23 04:36:18 PDT 2006
Rebuilding locate database:
Rebuilding whatis database:
find: /usr/local/man: No such file or directory
makewhatis: /usr/share/man/man1/fetchmailconf.1.gz: No such file or directory
Rotating log files: ftp.log lpr.log mail.log ipfw.log ppp.log secure.log
```

Note that the secure.log and ipfw.log files are being rotated. If you have requirements that force you to keep logs for long periods of time, then you can actually remove the weekly scripts or edit them to not rotate the required logs, but in most cases it's best to leave these as is.

monthly.out

The monthly.out log file is created by your monthly maintenance scripts and can be used to display what the monthly script did. As with the daily.out and weekly.out files, the monthly.out file will start with a date and time stamp. monthly.out can keep track of how long a user is logged into a system, a feature unique to this file. Login accounting is useful if you suspect that a user's password has been compromised and someone is illegally logging into a machine.

```
Fri Sep  1 23:11:45 PDT 2006
Doing login accounting:
        total        170.58
        cedge       170.50
        root           0.08
Rotating log files: wtmp install.log
```

The monthly.out script ends with a statement about the log files that it rotated. Monthly rotated logs generally do not get to be more than 150KB in size. The install log, for example, should be empty if you haven't installed any software in the past month. If you do see data in this file and you haven't installed software, then review what software it is and check it.

▓**Note** Older versions of Mac OS X will also rotate cu.modem.log, so you will see this noted in your monthly.out log file as well.

The monthly script is scheduled to run on the first of the month at 5:30 a.m. local time.

What to Worry About

Sunset Boulevard is a weird place to live. If we got worried and went for the bomb shelter every time we heard sirens, we wouldn't get a wink of sleep or any writing done, and you wouldn't be reading this book. To some extent, much of what could be considered worrisome simply becomes normal in a big city because of all of the "white noise" to which we're exposed.

The same goes for log files. There is a lot of information in your log files, and not everything is important. This can be overwhelming for anyone, even the most senior systems administrator. We'll now cover some of the items to be on the lookout for when reviewing your logs and some of the ways to reduce the amount of "white noise" in the logs.

One way to do this is by using keywords. The words `failed`, `error`, and `incorrect` are usually important to look out for. Read the content surrounding these for more information, or use an automated analysis tool. Sorting through a log file can also be automated by using a log analyzer to help keep track of events on user systems. One of these is LogPile, which is a utility that can make analyzing your log files easier. Another option is the open source product Swatch, which has been used by Unix systems administrators for a long time and has now been ported to Mac OS X.

Parallels and Bootcamp Logs

It's hard to imagine that discussing the methods that Windows uses to log events would ever factor into a book about the Mac. Who knew ten years ago that two competing technologies would ever converge? But converging they are. And if your computer is running either Parallels or Bootcamp with Windows, then security is going to be one of your top concerns. As we've discussed throughout this chapter, logs can give you a wealth of information about how secure your system is. Windows has its own tools that can help you to secure a Windows environment on the Mac.

Event Viewer

The Event Viewer is similar to the Console application on a Mac. It provides an administrator with one place to go to find information about service-oriented errors on the system itself.

The Event Viewer is split into three parts (see Figure 6-5) in Windows Vista. Windows XP and Server have more items to view, but for the sake of discussion in this book, we will concentrate on Windows Vista because it is what most Mac users are likely to be running:

- Application Logs contains events that are logged by programs. This includes database, Microsoft Exchange, and other applications that write data into logs that are not part of the core operating system.

- Security Audit contains information about security events that have occurred when logging onto the computer. If you have enabled audit trails on file access, then this can be a verbose log. Otherwise, it is usually a very small log. Look out for anything with the word *failure* in the log because this can signify a failure with a security process.

- System Logs shows you the events that get logged by the operating system. This includes drivers and other system components that could produce an error.

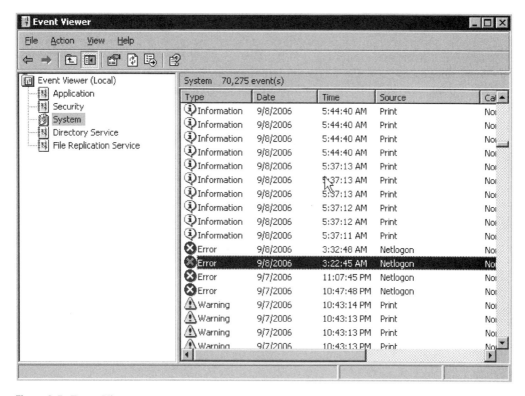

Figure 6-5. *Event Viewer*

There is a plethora of Microsoft event IDs in the Event Viewer. Microsoft has made it fairly simple to sift through these event IDs to find the errors by using color-coding. Blue means no action is necessary, yellow indicates that an item should at least be looked at, and red indicates a failure. By researching the contents of each of these entries, you will get a good handle on what Windows is having any problems with, including many events directly related to the security of your system.

Although it may seem daunting at first, you should know what every warning and error message means. The Microsoft Web site is a good place to research information about these events.

■**Note** In response to the need for a more comprehensive listing of event information, EventID.net publishes information about Windows events and links to Microsoft Knowledge Base articles and third-party Web sites to find more information on fixing issues you may find here. Searching for the event message, enclosed in quotation marks, on Google is also a good bet.

Task Manager

The Event Viewer is helpful for researching events that have already occurred on your system. But it doesn't go into detail about all the processes currently running on your system. The Task Manager in Windows is similar to the Activity Monitor on a Mac and will provide you with the ability to look (see Figure 6-6) at what processes are currently running.

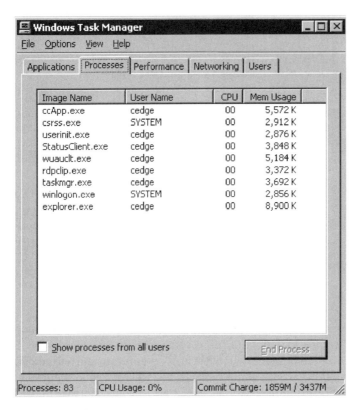

Figure 6-6. *Task Manager*

To see the Task Manager, press the Ctrl+Alt+Del keys on your keyboard, and click the button for Task Manager. Here you will see a few tabs. The first is Applications, which contains applications that your account has launched. The second is Processes, which contains the applications you have launched and any background processes that might be running, as well as the user who started the process and the CPU and memory being taken up by that application. You can use the Performance tab to check memory and processor utilization and get a chart that shows this.

To stop a process that is running, you can right-click it and click End Process. To find out more about a process, then consider using Google or the Microsoft Knowledge Base at http:// www.microsoft.com/support to research what each process is doing on the system.

Note You can use the Networking tab to view the network traffic running on your network interfaces.

Performance Alerts

You can use the Performance administrative tool (see Figure 6-7) to customize the amount of information that is being logged and to provide you with extremely detailed information about nearly every aspect of how your system is running. This tool is far more advanced than those available on the Mac platform for tracking down bottlenecks in speed, levels of inbound traffic, and other items that could introduce security issues. A comprehensive discussion about this tool is beyond the scope of this book but should definitely be consulted when trying to trouble-shoot why the Windows environment on your computer is running poorly.

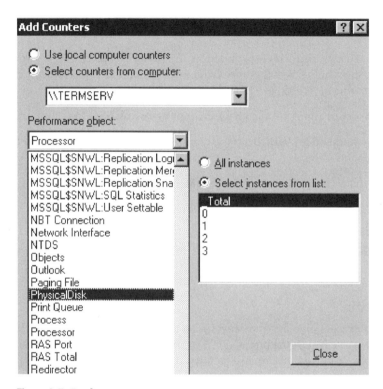

Figure 6-7. *Performance counters*

Review Regularly, Review Often

Reviewing logs is an integral aspect of security, and you should review them routinely. If you are the only person responsible for looking at logs, set up a recurring event in your calendar program to remind you to do this. This might be daily, weekly, or monthly according to how concerned your organization is about the health and security of your system coupled with how complex your environment is.

Accountability

Establishing some form of accountability is also important. Have you ever gone to the bathroom in a gas station where it has a sign-in sheet for the attendants to mark when cleaning the bathroom?

If there wasn't a sign-in sheet for cleaning the bathroom at a gas station, it might never get cleaned. Likewise, unless you establish some form of accountability, you will likely run into a situation where your logs haven't been checked in months, especially if you are dealing with multiple people in charge of log checking.

Using a spreadsheet or a sign-in sheet to indicate when log files have been reviewed is an excellent way to establish accountability for log checking. You can also track when logs are backed up to optical media if you choose to do so.

The following are the items to include in your regularly scheduled log reviews:

- When were the `periodic` maintenance scripts (daily, weekly, and monthly) last run? You can easily find this using `ls -l /var/log/*.out` to see when their log files were last updated. Was there anything out of the ordinary in those logs?

- Look for repeated bad password attempts in the log for any service that accepts a network connection, such as the `smb.log` file if there are Windows computers on your network or `ftp.log` if you are sharing files through FTP.

- Look for any bad password attempts, and check the privilege escalations in `secure.log`.

- Review the `history` command to check for strange commands and the `last` command to look for weird user logins.

- If you're running Parallels or Bootcamp, check your Windows Event Viewer.

- The `access.log` file in the `/var/log /cups/access_log` folder shows all the CUPS activity on your print server.

- The logs located in the `/var/log/samba` directory deal with access attempts from Windows computers.

Incident Response

Smart homeowners have a disaster plan put in place for what to do if their home is affected by a natural disaster or burglary. They post the phone number to the local police or fire department next to their phone. In California, earthquake country, they keep gallons of water and canned foods stored in their pantries. Whether they know it or not, they are developing an *incident response plan.*

If, in your searching through regular log files, you find something that concerns you, then you will want to also have an incident response plan for how you are going to handle these incidents. Incident response plans don't have to be very complicated, but the more people who are involved in the operations of your information systems, the more involved the incident response plan will be; therefore, the more complex the infrastructure, the more thought out the incident response plan should be.

The incident response plans can vary from location to location. For example, if you are troubleshooting your security logs at home, a typical incident response to a suspicious item in a log might be to spend an hour trying to discover what occurred. After that initial hour, if you haven't managed to discover the culprit, you will immediately clone your hard drive and then reformat and move your data back over from this backup. But at the office, you might decide that if a security event occurs and you cannot figure out what the problem is, you will open a ticket with AppleCare immediately, down the system, make a check-summed clone of it, install a new hard drive, install OS X on the new hard drive, and migrate data. Home incident response plans are typically easy to compile and really just offer you a task list of what to do in the case of a security incident. Office incident response plans are typically more comprehensive and need to go through committees or IT groups for approval, especially because they could contain some mission-critical systems with guaranteed uptimes that need to be maintained.

We cannot stress the importance of implementing an incident response system enough. Intellectual property theft is on the rise. Companies have lost billions of dollars in revenue over the years because of stolen intellectual property. When it occurs, generally it is not an overnight sensation; it happens over time. More often than not, the logs were giving clues to breaches in the security framework long before the actual theft occurred. Some have been put out of business because of it. An incident response plan coupled with routine backup checking spares everyone the heartache and devastation of stolen intellectual property and financial information.

Mac-based companies are growing. Many Mac deployments are moving from small into medium-sized or enterprise-class network environments. As your technology infrastructure grows, incident response plans and other similar plans will become a must in order to keep everyone in your organization on the same page.

PART 3

■■■

Network Security

CHAPTER 7

■■■

Securing Network Traffic

Infiltration is a very real problem for network administrators. Every day, new network attacks are developed to try to breach a network's security perimeter. Building a secure network requires that a number of key software and hardware components are implemented and configured correctly. But securing a network is not just about acquiring the right network hardware to block unwanted traffic. What is more important in a discussion about network security is understanding how a network works, how Internet traffic is managed, how information flows within that network, and what services need to be secured that control the traffic. Once these crucial elements are explored, discussing how to ensure data packet protection makes sense. In this chapter, we will explore the essential concepts of network structures. Within those concepts, we will then discuss what steps you can take to make your network stronger against security breaches and unwanted network traffic.

Understanding TCP/IP

The Internet works on a scheme generally known as the *TCP/IP stack*. This stack divides the task of moving data into its various levels of responsibility, known as *layers*. Each layer presents its own security problems, so effective security must address each layer independently.

Crucial to understanding network traffic is understanding what TCP/IP is. TCP/IP, which stands for Transmission Control Protocol/Internet Protocol, is the primary technology used with most modern network traffic and is one of the most common vectors exploited by network-based attacks. The Internet is now almost exclusively running on the Internet Protocol (IP).

TCP establishes communication over ports. Each port allows one server to communicate with another by mapping data to a particular process running on a computer. A prime example of this kind of communication is the way that e-mail travels on a network. SMTP runs, by default, on port 25 and is the protocol most commonly used to send e-mail from client computers to servers. SMTP also allows all mail servers to deliver messages to one another.

■**Note** There are several different "layer models" used to explain IP traffic. For the purposes of this condensed discussion on IP traffic, we will stick to the four-layer model.

The path that data takes over the TCP/IP stack begins and ends at the user-level *application layer*. Applications, from a network security perspective, are lower-level (behind-the-scenes) programs such as HTTP for serving web pages, POP and IMAP for receiving mail, and SMTP for sending mail. Securing the application layer can consist of limiting the applications a user has access to, as discussed in Chapter 3. It can also entail using application-level encryption— everything from manually encrypting sensitive data using PGP (explained in further detail in Chapter 5) to automatically encrypting data using a secure application such as Secure Shell (SSH, discussed further in Chapter 12).

Application data is then presented to the *transport layer* where a protocol, typically TCP, splits data into *packets*, manageable chunks of data with a source address and a destination address. If we were to use the analogy of commercial shipping, this most closely resembles the packing of items into boxes and attaching a shipping label that includes a delivery address and a return address.

The *control layer* is also responsible for receiving incoming packets, reassembling them, and sending them along to the appropriate application. It is represented by a port number. This is analogous to the name written above the street address on a package. Once the package is delivered to the appropriate building, it's the responsibility of the people in that building to ensure the package finds its way to the appropriate resident. One of the most important steps of securing any network is limiting the number of incoming ports to only the traffic that is necessary. For example, if a machine is not serving web pages, it should not accept traffic on port 80, the default port for HTTP, whether a web server on that port is running or not.

Moving packets from one address to another is handled by IP, from which the Internet gets its name. Packets move from machine to machine via a series of intermediate steps, called *hops*. This is much like the process of shipping packages from one drop-off point to another until it reaches its final destination.

■Note Packets are explained in further detail later in this chapter.

An example of security at the control layer is network address translation (NAT), which presents a single IP address to the outside world, while maintaining a separate internal addressing scheme for the local network. Although it doesn't necessarily secure your network from outside attacks, the less information an outside attacker knows about your internal network, the better. This concept of "security through obscurity" increases the difficulty of exploiting vulnerabilities. Having a single incoming access point rather than a large number of systems sitting on the Internet also makes it easier to deal with potential risks such as a Denial of Service attack when you are looking to secure systems from the Internet rather than from other hosts on your internal network.

Finally, there are the physical elements that make up the *physical layer*. This consists of how a network is physically implemented. For example, a wired Ethernet network consists of a network interface system, which consists of an Ethernet port and switches. Another example is a wireless AirPort network, accessed with AirPort cards in laptops and hosted by AirPort base stations. There are also fiber-optic ports, satellite signals, and DSL modems of the various Internet service providers, all parts of the physical layer.

The bigger your network is, the more vulnerable the physical layer. For a home user, physical security is as simple as using WPA2 encryption and a strong password on an AirPort network, as discussed in Chapter 9. For a large office, a larger number of hubs, switches, and routers need to be secured. It is also important to look out for and stop unauthorized access points, spoofed MAC addresses, and Denial of Service attacks that may be launched, even unwittingly, by users.

Each layer has its own part to play and is generally ignorant of the implementation details of the other layers, which allows the TCP/IP stack to be rather scalable. The post office doesn't tape up the package, and it isn't concerned with what is done with the contents of the package once the recipient receives it. All it cares about is moving the package from one address to another. Similarly, when you pack your boxes, you neither know nor care whether they will be put in the back of a truck and driven across the country or packed with other items into a large container and flown across the country on a cargo jet. All you are concerned with is that they get there.

However, as a security expert, you can't afford the luxury of this ignorance. You must be aware of that which you can control and mitigate that which you cannot control. Now that we've run through a quick synopsis of what network traffic is, we'll discuss some of the various network topologies, management techniques for that traffic, and ways to safeguard network traffic from possible attacks.

Types of Networks

To some degree, there are about as many types of networks as there are network administrators. But they are all built using varying themes on one of two network architecture types: peer-to-peer networks and client-server networks.

Peer-to-Peer

A peer-to-peer (P2P) computer network is a network that relies primarily on the computing power and bandwidth of the participants in the network to facilitate the interactivity on the network rather than concentrating it in a centralized set of network servers and routers. (See Figure 7-1 for a graphical representation of a P2P network.) P2P networks are typically used for connecting nodes via largely ad hoc connections. Such networks are useful for many purposes: assembling marketing materials, conducting research, and acquiring digital media assets (probably the most common use).

A wide variety of peer-to-peer applications are available for use, and each has its specific feature set that makes it popular. BitTorrent, LimeWire, Kazaa, and others allow you to publish music, documents, and other media to the Internet and access media published by others. However, peer-to-peer networking applications can use a considerable amount of bandwidth when they are not configured properly. Multiple computers running peer-to-peer applications can flood any network, from DSL to cable modems and even T3s. You will also need to configure them correctly to make sure you are not sharing private information, such as your address book or financial data.

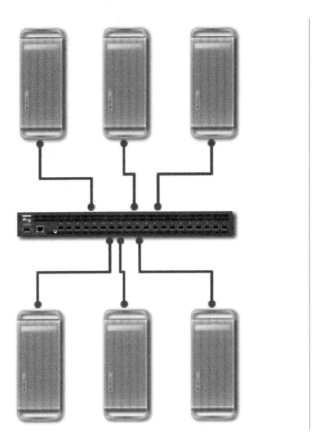

Figure 7-1. *Peer-to-peer networks*

Configuring Peer-to-Peer Networks

When configuring a peer-to-peer networking application, you will likely want to share files on your computer *and* download files from other computers. If you do not share files to the P2P network, then your download bandwidth will be automatically limited by the application, and some computers will not even allow you to download files from them. Sharing is part of peer-to-peer networking, so you will need to devote some bandwidth to others downloading your material. But you will need to limit the bandwidth these applications are using because it can affect other system processes on your computer that perform their duties on the Internet.

Each application will come with the ability to limit incoming access in some way. One way to limit the bandwidth is by limiting the number of incoming connections that are allowed to access your data. Each program does it a bit differently. When thumbing through the settings, look out for settings allowing you to configure the number of concurrent incoming and outgoing connections.

Another way to limit incoming connections is accomplished by throttling bandwidth. Consider that someone accessing your computer may be running a T1 or cable modem and have up to 7Mbps of speed available to access your files. If you are running only a DSL connection and they have a faster T1, their machine could cause your bandwidth to max out as your DSL tries to keep up the pace. This could also cause your Internet speed to slow to a crawl while accessing data outside your network. You can limit incoming connections (commonly limited to 375KBps) to make sure you always have plenty of speed available for browsing the Internet. When configuring the settings of a P2P application, look for a section that allows you to limit maximum upload and download speeds. By limiting concurrent connections, you help ensure that your network does not become flooded with P2P traffic (which can result in a Denial of Service attack on your entire network if you are not careful).

Another concern with peer-to-peer applications is limiting access to certain files. On P2P networks, users often share their entire Documents folder, exposing private data such as their mail database and financial information to the world. When installing a peer-to-peer application, make sure you know which folder is being shared and that the contents of that folder are limited to data you want accessible from outside your environment. For example, when installing LimeWire, you are asked whether the program should scan your entire system for files to share. Do not let it do this because it could include files that you may not necessarily want to share. Identify a folder within your computer to share data from, and allow it to share only from that folder.

One administrative concern with peer-to-peer file sharing can be its use to illegally upload copyrighted material to other file sharers on the Internet. Although preventing this type of traffic by blocking network ports is possible, it can sometimes be a moving target because some of these P2P protocols use random ports dynamically. Some Internet appliances and filtering packages can be configured to "tag" traffic that appears to be P2P, tracking the session based on these tags and thus overcoming any reliance on blocking traffic on any specific port.

Client-Server Networks

Over the years, as networks grew, they became unwieldy, making it more difficult to keep tabs on the computers that were linked together. This led to the development of client-server networks. Client-server networks are not ad hoc. Services on client-server networks are statically assigned and centrally managed, and settings on desktops are maintained by servers. Because the network does much of the management of itself through tasks such as assigning IP addresses, warehousing data, and managing bandwidth, client-server networks quickly became the primary weapon in combating unwieldy networks (See Figure 7-2 for a graphical representation of a client-server network.)

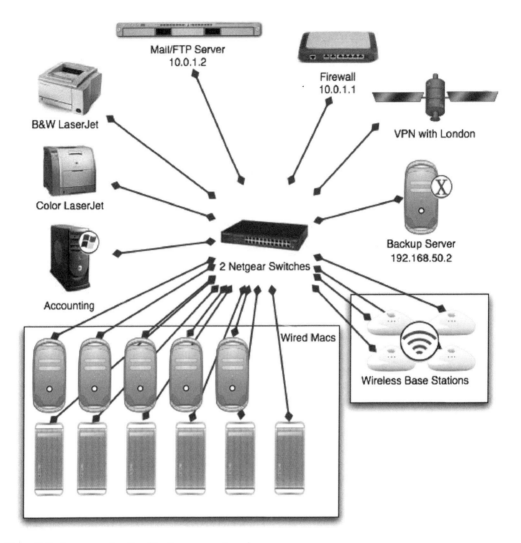

Figure 7-2. *An example of a client-server network*

Understanding Routing

As data moves between networks, you need to tell it where to go. Moving data through networks is called *routing*. In the following sections, we'll show how to route data packets and how to secure the routing techniques used to move that data along. First, we will explain a packet, and then we will move on to explain the various types of devices that packets will encounter as they traverse the Internet. This includes gateways, routers, and firewalls.

Packets

To understand how routing data works, we first need to explore what a packet is. A *packet* is a generic term for a bundle of data, organized in a predetermined way for transmission over computer networks. Packets consist of the data to be transmitted over the network along with information about how to control transmitting the packet, including its source and destination addresses.

■**Note** Packets are sometimes referred to as *datagrams*. The terms are not interchangeable, however. A datagram is a type of packet, but not all packets are datagrams.

Packets consist of three parts. The *header* marks the beginning of the packet, the *payload* contains the information to be carried in the packet, and the *trailer* marks the end of the packet.

■**Note** The term *payload* occurs consistently in computer terminology and should not be confused with the payload of a virus, which is different.

Different protocols use different conventions for distinguishing between the header, data, and footer elements and for formatting the data. The Ethernet protocol establishes the start of the header and the other data elements by their relative location to the start of the packet. Some protocols format the information at a bit level instead of a byte level. For the purposes of understanding other technologies discussed throughout this chapter, just keep in mind that there are different ways to form a packet based on the protocol that established the packet.

A good analogy when thinking about packets is to treat data transmission like moving into a new house. When moving our things, we tend to be efficient. Instead of loading one piece of furniture on to the truck, driving to the new house, unloading it, and then driving back for another piece, we move multiple pieces at a time. We also don't cram everything into one giant box either. We load our stuff from one room and put it in a box (or boxes) and label it. The header is the container (or box) for data (our stuff). It writes the name of the data on itself, much like we would write where the stuff in the box would go on the outside of it. This allows the network router (or movers) to know which room each box is destined for and typically which room the stuff came from. The router (or moving truck) will create a list of what was transmitted (moved). Most transfers of data will move more than one packet (box), breaking files into data packets (boxes) to move them more efficiently.

Gateways

A *gateway* is a device that connects two networks, the local area network (LAN) computers sitting behind the gateway and the wide area network (WAN) computers sitting outside of it. All gateways have a minimum of two IP addresses, the LAN and WAN addresses. The LAN IP addresses of computers connected internally are hidden behind the gateway. Computers on the WAN trying to connect to other computers on the network can see only the gateway's IP address. To allow traffic between the WAN and the LAN while hiding their IP addresses, the gateway uses NAT to mask the computers' network activity while allowing computers from the outside to talk to those on the inside.

> ■**Note** Not all gateways are configured correctly. Many environments behind routing devices still use public IP addresses on their local computers, a practice that should be avoided.

NAT is the act of presenting all the LAN traffic to the WAN as though it were coming from the gateway's WAN IP address. This element of network security is crucial for two reasons. One, there are simply not enough public IP addresses for all the computers that exist on networks worldwide to give each computer a public IP address. But more important, by putting your computers behind WAN addresses and filtering their traffic, you are greatly increasing the security of your network. If a computer is not easily accessible from outside the LAN, then another layer of protection has been added to it, securing it from the outside. Even if there were enough public IP addresses for every computer on a network, the amount of work necessary to secure each individual computer from the outside world would be overwhelming. By using a gateway with NAT enabled, we have conveniently implemented an extra level of protection.

> ■**Note** In NAT, the source and destination addresses of packets are rewritten as they pass through a gateway, and the way in which they are rewritten varies depending on whether they are going in or out of the network.

Routers

When a gateway is forwarding IP traffic between a LAN and a WAN, it is considered to be a *router*. A router forwards packets from one network to its destination network.

Routers use routing tables to help traffic reach its destination. A *route* is the path that is taken by data traveling from one system or network to another system or network. The routing table will record this path in temporary memory by caching the paths the data takes to get there. This makes communication between devices quicker. The address of each device that the data touches on the path to its destination is a *hop*. Each entry in a routing table specifies the next hop (or several hops), resulting in reduced lookups and improved performance. Each hop possesses its own routing table unless it is the device that initiated or terminated the connection. These routing tables need to be consistent, or routing loops can develop, establishing an inability for devices between the looped hops to communicate.

One way to view hops is by using the traceroute command in Mac OS X. The traceroute command will show each hop between your computer and a remote device. The traceroute command is followed by the remote hostname. For example, a traceroute for www.apple.com recently resulted in the following output:

```
traceroute to www.apple.com.akadns.net (17.112.152.32), 64 hops max, 40 byte packets
 1  192.168.1.1 (192.168.1.1)  3.501 ms  2.816 ms  2.659 ms
 2  10.67.152.1 (10.67.152.1)  4.271 ms  6.450 ms  6.128 ms
 3  10.1.176.1 (10.1.176.1)  4.670 ms  5.834 ms  5.067 ms
 4  147.225.49.89 (147.225.49.89)  4.686 ms  5.809 ms  5.337 ms
 5  152.161.241.70 (152.161.241.70)  10.346 ms  17.047 ms  10.958 ms
 6  72-254-0-1.client.stsn.net (72.254.0.1)  11.563 ms  12.283 ms  15.622 ms
```

```
 7  206.112.96.178 (206.112.96.178)  11.334 ms  10.764 ms  13.055 ms
 8  63.66.208.221 (63.66.208.221)  12.194 ms  14.915 ms  15.028 ms
 9  sc0.ar1.sjc5.web.uu.net (63.66.208.21)  32.809 ms  12.049 ms  10.935 ms
10  0.so-3-0-0.xl2.sjc5.alter.net (152.63.49.58)  10.811 ms  10.897 ms  10.336 ms
11  150.ATM4-0.XR1.SJC2.ALTER.NET (152.63.48.2)  18.823 ms  13.592 ms  14.346 ms
12  0.so-7-0-0.br1.sjc7.alter.net (152.63.48.253)  17.073 ms  16.109 ms  21.148 ms
13  oc192-7-1-0.edge6.sanjose1.level3.net (4.68.63.141)  12.819 ms  13.318 ms
16.430 ms
14  vlan79.csw2.sanjose1.level3.net (4.68.18.126)  15.149 ms
vlan69.csw1.sanjose1.level3.net (4.68.18.62)  15.668 ms
15  ae-81-81.ebr1. level3.net (4.69.134.201)  15.655 ms ae-61-61 13.229 ms
16  ae-4-4.car2.level3.net (4.69.132.157)  210.512 ms  182.308 ms  41.987 ms
17  ae-11-11.car1.level3.net (4.69.132.149)  15.889 ms  31.446 ms  16.157 ms
18  apple-compu.car1.level3.net (64.158.148.6)  18.413 ms !X *  21.754 ms !X
```

Firewalls

The term *firewall* as an appliance can be a gateway, but this is not always the case. Firewalls can be a dedicated appliance or software running on the host operating system. Firewalls function in a networked environment to prevent certain communications, filtering the traffic you want to be able to receive from the traffic you do not want to receive. Mac OS X has a built-in software firewall that you can use to limit incoming traffic to that machine. This will allow you to control traffic in a way that keeps attacks at a minimum. In Chapter 8 we discuss the software firewall in more depth.

Many firewalls will help reduce the likelihood of a Denial of Service attack against one of your computers. However, some firewalls are susceptible to these attacks themselves, opening your environment to the threat of not being able to do business. To help with this, most firewalls support the ability to have a fail-over firewall. A fail-over firewall can automatically become the active firewall in situations where the main firewall goes down.

Port Management

Since the introduction of malware and spyware, it is becoming more common to restrict outgoing access on commonly used ports, such as port 25. For example, if you don't need mail services in your environment (perhaps because e-mail is hosted elsewhere), then it is likely that you will want to eliminate outgoing mail server traffic (SMTP, POP, and IMAP) from passing through your router.

As discussed in previous chapters, most savvy network administrators will also restrict incoming access on networks to all but a select number of ports, and for good reason. Many older protocols such as FTP are not secure, or there are weak implementations of these protocols that should not be accessible from the outside. Restricting access is the primary job of most firewalls and is often called *access control*. When looking into configuring the access controls on your firewall, keep in mind that all open ports are security risks, and each needs to be treated as such. Allow incoming access only for services that are required.

Properly securing your backbone and perimeter means that you are securing the ports on the network. This will greatly reduce the likelihood of a successful attack. For example, many root kits will attempt to establish an outgoing connection over a certain port to an attacker's computer. If this connection cannot be established, the root kit is less likely to cause harm in your environment. Therefore, it is important to restrict outgoing access, as well as incoming access.

■**Note** We discuss root kits in more detail in Chapter 4.

■**Tip** Keep in mind that port management is a common task, and as an administrator, network management time should be allocated to this vital aspect of network security. Users on a network will frequently ask for certain ports to be opened that are not standard for many environments. Understand that this is common across many networks. For example, Apache Tomcat, a underlying component of the Apache web server, requires TCP port 8080 to be open for users to be able to access it from the outside, but it does not need to be enabled all the time. Tomcat is an example of just one web application that runs on a port other than 80 that users of most networks will require access to, in addition to other commonly used web, messaging, and file transfer ports.

DMZ and Subnets

A *demilitarized zone* (DMZ) is a perimeter network, or a network area that sits between an organization's internal network and an external network. A DMZ is used to house insecure segments of a network and bridge them into more secure segments of a network. It should never house important or sensitive information. On consumer-grade routers, a DMZ typically refers to an address on a network that accepts all traffic bound to a specified address. In home environments, the DMZ is often configured incorrectly. We often find that it is used to forward all traffic to a specific address, rather than researching which ports need to be accessible for each service and segmenting the network traffic that shouldn't be included in the DMZ. This becomes a big security threat to the computer or network device that has all the traffic forwarded to it.

Whether you choose to use a DMZ is not dependent on the size of your company but on whether you are using protocols that you think might easily be hacked and therefore would not want to live on your local network. For example, FTP is not a secure protocol. Relegating the use of FTP in your environment to a system that lives outside your local network would prevent standard FTP attacks, such as an FTP bounce attack (an all-too-common attack on FTP servers) from affecting the entire network infrastructure. To implement a DMZ, an administrator could simply put a second network between their firewall and the Internet or use their actual firewall to build the DMZ. Many firewall appliances even have a built-in DMZ port.

Some administrators might choose to use a second subnet instead of a DMZ to keep certain types of traffic separate from the primary network. A *subnet* is a smaller portion—a network segment, if you will—of a larger network. Subnetting an IP network allows a single large network to be broken down into what appears (logically) to be several smaller ones. Devices on the same subnet have the same subnet mask and are signified on the network by that subnet mask.

Rather than allowing your users to see one another, you could put them on separate subnets and not allow UDP-based protocols to bridge across the various subnets implemented in your environment. It is even possible to split a network into multiple subnets. Keep in mind, however, that the more complex the subnetting gets, the more difficult it becomes to troubleshoot problems on the network. For example, when an airport is introduced into an environment, a separate wireless subnet is created, and wireless users may have difficulty automatically finding printers that are located on the main network. The printers will need to be manually installed using their IP address.

Spoofing

When access controls are configured based on IP addresses vs. network security policies, access attacks can occur. *Spoofing*, or the act of masquerading around on a network with a valid IP address that was not legitimately given, is one of these access attacks and is a common way for attackers to establish access. To spoof an IP or MAC address, an attacker need only discover the MAC address or IP address of someone they know can access a network and then change their MAC address to the MAC address that the network is familiar with.

Let's take a command-line look at how to change your MAC address. First run an `ifconfig` command to get your current MAC address. Then, use the `lladdr` option of `ifconfig` to change your MAC address slightly.

```
ifconfig en0
en0: flags=8863<UP,BROADCAST,SMART,RUNNING,SIMPLEX,MULTICAST> mtu 1500
        ether 00:17:f2:2a:66:12
cedge:/Users/cedge root# sudo ifconfig en0 lladdr 00:17:f2:2a:66:21
cedge:/Users/cedge root# ifconfig en0
en0: flags=8863<UP,BROADCAST,SMART,RUNNING,SIMPLEX,MULTICAST> mtu 1500 .
        ether 00:17:f2:2a:66:21
```

For any application that is blocking traffic from your machine based on its MAC address, the traffic will now be allowed. Once a machine on a network changes its MAC address, other machines will see this change and issue a line similar to the following:

```
kernel: arp: 192.168.55.108 moved from 00:17:f2:2a:66:12 to 00:17:f2:2a:66:21
        on eth0
```

Armed with this information, you can now set up a scanner in your logs to be notified when this line appears and then investigate all changes of MAC addresses. One way to get around this type of attack is by redirecting the access to other sentry machines that are set up to monitor these kinds of spoofing attacks. This is a deceptive active response to fool attackers into thinking attacks are succeeding, allowing an administrator to monitor the activity of the attack. If you are running Snort/HenWen with the Guardian plug-in, discussed further in Chapter 14, then your system should notice the MAC spoof and disable communications from that host automatically, thus defending you against an attack from a spoofed IP address.

Stateful Packet Inspection

Using stateful packet inspection (SPI), a firewall appliance holds the significant attributes of each connection in memory. These attributes, collectively known as the "state of the connection," include such details as the IP addresses and ports involved in the connection and the sequence of packets traversing the connection. The most CPU-intensive checking is performed at the time of the start of the connection. All packets after that (for that session) are processed rapidly because it is simple and fast to determine whether they belong to an existing, prescreened session. Once the session has ended, its entry in the state table is discarded.

Most modern firewalls, including those in some Linksys and Netgear routers found at your local consumer electronics store, will have basic SPI features, as does the OS X Leopard software firewall. Appliances have a limited amount of memory and cannot inspect as many packets as rapidly or as closely as a more advanced device, such as some CheckPoints, SonicWalls, or Ciscos. Typically, SPI on these firewalls will check only the source of the packet against the source defined in the header.

Deep packet inspection (DPI) is a subclass of SPI that examines the data portion of a packet and searches for nonprotocol compliance, or some predefined pattern, in order to decide whether the packet is allowed to pass through the device performing the inspection. This is in contrast to shallow packet inspection (or more simply packet inspection), which checks just the header portion of a packet. DPI classifies traffic based on a signature database (as does SPI) and will allow you to redirect, mark, block, rate limit, and of course report based on the classification.

Many DPI devices can also identify flows rather than rely on signature-based packets by packet inspection. This allows devices to detect newer attacks rather than react to predefined attacks, giving more security to the environment. If your environment has the budget to acquire a firewall with DPI as a feature, heavily consider putting one into your network environment. For the security it provides, it is well worth the investment.

Data Packet Encryption

When two computers on different networks are communicating, they are often sending packets across multiple routers, allowing traffic to be susceptible to a variety of security holes at each stop along the way. Even with good inspection on a firewall, an attacker can still perpetrate a *man-in-the-middle attack*, or an attack where someone spoofs a server (trusted host) while sitting between your server and a user accessing your server. A man-in-the-middle attack is designed to intercept some form of data, such as a password or the data that a user is accessing. To keep prying eyes off your data, it is important to implement encryption techniques on that data between the two points, rendering the data unreadable to the interceptor. If your data is passing from your home to your office, for example, you would implement a VPN. If you are taking customer data over web sites, then you might consider using SSL. We discuss using VPN and SSL further in Chapter 11.

Understanding Switches and Hubs

Hubs are dummy devices that connect multiple computers, making them act as a single segment on a network. With hubs, only one device can successfully transmit data at a time. With hubs, when two computers submit data at the same time, a collision occurs, and a jam signal is sent to all the ports when collisions are detected. This makes one computer able to cause collisions and force an entire network to slow down while packets that were jammed are re-sent by all the computers that attempted to communicate during the jam. Hubs will also allow any computer to see the packets sent by other computers on the hub. Do not use hubs unless you have a very explicit reason to do so, because they can act as potential collision centers and cause security breaches.

Switches are more advanced than hubs and provide expandability, allowing more switches, ports, and computers to exist on a network. Switches perform collision detection and isolate traffic between the source of a packet and its destination. Because each computer is not automatically able to see all the traffic from other computers, this is a more secure communications environment. Switches are less likely to become flooded with collisions and more likely to offer faster throughput and lower latency than hubs in multiswitched environments. Although switches are more expensive than hubs, they are far less expensive than network downtime often caused by hubs.

Hubs do still have limited usefulness in networks. Switches respond to loops, hubs do not. When a cable is plugged into a switch twice, it can cause unwanted network traffic. In areas where many users are plugging in their laptops, a cable can get plugged back into a switch by accident, and some network administrators will use a hub to keep this from occurring. Additionally, protocol analyzers connected to switches do not always receive all the desired packets since the switch separates the ports into different segments. Connecting a protocol analyzer to a hub will allow it to see all the traffic on the network segment. Finally, some cluster environments require each computer to receive all the traffic going to the cluster. In these situations, hubs will most likely be more appropriate than switches.

Stacked switches are switches designed from the ground up to accommodate multiple switches in a network. When a switch is stackable, it will have dedicated ports for adding more switches that allow speeds of 10 or more gigabits between the switches, using special stackable cables. These are often converted into fiber connections so that latency is optimized over long distances.

Managed Switches

As networks and features of networks have grown, managed switches have become more popular. *Managed switches* can control internal network traffic and are used to split a network into logical segments, giving more granular control over network traffic and providing more advanced error detection. Managed switches also offer more advanced logging features to help network administrators isolate problem areas. Some managed switches are also stacked, although not all of them are capable of stacking.

A standard feature to look for on a managed switch is VLAN support. VLAN, short for *virtual LAN*, describes a network of computers that behave as if they are connected to the same wire even though they may actually be physically located on different segments of a LAN. VLANs are configured through software rather than hardware, which makes them extremely flexible. One of the biggest advantages of VLANs is that when a computer is physically moved to another location, it can stay on the same VLAN without any hardware reconfiguration. This also works the other way; one physical LAN can be split into multiple logical networks by the VLAN software running on switches. Nearly all managed switches have a VLAN feature set.

Newer and more advanced switches also have the capability to perform rogue access point detection, or detection of unwanted access points and routers on a network. Since Apple joined the ranks of operating system vendors that have introduced Internet Sharing as a built-in feature, many networks have been brought to a grinding halt by rogue routers providing IP addresses to networks. Problems with rogue access points has been most common in networks with large numbers of freelancers who bring their laptops into the office, connect to the wireless network, and are still using the Internet Sharing that they may have used at home. This establishes an ad hoc Denial of Service to the rest of the network because they receive bad DHCP leases with bad TCP/IP settings and can require administrators to comb through every machine on a network to isolate which user has enabled the Internet Sharing features on their computers. Rogue access point detection is also helpful for making sure that random users on networks do not plug in wireless access points or routers they may think are switches.

Most managed switches also provide some form of MAC address filtration. A *MAC address* is a unique identifier attached to most forms of networking equipment. In MAC filtration, a network administrator can define a destination address so that packets can be received only from a specific port and allow only those same packets to be forwarded to another port. Using MAC address filtering, only users who are connected to port A can access the server connected to port B; other packets from other ports, even those whose destination address is for the server on port B, will be dropped. MAC filtration is also referred to as *network access control*, although this could refer to port filtration rather than MAC filtration.

Here are some other features of managed switches:

PoE: Power over Ethernet allows network devices to run using power supplied over the Ethernet cable rather than over a power adapter.

Spanning tree: This closes loops on networks. If more than one open path were to be active at once (a loop), then a broadcast *storm*, or large amount of network traffic, could cause the network to become unstable.

Priority tagging: This specifies ports that are of a higher priority, allowing mission-critical traffic to be differentiated from non-mission-critical traffic.

Link aggregation: This uses multiple network ports in parallel to increase the link speed beyond the limits of any one single cable or port. Link aggregation, also known as *teaming*, is based on the IEEE 802.3ad link aggregation standard.

Flow control: This manages traffic rates between two computers on a switched network. It is not always possible for two computers to communicate at the same speed. Flow control throttles speeds for faster systems by pausing traffic when it is running too fast.

Using managed switches historically meant that large amounts of an IT budget would need to be spent on acquiring them. However, with the increased number of manufacturers now involved in developing managed switches, this is no longer the case. Managed Netgear and D-Link switches (like the one featured in Figure 7-3) provide many of the advanced features found in Cisco and other top-of-the-line switches for a fraction of the cost. This has made them increasingly popular. Features offered on D-Link and Netgear switches include link aggregation, flow control, network access control, spanning tree, and priority tags.

Figure 7-3. *D-Link 48 port managed switch*

Many administrators of Mac environments are not comfortable deploying managed switches in their environments because they are typically command-line-only configurations, and some of the protocols they use can be incompatible with other devices on the network. To address this concern, Apple has recently begun to align with industry network standards, enabling Mac network administrators to get more comfortable using managed switches to support extended features of Mac hardware products. One example of this is the use of link aggregation (using two network interfaces as one) on Mac servers, which requires a managed switch in order to properly configure this feature.

Restricting Network Services

Network services are the building blocks of many network environments. Connecting to the Internet, DNS, DHCP, and other protocols is the main reason for having a network in the first place. One of the best ways to ensure security for file sharing, web services, and mail services is to limit the access that computers have to them. Some computers may need access to these resources; denying them can be detrimental to the workflow. Others may not need access, and giving them access could be potentially damaging. For example, you might allow local users to your network to access your file server but might never want to allow access to the file server for users outside your network.

When architecting a network, each service needs to be handled separately. Analyze which services go in and out of every system in an environment. If protocols will be accessed only from inside the network, such as file sharing and directory service protocols, then they should not be routable. Restricting access to protocols to users outside your network can be handled using the firewall, as mentioned earlier in this chapter. For larger environments, restricting access to services from other computers within your network is often handled using the switches in your environment. Draft up a document, such as the one in Figure 7-4, that lists the servers in your environment, the services they will be providing, and which ports they run on. This can help tremendously when trying to secure all the services needed in a networked environment while maintaining their usability.

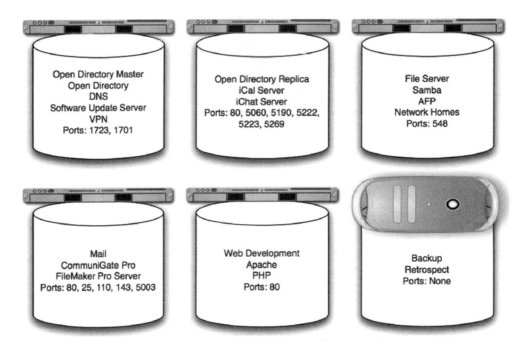

Figure 7-4. *Servers, services, and ports*

For smaller environments, restricting access between computers is usually handled on a per-service basis by using a local firewall running on the computer providing the service. For more information on configuring the software firewall in Mac OS X, see Chapter 3 and Chapter 5. For firewall configuration for Mac OS X Server, see Chapter 16.

Security Through 802.1x

802.1x is a protocol that Apple recently added to the Mac OS in Leopard. The 802.1x standard can greatly increase the security of a network environment by requiring users to authenticate before they can access the local network for Ethernet, Token Ring, and wireless networks. In fact, 802.1x must be supported by wireless and Ethernet equipment in order for an 802.1x environment to be supported. The 802.1x standard uses certificates to connect client systems to network resources by restricting access to users with valid certificates, network-based usernames, and passwords. Authentication to the network rather than just the computer is a fairly new concept for most Mac environments. This level of advanced networking is fairly complex and must be given an appropriate level of planning.

Enabling 802.1x is accomplished by going into System Preferences, clicking the Network pane, and then clicking the Advanced tab. As shown in Figure 7-5, 802.1x is a menu tab that can be enabled by clicking the Enable 802.1x button, selecting a certificate using the Get Certificate button, and then selecting the network to join.

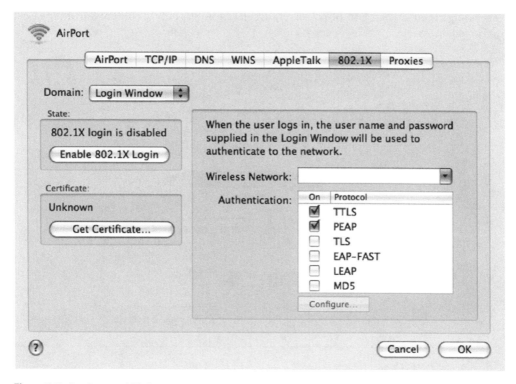

Figure 7-5. *Setting up 802.1x*

Once you have chosen your network, click the authentication protocol you want to use in the Authentication section and then click Configure. This will allow you to configure settings for the specific protocol to match the settings of your server.

■**Note** Settings can be exported as Internet Connect files. These can then be distributed through images, mail, or web sites.

Proxy Servers

One way of filtering traffic on your network is through the use of a proxy server. A *proxy server* allows services to establish network connectivity using one server as the traffic cop. The proxy server is situated between computers and the network connection and processes requests for external resources on behalf of the users of the network (see Figure 7-6). Using proxy servers, administrators can prevent users from viewing predetermined web sites. In addition to increasing security, proxy servers can increase network performance by allowing multiple users to access data from the proxy's memory or cache. On the first access of this data, there will be a performance loss, and the performance gain isn't seen until the second attempt at visiting the site or accessing the data. Therefore, proxy servers accelerate access only to content that is repeatedly accessed on systems.

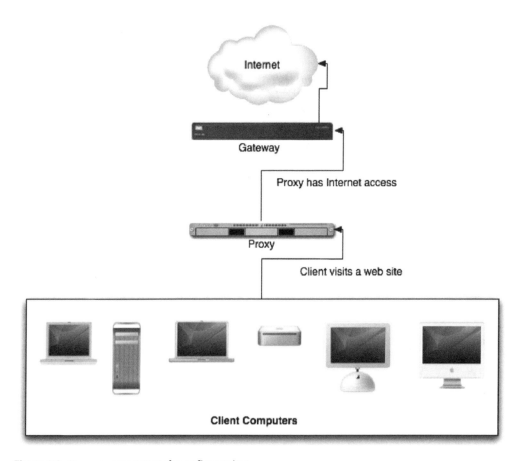

Figure 7-6. *Proxy server network configuration*

Proxies themselves can be exploited as a means to forward malicious HTTP traffic such as web-based spam e-mail referrals. When setting up a proxy, it is important to take into account security concerns, such as which clients on the network will have access to the proxy. Often proxy servers have a white list (a list of allowed addresses) that can be used to allow IP addresses by subnet to access the proxy; this should be configured to allow only those machines on the local area network to access the proxy services.

If external access is required, consider running the proxy on a nonstandard port and requiring authentication, perhaps utilizing an existing directory service such as Active Directory or Open Directory. This, combined with strong password policies, should help protect against unauthorized access to the proxy. Using proxy servers on desktop computers is discussed in more detail in Chapter 6.

Squid

Squid is an open source product that allows network administrators to easily configure proxy services. It has a robust set of access control options that can be configured to allow or deny access based on user or group access as well other criteria such as scheduling proxy servers to be enabled at certain periods of time. SquidMan is a utility developed by Tony Gray to provide Mac users with a GUI to assist with installing and configuring a precompiled version of Squid.

To install SquidMan, follow these steps:

1. Download the installer from `http://homepage.mac.com/adg/SquidMan`, and extract the SquidMan `.dmg` file.

2. Copy the SquidMan file into your Applications folder.

3. Open SquidMan, entering your administrative password to run the application.

4. At the preferences screen, enter the appropriate settings for the following fields (see Figure 7-7):

   - *HTTP Port*: The port that client computers will use to access the proxy.

   - *Cache Size*: The amount of space used to store data in the cache.

   - *Maximum Object Size*: The size limit for files that are to be cached by the proxy.

   - *Rotate Logs*: When to rotate log files.

   - *Start Squid on Launch After a _ Second Delay*: Enabling this option will automatically start Squid when SquidMan is launched and enable you to define a delay after launching SquidMan to start the Squid services.

   - *Quit Squid on Logout*: This allows you to choose whether to keep Squid running when a user on a computer logs out of a computer being used as your proxy server.

   - *Show Errors Produced by Squid*: This prompts users with pop-up windows that contain errors. This is helpful if someone is sitting at the desktop of the proxy server when it's running. However, if the desktop of the system is never looked at, then you will probably refer to logs to discover errors.

   - *Disable Initial Squid DNS tests*: This disables the DNS requirement to start the Squid services. Whenever Squid is started, it will perform a DNS test to verify that it can be started. If you are troubleshooting Squid issues, this option will come in very handy!

5. Click the Parent tab, and use this location to choose whether you will have your Squid server use another Squid server as its proxy server. This can make troubleshooting difficult in proxy environments. Keep the defaults here unless you have multiple Squid servers.

6. Click the Clients tab, and enter the appropriate IP addresses in the Provide Proxy Services For field. When entering IP address ranges, you will need to also enter the subnet for the IP range.

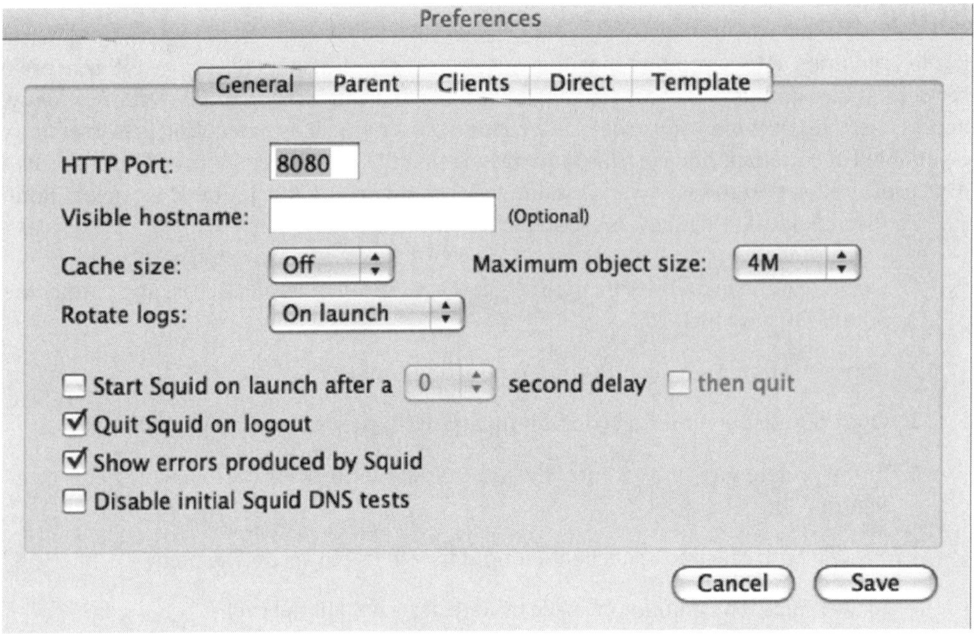

Figure 7-7. *SquidMan preferences: changing ports and hostnames*

7. Use the Direct tab to configure any exclusions to the domains that will be proxied by the server. This will be helpful when troubleshooting a parent proxy environment.

8. Click the Template tab, and use this location to edit the Squid configuration file manually. Here, the maximum object size and cache directories can be increased beyond the variables available in the GUI.

9. Once the settings have been configured for SquidMan, use the Start Squid button of the main SquidMan screen to start Squid (see Figure 7-8).

Once SquidMan is running, you can stop it by clicking the Stop Squid button on the main SquidMan screen. You can get more granular control over the Squid proxy services via command-line administration by editing the settings of the squid.conf file located in /User/ <username>/Library/Preferences/squid.conf once SquidMan is launched for the first time.

■**Note** The help files for SquidMan are very thorough in their explanation of configuring these settings.

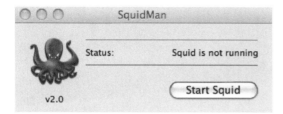

Figure 7-8. *Starting SquidMan*

A Layered Approach

Layers of security breed resilient networks. When securing networks, layer your approach. Start from the center, the computer itself, and move outward, looking at which services should be accessible by which computers. Then, layer the security levels by grouping the computers and building policies to limit access on each of those groups. Determine the firewall security, both internally and externally. Switches will also factor in heavily as you hand out security policies based on location within the network. This kind of layered approach gives strength to your network's security blueprint.

CHAPTER 8

■■■

Setting Up the Mac OS X Firewall

Put simply, a firewall is a network traffic moderator. It uses a set of rules to determine what kind of traffic is allowed in and out of your computer or network. The word *firewall* can be ambiguous because there are a variety of types of firewalls. In Chapter 2, we discussed the importance of using a firewall to act as a gateway into your network, denying and allowing network traffic on a network-wide basis between your computers and the outside world. This is what we refer to as a *hardware appliance firewall.*

For the purposes of this chapter, we will discuss the intricacies of the built-in firewall of Mac OS X, the software in your operating system that determines which traffic your computer will accept. This is referred to as a *software firewall.* The differences between a software firewall and a hardware firewall can be rather significant. For example, a software firewall primarily limits how services from other computers on the same network talk to services on your computer, something hardware appliances do not typically do. A software firewall can also act as a barrier to network traffic of any type that might slip past your firewall appliance. In this respect, a software firewall can act as a powerful second line of defense against malicious attacks.

It is important to note that the firewall built into Mac OS X should not be your only firewall defense. Inexpensive routers from companies such as Linksys, Netgear, D-Link, Xsense, and hundreds of other companies offer firewalls that cost less than $100 and have many features that are not configurable in the OS X firewall. In many smaller environments, such as homes and offices with fewer than ten users, these firewall appliances used in conjunction with the Mac OS firewall are more than adequate to protect computers accessing the Internet, because it hides their IP addresses from the Internet and exposes only the IP address of the router.

To explain how your software firewall works and how it can be configured, we'll discuss the specific services that your software firewall can listen for and how to teach your computer to allow or deny them. These services are often known as *network services.*

Introducing Network Services

The primary purpose behind most network traffic is for computers to communicate with one another. There are a wide variety of communication paths, or *routes*, that computers take to do this. And there are different purposes, or *roles*, for these varied communication paths. One communication path might have the intent of sending printing commands to a printer, while another might need to send an Internet request to an Internet gateway, or *router*. You can consider each type of communication path to be a *network service*, or *protocol*. For firewalls to manage these various protocols, they use rules. A *rule* is a set of parameters that enables the firewall to allow or deny access to a protocol on a computer.

In networking, there are a variety of protocols. Each protocol comes with a default port assigned to it. *Ports* are what computers use to sift through the variety of protocol traffic in order to understand what network service each protocol needs. Port numbers fall anywhere between 0 and 65,535, and each protocol is assigned a number so that each type of traffic can be handled differently. Although there is the possibility for thousands of different port numbers in use at one time, most applications use only a few common ports. When communications between computers occur, applications understand how to connect to each other based on the port number they use. Rules for applications and network services are then built using port numbers or sets of port numbers.

Fortunately, we usually don't have to keep track of port numbers because the programs we use to access ports (such as Safari for web browsing or Entourage for reading e-mail) usually standardize the use of port numbers. Some even allow us to customize the port number to our own liking. For example, if you access a web site, then you are probably using HTTP, which uses port 80 as its network port. If you send a friend an e-mail, Outlook is likely using port 25 because it is the default port for outgoing mail traffic. However, if you were to build a web server that runs over port 8080, such as the one built into many inexpensive routing or firewall devices, you would need to specify that web traffic moves through that port.

Note When working with firewalls, you will often need to know about port numbers in order to allow or block certain types of traffic. If you want to allow incoming access for the Web, for example, which would turn your computer into a web server, you would open port 80 on your computer. It's good practice to frequently reference port number tables in order to remember which ports typically work with various protocols. Apple publishes a list of commonly used ports at `http://docs.info.apple.com/article.html?artnum=106439`.

To demonstrate the way the network process structure works, let's look at an essential service of the Mac OS, the Apple Filing Protocol (AFP). AFP is a network communications service that allows the sharing of files between computers. It allows one machine to talk to other machines running AFP in order for files to move back and forth. AFP runs on the computer, sharing files as a process. That process listens on port 548. Another computer requests traffic over port 548, and when the host computer is listening, it responds, and a communication link between the two computers is established. And this all happens in a matter of milliseconds.

Many processes are easy to identify. Processes that listen for traffic can also be running as hidden processes or as a different user. mDNS (called Bonjour or Rendezvous in Mac OS X) is the protocol that allows other computers to discover information about your machine. mDNS (the process is known as the *mDNS responder*) runs over port 5353 as the root user, a user hidden by default. This means that if you were to log in as any registered user on a machine besides the root user and open the My Processes section of Activity Monitor, you would not find any processes running on the mDNS protocol, because root processes are hidden. If you were to change the filter from My Processes to All Processes, you would find the mDNS responder, which is the actual process that is typically referred to as Bonjour.

Now that we've discussed what a network service is and how it talks to your computer, we'll move on to taking control of these services.

Controlling Services

To get started controlling services, open System Preferences, and go to the Sharing pane (see Figure 8-1). If the padlock icon in the bottom-left corner of the screen is in the locked position, click it to be able to configure settings for the Sharing preferences. To enable a service, select the box that corresponds to each service; after you've checked the box, wait for it to start. This is the quickest and easiest way to enable a service.

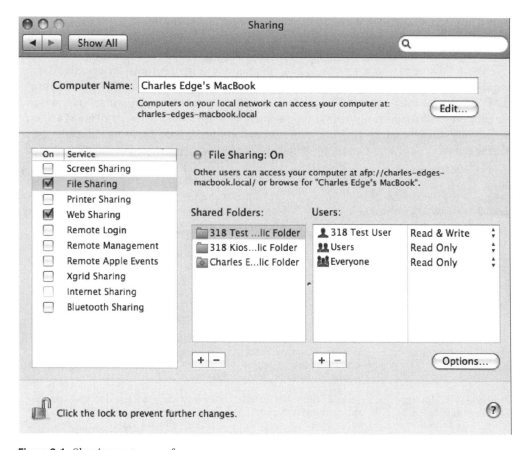

Figure 8-1. *Sharing system preferences*

To disable a service, open Sharing in System Preferences, highlight the service you want to disable on the Sharing pane, and click the Stop button. You can actually watch services appear and disappear in Activity Monitor as you start and stop them and review the resources (in terms of memory and processor utilization) that the services are using. This allows you to learn more about services as you go.

Services are accessible from any computer once they are started (we'll discuss fixing them later in this chapter). To simplify controlling services, Apple lists commonly used services by name rather than by port number. For example, you will see File Sharing on the Services pane versus port 548. By adding File Sharing and some of the other more common Apple-centric ports by default, Apple has made basic service management tasks simple to perform. This allows you to quickly enable or disable outgoing and incoming traffic for the ports you will most commonly need to access.

For another computer to connect to yours, you need to know your IP address or the computer name that corresponds to your IP address. To find the IP address of your machine, look at the bottom portion of the Sharing pane (Figure 8-1) where the computer name is also displayed. Usually when you connect to resources on another computer, you can browse to them using various programs, such as the Finder or Bonjour Browser, and you will see the computer referenced by name. This makes things easier for users wanting to connect to your computer from your local network. However, you might need the IP address when connecting over the Internet or when the name does not appear on its own.

When looking at which services to run, remember to run only those services that are required to receive *necessary* communications from other computers. Unless a service is absolutely required, do not enable it. Because they have direct access to your machine, each service running on your computer represents another possible vulnerability whereby an attacker, bot, bug, or other antigen might crawl into your system and wreak havoc. Table 8-1 indicates when the default services included with OS X should be run and what potential pitfalls enabling them could bring.

Table 8-1. *When to Enable a Service*

Services	When to Enable	Dangers
Personal File Sharing (AFP port 548)	Enable when you want other Mac users to have access to files on your computer.	If you have weak passwords (or no password), then others could gain access into your file system. There have also been a few exploits specifically targeting AFP that have been released.
Windows Sharing (SMB)	Enable when you want Windows users to have access to files hosted by your computer.	If you have weak passwords (or no password), then others could gain access into your file system.
Personal Web Sharing (WWW port 80)	Enable when you want to run your system as a web server.	Poorly written web code and Apache configuration could lead to vulnerabilities on your system.
Remote Login (SSH port 22)	Enable when you want a command-line or Secure Shell (SSH) interface into your system.	Systems with SSH exposed to the Internet are prone to brute-force attacks, where an attacker attempts repeatedly to guess your password. This will show up in your logs, waste your bandwidth, and, if you have weak passwords, give an attacker full control over your computer.

Table 8-1. *When to Enable a Service*

Services	When to Enable	Dangers
FTP Access (FTP port 21)	Enable when you want to turn your system into an FTP server.	FTP has not changed in 30+ years. Need we say more?
Apple Remote Desktop (VNC port 5900)	Enable when you want to allow remote control over the desktop of your computer.	Weak passwords and poor configuration could give an attacker access to everything on your computer.
Remote Apple Events (SNMP ports 161–162)	Enable when you want to turn on SNMP monitoring so other systems can review vital statistics about your system.	Others could gain too much information about your system if SNMP is not configured appropriately.
Printer Sharing (port 1179)	Enable when you want other users to access your printers.	There are very few access controls for printing services.
XGrid (port 4111)	Enable when your system is a grid node of an XGrid deployment.	Your computer could be abused as a grid client, reducing your performance.

Configuring the Firewall

Any time you are enabling the firewall on a Mac, you must first determine which services to enable and which to disable, as described in the previous section. Once you have enough information to understand what you are trying to control by configuring the firewall, you're ready to move onto the nuts and bolts of working with it. First things first—let's turn it on.

Working with the Firewall in Leopard

Out of the box, the firewall in any version of Mac OS X is turned off by default. Click the Firewall tab of the Security system preferences (see Figure 8-2). Then click the Set Access for Specific Services and Applications option (make sure the padlock icon at the bottom of the screen is unlocked). Enabling the firewall allows incoming connections only from certain Apple services such as Personal File Sharing or Web Services by default. To enable other services, you must add them based on the application rather than just the port number. This gives each application access to open ports on the firewall.

■**Note** The setting Allow Only Essential Services blocks all services except those running in the background of your system.

In Tiger, placing a check mark next to a service tells the firewall you are allowing that service to run, while unchecking the service tells the firewall you want to deny it. The same holds true for rules. By enabling the firewall, you are telling the firewall that the only default rules you want enabled are the rules that are generated for services currently running.

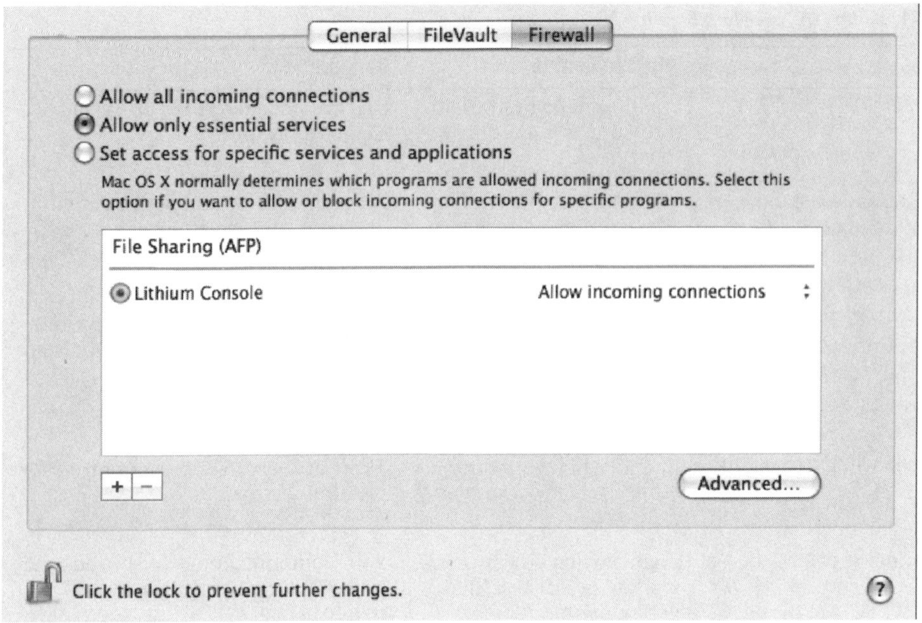

Figure 8-2. *The Firewall tab*

The firewall in Leopard is an application firewall. Application firewalls manage connections based on applications rather than ports. This makes it easier to configure initially (and for most users) but also causes control to be harder for more granular customizations. However, it is still possible, as we describe later in this chapter, to control the firewall more granularly using ipfw.

Because not all applications are trustworthy, if you attempt to allow access for an application that is not trusted by Apple to open a port (or set of ports) on your system, then you will be warned that the application is potentially dangerous. A digital signature is used for applications to determine whether they are trusted. If you attempt to install software that has a digital signature that is known by Apple and you still get the warning, then the application has been modified, making it untrusted. In early versions of Leopard, this feature is new, and the database is not yet extensive. But over time the database of software will grow and become a trusted way of determining which software is safe to install on your computer.

■Note For Tiger users, the firewall settings are on the Sharing pane.

Once you've enabled the firewall, you can control the rules for how you handle services requesting traffic from the computer. Remember, if a service is not running on the computer, then another computer cannot connect to that service regardless of whether the firewall is enabled. Conversely, when starting a service in the firewall, you're allowing anyone who can communicate with the computer to connect to it through this service. This poses a potential security risk if these services are not password encrypted; therefore, all services should use passwords. Thankfully, most services have their own access controls built into them, above and beyond what is available in the firewall. Make sure to verify that each service has been independently properly secured either with a password or with some other form of security mechanism such as shared key exchanges.

■**Note** If you encounter services that cannot function once you have enabled the firewall, you can quickly determine whether the firewall is the problem. Try disabling the firewall to see whether it is blocking those services (click the Stop button on the Firewall tab of the Sharing pane), and restart your computer. If the problem persists, then the firewall is not the culprit. If this resolves the issue, then the firewall is most likely the problem.

To open the firewall for a non-Apple-based application, you will need to click the plus (+) icon in the lower-left corner of the firewall screen (see Figure 8-2). Once you have done this, browse to the application you want to allow access to, and click Add. Provided that access has been allowed for specific services, then the application selected will now be allowed to open a listener on the computer.

Working with Default Services in Tiger

If one of the default Apple services has been enabled using the Services button on the Sharing pane (as shown in Figure 8-3), then you will not be able to block access to that service. On the Firewall tab, the service will be checked but grayed out.

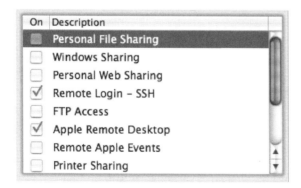

Figure 8-3. *Disabling shared services*

Attempting to disable the service will generate an error stating that "you cannot edit default services that have been enabled."

■**Note** You can add and remove rules that are manually created or automatically inserted by a third-party software installation. You cannot delete the default rules created by Apple.

Allowing Non-Apple Services in Tiger

When the firewall is running, you are denying all traffic except that which you specifically allow into the system. But what if you want to run a non-Apple program (such as Webmin, Retrospect, or Timbuktu), which requires talking to other computers but doesn't automatically add a rule to the firewall? In that case, you need to manually add these firewall rules.

To create a new firewall rule, click the New button on the Firewall tab of the Sharing system preferences. As shown in Figure 8-4, you will be asked to select a service to enable. You can add any service in the list of predefined services using the Port Name field on this dialog box. If the service you want to add is listed, select it, and click the OK button. You should see it listed in the Allow list, and the On box should be checked. This is called a *port forward*.

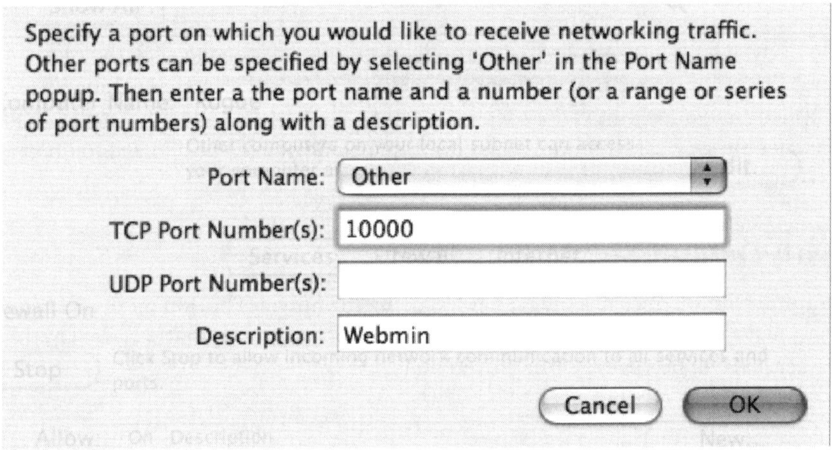

Figure 8-4. *Adding a custom service*

■**Note** To disable this port forward later, simply uncheck the box for the port.

If the service is not listed, you will need to add a custom service. To do this, select Other in the Port Name field. This allows you to create a custom rule in the services listing for your firewall. There is a section in this dialog box for specifying TCP and UDP port numbers. As we discussed earlier in the chapter, port numbers are the way the router knows how to maneuver the service through the firewall. And this is where you would specify the port numbers you wanted to use to pass the service through the firewall.

■**Note** In the TCP Port Number(s) field, you can enter multiple port numbers by separating them with a comma. Many applications will use more than one port number for communication. For example, Timbuktu will use port 407 for logging into a system but use 1412 for other operations such as transferring files.

TCP and UDP ports vary from service to service, and most services require at least some sort of specification in the TCP Port Number(s) field for the service to be served correctly. Sometimes services allow you to choose the port numbers that they will use to move across a network. Other services are fixed to use only certain port numbers, and they must be accurate for them to work correctly. For example, AFP will move only over TCP port 548. You cannot specify a different port for it to transport over. Determining the correct port number used for a specific service can take some effort; however, the heightened security achieved by tightening down ports with rules is definitely worth the extra time. If there is some confusion regarding which numbers to use, try consulting the software documentation for the service and the developer's web site for information on which port numbers are used. Search engines are a good resource as well for port number assignments for services if there is no documentation and the developer's web site comes up short.

Note You can find more information on UDP access in the "Setting Advanced Features" section of this chapter.

The Description field of this screen allows you to enter a short explanation of what the service is. The Description field is there merely as a reference for tracking rules you have created for this service. It has no bearing on how the computer interprets the port rule you have created. Once you have entered all the appropriate information for your custom service, you can click OK, and you will see it listed and enabled in the Allow section of your Firewall tab.

It is possible to enable all ports in a range on the Custom screen. However, you should implement this with care. Remember that when security is a concern, you always want to allow the least amount of privilege to any resources, especially when configuring a firewall. Your goal should be to lock down access to your network. If you were to allow all traffic, not only would your network be unsecured, but you would have effectively defeated the reasoning behind using a firewall in the first place.

Note TCP and UDP ports can and do change with updates to software packages as vendors add new features to their applications.

Setting Advanced Features

Apple has made available some nice features on the Firewall tab of the Sharing pane that allow for more extensive tightening of security in the operating system. They may seem rather unimportant, but they actually are crucial elements in securing your Mac. Clicking the Advanced button on the Firewall tab of the Security pane displays three new options (see Figure 8-5) for working with traffic: Block UDP Traffic, Enable Firewall Logging, and Enable Stealth Mode. We will go through these options in order of complexity rather than order of appearance.

■**Note** These settings are similar in both Tiger and Leopard but are accessed using a different set of steps in the two versions. Tiger uses the Advanced button on the Firewall tab of the Sharing pane instead.

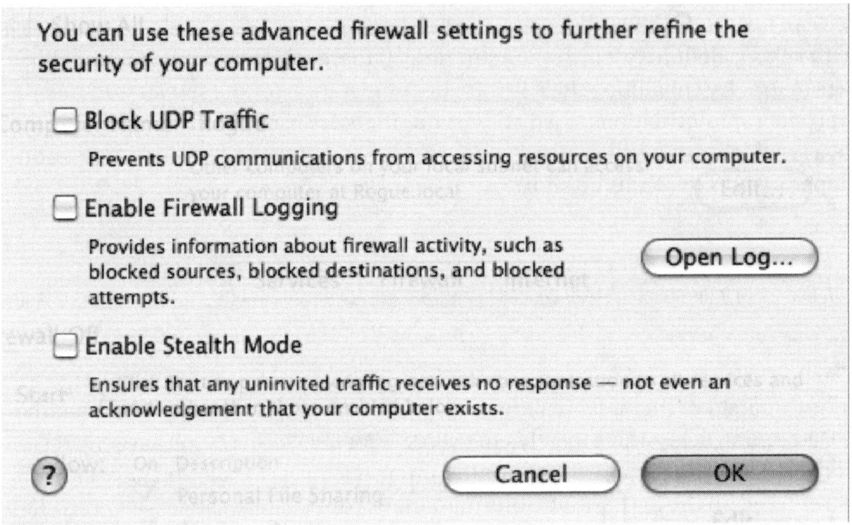

You can use these advanced firewall settings to further refine the security of your computer.

▢ Block UDP Traffic

Prevents UDP communications from accessing resources on your computer.

▢ Enable Firewall Logging

Provides information about firewall activity, such as blocked sources, blocked destinations, and blocked attempts.   (Open Log...)

▢ Enable Stealth Mode

Ensures that any uninvited traffic receives no response — not even an acknowledgement that your computer exists.

(?)   (Cancel)   (OK)

Figure 8-5. *Advanced firewall options in Tiger*

Enable Stealth Mode

When Computer A requests traffic to Computer B, Computer B determines how to respond. Responses contain either the data requested or a rejection to the request, which is sent back to the requesting computer. If a process is running and traffic is allowed, then Computer A, requesting traffic, will get a message from Computer B allowing it to connect. If a process is not running or a firewall rule is active that prohibits Computer A from connecting to a given port, then Computer A will get a deny message from Computer B. This process occurs before a web page is loaded or before a password is requested.

This seemingly innocuous process is the basis for much of how computers can communicate and can be used to expose rather important details about your system. By analyzing the patterns in delivery times and the actual content of responses to requests for traffic, it is possible to determine the operating system you are running, the patches you have installed on your operating system, and in many cases the type of hardware that is in your system. Armed with this information, a hacker can easily attack a system. So, how do you protect against this? Stealth mode.

If a computer does not appear to exist, rather than sending a response denying a message, it simply will not respond at all. The Enable Stealth Mode option in Mac OS X tells the system not to reply to traffic that is not specifically allowed. By not responding to requests, your system will make it more difficult for other computers to fingerprint the machine and locate the system on a network. By making it more difficult to *enumerate*, or discover the essential details of, a system's operating system, you make the system more secure. If you are running a firewall on a Mac, you should definitely be running stealth mode with it.

Stealth mode causes the system to not reply to response requests, or *pings*. However, this doesn't make it completely impossible to locate a system on a network. It is still possible to get the system time information or *netmask requests* (which show details about the network settings on your computer) on a machine that is running stealth mode. One reason for this is that stealth mode simply tells the computer not to respond to network requests that aren't running. However, because of the zero-configuration networking that Apple has built into the operating system, there are a large number of services that are running and easily discoverable, making it easy to enumerate the Mac OS. One way to help mitigate this discovery is to block UDP traffic.

Blocking UDP Traffic

Most networking traffic runs on TCP. TCP is a direct connection–oriented way to communicate on networks. It sends its communications only to the intended recipient and is used when reliable network connections are required. But TCP/IP, a common way for computers to talk to each other, consists of both TCP and IP traffic. IP traffic, an older technology, employs the use of UDP traffic and TCP traffic when used in conjunction with TCP/IP. UDP does not have the reliability of TCP and is used in many cases to send more lightweight packets in bulk. This makes it good for broadcasting large chunks of network traffic to all users of the network. UDP is used in a variety of ways such as through DHCP, for distributing IP addresses, and with some streaming media providers. However, UDP does not guarantee the delivery or reliability of communications and sends the information to many users. Without a guaranteed target, this often makes it less secure. In an effort to make the network more secure in environments where there are not many users or where incoming UDP-based services are not being used, it is a good idea to block UDP traffic. This can help mitigate the possibility of someone obtaining more information about your computer or flooding your computer with UDP traffic with a Denial of Service (DoS) attack.

The Block UDP Traffic button on the Advanced screen of the Firewall tab disables all incoming requests for UDP traffic on your system. In many iterations of the Unix operating system, this is enabled by default. However, on the Mac, you will need to enable it manually.

■**Note** Blocking UDP ports does not always work. If the system needs to run a listener for a built-in service, then the service will not be blocked. Other non-Apple services are the target of this feature.

It is important to note that by checking the Block UDP Traffic box, the rules aren't always built properly, because other rules in the firewall may override them. This can expose the system to UDP-based attacks. These attacks can occur over Network Time Protocol (NTP), commonly used to keep computer times in synchronization; Bonjour, a device discovery protocol; Microsoft Word (when it is left open); and CUPS when Printer Sharing is enabled. NTP attacks date back to 2001, and there are more than 30 attacks designed to exploit the vulnerabilities in CUPS, which will automatically respond even if you do not have Printer Sharing enabled. There is very little security risk with the utilization of Bonjour in smaller environments, such as those with 25 computers or less. Bonjour does offer a way to discover networks in larger environments and should be replaced with DNS in networks with more than 25 computers.

Note In OS X 10.3, the firewall doesn't block UDP or ICMP traffic.

Enable Firewall Logging

By default your computer does not log firewall events. Using the Enable Firewall Logging option on the Advanced screen turns on the ability for the computer to write events that occur in the firewall to a log file. This is disabled by default but should always be enabled so that you can read the logs and find out what kind of traffic the computer has been moving in and out of the firewall. At the command-line level, `ipfwloggerd` is a process that writes firewall logs into the `ipfw.log` file, located at `/private/var/log/ipfw.log`. Once you enable the firewall-logging feature, you will see this process running in the background in Activity Monitor. Once firewall logging has been enabled, you should review the log files regularly for any kind of suspicious behavior. For more information about what to look for in the firewall logs, see Chapter 14.

Testing the Firewall

Once you have closed the ports and configured your firewall to your liking, you will want to test the configuration and make sure the services you have denied are no longer accessible. Performing a port scan is the best way to test the configuration. A port scan will check whether a service is available to other systems. Apple has included a port scanner in Network Utility, which is located at `/Applications/Utilities` on your system (see Figure 8-6). Port scanning is explored in more depth in Chapter 4.

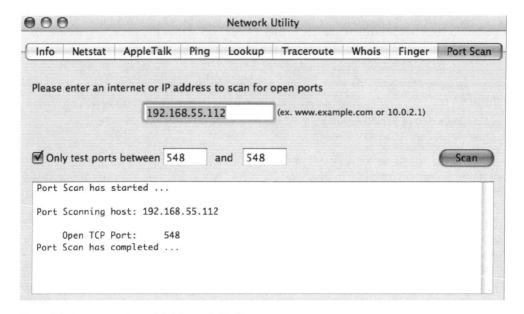

Figure 8-6. *Port scanning with Network Utility*

Note The ability to run a port scan on versions of OS X older than Tiger is disabled unless the BSD subsystem is installed. The BSD subsystem is installed by default; however, if it is explicitly not installed and the system is then upgraded to newer versions of OS X, in some cases the BSD subsystem does not get installed.

Network Utility, although robust, can tend to run rather slowly. For a quicker, dirtier port scan, there is a hidden command-line scanning utility, called `stroke`, that will allow you to use the port scanner included with Mac OS X much more quickly to scan ranges of ports. `stroke` is just the command-line version of the port scanner in Network Utility, separate from the GUI, causing it to run much faster. It is located in the `/Applications/Utilities/Network Utility.app/Contents/Resources` folder. To invoke the `stroke` command, you will need to use the Terminal application to access it. For example, if you wanted to scan ports 25 (SMTP) to 80 (HTTP) of a mail server to see what services are listening on what port using the `stroke` command, you would type the following:

```
Stroke mail.mydomain.com 25 80
```

This command would result in something much similar to what Network Utility would display, only it's quicker because it's coming from the command line:

```
Port Scanning host: 208.57.132.195
          Open TCP Port:      25
          Open TCP Port:      53
          Open TCP Port:      80
```

Using Mac OS X to Protect Other Computers

Mac OS X provides users with the ability to share an Internet or network connection with other computers. Internet Sharing is a handy utility that Apple included in its operating system. Using Internet Sharing allows you to use your computer as a router in much the same way that a firewall appliance is used, as discussed in Chapter 2.

Enabling Internet Sharing

The controls for turning Internet Sharing on are located on the Internet tab of the Sharing pane (see Figure 8-7). This pane allows you to choose the port connection you want to share from, which is similar to how you would configure your WAN (or Internet connection coming from the outside) option, on a firewall appliance. You can also choose which network adapter you want to share. This option is similar to the LAN (or internal network accessing clients) option on firewall appliances.

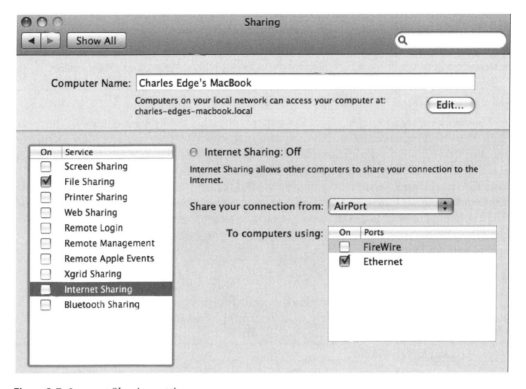

Figure 8-7. *Internet Sharing settings*

Once you have set your sharing settings and started the Internet Sharing service, you need to assign IP address information for client computers for them to access the Internet. If they are set to use Dynamic Host Control Protocol (DHCP), a protocol used specifically for handing out IP addresses, the Internet router (which could be your computer or an AirPort using Internet Sharing) will provide dynamic IP addresses to them. Or you can assign static IP addresses to them. To use a static IP address, you will need to know the network settings on your computer or router and configure the other computers in the same way. At this point, any system that can connect to your computer's IP address can access the Internet, provided it has the correct information and is firewalled behind your computer.

Client IP Addresses

The first network you establish using Internet Sharing on your system will use the IP address of 192.168.2.1. This will allow all client systems that are connected to the network to connect to the Internet. To connect to the Internet, client computers will need an IP address that falls between 192.168.2.2 and 192.168.2.254. The subnet mask that would be used in this setup is 255.255.255.0. All subsequent subnets and networks would use the same subnet mask as the first.

IP and gateway settings do change when establishing multiple networks. The second network uses the IP address 10.0.2.1, and computers using the IP addresses from 10.0.2.2 10.0.2.254 can communicate with it. A third adapter would use 192.168.3.1, and clients would communicate using 192.168.3.2 to 192.168.3.254.

Clients connected to each network will use the IP address of the adapter as their Default Gateway or Router setting (the name of this option varies per operating system). This routes all traffic bound for the Internet through the system you have enabled Internet Sharing on. In many cases, you need to add firewall rules for each IP range.

Dangers of Internet Sharing

When implementing Internet Sharing, it is important to check the configuration to make sure it is set up correctly. One reason for this is that your computer, when running Internet Sharing, will by default give IP addresses to other computers using DHCP. If you set it up improperly, you can cause entire networks that are not protected sufficiently against rogue DHCP servers to go down. Rogue DHCP servers can be difficult to track down in environments that use inexpensive switches and are fairly common in creative environments where different freelancers move in and out of the company on a daily basis (a common situation with Mac environments). Because the first interface that provides connections to other computers issues 192.168.2 IP addresses, any time your client systems begin getting an IP address that starts with 192.168.2, you know to look for a Mac running Internet Sharing. This is often the place to look if you are the network administrator of a network and you notice that many of your computers are getting bad dynamic IP information.

Also, if you try to connect to a network and share a connection using the same adapter for both your Internet connection and your client computers, then you can cause serious network problems. If you do this in a cable modem or DSL environment, then you will likely cause your service to be turned off. If your service does not get cut off, then you have successfully bridged your network to the network of your Internet service provider. This can cause any computer on their network, of which there are likely tens or hundreds of thousands, to have the ability to access any computer on your network.

If we wanted to share a network connection and had only one network interface, such as an Ethernet card, our best way to accomplish this would be to install a second Ethernet card into the system to share the connection.

If you are sharing your network connection over an AirPort card, you need to address some security concerns. Specifically, these include the fact that the security of the network is based on wireless protocols that by their very nature are not always properly secured. Traffic sent over a wireless network is easily interceptable, potentially exposing passwords and other private information. We will discuss this further in Chapter 19.

■**Note** The Firewall and Internet tabs will not be present in Mac OS X Server. You configure these options, covered in Chapter 13, using Server Admin on Mac OS X Server.

Using Third-Party Firewalls

What we have discussed thus far in this chapter is only a portion of what you can do using the built-in firewall. It is highly configurable and provides many features that are typically accessed in a Unix environment using the command line. Later in this chapter, we will round everything out by discussing how to use the command-line tools in Terminal to configure the firewall. But before we do that, it's important to discuss some other third-party graphical user interface (GUI) tools that you can use to configure the firewall, instead of using the command line.

Third-party products have become fairly popular lately in part because of consumers' growing need to more securely lock down their systems. Although the Sharing system preferences has nice features, third-party applications have many more advanced features that enable you to lock down services, giving you much more granular access to the firewall rules.

A limited number of specific firewall products are available for Mac OS X. Of the products that are available, the features and popularity of each have not changed much in years; new products only rarely appear in the marketplace. To provide some insight into how to use these third-party applications, we will discuss the two most popular third-party firewall products, focusing on some of the key elements that are common among most third-party firewall products.

■**Note** This is not a review or an endorsement of either product but is merely an overview of what each is capable of in order to provide guidance on what to look for in third-party firewall software.

Doorstop X

As with many OS X firewall products, DoorStop X allows you to configure the OS X firewall in a friendly yet useful manner. This makes it a nice solution for people who like the idea of configuring the OS X firewall without resorting to the Terminal.

Installing DoorStop X is pretty straightforward. A wizard walks you through choosing the access other computers will have to resources that are hosted on your computer. By default, DoorStop X gives visitors no access and has you grant access to each service. (This is in stark contrast to the OS X firewall, which is disabled by default.) Once you select the services you want to make available to other users, DoorStop X lists all the services currently available with a lock icon that, when clicked, can block access to those services.

The DoorStop X application has a nice feature that allows you to disable outgoing access to resources outside your computer. This can be extremely helpful to mitigate the risks of malware and root kits. DoorStop X Security Suite (the enhanced version of DoorStop X) also comes with a second application called Who's There? that gives you detailed information about visitors and tracks the types of outgoing connections that are being made by your system and their targets. DoorStop X then gives you suggestions on possible firewall configuration changes to fill these holes.

Flying Buttress

Flying Buttress, known at one time as BrickHouse, is another third-party firewall with some unique features. Like DoorStop X, when you first open the program, it uses a wizard to help you determine which ports it should enable or disable. One nice feature is that it can use a syntax checker to review your changes made to the configuration and notifies you whether any are not entered properly. After the wizard finishes, you can manually add or remove ports and services that are monitored by the firewall if they weren't covered in the wizard. Flying Buttress has an expert mode that can be used to edit the firewall configuration file, in much the same way we will be discussing later in the chapter.

Flying Buttress comes with little documentation, which means it is definitely not for the technically challenged. Flying Buttress requires a bit more networking savvy than DoorStop X. However, Flying Buttress is shareware and can be downloaded and used for free.

■**Note** Utilities such as DoorStop X and Flying Buttress, although powerful utilities, can definitely have learning curves to them. Updating the firewall with a firewall utility requires more knowledge of networking than the standard user. And it can be difficult at first, but as you will find when reading the command line–oriented portions of this chapter, it is far easier to learn how to configure the firewall with these utilities than using the command line. And the effort spent training your firewall is definitely worth the heightened security you will be implementing on your network.

Working from the Command Line

Although it is possible to adequately configure the firewall through the Mac OS X Sharing system preferences or through the third-party applications covered earlier, sometimes you'll want to get even more granular. For example, you might want to perform a more advanced security lockdown such as denying outgoing traffic for certain ports while continuing to allow incoming traffic on those same ports. This cannot be accomplished with the GUI. Or you might want to disable communications to and from certain IP addresses rather than across the board. These and other specific tasks can be accomplished only by using the command line. You will also need to use the command line if you want to throttle bandwidth, for example, by using the dummynet program (more on that later). Before we delve into the specific commands, we need to discuss some of the ways in which you can get more granular with control of your firewall and why it is important to maintain this control.

Getting More Granular Firewall Control

A *network adapter* is a physical connection that your computer makes to a network. Network adapters include your Ethernet card (or cards if you have a MacPro), your AirPort interface (whether it is built into your computer or a card that you have added), your FireWire interface, modems, and any other item that allows your computer to access other computers.

Because of the nature of complex networking, sometimes you'll want to assign differing rule sets to different interfaces or different IP addresses within different interfaces. For example, you might want to put multiple e-mail domains on separate IP addresses within the same network interface. There are definite benefits to this. The configuration of multiple IP addresses can bring a more fault-tolerant network connection to the server, it can provide other features with the mail server, and it could be used to run various services over the same port on the same system. However, these configurations can be difficult to set up using the graphical tools built into the OS, because each instance of a network interface must be configured separately. By default, all firewall rules created on the Sharing pane are applied to all network interfaces. To make these configuration changes possible, you will need to use the command line to configure the firewall.

Configuring multiple IP addresses on a Mac is a fairly straightforward process. Each network interface is not limited to using one IP address. Figure 8-8 shows a second IP address configured on a Mac. You can do this by opening the Network system preferences pane, clicking the + icon, choosing the appropriate adapter, and clicking the Add button. This creates a second listing for the duplicated network interface and allows you to give it an IP address. If you have multiple IP addresses, you will notice that although network requests can be sent to multiple interfaces on the system, they will always reply from the one that is the primary interface. An example of a system using multiple IP addresses for the same interface, in Figure 8-8, shows that the instance of the AirPort occurs twice: once under the heading of AirPort and once under the heading of AirPort 2.

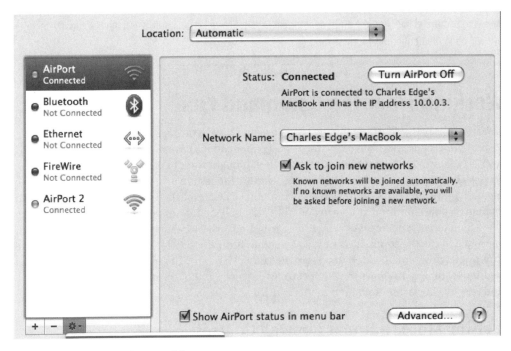

Figure 8-8. *Adding another IP address*

As mentioned previously, a really important security measure to take with your network is to lock down certain types of outgoing traffic on specific ports. For example, in an educational environment, a system administrator may want to lock down most types of outgoing Internet traffic. Remote control applications, instant messaging applications, and file-sharing peer-to-peer software all tend to be unnecessary in a classroom environment. Because these programs make requests for outgoing traffic, they will need their ports locked down for them to be properly secured. In the workplace, you might want to block streaming Internet music stations to help conserve precious bandwidth, or you might want to restrict staff from using a file-sharing protocol to keep them from taking creative assets out of your environment. All of this must be configured using the command line.

Some outgoing network traffic blocking can be configured using a firewall device at the edge of your network, but not all. Even if it is possible at the firewall device level, it's wise to impose a rule at both the software level and the hardware level to circumvent a breach at one of your layers of defense. This layered, or tiered, approach to security helps keep your network as secure as possible. But little of this would be possible without `ipfw`. Another reason to use `ipfw` to configure your firewall is to block outgoing traffic for certain ports, a feature not available otherwise.

■Note Later in this chapter we will discuss blocking outgoing traffic, but it is important to point out that you can block outgoing traffic only by using either the command line or a third-party application. You can block incoming traffic by using the built-in firewall in System Preferences.

Using ipfw

As previously discussed in this chapter, the firewall located on the Sharing pane in Tiger is based on the open source program `ipfw`. `ipfw` is short for Internet Protocol Firewall and can also be used with Leopard. The `ipfw` program has the ability to configure the firewall in OS X more securely than any other program. However, there is a rather steep learning curve when configuring the firewall with the `ipfw` interface for the first time, especially if you aren't very experienced with BSD. But learning curves are good. They offer you a chance to know more about the firewall on your system, what it is doing, and the key factors you should consider to make your network more secure. You also have the opportunity to get to know more about the inner workings of your system and how the different pieces to the security puzzle fit together.

Because `ipfw` works at the kernel level, or innermost level, of the operating system, it is a highly secure command set to use and requires that you run it from a superuser account. This is accomplished by using the `sudo` command to issue commands and create rules for it. Applications such as LimeWire or Samba (the Windows file-sharing component of Mac OS X) cannot override rules enforced by `ipfw` because of the secure nature of the command. This provides for a far more secure way of controlling threats to the system. The official syntax for the base `ipfw` toolkit is as follows:

```
ipfw [-cq] add rule
    ipfw [-acdefnNStT] {list | show} [rule | first-last ...]
    ipfw [-f | -q] flush
    ipfw [-q] {delete | zero | resetlog} [set] [number ...]
    ipfw enable {firewall | one_pass | debug | verbose | dyn_keepalive}
    ipfw disable {firewall | one_pass | debug | verbose | dyn_keepalive}
```

The Anatomy of an ipfw Rule

To understand how to make the firewall perform many of its more complex features, you first need to understand what the firewall is doing and how it interacts with rules and the rule set. An `ipfw` rule is a line of code that informs your firewall about what is acceptable to allow and what to do when a pattern that you indicate is encountered. The `ipfw` rule set is the combination of all the `ipfw` rules that need to be invoked to provide the proper security for the policy. `ipfw` applies this rule set as criteria for whether network traffic that is being scanned is acceptable to enter the network. This can include which rules to log, what to do when a pattern matches a rule, and how much bandwidth is possible on a rule (using dummynet).

Rules in an `ipfw` rule set are processed based on their numerical priority. Each rule requires a unique five-digit number in the first column of the rule that tells `ipfw` what priority to assign it in a rule set. They are then processed in order from highest to lowest. This is an example of an ipfw rule:

```
01000 allow log all from any to any via en0
```

■**Note** The rule number of this rule is 01000. Multiple rules can share the same number, but this is typically discouraged because it can make troubleshooting difficult.

This particular example rule allows all traffic into or out of the computer from any source over the en0 network interface and logs the activity (more about logging later).

The en0 signifies the particular network interface our computer is using for the rule. To find out what names a computer uses for its network interfaces, reference Network Utility, located at /Applications/Utilities, to list the various network interface names. Network Utility shows each network interface, and when you click an interface, it shows detailed information about the interface on the screen (see Figure 8-9).

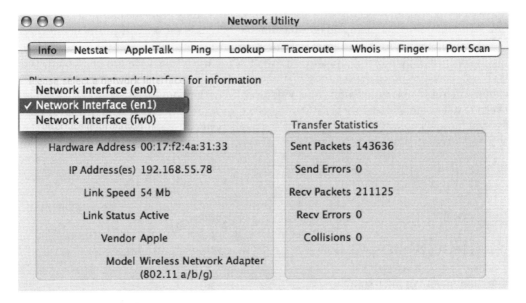

Figure 8-9. *Network Utility*

You can see a list of all the rules that are applied to your system by running the ipfw show command. When you run this command, you will see something like this:

```
00001      0  0 allow udp from any 626 to any dst-port 626
12301  11552 669920 allow tcp from any to any out
12302      0  0 allow tcp from any to any dst-port 22
12302      0  0 allow udp from any to any dst-port 22
12308      4  336 deny icmp from any to any icmptypes 8
12309      4  336 deny icmp from any to any icmptypes 0
12311      0  0 allow tcp from any to any dst-port 497
12311  20649 462537 allow udp from any to any dst-port 497
65535   4270 469852 allow ip from any to any
```

■Note Notice that each service on the Sharing pane corresponds to a line in the `ipfw show` command.

The first column of the `ipfw show` output contains the rule's unique number. The second column shows the number of packets that matched each rule. The third column shows the number of bytes processed by that rule. The rest of the data indicates (in this order) whether the rule allows or denies traffic, the type of traffic it is moderating, the target of the traffic, the source of the traffic, and the port the traffic is using. What is of particular importance is the second column of numbers that shows you the amount of packets matching a rule. This allows you to see how often a rule is being processed and can help you determine whether you should block traffic on another device interface if the system is running slowly on this one.

To add a new rule to the current rule set, type `ipfw add` and then the rule you want to add. For example, the following command would add a rule to our firewall that limits outgoing traffic on port 80, effectively removing our ability to open or serve web sites (a common use for `ipfw`) on our local computer:

```
ipfw add 500 deny tcp from any to any dst-port 80
```

After invoking this rule, if we attempted to open a web browser, we would see something similar to Figure 8-10.

The `add` statement tells `ipfw` to add that rule to the current `ipfw` rule set using the unique number provided by `ipfw`.

To delete a rule from the current rule set, type `ipfw delete` followed by the unique number of the rule you want to remove. To delete the rule that is now blocking us from being able to access web sites, we type the following:

```
ipfw delete 500
```

■Note The first rule entered by a user (so it doesn't conflict with any autogenerated rules) should be 500. Rules can be numbered all the way up to 65,535.

Unable to connect

Firefox can't establish a connection to the server at www.google.com.

- The site could be temporarily unavailable or too busy. Try again in a few moments.
- If you are unable to load any pages, check your computer's network connection.
- If your computer or network is protected by a firewall or proxy, make sure that Firefox is permitted to access the Web.

Figure 8-10. *Connection Error dialog box*

If you want to allow traffic to be processed only on a specific network adapter, then use the network interface ID being controlled, and append `via <network interface>` to the end of the line. For example, you would use the following code to allow any traffic at all to pass through your primary Ethernet interface:

```
ipfw allow ip from any to any via en0
```

A Word About Logging

Logging is a tricky thing. Too many logs, and you have too much data to make heads or tails of anything. Too little data, and you don't have enough logs. When using `ipfw`, you can set logging options per rule. This allows you to prioritize which rules you consider important enough to receive logs about. To enable logging, add the word `log` following your `allow` or `deny` variable. In the following rule, we will log any attempts to access the popular game World of Warcraft III:

```
ipfw allow log tcp from any to any dst-port 6112-6119
```

ipfwloggerd

Once you are finished customizing your `ipfw` rule set, you can start looking into reviewing the logs that you set up to receive from your firewall. These can be pretty lengthy because many systems receive a lot of traffic. You can tell `ipfw` to log every packet that comes into your system or leaves your system by adding `log` to each rule.

Logging high loads of traffic can be far too much of a workload for `ipfw` to handle on its own, but many administrators require it for security tracking purposes. Since `ipfw` sometimes cannot handle the immense logging load, a daemon was written that unloads logging of `ipfw` events to another process. `ipfwloggerd` is the process that manages logging `ipfw` events. Logs containing information about traffic that is dropped are stored at `/var/log/system.log` and can be viewed using the Console application located at `/Applications/Utilities`.

For a more thorough discussion of reviewing logs and the `ipfw` log, see Chapter 14.

/etc/ipfilter/ipfw.conf

At this point we have shown how to create rules and check the logs for attempts to access resources that match the rules. But none of the rules that have been created will still be active on the next restart. When using ipfw interactively, any rule changes that are made to the ipfw rule set are not saved on the next reboot. Experimenting with firewall rules can cause harsh problems on systems if done without taking precautions. So, it is a good idea to avoid applying rules permanently until you are savvy enough to remove them if you get into trouble.

When your computer is booted up and ipfw first starts, it processes the ipfw.conf file. To make these changes persistent, you need to update this .conf file. But, before we jump into that, let's discuss how to get yourself out of a jam if you make a mistake. In the ipfw.conf file, there is a significant amount of commented-out text that tells you the proper syntax to use in the file. This is a way for you to undo what you've done. To exclude or comment text out from /etc/ipfilter/ipfw.conf, you need to add # in front of the rule. Adding # in front of a rule tells the system not to process the rule when booting.

■**Note** If you do not see a /etc folder on the root of your boot volume, then cd to the /private folder, and then look for the /etc folder in that directory.

Any time you change your ipfw.conf file, you should back it up first. You can and probably should keep multiple versioned backups as you edit the ipfw.conf file. Once you update the ipfw.conf file and save it, you will need to restart ipfw for the changes to take effect, which you can do easily by stopping and starting the firewall in your System Preferences. Don't forget to scan blocked ports to verify your changes were applied after restarting the firewall.

Using dummynet

On a drive down from San Francisco to Los Angeles, one of the authors of this book was very safely speeding down the 101 freeway. While coming through Santa Barbara, a police officer sped up behind him, sirens blazing. Prepared for the worst, he slowed down, expecting to get pulled over. To the author's pleasant surprise, she raced past his car heading toward the traffic ahead of him. As he came around the corner into a wall of fog, he noticed that what she was actually doing was slowing the pace of traffic down to prevent everyone from crashing into what he later learned was a 13-car pile-up. He immediately made the connection—this is what can happen with DoS attacks.

A variety of attacks take place against systems by flooding the computer with traffic and causing them to crash. These attacks are typically referred to as DoS attacks and can often be protected against by limiting the bandwidth that is available for a specified port—in effect, slowing the traffic down before it crashes into itself. Network traffic can accidentally attack itself by simply using too much bandwidth when connecting to a computer. Limiting bandwidth, often referred to as *throttling* or *traffic shaping*, is a good way to keep from overloading a system and crashing into a pile-up of network traffic.

dummynet is a built-in Mac OS X tool that can be used to throttle traffic on a network. It allows the administrator to limit bandwidth for certain ports or IP address groups on the network. This is more than a basic Boolean, or true/false, argument indicating that traffic can or cannot be allowed. dummynet works in conjunction with ipfw to limit the throughput of traffic that matches certain criteria when ipfw rules are created. dummynet is not run as a command but is instead called by using pipes and queues, which we will discuss next.

Note Like ipfw, dummynet is a kernel-level process.

Pipes

To use dummynet, you start by creating a pipe or a set of pipes for traffic to flow through. A pipe is created by inserting a pipe command into an ipfw command, while using a unique numerical identifier to access it in the ipfw rule. The official syntax for the ipfw pipes is as follows:

```
ipfw {pipe | queue} number config config-options
```

Each pipe has a maximum amount of throughput that can flow through it. The following example creates pipe 1 that allows for 752KB worth of traffic to travel through the pipe per second:

```
ipfw pipe 1 config bw 752KByte/s
```

The previous command creates a pipe that limits traffic coming through the pipe and caps it at half a T1 worth of traffic. That is all it does. If you want to attach services to it, you need to augment the command with more specific criteria.

Let's say you want to create a rule that enforces a pipe to a specific port range. In the following example, we will limit AFP traffic to half of our T1 by binding pipe 1 to port 548.

```
ipfw add 1 pipe 1 src-port 548
```

Note The maximum number of pipes by default is 16. This is primarily because the net.inet.ip. dummynet.max_chain_len variable, which controls the maximum number of pipes, is set to 16. You can change this by editing the file. If you need more than 16 pipes, then you may have stability concerns with high-traffic loads.

The final task with bandwidth throttling will be to limit the amount of throughput that each individual connection can take. In this case, you will use something known as *address masking*. When you use masking, you are telling the system to limit a specific IP address or set of IP addresses to a specified pipe size rather than applying a pipe to a port. To configure a pipe that limits each AFP connection (port 548) to 75Mbps, you would add the following series of lines to the system:

```
ipfw add pipe 1 ip from any to any src-port 548
ipfw pipe 1 config mask src-ip 0x0000ffff bw 75Mbits/s
```

■**Note** As with other `ipfw` rules, your pipes must be added to your `ipfw.conf` file in order to be persistent after restarts.

Pipe Masks

Pipes can allow multiple queues per traffic flow. This allows you to cap the bandwidth of each server and not just the aggregate bandwidth of all traffic moving through the pipe. This allows an administrator to manually create a pipe for each server when using Mac OS X as a gateway device (router).

Masks are used to define which hosts belong to a pipe. Masks can be specified as follows:

`dst-ip`: IP packets sent using the pipe they're bound for

`src-ip`: Mask for the specified source

`dst-port`: Mask for the specified destination port

`src-port`: Mask for the specified source ports

`proto`: Mask for the specified protocol

`all`: Mask for any computer

For example, if you have a network behind a firewall and all your systems have a desired 500Kbit/s bandwidth maximum, all the traffic can be sent through a pipe. The cap of the pipe will then be applied to the aggregate traffic from all the hosts and not applied to each pipe individually. If the traffic for each host is sent into a separate queue and applied the bandwidth limit separately, you could use the following rule:

```
pipe 20 config mask src-ip 0x000000ff bw 500Kbit/s queue 100Kbytes
pipe 21 config mask dst-ip 0x000000ff bw 500Kbit/s queue 100Kbytes
add 10101 add pipe 20 all from 10.0.0.0/16 to any out via <IP of server>
add 10102 add pipe 21 all from 10.0.0.0/16 to any in via <IP of server>
```

■**Note** Pipe masks get very complicated. We are looking to help you get started with using them, but mastering pipe masks is beyond the scope of this book. Refer to the manual page for `ipfw` in order to gain a mastery of them.

Queues

Sometimes you may want to assign priority to certain protocols. For example, you may be surfing the Internet from your home office computer and notice that the Internet is running very slowly. You have already designated certain pipes to allow certain bandwidth capacities. However, you would rather have Internet traffic take priority over other protocols on your network. This is different from throttling in `ipfw` rules. You have already told each service that it can take only a certain amount of resources. At this point you want to control which service will receive priority when two services compete for those resources.

A *queue* is one way to prioritize traffic that runs over a certain pipe. Queues have weights (similar to priorities) assigned to them using a range of 1 to 100. A weight can take up a certain percentage of a pipe. If you have two queues with weights of 20 and 80, they will take up 20 percent and 80 percent of a pipe, respectively. However, if you specify weights that do not equal 100, the pipe will assume you are splitting the weight between the two and divvy the weight up proportionately. For example, if you have two queues with weights of 10 and 40, it will compute that they will take up 20 percent and 80 percent of the pipe, respectively. By allowing traffic shaping in such a highly configurable manner, it is possible to have many different groupings, or *queues*, of systems that can receive various proportions of throughput to a pipe.

For example, a creative workgroup environment accessing a computer with File Sharing enabled will need some throttling to prevent the computer from being overloaded with requests. We know that the system will choke if it receives more than 800 megabits worth of connections, so we will build a pipe allowing only 800Mb at a time. Of the connections we have coming into that pipe, we will build four queues. These will receive weights proportional to the bandwidth we want them to have.

In our example, we'll consider a typical creative workgroup. Queue 1 contains our creative users who are accessing the server using AFP (548). Queue 2 has our executive producers who are accessing the server through HTTP (80). Queue 3 contains our external users that access the server over FTP (21), and queue 4 has our backup system that uses Retrospect (497). The following represents a series of commands to build the appropriate queues for pipe 1 using what would typically be proportional weights:

```
ipfw pipe 1 config bw 800Mbit/s
ipfw queue 1 config pipe 1 weight 90
ipfw queue 2 config pipe 1 weight 80
ipfw queue 3 config pipe 1 weight 30
ipfw queue 4 config pipe 1 weight 10
ipfw add 40 queue 1 from any to any dst-port 548
ipfw add 41 queue 2 from any to any dst-port 80
ipfw add 42 queue 3 from any to any dst-port 20-21
ipfw add 43 queue 4 from any to any dst-port 497
```

In the previous rule set, we first created a pipe with an 800Mb limit. Then we created four queues with varying weights to create the various pipes for traffic to move through. From there we added four firewall rules (40 through 43) and assigned a destination port to each individual queue, allowing traffic from different ports to travel on their respective pipes. We also could have replaced the any statements on a per-rule basis to limit which IP addresses or ranges of IP addresses on which each queue is processed. For example, if you wanted to limit Retrospect traffic from one bandwidth-hogging computer (192.168.55.89) but not to the other computers, then you would be able to use the following in place of the last line of the previous code:

```
ipfw add 43 queue 4 from 192.168.55.89 to any dst-port 497
```

Now our creative group is functioning with traffic shaping based on their prioritized needs for accessing data. As you've seen throughout this chapter, the firewall in Mac OS X can be both highly configurable and easy to use.

CHAPTER 9

■■■

Securing a Wireless Network

This just in about wireless security on a Mac: at the Black Hat conference in August 2006, David Maynor and Jon "Johnny Cache" Ellch demonstrated to the rest of the world something that hackers had known for a long time. Maynor and Ellch, two security professionals with long careers in the security industry, were able to release what is known as a *proof-of-concept attack* by exploiting the wireless Atheros drivers built into the Mac operating system. Using a script called setup.sh, which turned a Mac computer (with its wireless card turned on) into an access point, an attacker could gain control of an unsuspecting Mac user's laptop. Another hacker script, bad_seed, could then be run from the host computer to exploit the vulnerability in the target computer's wireless driver; this would give an attacker access to a Terminal session on the target computer running root (which is a "superuser" that is allowed full control of the computer). The exploit was not released, but it did provide proof that the Mac community was a long way away from an operating system that is immune to wireless attacks. The concept used in the wireless exploit was not specific to Apple computers but pointed instead to general flaws in wireless networking protocols as a whole.

Although it may not be a completely secure technology, wireless networks have a lot of positive features. Going wireless offers flexibility for computers to move around from location to location. In addition, wireless networking allows for fast expansion when a company or residence is looking to increase the amount of computers on a network, especially temporary networks in larger environments such as those found at conferences and schools. Entire cities have begun to deploy wireless networks for their residents citywide, making the Internet accessible to anyone with a computer and a wireless network card. And let us not forget how wireless networks relieve the eyesore of unsightly cables.

In this chapter, we'll cover securing Apple AirPort–based wireless networks. This starts off with an introduction of wireless networking in general and then moves into how to go about securing an Apple AirPort base station. Later in the chapter, to help show the importance of wireless security, we will showcase some of the wireless hacking tools and illustrate just how easy it is to listen in on wireless traffic and why the security measures are so important.

Wireless Network Essentials

From a security perspective, wireless networks can be rather challenging. Most amateur wireless setups are usually left unsecured, exposing user credentials, e-mails, and other data submitted over the network to the world and causing unnecessary security risks to sensitive information. It is also possible to discreetly plug in an open wireless device on a wired network, allowing someone to then tap in from an outside location, such as a parking lot or nearby coffee shop. These and other security threats make it important to practice good security when dealing with wireless networking.

To properly secure a wireless network, it is key to first have a fundamental understanding of what a wireless network is. A wireless network is different from an Ethernet network or a LAN, although the topologies often follow many of the same standards covered in Chapter 7. In fact, a wireless network is often referred to as a wireless LAN (wLAN).

Logging into a wireless network is like connecting to a hub with all the other users of that network. But rather than traveling across copper wires to interconnect devices like LAN networks, wireless networks use channelized, low-powered radio waves running on the same frequencies as microwave ovens and cordless telephones. The 2.4GHz band is pretty crowded these days now that the Bluetooth technology also runs on this frequency. This can often place a large quantity of traffic on these channels, causing data to get lost or fragmented in transit.

▓**Note** A key element of wireless security is what happens with data that is not properly delivered between wireless devices.

The speed and reliability of a wireless network depends on the hardware and proximity between the devices. Ranges between wireless devices are typically limited to a few hundred feet. The greater the distance, the greater the chance that packets will be intercepted.

Wireless networks that need to encompass a large area will be composed of multiple wireless devices because of the short-range capacity of wireless connectivity. Wireless access points (WAPs) are the devices used to distribute the wireless signal across this network. They accomplish this using a *radio*, the device within the WAP that talks to the client computer's wireless card, creating a wireless signal. WAPs will often connect directly into a wired network, piggybacking on the wired network via Ethernet, to distribute connectivity to the wireless network. This connection is known as a *backhaul*.

Wireless networks use the IEEE 802.11 protocol, which is different from other wireless protocols in how it processes the wireless signal and the frequency used for connectivity. This isn't to say it is more efficient.

There are four flavors of 802.11 used in wireless networking as it applies to Macs. Each of the four primarily distributed wireless protocols runs at a different speed. The most common flavors are 802.11b running at 11 megabits per second, 802.11g running at 54 megabits per second, 802.11n running at 108 megabits per second, and 802.11a, which uses the 5GHz band for communications.

Introducing Apple AirPort

Over the years, Apple has released a variety of products in its family of WAPs, typically referred to as Apple AirPorts (see Table 9-1).

Table 9-1. *Types of Apple AirPort*

Product	Description
AirPort (Graphite)	The original gray AirPort. This AirPort ran at 802.11b.
AirPort Extreme (snow)	This AirPort ran at 802.11g and included a pair of Ethernet interfaces (one LAN and one WAN) and a USB port for printer sharing across a network.
AirPort Express	This is the first device Apple released with the ability to communicate with audio equipment. The AirPort Express has only one network connection and is limited to ten users, making it perfect for a home or small office.
AirPort Extreme (N)	This square white AirPort is the latest and greatest. It incorporates the newest 802.11 protocol, 802.11n, and also facilitates file sharing for smaller networks.

AirPort supports a variety of encryption protocols that can be used to secure the wireless network. Encryption protocols that are specific to wireless networking include the following:

WPA2: Also known as 80211i, WPA2 uses the AES block cipher to make cracking keys difficult. Unless you have a RADIUS server, WPA2 is the best form of encryption to use on an AirPort with Apple clients.

WPA2 Enterprise: Similar to WPA2 in supported encryption standards, WPA2 Enterprise also adds support for usernames, which can be obtained using a RADIUS server, such as FreeRadius, Mac OS X 10.5 Server, and Microsoft Windows Active Directory servers.

WEP: This is the weakest of the security features supported by Apple AirPort. Windows computers need to use the hex equivalent to log into the network. This can be found using the Equivalent Network Password option in the Edit menu of the AirPort Utility or AirPort Admin Utility.

The Apple AirPort devices were designed to be easy to use. In many environments, the Apple AirPort will work right out of the box. However convenient this may be, the default settings are widely known, so an AirPort left with the default settings running represents a considerable security risk for any network.

AirPorts do not always need an Ethernet cable connection to become part of the network. If there are other AirPorts on the network, it is possible to use the wireless network of an existing AirPort network as the network connection that the AirPort will use. This is what is known as a wireless distribution system (WDS) *cloud*. A WDS network can allow you to extend a wireless network for great distances and create a wireless network that goes far beyond the 300-foot limitation documented by Apple.

Configuring Older AirPorts

The first generation of Apple AirPort, the AirPort (Graphite), the AirPort Extreme (snow), and the AirPort Express, shipped with the AirPort Admin Utility. To configure an AirPort using the AirPort Admin Utility, open the application from /Applications/Utilities, and select the AirPort to configure from the list of AirPorts the computer can detect (see Figure 9-1).

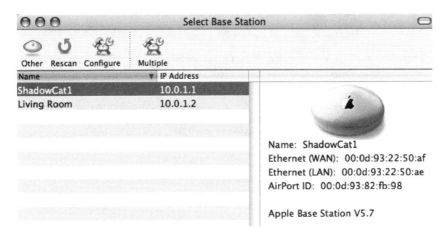

Figure 9-1. *The AirPort Admin Utility*

   To add basic security using the AirPort Admin Utility, start by entering the appropriate contact information in the fields supplied (see Figure 9-2).
   The most important setting to change on the older AirPorts is the password to configure the device. The default password for an AirPort base station is *public*, and it is fairly common for users to leave the password set to this. You should always change this by clicking the Change Password button and entering a new one.
   To set the form of encryption on an Apple AirPort using the AirPort Admin Utility, click the Wireless Options button. On the next screen (see Figure 9-3), select the form of security you want using the Wireless Security option. Then enter the password, and click OK.

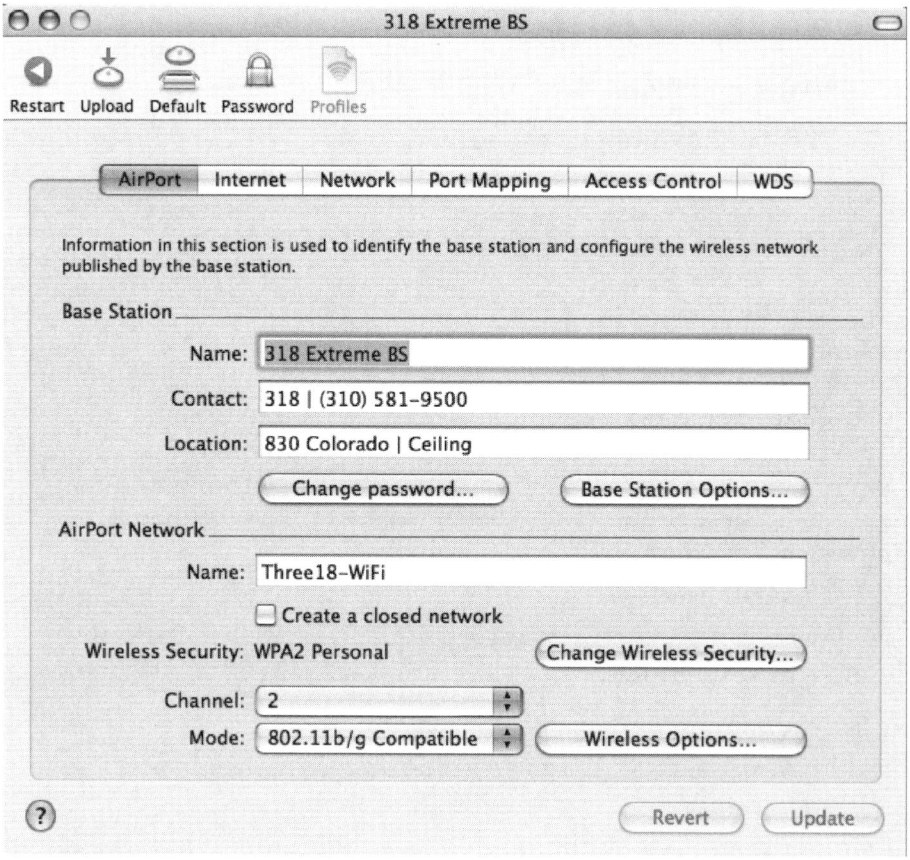

Figure 9-2. *Basic AirPort settings*

■Note If you are changing the form of encryption on a network with WDS enabled, you will likely break the WDS network and need to set it up again. The WDS protocol requires all AirPorts to use the same security settings.

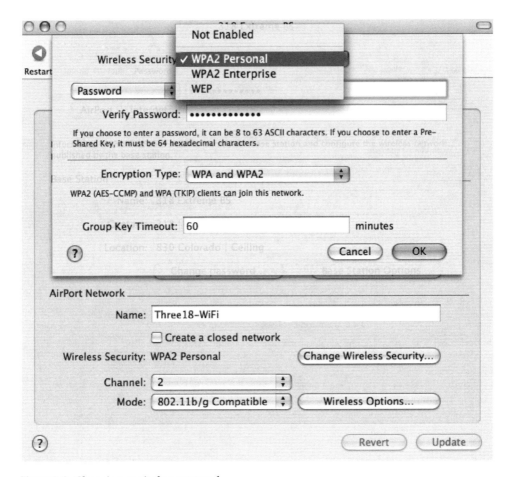

Figure 9-3. *Choosing a wireless protocol*

AirPort Utility

In the winter of 2007, Apple released the AirPort Utility, which shipped concurrently with the AirPort Extreme (N). The AirPort Utility, an upgraded version of the AirPort Admin Utility, has built-in controls for disk sharing and a more user-friendly, wizard-like approach to configuring AirPorts of all types, including older AirPorts. The newer AirPorts can be configured to do a lot more than the older AirPorts could. These newer features include printer and disk sharing.

Configuring Current AirPorts

When you start the AirPort Utility, you're immediately able to browse all the AirPorts on the network at once in a list on the left side of the screen. This list includes all AirPorts that are visible over the Ethernet interface as well as AirPorts on the wireless network. To configure a specific AirPort, click the AirPort to configure, and then click the Configure button. The next screen lets you choose whether you want to use a wizard to configure the AirPorts or configure them manually. Clicking Manual Setup opens the screen shown in Figure 9-4.

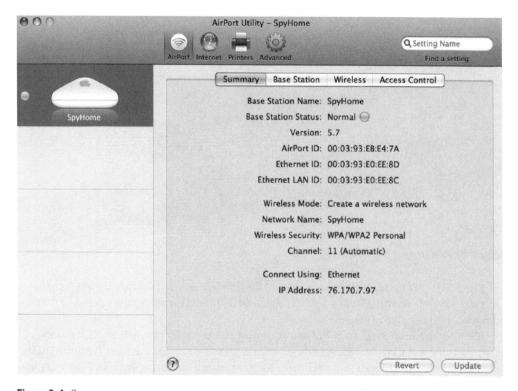

Figure 9-4. *Summary screen*

Once you have logged into the appropriate AirPort, click the AirPort icon in the toolbar, and click the Base Station tab. On the Base Station tab, you will be able to reset the password to administer the AirPort, rename the base station, and add a network time server so the base station's time is always up-to-date (see Figure 9-5). Once you have set an administrative password, click the Wireless tab.

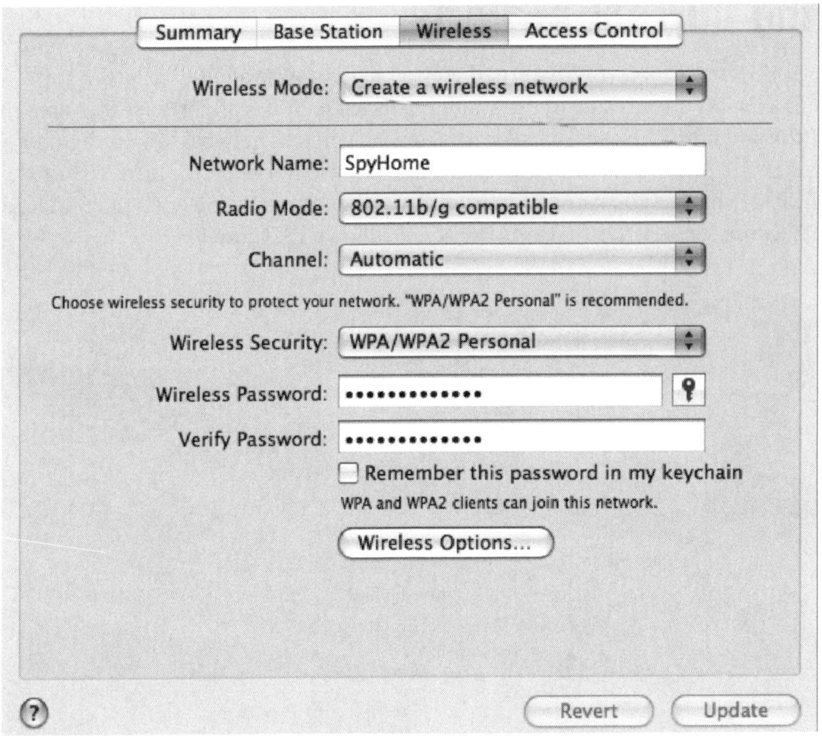

Figure 9-5. *Base station configuration*

From here, the first priority is to configure the wireless encryption type by selecting the encryption type from the Wireless Security drop-down list and entering the password that should be used to join the wireless network.

It is also important to change the administrator password for the AirPort. This is done in much the same way that you changed the password for the AirPort in the AirPort Admin Utility. Click the AirPort to configure, and click the Configure button to change the administrator password. Then click the AirPort icon in the toolbar, and enter the new administrator password. This section also allows the administrator to set the time on the AirPort automatically by clicking Set Time Automatically. This is important for making sense of system logs and can play a critical role in dealing with encryption keys.

Once the wireless network type is configured, if the AirPort receives an Internet connection from a DSL modem or some other publicly accessible source, it is probably a good idea to enable the basic firewall feature of the AirPort, also known as NAT, if it is not enabled by default. To enable NAT, click the Internet icon on the AirPort Admin Utility's toolbar, and then click the Internet Connection tab (see Figure 9-6). Selecting Share a Public IP Address enables NAT on the AirPort, making it act like a router/firewall. (For more about NAT, see Chapter 7.)

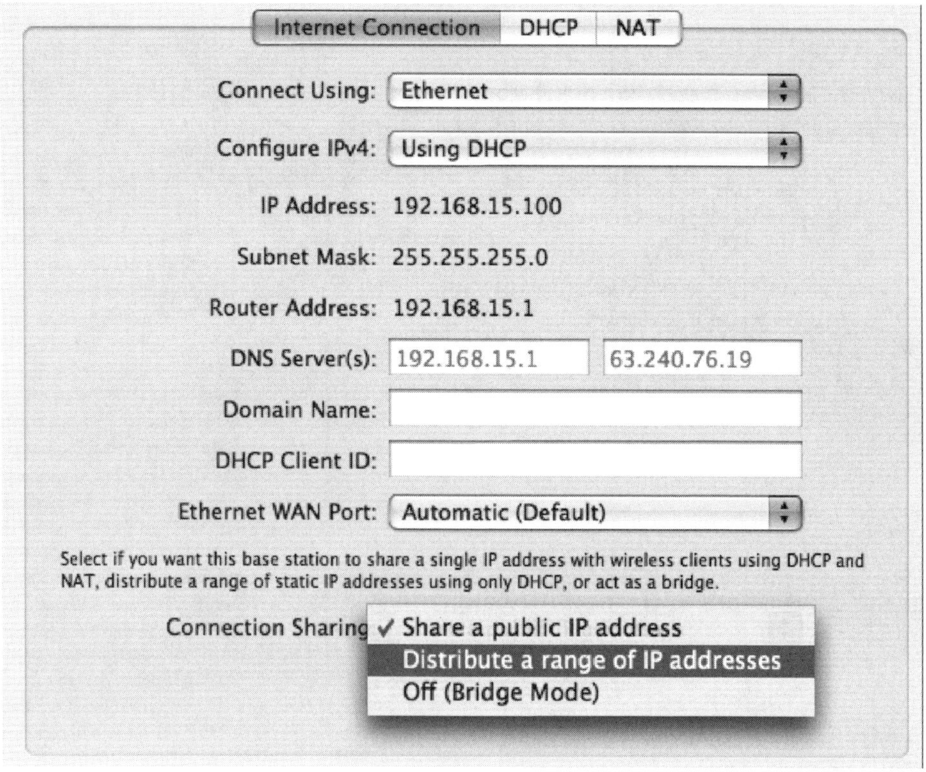

Figure 9-6. *Enabling routing on a base station*

Once router/firewall services are configured on the AirPort, it might be desirable to direct traffic to a local computer on the network. For example, if there is a web server on the network, web traffic may need to be directed to it. Or if one user wants access to files hosted on another computer on the network, traffic may need to be guided toward that computer. This is accomplished via port forwarding. To enable port forwards on the AirPort, click Internet in the AirPort Utility, and then on the NAT tab, check the Enable NAT Port Mapping Protocol box (as shown in Figure 9-7).

Once NAT is enabled, you need to specify the port (or ports) that are to be forwarded. You can do this by clicking the Configure Port Mappings button on the NAT tab. This opens a dialog box (see Figure 9-8) asking for the public and private port numbers that the forwarded port should point to as well as the IP address to which traffic should forward.

Using public and private ports allows the administrator to have more control over the network by redirecting traffic to different ports. For example, if incoming traffic comes in on port 80 but for heightened security should point to port 81 on the server, then you'd enter **80** in the Public Port Number field and **81** in the Private Port Number field.

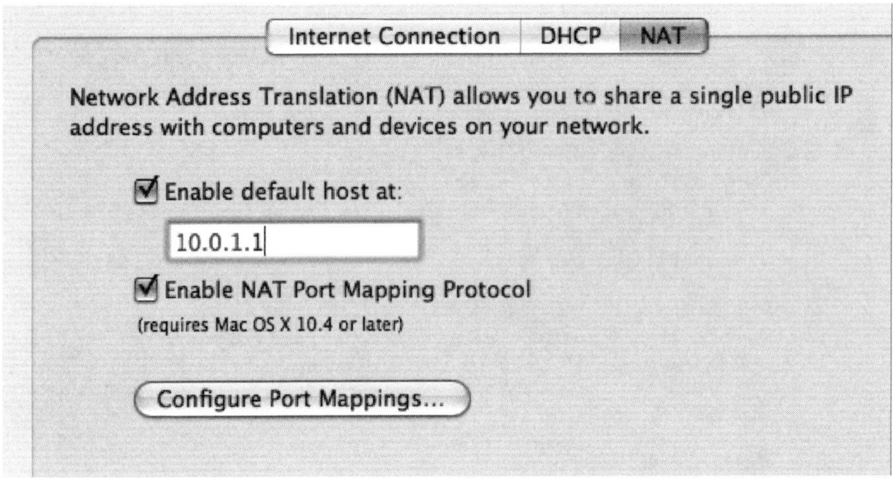

| Internet Connection | DHCP | NAT |

Network Address Translation (NAT) allows you to share a single public IP address with computers and devices on your network.

☑ Enable default host at:

10.0.1.1|

☑ Enable NAT Port Mapping Protocol
(requires Mac OS X 10.4 or later)

(Configure Port Mappings...)

Figure 9-7. *NAT settings*

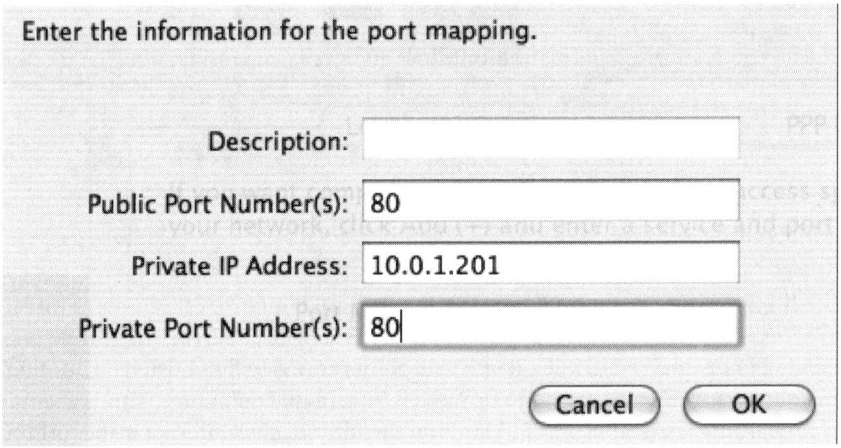

Enter the information for the port mapping.

Description:

Public Port Number(s): 80

Private IP Address: 10.0.1.201

Private Port Number(s): 80|

(Cancel)   (OK)

Figure 9-8. *Port mappings*

Limiting the DHCP Scope

If the AirPort is acting as a routing device and there are multiple computers that the AirPort is directing traffic for, then you should use the built-in DHCP feature on the AirPort. The DHCP feature will configure the AirPort to hand out IP addresses to client computers on the network. A good way to secure the network is to limit the number of IP addresses assigned to networked computers. Limiting the number of assignable IP addresses that can be given out by the router to the exact number of computers on the network is a good way to ensure that only certain computers are able to use it. Taking away the ability for an unlimited number of computers to join the network limits the ability for a rogue computer to automatically have an IP assigned.

To enable DHCP, click the Internet icon in the toolbar of the AirPort Utility, and select the DHCP tab (see Figure 9-9). Next, click the DHCP Range field, and select the IP address scheme to use. When choosing an IP scheme, make sure there are no other IP schemes already in place on the network that might conflict. Once an IP scheme is selected, enter the first IP address the router should use in the DHCP scope in the DHCP Beginning Address field. Then enter the last IP address in the scope in the DHCP Ending Address field. For example, if five computers need to have IPs distributed to them, then you'd use 10.0.1.2 as the first address and 10.0.1.6 as the last address. Clicking the Update button commits the changes to the AirPort.

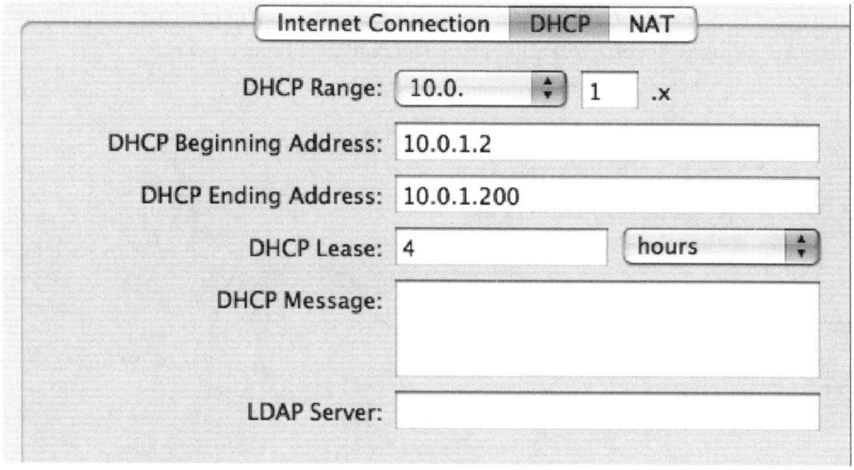

Figure 9-9. *DHCP settings*

Hardware Filtering

The AirPort can also restrict computers that are allowed to log into it based on the MAC address of each client computer. The MAC address is a unique address on network adapters (wireless and wired) that is stamped by the vendor during assembly and is unique to the card. There should never be two cards with the same address. By using the actual hardware address of a computer to decide whether the computer can log into the wireless network, a second layer of security is added to the wireless network (encrypted passwords providing the first layer, as discussed earlier).

To filter by MAC address, it is important to find the AirPort ID (the MAC address on a Mac) of each computer. This is located on the Network pane of System Preferences on the client computer. Clicking the Network tab and then clicking the AirPort tab opens a list of various protocols that the Mac will use to communicate on the network. Clicking the AirPort tab will open the AirPort ID (see Figure 9-10).

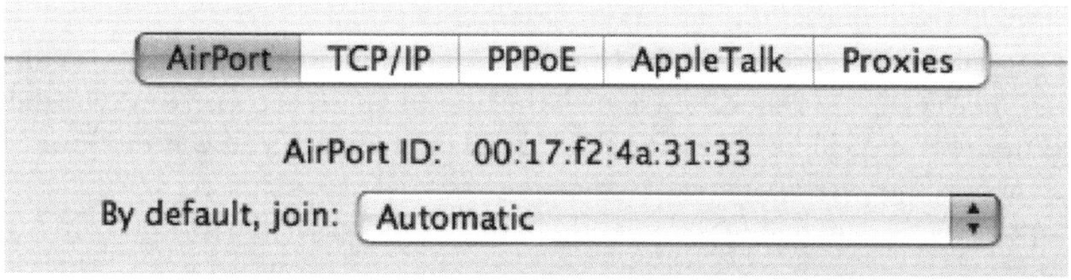

Figure 9-10. *Identifying your MAC address*

■**Note** We suggest writing down all the AirPort IDs on your network before beginning this process and adding them during the initial setup of the AirPort.

Once the AirPort IDs have been assembled, enable MAC filtration on the AirPort by opening the AirPort Utility and clicking the AirPort icon in the toolbar. Then select the Access Control tab, and set the MAC Address Access Control feature to Local (see Figure 9-11).

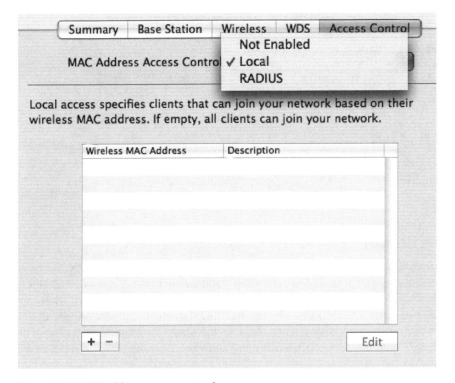

Figure 9-11. *MAC address access controls*

■**Note** RADIUS requires Mac OS X Server to be configured in a Mac environment.

Before clicking Update, make sure to add the computers you want to give access to on the wireless network. To add a computer, click the + sign at the bottom of the screen. Now type the AirPort ID of the computer that will be accessing the wireless network. If you want to limit which machines can access the wireless network, then you can click the + sign. As you can see in Figure 9-12, this opens a screen allowing you to enter the MAC address of the AirPort card (or other wireless adapter). If you are using MAC addresses, only the systems listed will be able to join the wireless network.

Caution If the computer configuring the MAC filtering is not configured, once Update is clicked, that computer will not be able to tap back into the wireless network and will need to use a wired computer for access.

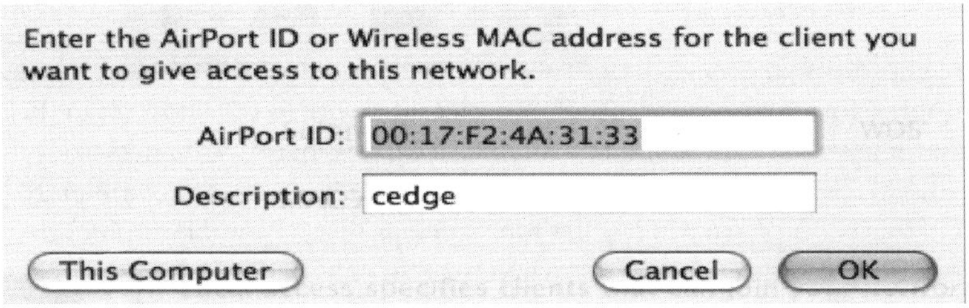

Enter the AirPort ID or Wireless MAC address for the client you want to give access to this network.

AirPort ID: `00:17:F2:4A:31:33`

Description: `cedge`

This Computer   Cancel   OK

Figure 9-12. *Using the MAC address*

AirPort Logging

The AirPort does not keep logs for an indefinite amount of time. For longer log retention, an OS X Server should be configured with the syslog service option to keep AirPort logs long-term. Syslog is a built-in configurable service of OS X Server. To enable the syslog function of OS X Server, click the Advanced button in the toolbar of the AirPort Utility. Then, click the Logging & SNMP tab (see Figure 9-13), and enter the IP address for the syslog OS X Server. Choose the level of alerts that are sent to the server using the Syslog Level drop-down list.

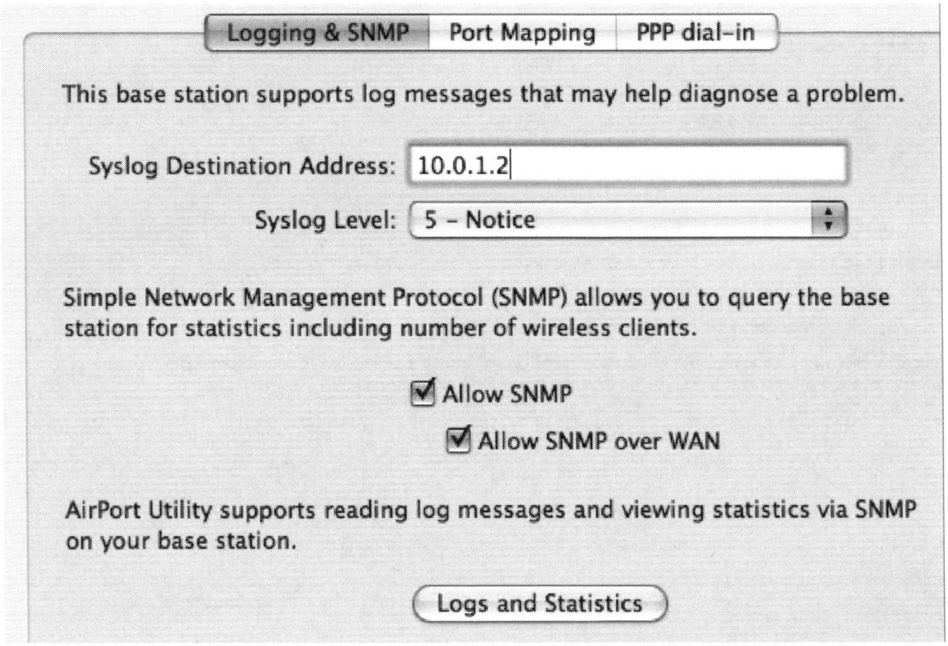

Logging & SNMP │ Port Mapping │ PPP dial-in

This base station supports log messages that may help diagnose a problem.

Syslog Destination Address: `10.0.1.2`

Syslog Level: `5 – Notice`

Simple Network Management Protocol (SNMP) allows you to query the base station for statistics including number of wireless clients.

☑ Allow SNMP
☑ Allow SNMP over WAN

AirPort Utility supports reading log messages and viewing statistics via SNMP on your base station.

Logs and Statistics

Figure 9-13. *Enabling logging*

■**Note** If a syslog server is not available, you can still click the Logs and Statistics button to review logs. However, the AirPort will erase these log files the next time it loses power or is reset.

Hiding a Wireless Network

Another good measure to protect an Apple wireless network is to hide the SSID of the network, also known as SSID suppression, which will cause the wireless network to not show up in the list of available networks for users. If fewer people can discover a wireless network, it is less likely to be hijacked and abused. This isn't to say that hiding the SSID makes the network completely undiscoverable. Later in this chapter, we will discuss tools such as KisMAC and iStumbler that will allow those who wardrive to see networks even when the SSID has been suppressed. SSID suppression is a good mechanism for security, but only when used in conjunction with other security measures.

To suppress the SSID for your Apple AirPort, click the Wireless tab for your AirPort, and then click the Wireless Options button. This opens a screen similar to Figure 9-14, which allows you to click Create a Closed Network. An AirPort environment with the SSID suppressed is synonymous with a closed network in Apple terminology.

■**Note** *Wardriving* is the act of searching for wireless networks by a person in a moving vehicle using a computer or a PDA to detect the networks and possibly break into them.

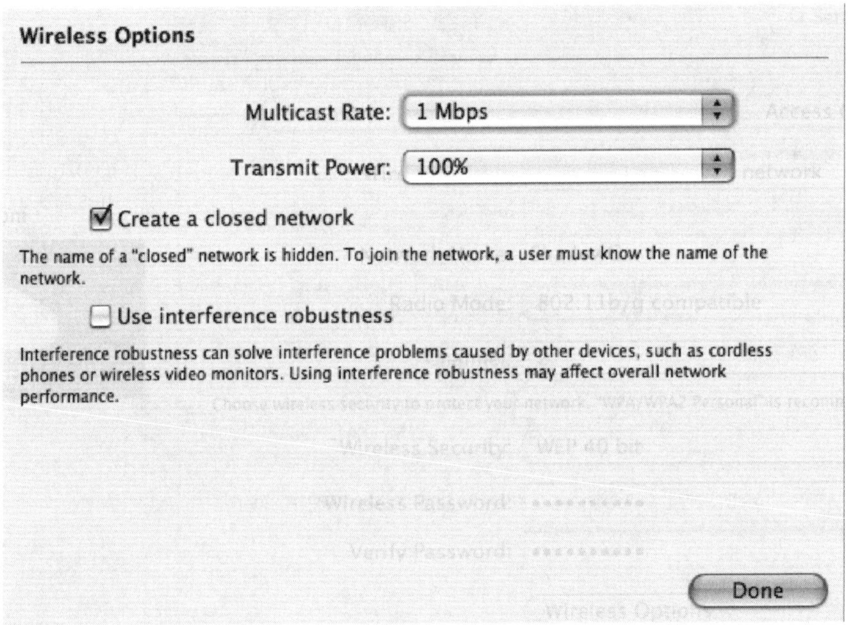

Figure 9-14. *Creating a closed network*

Base Station Features in the AirPort Utility

Every Apple computer comes with a utility to manage Apple AirPorts. This means that every Mac on your network has the ability to configure your AirPorts, which is dangerous. But imagine if every Apple computer on the Internet were able to configure your AirPort. If you select the Allow Configuration Over Ethernet WAN Port box (see Figure 9-15), then this is exactly what you are doing. Do not use this feature unless you have to use it. If it is absolutely necessary to allow administration over the Ethernet, make sure to put an administrative password on the AirPort and give the password only to those who absolutely need it.

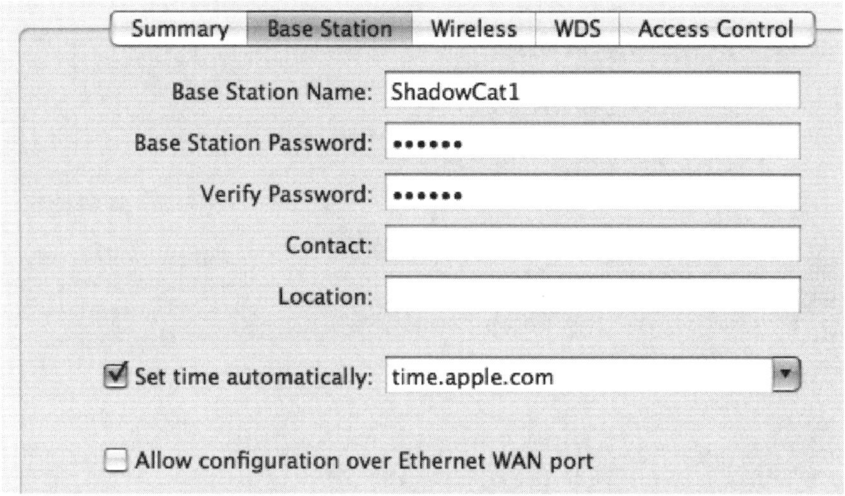

Figure 9-15. *Setting a time server*

The AirPort Express

From a security standpoint, the Apple AirPort Express closely resembles the Apple AirPort. The key difference is that the AirPort Express has a port dedicated for playing audio. iTunes has a field that can be used to log into an AirPort Express and play audio to the device.

■**Note** The future of the AirPort Express is somewhat questionable, because Apple has introduced the AppleTV with far more features to eventually replace the AirPort Express. However, it is widely used in the world of Mac networking, and therefore it's worth discussing.

To reliably secure the AirPort Express features for playing audio, log into the AirPort Express, and click the Music Icon in the toolbar. This opens a screen that allows you to disable AirTunes, which you should do if you are not using this feature. If you are using AirTunes, then create a speaker password using the AirTunes option in AirPort Setup (shown in Figure 9-16), which will then be required by anyone using the AirPort Express to listen to music.

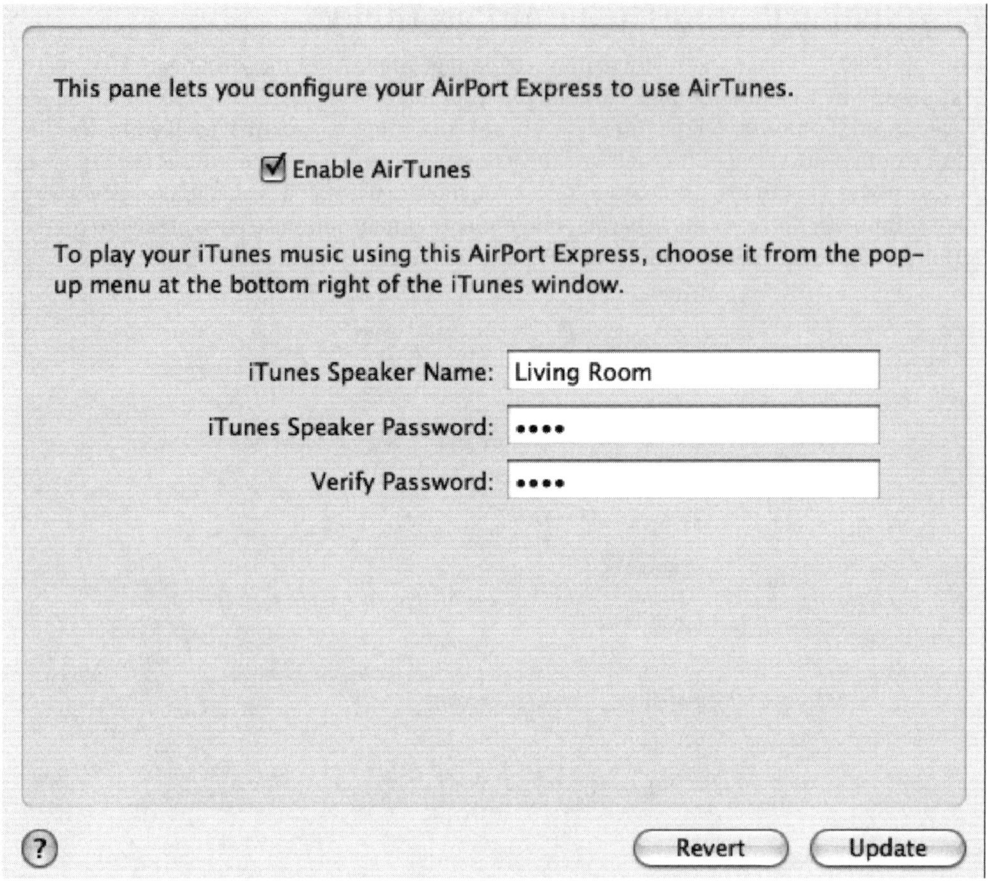

This pane lets you configure your AirPort Express to use AirTunes.

☑ Enable AirTunes

To play your iTunes music using this AirPort Express, choose it from the pop-up menu at the bottom right of the iTunes window.

iTunes Speaker Name: Living Room

iTunes Speaker Password: ••••

Verify Password: ••••

?   Revert   Update

Figure 9-16. *Enabling AirTunes*

Wireless Security on Client Computers

As mentioned, David Maynor clearly demonstrated that Apple client computers are not immune to wireless attacks. When using a public wireless network, it is often best to make sure you are using a secure means of authenticating and transmitting data. For example, when traveling, we always use a VPN to connect to our office network and access resources. This extra layer of authentication keeps the data away from prying eyes that may be watching these public networks.

Note When your AirPort connection is not in use, make sure to turn off the AirPort. Any time you are not using the wireless, try to keep it turned off. To disable it, just click the AirPort icon at the top of the screen, and click Turn AirPort Off (see Figure 9-17).

Figure 9-17. *Turning your AirPort off*

Securing Computer-to-Computer Networks

A *computer-to-computer network* is similar to other wireless networks except that it is a network without a central base station. In previous versions of OS X, computer-to-computer networks were known as *ad hoc networks*.

The security features available on computer-to-computer networks are limited. When creating a computer-to-computer network, WEP is disabled by default, and WPA is not available. To create a secured computer-to-computer network, click the wireless icon at the top of your screen (see Figure 9-18), and choose the Create Network option.

From here, click the Enable Encryption (Using WEP) option, and choose the level of encryption you want to use (128-bit is typically the best). Once you have selected your encryption level, enter a password, and click the OK button to establish the wireless network.

Figure 9-18. *Encryption levels*

Wireless Topologies

Where a wireless network is placed on the network can greatly impact the security level of the network. Many wireless networks, for ease of use, will want to have NAT disabled, allowing AppleTalk and Bonjour connections into devices on the wired network. For larger networks where security is paramount, network administrators should strongly consider putting an Apple AirPort in a demilitarized zone (DMZ). A DMZ sits outside the corporate firewall and can have a completely different set of rules for how network traffic works as compared to the internal corporate network.

The default configuration of an Apple AirPort has NAT enabled. This removes the ability of the wireless clients to communicate over broadcast networks with upstream networks. However, clients can still communicate by IP address with upstream networks. Therefore, this is not actually a DMZ but instead a subnetwork of your main network. Communications are still possible and less controllable.

The preferred location of AirPorts and wireless access points is in a demilitarized zone. By placing the wireless access point in a network above rather than below in terms of the network architecture, your corporate NAT wireless clients will not be able to communicate directly with your corporate network. From here, users can establish a VPN tunnel into the network, and traffic will be most effectively encrypted.

This topology requirement is often employed in larger companies, and in the future you'll probably see more and more wireless protocols developed around it.

Wireless Hacking Tools

Several tools can be used when looking to enumerate or crack into wireless networks. Many of these have GUIs that allow less-savvy users to perform very complicated tasks such as mapping out WEP keys for physical areas and cracking wireless networks with relative ease, even if they don't have any background in hacking. We'll spend some time covering these tools so you know what to keep an eye out for and to increase your awareness of the need for strong wireless security if you are using any wireless devices like the Apple AirPort.

KisMAC

KisMAC is a utility that can be used to find and crack into wireless networks. When scanning, KisMAC shows networks in four colors, based on their level of encryption. Green is open, yellow is unknown, red is WEP, and blue is WPA (see Figure 9-19).

Figure 9-19. *KisMAC*

Figure 9-20 lists all the wireless networking that can be seen at the time of running KisMAC. Having easy access to see the signal strength and type of encryption makes it easy to find AirPorts that are close to you. But it also makes isolating networks with weak signal strengths possible. The better your signal strength, the less likely a packet will get missed by the AirPort.

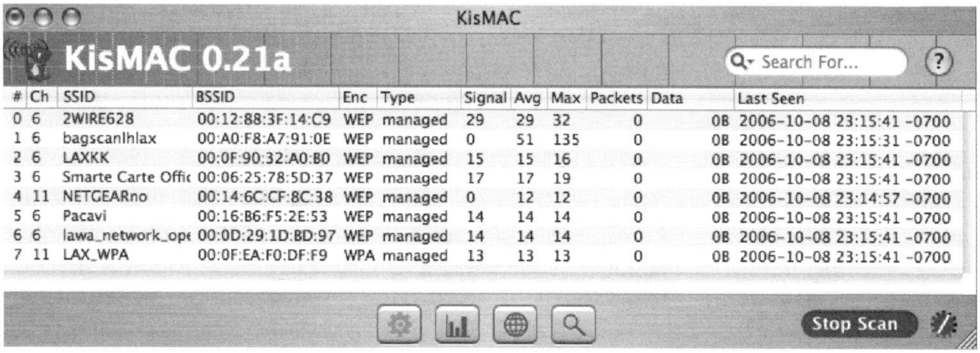

#	Ch	SSID	BSSID	Enc	Type	Signal	Avg	Max	Packets	Data	Last Seen
0	6	2WIRE628	00:12:88:3F:14:C9	WEP	managed	29	29	32	0	0B	2006-10-08 23:15:41 -0700
1	6	bagscanlhlax	00:A0:F8:A7:91:0E	WEP	managed	0	51	135	0	0B	2006-10-08 23:15:31 -0700
2	6	LAXKK	00:0F:90:32:A0:B0	WEP	managed	15	15	16	0	0B	2006-10-08 23:15:41 -0700
3	6	Smarte Carte Offic	00:06:25:78:5D:37	WEP	managed	17	17	19	0	0B	2006-10-08 23:15:41 -0700
4	11	NETGEARno	00:14:6C:CF:8C:38	WEP	managed	0	12	12	0	0B	2006-10-08 23:14:57 -0700
5	6	Pacavi	00:16:B6:F5:2E:53	WEP	managed	14	14	14	0	0B	2006-10-08 23:15:41 -0700
6	6	lawa_network_ope	00:0D:29:1D:BD:97	WEP	managed	14	14	14	0	0B	2006-10-08 23:15:41 -0700
7	11	LAX_WPA	00:0F:EA:F0:DF:F9	WPA	managed	13	13	13	0	0B	2006-10-08 23:15:41 -0700

Figure 9-20. *KisMAC base stations*

It is also possible to see detailed information about the wireless networks that KisMAC accesses. Other programs can give the same information, such as Mac Stumbler and iStumbler, but the more advanced cracking and wireless scanning features found in KisMAC make it a more compelling application to use.

Cracking wireless networks with KisMAC is possible only if a second wireless network interface is installed on the machine. The second network interface runs in a passive monitoring mode, while the first active network interface sends out probe requests and waits for answers.

Packet reinjection is a WEP cracking technique used to crack wireless networks. With this attack, KisMAC will try to send captured packets of data in order to cause another computer to respond. If the computer responds, KisMAC will send these packets repeatedly. If KisMAC detects any answers, then it will go into injection mode. Injection mode generates a lot of traffic, causing more easily captured pieces of data to be generated. Wireless networks with WEP can be broken within an hour, sometimes only ten minutes, maybe even five. Be aware that this is no longer the bleeding edge of hacking technology, but it is also not standardized, so it may not work with all cards and equipment.

A lot of wireless access points offer a key generation process using an easy-to-remember passphrase. Unfortunately, many wireless manufacturers implemented a very dangerous algorithm, called the Newsham 21-bit attack, for the generation of 40-bit WEP keys. This algorithm generates keys with an effective strength of only 21 bits. KisMAC is able to *brute-force*, or attempt all possible combinations until the correct password combination is found (see Figure 9-21), finding these keys quickly. Wireless access points from Linksys, D-Link, Belkin, and Netgear are confirmed to be vulnerable to the Newsham 21-bit attack.

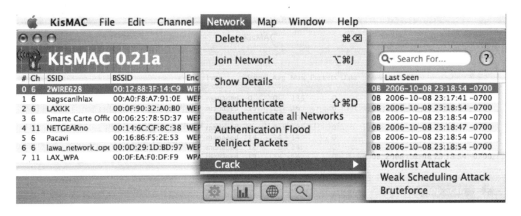

Figure 9-21. *Cracking into base stations*

Most network interfaces that are available are PCMCIA cards, which is an interface that MacBook and MacBook Pro users cannot use because of the lack of a PCMCIA interface on the machines. The Netgear MA-111 USB adapter is a good alternative for Mac users. However, make sure to check the KisMAC site before purchasing a card, and make sure it is still supported or that there aren't other interfaces that might be more readily available to purchase for the Mac.

Detecting Rogue Access Points

If a rogue access point is suspected on the network, it is possible to use KisMAC to quickly locate the WAP. If you have a GPS unit, the Map menu provides users with the ability to set their current position on a map and then follow the wireless signal to the rogue access point's source using signal strength readings.

To set up a map, you will need to import an image and switch to the Map tab. You should now see a map. Click the Set Waypoint 1 entry in the Map menu and click a position in the map that you know the geographical position for. KisMAC will now ask you for this position. If you have a GPS device attached to your computer, you current position is set as default coordinates.

Now use the Set Waypoint 1 entry to set up a second waypoint. After you have set up these two points, KisMAC can use the image as a map (see Figure 9-22). Networks are automatically displayed. You can also show your current position by clicking the Current Position entry in the Map menu.

Figure 9-22. *Setting up a map for KisMAC*

Note You may be using a second machine that supports classic mode. When classic mode is running, KisMAC will not be able to function as intended.

---

iStumbler and Mac Stumbler

iStumbler is a good discovery tool for Mac OS X, available under a BSD-style open source license, that allows users to find AirPort networks, Bluetooth devices, and Bonjour services. To install iStumbler, download it from http://www.iStumbler.net. After downloading it, open the application, and it will automatically scan the wireless networks that are accessible to the computer running it. The default graph (see Figure 9-23) will show the wireless network name, the type of security employed on the wireless network, the signal, the vendor of the WAPs, the wireless channel, and the Mac address of the wireless base stations.

	Secur	Mode	Network Name	Signal	Noise	Chann	MAC Address	Vendor
○	Secure	managed	ShadowCat	60%	0%	2	00-11-24-0B-E6-E;	Apple
○	Secure	managed	2WIRE169	19%	0%	6	00-0D-72-65-C2-5	2wire
○	Secure	managed	2WIRE314	29%	0%	6	00-12-88-E9-28-8	2wire
○	Secure	managed	2WIRE542	70%	0%	6	00-12-88-A5-1A-E	2wire
○	Secure	managed	2WIRE674	19%	0%	6	00-14-95-7F-05-0	00-14-95
○	Secure	managed	2WIRE744	19%	0%	6	00-12-88-CA-11-4	2wire
○	Secure	managed	2WIRE749	18%	0%	8	00-18-3F-E9-88-7	00-18-3F
○	Secure	managed	2WIRE785	16%	0%	6	00-12-88-C5-8E-3	2wire
○	Secure	managed	2WIRE790	35%	0%	6	00-14-95-A8-4D-C	00-14-95
○	Secure	managed	Aervox	16%	0%	1	00-03-93-E8-5F-F;	Apple
○	Secure	managed	Barksdale	21%	0%	11	00-18-4D-87-9B-1	00-18-4D
)(	Open	managed	dale3	14%	0%	1	00-13-10-B0-E4-2	Cisco-Link.
○	Secure	managed	hectorbojangles	29%	0%	6	00-13-10-A3-33-E	Cisco-Link.
○	Secure	managed	Hlywd Std	18%	0%	11	00-13-10-E2-F2-D	Cisco-Link.
)(	Open	managed	karnell	20%	0%	11	00-18-F8-E2-DB-0	00-18-F8
)(	Open	managed	LBPNet	16%	0%	11	00-09-5B-51-68-1	Netgear
)(	Open	managed	panther	27%	0%	6	00-0F-66-21-D4-F	Cisco-Linksy
○	Secure	managed	PChase	14%	0%	11	00-18-4D-54-6D-:	00-18-4D
○	Secure	managed	Pinto Avenger	21%	0%	11	00-14-BF-8D-22-5	00-14-BF
○	Secure	managed	ShadowCat	46%	0%	2	00-0D-93-82-FB-9	Apple
○	Secure	managed	Spencer	19%	0%	6	00-13-10-AF-BE-2	Cisco-Link.
○	Secure	managed	SSI	17%	0%	9	00-14-A9-F6-36-B	00-14-A9
○	Secure	managed	2WIRE437	17%	0%	11	00-19-E4-49-30-8	00-19-E4
○	Secure	managed	2WIRE578	18%	0%	6	00-14-95-AF-23-3	00-14-95
)(	Open	managed	linksys	17%	0%	6	00-0C-41-3D-35-9	Linksys Gr.

Figure 9-23. *iStumbler*

It will also compute a graph that displays a history of the wireless network's signal strength. You can see this in a stand-alone window by selecting Monitor from the AirPort menu. You can use the monitors to help in troubleshooting wireless signal issues by finding overlapping SSIDs, finding rogue access points, and helping determine what channel to use in a physical location highly saturated with wireless access points.

Another nice feature of iStumbler is the ability to view details about wireless networks using the AirPort Inspector. The Inspector includes details such as the noise level and the average signal level of the network. The advanced information that can be obtained using AirPort Inspector (see Figure 9-24) is accessible in the Edit menu. iStumbler provides you with a lot more information than we can cover in this chapter. However, suffice it to say that this level of detail can be handy if you are troubleshooting an issue on the phone with a vendor or looking to hack into a wireless network to test the security of your environment.

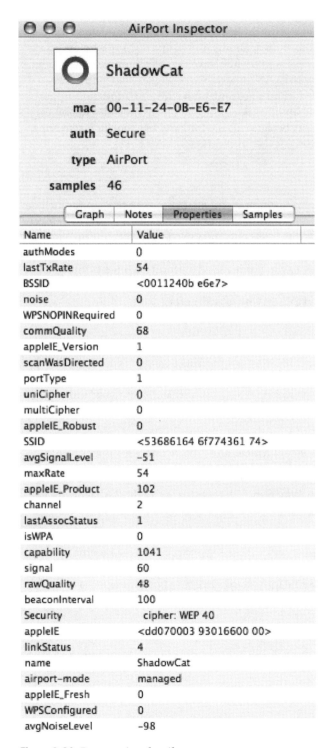

Name	Value
authModes	0
lastTxRate	54
BSSID	<0011240b e6e7>
noise	0
WPSNOPINRequired	0
commQuality	68
appleIE_Version	1
scanWasDirected	0
portType	1
uniCipher	0
multiCipher	0
appleIE_Robust	0
SSID	<53686164 6f774361 74>
avgSignalLevel	-51
maxRate	54
appleIE_Product	102
channel	2
lastAssocStatus	1
isWPA	0
capability	1041
signal	60
rawQuality	48
beaconInterval	100
Security	cipher: WEP 40
appleIE	<dd070003 93016600 00>
linkStatus	4
name	ShadowCat
airport-mode	managed
appleIE_Fresh	0
WPSConfigured	0
avgNoiseLevel	-98

Figure 9-24. *Base station details*

MacStumbler

MacStumbler displays various bits of information about 802.11b and 802.11g wireless access points. Designed to be a tool to find access points while traveling, MacStumbler can also be used for wardriving and coordinating with a GPS unit while traveling to help map access points. MacStumbler requires an Apple AirPort Card and, unlike KisMAC, does not support PCMCIA and USB wireless devices. MacStumbler does not generate as much useful information as iStumbler but is worth mentioning because of its popularity as a tool for discovering unsecured wireless networks.

Ettercap

Ettercap is a tool used to perpetrate "man-in-the-middle" attacks on a LAN. Features include sniffing network traffic, network analysis, and content filtering. It can also be used to intercept packets, to perform ARP spoofing, and to perform character injection. It will perform password collection for a variety of protocols including Telnet, FTP, POP, SSH, ICQ, SMB, MySQL, HTTP, IMAP, MSN Messenger, and Yahoo Messenger. Ettercap can perform OS fingerprinting, kill network connections, and check for other poisoners. It can also do all of this on wired networks.

You can download Ettercap from `http://ettercap.sourceforge.net`.

EtherPeek

EtherPeek is closed source software available from WildPackets.com that is used on Ethernet networks. It can perform traffic monitoring and packet capture. It will also capture traffic, set triggers, view packets in real time, and deliver updates on packet statistics in real time.

There are three versions of EtherPeek, available from WildPackets.com:

EtherPeek VX: EtherPeek VX, WildPackets' Expert VoIP Network Analyzer, is the application that is used for diagnosing VoIP deployment and Ethernet network issues within enterprises.

EtherPeek NX: This provides network analysis with tools to troubleshoot, diagnose, and configure networks.

EtherPeek SE: WildPackets' Ethernet Protocol Analyzer is an intuitive, powerful network and protocol analyzer for Ethernet networks. It gives visual access to the Ethernet network through real-time views of the LAN and can perform baseline analyses of the Ethernet network. It also has triggers that can be tripped to deliver notifications when settings are activated.

▓**Note** EtherPeek is not sold for the Mac platform. To use it as a means to secure a Mac environment, it will need to run from a Windows computer.

Cracking WEP Keys

To drive home why it is so important to practice good security with your wireless environment, let's look at cracking a few types of wireless security protocols. There are three steps we will need to go through in order to crack a WEP key. First, we need to locate the AirPort using a tool such as KisMAC.

Second, we need to generate a minimum of 400,000 WEP initialization vectors (random bits of data used to decrypt wireless traffic). We will capture the traffic using Aireplay to generate the required initialization vectors. Aireplay is available at `http://www.wirelessdefence.org/Contents/Aircrack_aireplay.htm`. Once captured, Airodump will be used to save the captured initialization vectors into a file.

Run the Airodump command, as shown in the following example:

```
./airodump <wireless interface> <outputfilename> <MACfiler>
```

■**Note** Aireplay and Airodump are free to download and use.

Make sure your output filename ends with the file extension `.cap`. The MAC filter would be used when you have more than one access point or AirPort on the same channel within range of the system you are launching the attack from, in which case you would use the MAC address of the access point you are targeting. With Airodump still running, open another Terminal session, and run Aireplay with the following command:

```
./aireplay -b <maca ddress of wireless access point> -x 512 <wifiport>
```

■**Note** The b in the previous line of code is the `bssid` (MAC address of the access point), and the x is the `nbpps` (number of packets per second).

This will catch an initialization vector packet and replay it against the AirPort to get enough raw data to allow you to crack the WEP password. You can tell when you have enough initialization vectors by watching the IV column in Airodump. The more traffic running through the AirPort, the faster packets will be caught (if the AirPort is not being used, the AirPort might take a long time to crack). Once you have reached 400,000, use the Ctrl+C shortcut to exit Aireplay and Airodump. This will save the file you specified in Airodump and stop Aireplay from re-sending the IV packet out to the AP.

Once you have our initialization vectors in a file, you can analyze the packets to recover the actual WEP key using Aircrack to analyze the file and recover the WEP key. Aircrack is a set of tools used for auditing wireless networks by allowing you to crack WEP and WPA keys:

```
./aircrack -n 128 <outputfilenamefromairodump>
```

Note n is the "nbits" or WEP key length (listed in KisMAC).

If the attack that you have just launched was executed correctly, then you will get the key in red text followed by "KEY FOUND."

Cracking WPA-PSK

Of the wireless encryption protocols, WPA is one of the hardest to hack. Let's explore a way to do it. For this we will use two open source security tools, Airforge and Aircrack.

Once a target network using a WPA access point has been identified, using a tool such as KisMAC, you can begin to launch the attack using Airforge to create a deauthentication packet.

```
./airforge <MACaddressofap> <MACofclient> filename.cap
```

What Airforge will do is cause a user who is connected to the WAP to become deauthenticated from the network. Once disconnected, the deauthenticated user's system will attempt to reauthenticate, and the SSID will be sent over the air in plain text. You will typically want to set the packet length to 26, -u 0, -v (to specify sub), -w0, -x1 (number of packets), -r (to redirect to file), and eth0 (adapter to inject to).

While you're running this, you'll want to open Ethereal (or another packet capturing application) and start catching packets. After you are done packet catching (after about 5,000 to 10,000 packets), you want to sort by EAP over LAN (EAPOL). After filtering by EAPOL, analyze the remainder of the packets for the password. Once you find the four-way packets, save the packets. Then you will be able to use a tool called cowpatty or Brutal Gift to run a dictionary attack on the saved packets, and after some time you will be able to crack the WPA password. Most WPA passwords are simple for users to remember. It is often words such as *abcd* or *1234* or something with the name of the location. You can first try a combination of these. However, keep in mind that the Apple AirPort requires a minimum of eight characters for WPA on the Apple AirPort.

Note It is possible to further secure WPA by using WPA2 enterprise security.

General Safeguards Against Cracking Wireless Networks

Encryption should always be implemented on wireless networks. It is one of the best safeguards against allowing users to crack your WEP keys.

Determining the strength of encryption is always a trade-off between security and speed. The more encrypted, the slower the network will be. But increased levels of encryption mean increased time to crack. Most wardrivers will not bother with heavily encrypted networks, moving on to less well-protected environments. Keep in mind that the encryption strength is not only determined by the number of bits that the encryption is using but also by the complexity of the passphrase being used. More complex passwords are harder to crack using a dictionary attack. Businesses concerned about wireless security will use WPA2 Enterprise, which goes beyond simple WEP keys by employing a RADIUS server (included in Mac OS X 10.5.*x* Server) on the network. This allows the administrator to use a server that can lock accounts if someone is attempting to break into them using password policies and the other account management security measures described in Chapter 13.

■**Note** WPA2 requires a RADIUS server.

Having good signal strength helps keep packets from becoming orphaned. Since orphaned packets make cracking wireless networks easier, maintaining good signal strength is another good way to keep wireless networks protected.

Using the MAC address filtration feature of the Apple AirPort is another good security technique. This should, again, not be the only mechanism used for securing wireless networks, but it is a good step in wireless security.

PART 4

■ ■ ■

Sharing

CHAPTER 10

∎∎∎

File Services

Manual configuration of file sharing security can be one of the more challenging aspects of working with shared data on computers in a networked environment. The challenge is twofold—how do you keep files accessible to those who need them while simultaneously keeping them inaccessible to those who don't? Sharing files over a network is also an inherently dangerous activity. Other computers' users can access files on your system without physically gaining access to your computer; thus, if configured incorrectly, the wrong data can get into the wrong hands, which can prove to be catastrophic. However, in most environments, it is crucial that multiple computers have access to data on a single computer. So, how do we manage this file-sharing conundrum?

In Chapter 3 we discussed how to apply security settings to users. In this chapter, we will discuss these security settings as they apply to file sharing. We'll explore the security differences between file sharing between Macs on a peer-to-peer network vs. a central file-sharing networked system, and we'll look at how to strengthen these file-sharing policies in a networked Mac environment using the native tools within Mac OS X and also with third-party software.

The Risks in File Sharing

Giving others access to files on your computer can be risky on many levels. First, you risk someone obtaining access to the system who shouldn't. For example, when a file is remotely deleted from your system, the file does not go to the trash, you do not get alerted of the deletion, and anyone who knows the right password typically has access to delete files. If the wrong folders on a system are shared, you can also give someone the ability to delete critical files, whether intentionally or not. For all of these reasons, you need to properly lock down the security of any file sharing you do on your systems.

■**Note** In Chapter 3, we discussed creating a limited Sharing Only account. This was added into Mac OS X Leopard for this very reason, and when creating accounts solely to give access to files, use this kind of account instead of any other.

Peer-to-Peer vs. Client-Server Environments

Before we discuss how to configure file-sharing permissions correctly, it's important to examine the differences between peer-to-peer and client-server file-sharing environments.

It is common in a networked Mac environment to have a handful of computers, each with file-sharing enabled, with users trading files back and forth between each other without a central repository for the files. This type of environment is known as *peer-to-peer networking* (P2P). Security in a P2P environment is generally straightforward and tends to be rather loose. Anyone with access to the computer usually has access to files on that machine.

As environments mature and grow larger, the distributed file sharing of P2P will give way to centralized file servers in what is typically described as a *client-server*, or *two-tier*, environment. Client-server environments offer a single and centralized location for users to access files that are needed by multiple users. In a client-server environment, backup and security begin to play a much more critical role because files are now accessible by multiple users who have access to that repository. File permissions are critical to maintaining security.

There are some inherent challenges to migrating from a P2P to a server-based file-sharing environment. Some users might have a hard time moving away from their old method of sharing files. The proper permission controls are often not set up correctly on the centralized data, if they are set up at all. Client machines might continue to share files after the transition simply because they weren't configured to not share them. This can lead to security issues that can be disastrous if not managed appropriately. Before we dive into how to properly secure file services, let's discuss some fundamentals of file security in Mac OS X.

Using POSIX Permissions

Mac OS X is a fully POSIX-compliant operating system. POSIX is a standardized feature set developed to make operating systems compatible with Unix-based operating systems. POSIX permission levels are divided into three categories: read (users can access the file), write (users can write data to it), and execute (users can run the file, such as an application). When viewing these permissions from the command-line application ls, read is indicated by an r, write is indicated by a w, and execute is indicated by an x. When you look at the permission designations for files, you'll see they are displayed in the order of owner, group, and (if needed) everyone. The owner is the user who owns a file, can set permissions on files, and is listed in the text following the permissions of a file. The group of a file is listed next. The everyone group is every user accessing a file who is not listed in either the owner or the group slot and who is also known as a *guest user* of that file.

■**Note** When looking at file permissions, you might find that an admin or wheel group is listed in a file's permissions. These are part of the built-in users and groups that a system starts out with upon installation of the operating system. We discuss these in more depth in Chapter 3.

The output of the permissions for a file will use the following syntax:

```
(permissions) (owner) (group) (everyone) (file size) (last modified)
```

The ls command followed by the -al option can show you the permissions, as indicated in the following example:

```
cedge:/Users cedge$ ls -al
```

```
total 16
drwxrwxrwx   8 root      admin       272 Dec 24 22:07 .
drwxrwxr-t  35 root      admin      1292 Apr 13 20:27 ..
-rwxrwxrwx   1 cedge     admin      6148 Oct 23 13:55 .DS_Store
-rwxrwxrwx   1 root      wheel         0 Jul  1  2006 .localized
drwxrwxrwx  16 318admin  318admin    544 May 26  2006 318admin
drwxrwxrwt  10 root      wheel       340 Oct 23 13:14 Shared
drwxrwxrwx  38 cedge     cedge      1292 Apr 13 15:40 cedge
drwxrwxrwx  12 postgres  postgres    408 Dec 24 22:22 postgres
```

■**Note** The permissions of these files are also discussed in Chapter 3.

■**Note** The d in front of the permissions in the previous example indicates that the item is a directory rather than a file.

Getting More Out of Permissions with Access Control Lists

Traditionally, Mac OS X has been limited to the standard POSIX permission model of read, write, and execute. This system has served UNIX-based operating systems well for many years now; however, it is starting to show its age. The main concern is that it isn't very flexible, and several special modes, such as the *sticky bit* (a setting that indicates that only the owner can delete a file from the respective folder), have been added over time.

For more complicated permission structures, access control lists (ACLs) provide you with the most granular control available over permissions for files and folders. An ACL is a list of permissions attached to files and folders. These replace POSIX permissions in the traditional sense of Mac OS X security. ACLs give the Mac an equal set of permissions that is found in Microsoft Windows. ACL information is stored in the extended attributes of the Mac OS Extended file system (HFS+).

It's easiest to understand the ACLs if we break down how they work and are applied. These are the three key system properties that allow ACLs to function:

- The generated unique identifier (GUID) a number value that is used many times in Mac OS X because it can be guaranteed to be unique across computer systems and, in fact, time and space. Your user account has both a traditional Unix-style UID and a new GUID.

- An access control entry (ACE) is the individual rule that determines what access is given to any particular user or group.

- An ACL is a list of ACEs that can be attached to a directory or file.

The following are the possible permissions that can be applied to files and folders with the new ACL model. This is a huge jump from the read-write-execute model we are used to on Mac OS X. Here are the permissions:

- Change Permissions
- Change Owner
- Read Attributes
- Read Extended Attributes
- List Folder Contents
- Traverse Folder
- Read Permissions
- Write Attributes
- Create Files
- Create Folder
- Delete
- Delete Subfolders and Files

■**Note** When defining ACLs, do it at a group level. Reserve user-level ACEs for special cases such as deny rules.

Sharing Protocols: Which One Is for You?

Computers can connect in various ways in order to talk to each other. The way in which computers communicate to each other is known as a *protocol*. When configuring global settings for a file-sharing environment, you must consider that computers connecting to each other will more than likely use different protocols to do so. For example, one protocol, Apple Filing Protocol (AFP), will typically be used when connecting two Macs, and an entirely different protocol, Samba (SMB), will be used to connect a Windows-based machine to a Mac. However, one fact remains constant among these protocols: permissions must be set when accessing resources from one computer to another.

■**Note** For more information on changing permissions from the command line, see Chapter 3.

Apple Filing Protocol

AFP is a presentation-layer network protocol that is the primary protocol for providing file services for Mac computers. AFP is rarely used outside the Mac platform, so little security attention has been paid to it as a protocol. However, you should take certain steps to ensure the security of the files and data on your computer.

To configure AFP sharing, you must first enable AFP on the computer. To enable AFP in OS X, open your System Preferences, and click the Sharing preference pane (see Figure 10-1). Select the File Sharing check box. The File Sharing indicator button will turn green.

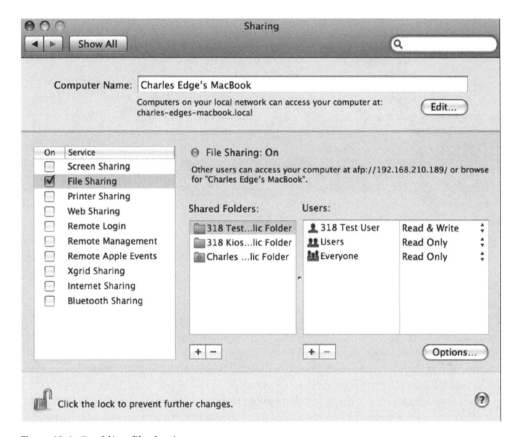

Figure 10-1. *Enabling file sharing*

■Note Configuring AFP is different and much more feature-rich in Mac OS X Server than in the Mac OS X client. For more information on this portion of AFP configuration, please see Chapter 13.

Now that you've enabled file sharing, you will want to limit access to files and folders. To do so, review the shared folders in the Shared Folders list. Here you can stop sharing any folders that should not be shared by clicking the minus (–) button in order to unshare them. Once you have verified that everything in the list should be there, you can now create new shared folders. To do so, click the plus (+) button, which will open a window that allows you to browse your folders (see Figure 10-2). In this window, find the folder you want to share, and click the Add button.

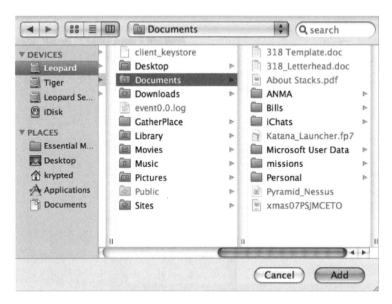

Figure 10-2. *Browsing to a folder*

Once you have shared a folder, you can then move on to setting permissions, which is how you control who accesses the files and folders in the shared directory. To do so, first review the list of users and groups (for more information on configuring users and groups, see Chapter 3) in the Users list. Click any of the users and groups that should not have access to the data in the Shared Folders list, and click the – button (while those users or groups are highlighted) to deny access. After you have removed users who should not have access to the folder, click the + button to add users who should have access. At this point, you will see a window similar to Figure 10-3. Any users who already have access to the directory will be disabled. Find the users you want to grant access to, select them, and click the Select button to add them to the Users list.

When adding users to this list, you will be asked to enter a password (see Figure 10-4). The reason that you are prompted for a password is that the respective user's password file must be modified to allow for an older style of password, which is used by the Samba Windows file sharing engine. Apple does not enable the storage of these weak passwords by default because dictionary attacking these older LAN Manager (LM MD4) passwords has been refined to a simple science. Be aware that you are decreasing the overall security of your system by using this service. Any attacker who has gained root access to your system could view this weak password "hash" in your password file and potentially recover your login password. This might seem counterintuitive to worry about security concerns for someone with root access, but remember that even the root account cannot view a user's encrypted keychain file without knowing that user's password. Therefore, in this instance, if an attacker has gained complete control of the system, they could be able to decrypt files that are based on the user's login password, such as keychains or file vaulted home folders.

Figure 10-3. *Defining an SMB/Windows user*

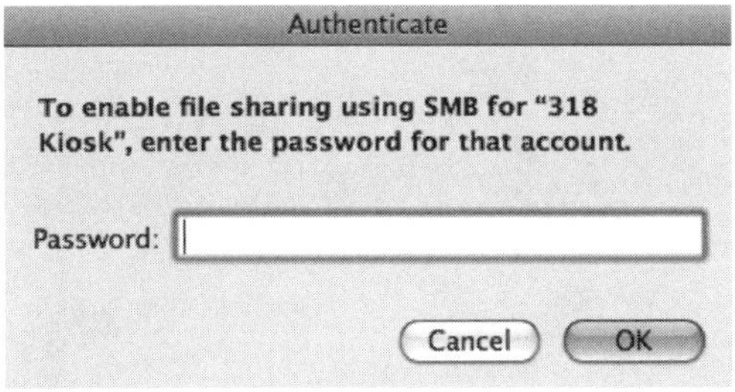

Figure 10-4. *Providing the password for a Windows user*

Once you are satisfied that your files and folders have an appropriate level of permissions assigned to them, it's time to turn to other protocols that computers will be using to access resources on your Mac. First on the list is the Samba protocol.

Samba

Samba is the default file sharing protocol for Windows computers. Samba must be enabled and configured on your Mac in order for Windows computers to be able to access the files natively.

To enable Samba sharing on a Mac, open the Sharing preference pane of System Preferences (like you did for sharing via AFP), and click File Sharing. From here, check the Share Files and Folders Using SMB box (see Figure 10-5). This will enable sharing but not allow any users to connect. To choose the users who are able to connect, you will need to select the On box for each user who should be able to connect.

Once you have enabled a Windows user, then you will be able to connect to the system using SMB. To test this from a Mac, click the Go menu from the Finder, and select the Connect to a Server option. In the Connect to Server window (as shown in Figure 10-6), type **smb://** followed by the IP address of the computer to which you are connecting. When you click Connect, you will be asked to enter the password and will be given a list of share points that have access through SMB. Make sure the user you are logged in as has access only to the locations that you want the user to be able to access.

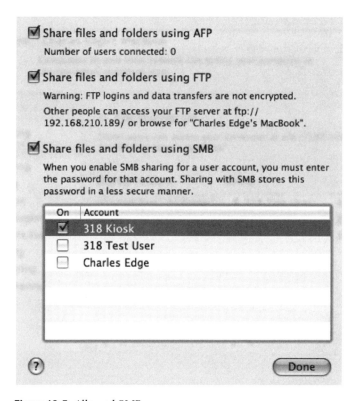

Figure 10-5. *Allowed SMB users*

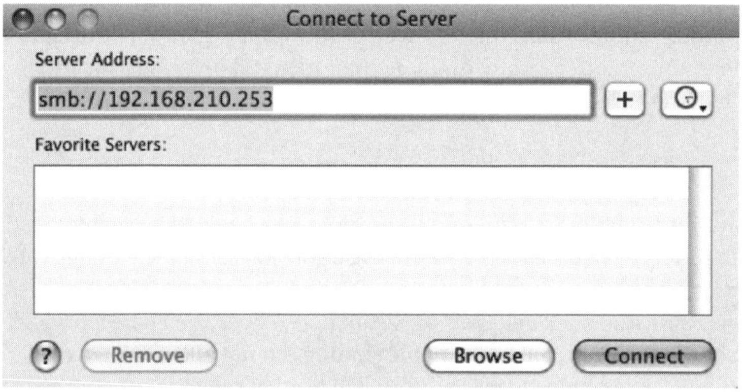

Figure 10-6. *Connecting to an SMB share point*

The SMB.conf File

The Windows file-sharing feature of a Mac OS X computer is provided by the open source Samba framework. Samba provides file-sharing services for a variety of platforms including Linux, Unix, and Mac OS X. The following is the basic/default smb.conf file for the Windows service:

```
Apress-MacBook-cedge:/private/etc cedge$ cat smb.conf
 [global]
  guest account = unknown
  encrypt passwords = yes
  auth methods = guest opendirectory
  passdb backend = opendirectorysam guest
  printer admin = @admin, @staff
  server string = 318 Administrator?s iBook G4
  unix charset = UTF-8-MAC
  display charset = UTF-8-MAC
  dos charset = 437
  client ntlmv2 auth = no
  os level = 8
  defer sharing violations = no
  vfs objects = darwin_acls
  brlm = yes
  workgroup = Workgroup
; Using the Computer Name to compute the NetBIOS name.
netbios name = 318-Administrat
    use spnego = yes
[homes]
    comment = User Home Directories
    browseable = no
    read only = no

;[public]
;    path = /tmp
;    public = yes
;    only guest = yes
;    writable = yes
;    printable = no

[printers]
  path = /tmp
  printable = yes
```

Review each section of the previous file. Make sure that any file shares (denoted as being between two [ ] symbols) have been planned and that the permissions are appropriate. Try to always disable guest access by changing the public variable to no. Try to always set the read only variable to yes, thus making many shares read-only. Also try to not make shares browseable unless otherwise required. In some instances, these settings may be too general, but if not, use these settings because they will give you a maximum level of security on these files.

Using Apple AirPort to Share Files

The File Sharing feature of Mac OS X provides the most granular approach to a workgroup-oriented file-sharing scenario that you can get without upgrading to Mac OS X Server. There will be instances, however, when users may want to configure the File Sharing feature to run off an AirPort base station. The Apple AirPort N (the square one) has the capacity to share files using a portable hard drive connected over USB to the AirPort device. To share files using the Apple AirPort, plug an external hard drive into the AirPort, and open the AirPort Utility in the /Applications/Utilities folder.

From here, you will see a window similar to that shown in Figure 10-7. This window will list the disks attached to your AirPort along with their names and capacities. It will also list the users attached to the AirPort and allow you to disconnect any users you would prefer to not use the disk.

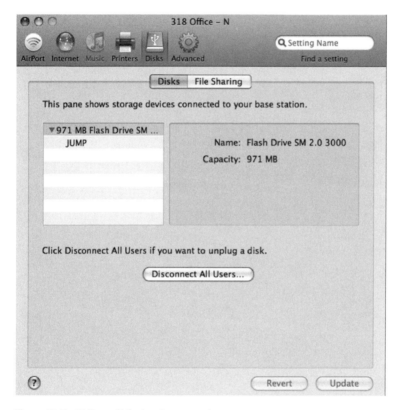

Figure 10-7. *AirPort disk sharing overview*

Once you have verified that the disks you want to use are plugged into the AirPort N, then you will need to enable file sharing on the AirPort. To do so, click the Disks toolbar icon in the AirPort Utility. Then click the File Sharing tab, and select the Enable File Sharing box. You can now configure the permissions for the disks you need to edit. The most secure setting to use for the Secure Shared Disks option is With Accounts, which allows you to create accounts for use with the disks attached to the AirPort. For security purposes, the Guest Access field should always be set to Not Allowed unless you absolutely need to allow guests to access the data.

In most cases, you can disable the Advertise Disks Globally Using Bonjour setting (as shown in Figure 10-8). Enabling this setting allows systems to automatically discover the storage and start using it. However, in a networked environment, the number of users with access to the drive should be limited and not using Bonjour to discover the drive. Having said this, this is one of those rare instances where ease of use can trump security, based on your preference. Although it may not be a good idea to easily make the drive accessible, organizations will enable this feature anyway to allow machines to easily access the drive.

■**Note** It is common to refer to the feature of a wireless access point, such as an Apple AirPort, that provides simple disk sharing as *network-attached storage* (NAS).

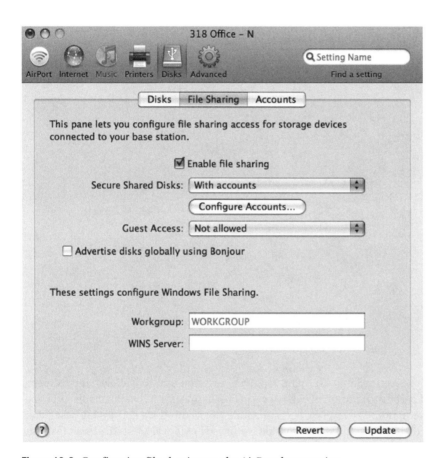

Figure 10-8. *Configuring file sharing on the AirPort base station*

Once you have set your base station to use accounts for shared storage, you can also configure the Workgroup setting, which allows the Windows systems on your network to browse the AirPort and access the shared media. The WINS Server option allows you to assign a WINS server that can be run on OS X Server, Windows NT Server, Windows 2000 Server, Windows 2003 Server, Samba on Unix or Linux, and Windows 2008 Server. These settings have little bearing on the security of your sharing structure if you are not using Windows in your environment. In other words, if there are no Windows machines in the environment, do not enable them.

Once you have configured the sharing settings for the AirPort, click Accounts to set up the users who can access the data on the disks attached to your AirPort base station. In the Accounts window, click the + icon to add accounts that can access the drive (see Figure 10-9).

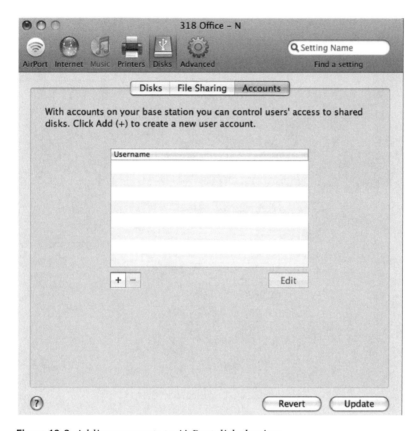

Figure 10-9. *Adding accounts to AirPort disk sharing*

This opens the Account Setup Assistant. The Account Setup Assistant allows you to enter a simple name and password, along with what level of access the user has to the media attached to the AirPort base station. The levels of access include Not Allowed, Read Only, and Read and Write (see Figure 10-10). These are similar to what is allowed in Mac OS X but with fewer features.

■**Caution** With these accounts, there is little protection: the usernames and passwords do not benefit from policies, the users and passwords are not shared between various systems, and there is no adaptive firewall as with OS X or OS X Server to protect the device whatsoever.

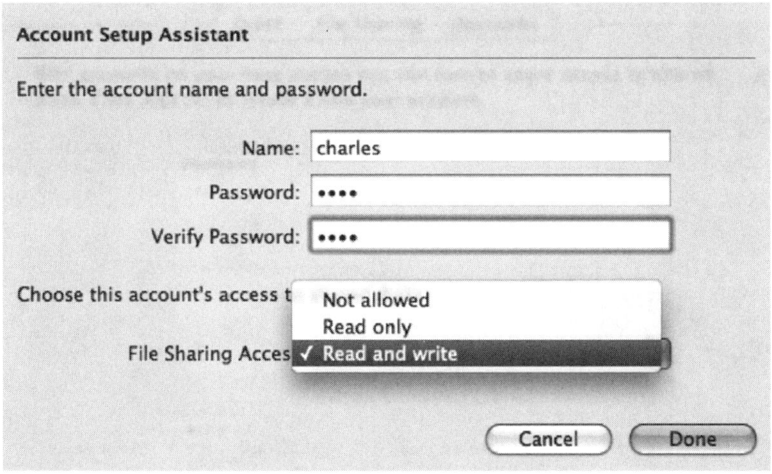

Figure 10-10. *AirPort disk sharing Account Setup Assistant*

DAVE

The default capabilities of Samba in OS X are often not enough, such as when you need to use SMB signing to communicate with Windows servers. From time to time, file and application incompatibilities will arise that cannot be solved by enabling the Samba protocol. Thursby Software (http://www.thursby.com) sells a software product called DAVE that enables file and printer sharing compatibility between Windows and Mac operating systems.

To get started with DAVE, you can purchase and download the installer from the Thursby web site. Install the software using the default configuration.

■**Note** Before installing DAVE, disable Samba on the Sharing preference pane in System Preferences. DAVE cannot be installed if Samba is currently enabled.

Once installed, DAVE will open the DAVE Setup Assistant. Click Continue on the first screen. DAVE will set up the network interface's configuration, and you will be asked to enter license information when it is complete. Enter the license codes (see Figure 10-11), and click Continue.

Next, DAVE will ask whether you have a Windows server in your environment (see Figure 10-12). If you are going to be using DAVE to communicate with an Active Directory controller, then you will need to check the Use Windows Server box on this screen and click Continue. Otherwise, leave this box unchecked and click Continue.

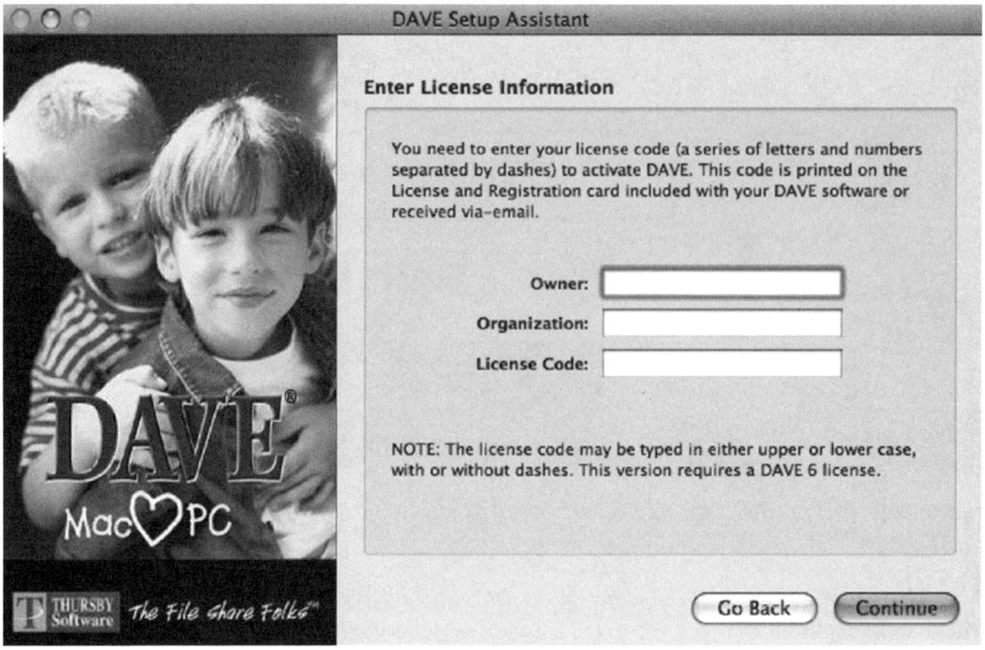

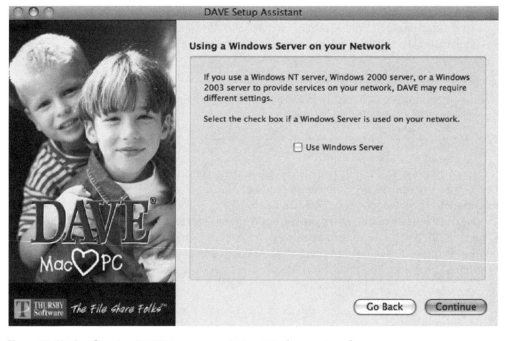

Figure 10-11. *Entering the license codes*

Figure 10-12. *Configuring DAVE to use an existing Windows network*

Next you will enter your computer name (see Figure 10-13). This is the name that will be broadcast to other Windows systems when they browse to see your computer on the network. It should be a unique name that no other computer on the network shares. This is also known in Microsoft networking as the *NetBIOS name*.

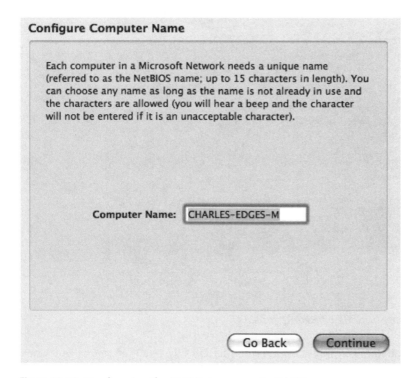

Figure 10-13. *Configuring the SMB Setup name in DAVE*

Once you have named your system, the wizard will prompt you for the workgroup to join (see Figure 10-14). This setting is used to connect multiple Windows systems in a group (much like AppleTalk zones from the OS 9 days). Enter the workgroup name, or select the name from the drop-down list of existing workgroups.

On the next screen, enter a friendly description of the computer (this setting has little ramification on the network or on network security). Once you have entered a brief description of the computer, click the Continue button. This will trigger the CIFS daemon of DAVE to be restarted, prompting you to enter an administrative username and password. Once the CIFS daemon and the Directory Services daemon are restarted, click Continue.

On the next screen, you will be prompted for whether you will be using DAVE to share data through Samba, which will allow you to share data using Samba to other systems on the network. Dave cannot coexist with the built-in Samba file-sharing feature, so make sure to disable it. If you will be sharing data to other Windows computers, use the Set Up DAVE Sharing option, and click the Continue button. Click Quit, which will finish the installation.

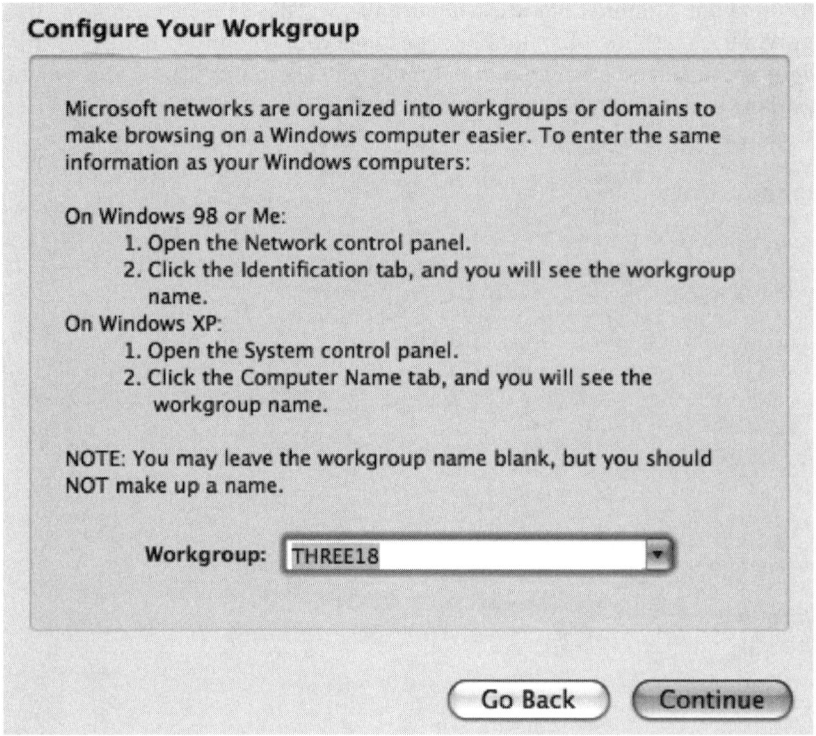

Configure Your Workgroup

Microsoft networks are organized into workgroups or domains to make browsing on a Windows computer easier. To enter the same information as your Windows computers:

On Windows 98 or Me:
1. Open the Network control panel.
2. Click the Identification tab, and you will see the workgroup name.
On Windows XP:
1. Open the System control panel.
2. Click the Computer Name tab, and you will see the workgroup name.

NOTE: You may leave the workgroup name blank, but you should NOT make up a name.

Workgroup: THREE18

Go Back   Continue

Figure 10-14. *Configuring the SMB workgroup for DAVE*

Now that the installation is complete, open your Mac OS X System Preferences, and you will notice three new preference panes. They are DAVE Login, DAVE Network, and DAVE Sharing. If you click the DAVE Login preference pane, then you will be able to configure your system to log into a Microsoft domain environment. The Log In button allows you to join a domain provided you have the credentials for an account with the appropriate levels of access. The Change Password button (see Figure 10-15) allows you to change your password for the domain you have joined. The Change Password feature is not one that is native to Mac OS X for Windows-based domains and thus enables a greater level of account-based security to be applied for user accounts.

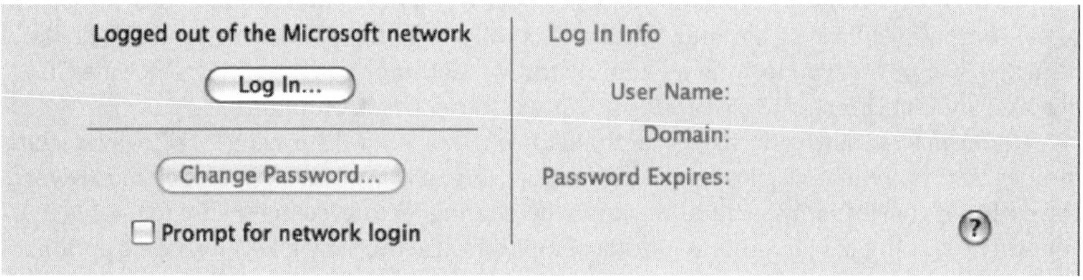

Logged out of the Microsoft network   Log In Info

Log In...   User Name:

                                                  Domain:
Change Password...   Password Expires:

☐ Prompt for network login   ⑦

Figure 10-15. *Logging into a Windows network with DAVE*

If you click the DAVE Network preference pane, then you will be able to configure how your system is perceived by Windows and Samba systems in the domain environment. This includes the computer name, which is how other Windows systems see your computer (using NetBIOS); the description, which is a simple text field; and the workgroup. The workgroup setting (see Figure 10-16) is meant to allow systems of a like type to see each other. Although Windows computers can see the systems in their workgroup, they can also see systems in other workgroups, and therefore this feature will not hide your system completely from Windows computers.

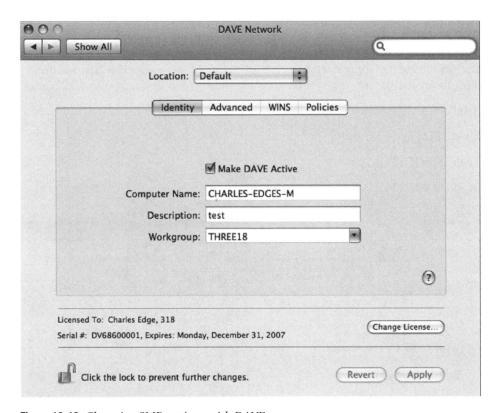

Figure 10-16. *Changing SMB settings with DAVE*

By clicking the Policies tab of the DAVE Network preference pane, you will be able to configure signing and the acceptable authentication levels for the Samba sharing. A *man-in-the-middle* attack is when an attacker is able to read or modify communications between two parties. Digital signing for SMB, or *SMB signing*, allows you to protect against man-in-the-middle attacks by placing a digital signature in each packet. If the packet is then intercepted in transit, the digital signature will be altered, and the parties will drop the connection. SMB signing is one of the best ways to protect SMB traffic. Many corporate security policies require SMB signing for communications over SMB to their file servers, a default option for Windows domain controllers. Therefore, this is a much-needed option for those in corporate environments that have SMB signing requirements.

SMB communications primarily occur over LANMAN, NTLMv1, and NTLMv2. LANMAN used a weak (by modern standards) authentication protocol known as LM Hash. NTLMv1 was a great step forward and represented the introduction of a challenge-response protocol. The server authenticates the client by sending a random number, known as the *challenge*. The client then uses the challenge and a password, or *ticket*, known by both the client and the server. The client identity then is configured using the result of combining the two. The server verifies that the client has calculated the correct result and verifies the identity of the client. NTLMv2 is also a challenge-response protocol, but with more steps involved to enhance the security of the challenge-response process. Of these, NTLMv2 is by far the most secure; however, it has been replaced in many situations by Kerberos.

If Kerberos is available, then the DAVE client will always use it. The Policies box of the DAVE Network preference pane (shown in Figure 10-17) allows you to set the minimum acceptable security level. The LAN Manager Authentication Level setting should be set to the highest possible, eliminating all other protocols from the options available to DAVE for authentication. If you are in an environment that supports NTLMv2, then you should be using NTLMv2 response only. Otherwise, the order of security for these options, from most secure to least secure, is as follows:

- Send NTLMv2 Response Only

- Send NTLM Response Only

- Send LM & NTLM Responses

- Send LM & NTLM

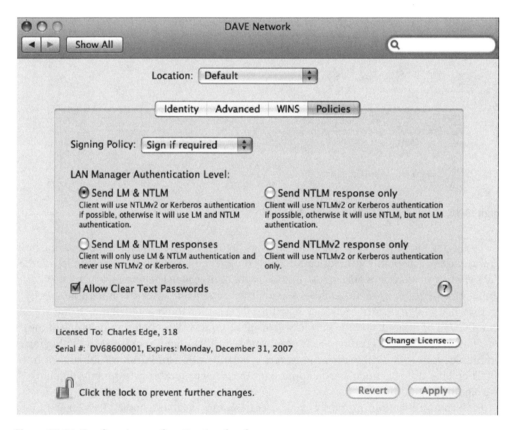

Figure 10-17. *Configuring authentication levels*

DAVE is a great tool to allow the Mac to thrive in a more corporate Microsoft-based environment. There are also some nice file-sharing features in DAVE, which make it a must in testing if you are performing file sharing in a Windows-based environment. If the features make it worth obtaining a third-party package, then look into volume licensing it.

FTP

FTP is a very old protocol, much older than SMB and AFP. FTP is most commonly used to transfer files over the Internet. However, FTP does not encrypt data and should not be used as a sharing protocol unless absolutely required (and if you think it's absolutely required, we urge you to continue to research other means because there usually is a better way). To enable FTP, click the Sharing preference pane, and click the Options button. Select the Share Files and Folders Using FTP box (see Figure 10-18).

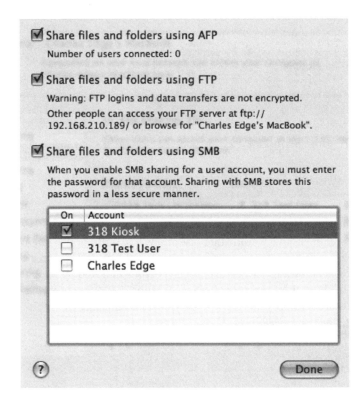

Figure 10-18. *Enabling FTP sharing*

Once you have enabled FTP sharing, you can connect to the FTP share by clicking Go and then Connect to Server in the Finder. From here, you can enter **ftp://***ipaddress* in the Server Address field (as shown in Figure 10-19). Once you have entered the address, click Connect.

Attempting to edit data that has been accessed via FTP will result in an error similar to that shown in Figure 10-20. When folders are accessed by FTP using the Finder, the files are mounted as read-only to your user account and cannot be modified.

Connect to Server
Server Address:
ftp://192.168.210.253
Favorite Servers:
Remove
Browse
Connect

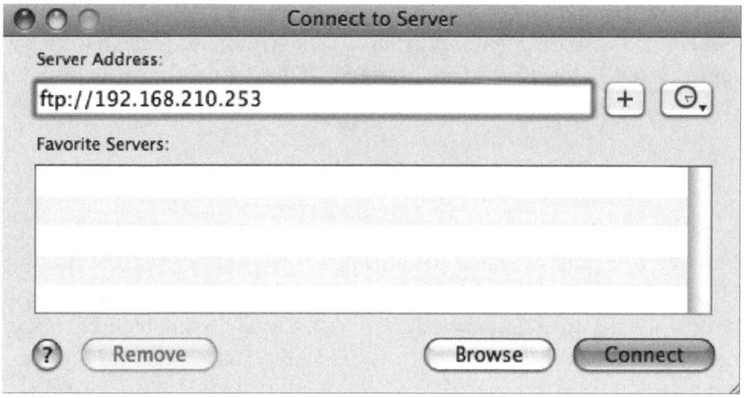

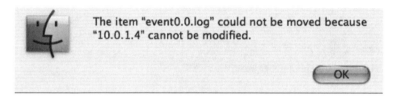

Figure 10-19. *Connecting over FTP*

The item "event0.0.log" could not be moved because "10.0.1.4" cannot be modified.
OK

Figure 10-20. *Trying to write to FTP through the Finder*

If you need to write to this folder, then you will want to connect to it using an FTP client such as Fetch or Transmit.

FTP security is a bit thin. FTP bounce attacks allow users to establish a connection between FTP servers and an arbitrary port on another system while connected to the server. This connection can then be used to bypass access controls that would otherwise apply. FTP traffic is also unencrypted, which can lead to the exposure of passwords. There is also a mode for FTP known as PASV, which allows FTP to work with firewalls. PASV sessions can become hijacked by other users using a PASV theft attack. In short, there are a lot of other solutions to FTP, such as web-based browsing through Rumpus or WebDAV that can be used. Consider replacing FTP with one of them in order to eliminate the use of FTP in your environment.

Permission Models

In larger environments, system administrators have been grappling with various methods to handle file permissions for years. Over the years, the Mac administrative community has developed a few different methodologies as standard practices for managing permissions. In this section, we'll touch on these permissions models to give you a better understanding about the ways that file sharing permissions policies can be implemented on Mac networks.

Discretionary access control (DAC) allows data owners to administer file permissions themselves. In a DAC model, administrators often spend less time assigning permissions (which often means spending more time restoring accidentally deleted files). Discretionary access control systems permit users to entirely determine the access granted to their resources, which means they can (through accident or malice) give access to unauthorized users. The owner of any resource has access to control the privileges to that resource. There are often no security checks ensuring malicious code is not distributed or that the owner of a file or folder is well trained enough to be assigning permissions in the first place. This is the default model and, unfortunately, the most common model for controlling permissions. However, in addition to time spent on restoring deleted files, DAC is also limited in that security breaches can be caused when users who do not understand the appropriate access levels for files within their organization assign permissions that cause security breaches.

Mandatory access control (MAC) is a model that can augment or even replace DAC for file permissions. MAC's most important feature involves denying users full control over the access to resources that they create. The system security policy (as set by the administrator) entirely determines the access rights granted, and a user cannot grant less restrictive access to their resources than the administrator specifies.

MAC has the goal of defining an architecture that requires the evaluation of all security-related information and making decisions based on what is done with data and the various data types in use in your organization. MAC is a strict hierarchical model usually associated with governments. All objects are given security labels known as *sensitivity labels* and are classified accordingly. All users are then given specific security clearances as to what they are allowed to access. A common term when working with MAC is *lattice*, which describes the upper and lower bounds of a user's access permission. In other words, a user's access differs at different levels.

Role-based access control (RBAC) involves limiting access to files based on the responsibilities of a user. When using a role-based security model for access controls, each role in an organization is created for various job functions. The permissions to perform certain operations are assigned to specific roles. Users are then assigned particular roles, and through those role assignments they acquire the permissions to perform particular system functions. Role-based access requires that an organization review the various positions and build access levels for resources based on those roles.

As an organization looks to scale, it should define roles based on potential future hires. As organizations grow, they are more likely to build out new organizational charts that contain current and future positions within the organization. This often represents a good building block for developing roles, which become users or groups in the directory structure. Security groups can then be used within any document management system or enterprise resource planning (ERP) solution that an organization might decide to deploy. This is the most common permissions model being used today because it accommodates growth within an organization while being careful to limit permissions definitively.

CHAPTER 11

■■■

Web Site Security

Down in the trenches, we hear it all the time: "My web site is hosted on a Mac. How could it be hacked?" or "My web site is too small. Why would anyone want to hack it?" This is a very common misconception in the Mac world. And hackers know this. Hackers have more than one reason to break into a web site. They are not just hacking sites to gather information. Although it's true that infiltrating and grabbing personal or business information from your web server might be significant, they are often looking to do more than that. Hackers want to exploit and control the largest amount of servers in the shortest amount of time, creating zombie systems to do their bidding.

An obscure niche web site is not safe just because it isn't a household name like Amazon.com or PayPal.com. In the past few years, we've seen time and time again that although obscurity may seem like a safe haven, in today's modern security landscape it's not enough to fall off a hacker's radar. Thus, this chapter is devoted to exploring the ways in which you can further secure your Mac OS X web server from intruders. First we'll discuss how to set up web services on a Mac.

Securing Your Web Server

Enabling Web Sharing on a Mac is as simple as clicking a few buttons. However, making it secure is another story altogether.

To enable the Apache 2.2 web server, the default web server in OS X Leopard, open System Preferences, and click the Sharing preference pane. Then, select the Web Sharing box (see Figure 11-1). That's it. You've just configured web services in OS X. But what exactly is the web server in OS X?

The Apache web server in Mac OS X Server is a powerful Unix and Linux web server capable of running on anything from a small web appliance to massive mainframes built in clusters. Apache is the most widely distributed web server running on the Internet and is used for small and big sites alike, from small web sites run out of people's homes to large corporate sites with hundreds of servers that process web requests from thousands of users every second.

Web Sharing allows Mac OS X users to host web sites on their computers. As you can see, it's fairly easy and enabled right there in the Sharing preference pane. However, using the options available in the Sharing preference pane does not allow administrators to properly secure the web server. To do this, you need to dig deeper. Let's examine how you accomplish this.

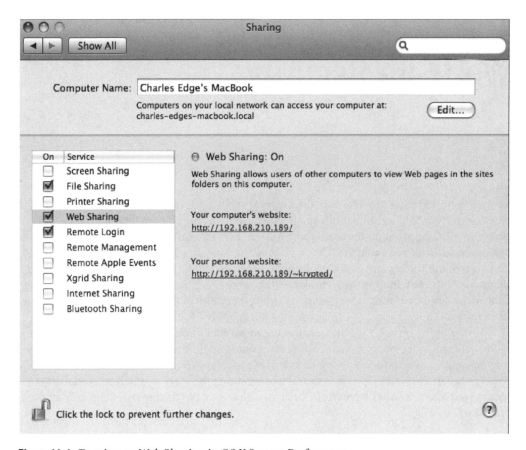

Figure 11-1. *Turning on Web Sharing in OS X System Preferences*

Introducing the httpd Daemon

Once the web services are turned on, if you open your Activity Monitor, and look for the httpd service (short for *HTTP daemon*), you will not find it there. Why is that? As you can see in Figure 11-2, the web httpd runs as the root user, giving it a high level of access. It is possible to modify the start-up scripts for httpd and have it run as a dedicated Apache user. This can help to mitigate the risk of further damage being done if someone were to exploit the web server.

Note In Leopard, it is also possible to use Sandbox to reduce the risks of an exploited httpd daemon.

■**Note** The `httpd` daemon listens for web traffic over port 80 (by default) and processes those requests using the Hypertext Transport Protocol (HTTP).

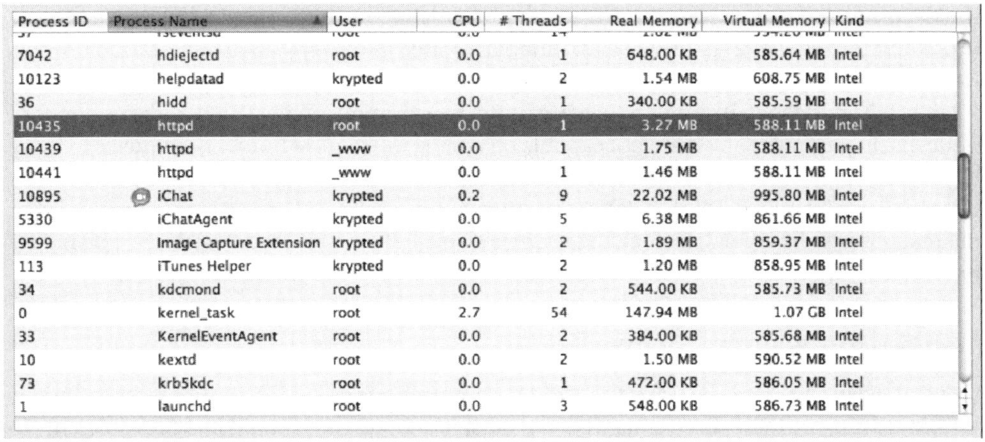

Process ID	Process Name	User	CPU	# Threads	Real Memory	Virtual Memory	Kind
37	rseventsd	root	0.0	14	1.02 MB	554.20 MB	Intel
7042	hdiejectd	root	0.0	1	648.00 KB	585.64 MB	Intel
10123	helpdatad	krypted	0.0	2	1.54 MB	608.75 MB	Intel
36	hidd	root	0.0	1	340.00 KB	585.59 MB	Intel
10435	httpd	root	0.0	1	3.27 MB	588.11 MB	Intel
10439	httpd	_www	0.0	1	1.75 MB	588.11 MB	Intel
10441	httpd	_www	0.0	1	1.46 MB	588.11 MB	Intel
10895	iChat	krypted	0.2	9	22.02 MB	995.80 MB	Intel
5330	iChatAgent	krypted	0.0	5	6.38 MB	861.66 MB	Intel
9599	Image Capture Extension	krypted	0.0	2	1.89 MB	859.37 MB	Intel
113	iTunes Helper	krypted	0.0	2	1.20 MB	858.95 MB	Intel
34	kdcmond	root	0.0	2	544.00 KB	585.73 MB	Intel
0	kernel_task	root	2.7	54	147.94 MB	1.07 GB	Intel
33	KernelEventAgent	root	0.0	2	384.00 KB	585.68 MB	Intel
10	kextd	root	0.0	2	1.50 MB	590.52 MB	Intel
73	krb5kdc	root	0.0	1	472.00 KB	586.05 MB	Intel
1	launchd	root	0.0	3	548.00 KB	586.73 MB	Intel

Figure 11-2. *The* httpd *process in Activity Monitor*

Removing the Default Files

One of the first steps you should take to secure the Mac OS X web server is to remove the default web site files. The files are stored in the `/Library/WebServer/Documents` folder and have no other purpose except as a test site to determine whether the web server is working properly. Leaving the default files in place will eventually get your test web site "crawled" by a search engine such as Google. The test web site documents display machine-specific information such as the version of Apache and the version of OS X that is running on your web server. Once the crawling occurs, this information will be made public. A fingerprint of your server would then give unsavory characters the ability to know which exploits would be able to run as an attack against your web server.

Changing the Location of Logs

Changing the location of where logs are written can give a hacker one less place to look for pertinent information about your web site. Writing logs to a separate location can also help centralize them, which comes in handy when needing to quickly troubleshoot hack attempts. It can also take some of the headache out of developing web scripts that grab information from these logs, such as the number of visitors to the site. These logs can be written to a local server or to a different destination entirely. The default location of your logs is `/private/var/log/apache2/access_log`. To change this, open the `httpd.conf` file from `/private/etc/apache2/`, scroll down to the `CustomLog` variable, and change the path using the fully qualified path of the file to which you want to write your logs.

Managing httpd

You can manage httpd in a few ways.

Using ModSecurity

ModSecurity 2 is an open source intrusion detection and prevention engine for web applications, but ModSecurity 2 can be used for other tasks such as running an Apache-based firewall. Web servers are typically well equipped to log traffic in a form useful for marketing analyses, but they fall short when it comes to logging traffic to web applications (such as the contents of requests). In particular, most are not capable of logging the request bodies or requests to those applications.

ModSecurity makes full HTTP transaction logging possible, allowing complete requests and responses to be logged. Its logging facilities also allow fine-grained decisions to be made about exactly what is logged and when, ensuring that only relevant data is recorded.

Restricting Apache Access

As discussed in Chapter 8, by using the Mac OS X firewall, it is possible to limit access to various ports in OS X using the ipfw command. If you host a web site that should be accessible only to computers on the internal network, you need to configure your firewall to restrict access to the web server, allowing only internal traffic to access it. You can also give access to computers outside of your network by adding new firewall rules to the system.

You can extend access restrictions in order to enforce restrictions on possible internal rogue access points as well. A *rogue access point* is a misconfigured device on the network that is acting as a wireless router. Many rogue access points are unknown to staff administrators and can be used to extend a localized form of access into your network from external hosts. An example of an access restriction policy might be to configure your router or firewall to allow only those systems on the corporate LAN to access a certain destination address on your web server. You can find more information about this in Chapter 7.

■**Note** If you restrict access to your internal site based on IP addressing, make sure that as new IP schemes are added to your network environment, these changes are accounted for in later revisions of your ipfw tables.

Running on a Nonstandard Port

There are a variety of protected ports in Mac OS X. These ports require any application that attempts to run and listen over them to run as the root user. This is a security feature used to control access to commonly exploitable ports. However, there is one service that cannot be configured this way, and that is your web server. Because of its very nature, any level of user can spawn a process that accesses the web server through its default port, which is port 80.

A great way to get around this is to run Apache over a port other than port 80. If your web site is Internet facing, then you can redirect incoming port 80 to a different system on your network. This is not entirely foolproof, however, because some visitors who have outgoing traffic limited by their own firewalls may have trouble getting to your web site if it runs over a different port. This is something that is becoming more and more common as larger corporate environments are tightening their own web security.

To customize the port on which the web server runs, open the `httpd.conf` file from the `/private/etc/apache2/` folder. From here, scroll down until you see the `Listen` variable. Edit the number for the listener to reflect the port you want the web server to run on, and save the information. When you restart the web server (or the computer), it will be running on the new port.

■**Note** If you are using a Mac as a dedicated web server, you should disable any ports that are not being used. Port 80 (unless it has been redirected) and port 443 are the two ports you'll need open for web access. See Chapter 8 (for OS X Client) or Chapter 13 (for OS X Server) for more details about disabling ports.

Use a Proxy Server

Web servers do not have to run on the frontline right behind your firewall. It is possible to use the IP address of another server to masquerade as your web server, filtering out unwanted visitors and then relaying the important information it needs to process back and forth to the Internet.

Using CGI

Directives also allow administrators to disable the Common Gateway Interface (CGI) and server-side includes. CGI is typically used as a server-side program or script that can process data entered in a form on a web site. Server-side includes are used for including dynamic information in documents sent to clients, such as the current date, the last modification date of the file, and the size or last modification of other files. As with other options within Apache, these should be enabled only if required. To disable them, use `-Includes` or `-ExecCGI` in your options line. These options can be used on a per-directory basis using Apache directives in the `httpd.conf` file.

Web designers will often place CGI files in locations that are not secure or attempt to assign them rights that are insecure and give wrong permissions to users who access these files and scripts. Restricting the location of the CGI executable allows administrators to keep all CGI scripts in a central location to ensure proper security for these scripts. This also limits the damage that can be done by scripts that may be uploaded to a web directory and executed by someone with improper permissions.

Many administrators are already familiar with using a dedicated directory for running CGI scripts or includes. The industry standard is to use the `CGI-BIN` directory on web servers. In Mac OS X, this folder is called the `CGI-Executables` directory by default. To maintain standards, you will notice the following line in the `httpd.conf` file:

```
ScriptAlias /cgi-bin/ "/Library/WebServer/CGI-Executables/"
```

This line allows references to directories called `cgi-bin` to point to the `CGI-Executables` directory. The default permissions on this directory allow only the everyone group to execute the contents of the directory. By using `ls -al` on this directory, you can see the appropriate permissions for files Apple already has there.

Disabling Unnecessary Services in Apache

The immense popularity of Apache is due in part to the large number of modules that have been developed for it. However, when used improperly, these modules can represent a security risk. To reduce the risk associated with running a web server, all modules not required should be disabled by placing a # in front of the LoadModule section of the line.

To learn which modules are required, look to the manual pages at Apache.org to get a better idea of what they are, or simply disable them one by one to see which modules will break the site if disabled. The modules that load in your httpd.conf file include any that begin with LoadModule and do not have a # in front of the line.

One example of a module that can be easily disabled without impacting the performance of the web server is bonjour_module, a module used to allow your web server to be discovered through Bonjour. Because most users will be visiting your site using a browser, it is not important for the server to work with Bonjour. To disable bonjour_module, place # at the beginning of the LoadModule so the full line reads as follows:

```
#LoadModule bonjour_module    libexec/apache2/mod_bonjour.so
```

Now restart the web server, and the bonjour_module will no longer be running.

■**Note** Mac OS X runs Apache 2.2. You can review any module on the Apache vulnerabilities site at http:// httpd.apache.org/security/vulnerabilities_22.html to review whether it is safe to run.

PHP and Security

PHP Hypertext Preprocessor (PHP) is a programming language that allows web developers to create dynamic content that interacts with databases. PHP is most often used for developing web-based software applications. Not all web sites use or need PHP. For web servers with sites that do not need PHP, you can leave the module disabled. But if you need to enable it because you are developing PHP code for the site, then you can do so by removing the commenting from the line in the httpd.conf file that loads the PHP module. You can do this by finding the following line and removing the # in front of it:

```
#LoadModule php5_module       libexec/httpd/libphp5.so
```

to look like the following:

```
LoadModule php5_module        libexec/httpd/libphp5.so
```

■**Note** Perl, a scripting language discussed later in the chapter, can be disabled in the same manner:

```
LoadModule perl_module        libexec/httpd/libperl.so
```

Securing PHP

If PHP is required to make your web site function, there are ways in which it can be further secured. For this, you should know every setting of the PHP configuration file if you choose to enable PHP. The file is located at /private/etc/php.ini. The php.ini file is like the httpd.conf file but for PHP.

■**Note** The following sections are designed for those familiar with the inner workings of PHP.

---

register_globals, an option in PHP for pre-Leopard systems, is the most insecure part of PHP, and many security auditors inform system administrators to turn this option off when following PHP security best practices. The PHP directive register_globals was disabled by default in PHP 4.2.0 but can still be enabled if necessary. Relying on this directive was quite common, and many administrators had no idea that it even existed or, if they did, assumed it was at the core of how PHP works. When enabled, register_globals will inject your scripts with all sorts of variables, such as request variables from HTML forms. This, coupled with the fact that PHP doesn't require variable initialization, means that the PHP code that is written will be much less secure.

■**Note** You should also be careful to review how you use cgi-redirect and other features of PHP. For a full review of PHP security, refer to *Pro PHP Security* by Chris Snyder and Michael Southwell (Apress, 2005).

Tightening PHP with Input Validation

Form data can be an entryway into a web site's inner workings. Any information can be entered into a form, and remote code could be executed through the forms (provided you have not disabled the ability to execute any code that is sourced from outside the system), allowing a potential hacker to infiltrate your machine through the form on your web site. The following code will remove all data from a variable except letters and numbers using regular expressions in PHP. This is a good way to eliminate the possibility of arbitrary data being entered into a form.

```
<?php
$string = "This is some text and numbers 12345 and symbols !£$%^&";
$new_string = ereg_replace("[^A-Za-z0-9]", "", $string);
echo $new_string
?>
```

Allowing users to input file names should be done only on secured pages such as those using an .htaccess file or realm for security, discussed later in this chapter. Allowing users to create file names can be dangerous and should be allowed only under highly restricted circumstances because it opens your site up to injection attacks, such as opening files that weren't meant to be opened using directory traversal attacks. Directory traversal attacks allow attackers to access restricted directories and execute commands that are located outside the web server's root directory. If you do use these types of scripts, do not allow two periods (..) in your file names. You can also use basename to determine the name of a file and to keep from putting path information in your scripts.

Directives are important in securing PHP code in regard to input validation. A PHP directive directs the operation of a feature of PHP or Apache. For example, you can use the open_basedir directive in the php.ini file to limit paths that files can be opened from. You can put all user files into a directory set in the include_path and restrict use outside of your include_path.

Taming Scripts

Writing scripts can be risky if you don't consider security issues when creating them. Insecure scripts can leave gateways for others to take over your web server. This includes defacing your web site but can also extend to controlling the operating system. Once the operating system has become unstable from a wayward script, the only reliable way to restore integrity to that web server is to reload it from scratch (something we like to refer to as "nuke and pave"). There is no magic bullet that can properly secure scripts, which is why they are so risky to implement in the first place. Practicing good scripting techniques is the best way to secure a script. Additionally, you should consider a mixture of editing httpd.conf, using mod_security, and using dosevasive. These and other script-hardening techniques are covered in more detail in the book *Hardening Apache* by Tony Mobily (Apress, 2004).

Many of the scripts contained in this book (and anywhere else in the world) are not, in and of themselves, secure. They should be treated with some degree of caution. The same is true for scripts that you find on the Web or elsewhere. These scripts, even those from reliable sources, can and often do contain security holes. Before deploying scripts that you find on the Internet, always perform your own security checks on them.

Securing Your Perl Scripts

▪**Note** This section is intended for scripting professionals.

Perl is an extremely powerful language built into every Mac system. What makes Perl so powerful is the way in which it deals with variables. Variables can signify a number of things, including file names. One example of securing Perl is dealing with opening a file name where the file name is stored in a variable. Using file names as variables can be an issue if a visitor of a site can change the variable. The visitor can be tricked into running and showing the output of arbitrary commands, showing the wrong files, or showing the contents of directories. To avoid this problem, always specify a redirection statement such as using the > character before a variable. You should also include a space between the redirection statement and the variable that contains a file name. Newer versions of Perl improved the open function to avoid this problem by introducing the three-argument call to use when opening a file.

■**Note** If your Perl code will run only on newer versions of Perl, always use the three-argument version.

In Perl, backticks (``) allow the Perl exec functions to run external programs. Although easy to use, backticks can result in security problems from their use in environments with user input.

The following is a simplistic method for validating user input based on the HTTP_REFERER variable, which contains data about the person who sent information to a server. This variable can be faked by visitors, but it is meant to be used as the first line of defense and can thwart a number of attacks. You should always check the HTTP_REFERER variable to ensure that the user is sending referral data to the server rather than a user. Generally, a user should not be sending data directly to a script as it is more than likely malicious activity.

```perl
#!/bin/perl
require "subparseform.lib";
&Parse_Form;
$referer=$ENV{'HTTP_REFERER'};
print "Content-type:text/html\n\n";
if ($referer =~ m#^http://www.apress.com/#){
    print "insert the scripts processes and code in place of this line";
} else {
    print "The server has encountered an error.  Please go back and try again.";
}
```

The following code shows a way of capturing and printing information about a visitor to a page. This data could also be passed to another variable and captured with a form. Obviously, the security implications for these variables are substantial. For example, validating the remote address could be a good way to add a layer of protection to scripts against the possibility of man-in-the-middle attacks.

```php
<?php
echo "<p>IP Address: " . $_SERVER['REMOTE_ADDR'] . "</p>";
echo "<p>Referrer: " . $_SERVER['HTTP_REFERER'] . "</p>";
echo "<p>Browser: " . $_SERVER['HTTP_USER_AGENT'] . "</p>";
?>
```

Another method for protecting Perl scripts is to restrict the script from using any data coming from outside the script. This can include visitor input and environment variables. Alterations to script data are thought of as tainted data. One possible way to instruct Perl to restrict the use of tainted data is to use a -T at the end of your line, calling up Perl at the beginning of each script. You can still use tainted data, but you must first untaint it. To do so, you assign part of the data to a scalar variable. By definition, the scalar variable will not be tainted.

This forces you into properly scripting regular expressions that will untaint data. To do so, use the following script:

```
$outside_Data =~ /regex/ //where some regular expression is to be used
$clean_data=$1 //Scalar variable contains regular expression from the above
```

The following code will convert specified information into regular expressions to make them more difficult for bots to decipher:

```php
<?php
function Convert2Regex ($text) {
  $text = eregi_replace('((((f|ht){1}tp://)[-a-zA-Z0-9@:%_\+.~#?&//=]+)',
    '<a href="\\1">\\1</a>', $text);
  $text = eregi_replace('([[:space:]()[{}])(www.[-a-zA-Z0-9@:%_\+.~#?&//=]+)',
    '\\1<a href="http://\\2">\\2</a>', $text);
  $text = eregi_replace('([_\.0-9a-z-]+@([0-9a-z][0-9a-z-]+\.)+[a-z]{2,3})',
    '<a href="mailto:\\1">\\1</a>', $text);
return $text;
}
$text = "yourmail@yourdomain.com";
echo Convert2Regex($text);
echo "<br /><br />";
$text = "http://www.yourdomain.com";
echo Convert2Regex($text);
echo "<br /><br />";
$text = "ftp://ftp.yourdomain.com";
echo Convert2Regex($text);
?>
```

Next, you would pass the $clean_data variable into your scripts. Be mindful that using these lines of code will not guarantee security in situations where you're protecting your Perl scripts with the –T option in Perl. If you use the Perl command line to test syntax, you can still do so by using perl –cT scriptname.pl.

Securing robots.txt

If you have a web site, you can assume that search engines will find it and add the text and code of your site into their extensive catalog of sites for users to be able to search. Many administrators do not want their sites to appear in search engines for a variety of reasons. The robots.txt file is a simple text file script at the root of your web host that tells a robot whether it has access to a certain file or directory. It is designed for companies that want to keep their data from being scanned by bots, preventing search engines from scanning or crawling their web site. It's flexible in that different rules can be specified based on the robot's user agent. A sample robots.txt is as follows:

```
User-agent: *
Disallow: /secret-files/
```

This simple file tells all robots not to enter the /secret-files folder.

A more complex `robots.txt` or `robots(AllowRoot).txt` file looks like this:

```
User-agent: *
Disallow:   /_vti_bin/
Disallow:   /clienthelp/
Disallow:   /exchweb/
Disallow:   /remote/
Disallow:   /tsweb/
Disallow:   /aspnet_client/
Disallow:   /images/
Disallow:   /_private/
Disallow:   /_vti_cnf/
Disallow:   /_vti_log/
Disallow:   /_vti_pvt/
Disallow:   /_vti_script/
Disallow:   /_vti_txt/

Allow All traffic:
User-agent: *
Disallow: /
```

Blocking Hosts Based on robots.txt

This is all well and good, and most robots such as those from Google, Yahoo, and MSN respect your rules, but what happens when a robot blatantly ignores your rules? The simple answer is, whatever it wants. Since it's up to the robot to obey or ignore the rules, any disreputable robot can download your entire site.

The solution to this problem is to proactively block wayward robots. There are a few different ways to do this, such as blocking known bad robot user agents and blocking IPs. Blocking certain user agents is easy, but it's also easy for the user agent to spoof itself, so you'll find that you have to continuously update your list of bad user agents. Blocking IP addresses is effective too, but you'll also need to consistently update your blocked IP list. The best solution involves a combination of techniques that, once implemented, requires little or no maintenance and lays a trap for bad robots.

First, put a hidden link into the main page of your site. This hidden link is a zero-by-zero-pixel image that links to a script within /secret-files/.

```
<a href="/secret-files/robot.cgi"><img border="0" width="0" length="0" src="images/
spacer.gif">
```

Since this image isn't viewable in a browser, the only way it's ever going to be accessed is if a robot is crawling your site. Since your `robots.txt` file is blocking access to that folder, the only time this script will actually get called is if a robot is crawling the site while ignoring `robots.txt`. Once the script within /secret-files/ is run, it blocks the user's IP.

Tip Typically, sites have more than one entry point, so it is wise to place this hidden link in more than one page. If you take advantage of server-side includes (SSIs), then placing it inside the `header.html` or `footer.html` file offers excellent protection.

The following are the contents of the `robot.cgi` script (big thanks to Erin Scott for whipping this up):

```
#!/usr/bin/perl -w
$htaccess = "/home/alt229/www/.htaccess";        # needs to be the full path
open (HTACCESS, ">> $htaccess") or die $!;
print HTACCESS "deny from $ENV{REMOTE_ADDR}\n";
close (HTACCESS);
```

Another benefit to this script is that it stops robots from crawling your site *before* they download anything more than your front page.

If you have other domains that are using Apache's `mod_rewrite` module in the root of your web folder, they will also be inaccessible by the bad robot's IP address. Ninety-nine percent of the time, this is preferable.

Protecting Directories

You can provide access to directories based on passwords in a variety of manners, including using Kerberos, `mod_auth`, `ldap`, or the `.htaccess` file. The `.htaccess` file is common when dealing with web hosting environments and when creating files using scripts to control access to directories and files. When using `.htaccess` and `.htpasswd` files, you are building simple text files that control certain permissions of files.

An `.htaccess` file is a simple ASCII text file that allows administrators to personalize error pages, password-protect directories, and redirect traffic. The `.htaccess` file is stored in your main site directory and/or in any subdirectory that you want to protect. You can use a regular text editor such as Notepad, SimpleText, vi, or pico to create and edit an `.htaccess` file. Not all web hosts will support `.htaccess` files, so you should consult your hosting administrator if you are in a shared hosting environment. `.htaccess` files will also not be available if you are running Apache on Windows.

Tip Before editing the `.htaccess` file, keep a backup of the original `.htaccess` file and web site configuration handy in case you have any problems with the file.

Although the `.htaccess` file can be stored in the main site directory, or any of the subdirectories, the commands in the `.htaccess` file will directly affect the directory and any subdirectories it is in. If it is stored in your main directory, it will affect the whole site. If it is stored in a subdirectory, it will affect only the files in that subdirectory. Each file in a directory is affected by the most immediate .htaccess file available, the folder itself, or the directories above it. The same is true for .htgroup and .htpasswd files.

There are many ways to create an .htaccess file. You can use the mkdir shell command to create the file. You can also create the file in Notepad or SimpleText and use an FTP program to upload the file into the proper directory. When you are uploading an .htaccess file, it must be created and saved in ASCII mode to avoid any initial errors when working with the file.

The permissions on an .htaccess, .htgroup, or .htpasswd file should typically be 644 (RW- R-- R--). This will give the group and user read-only access to this file. For more information on reading permissions, refer to Chapter 10.

■Note Commands in the .htaccess file are meant to be on one line only. Be sure that your text editor has Word Wrap turned off.

Using the .htaccess File to Customize Error Codes

The .htaccess file gives you the ability to redirect visitors to a different page if they try to access an invalid page. You can use a custom error page for any type of error that corresponds with its unique error number. One of the most common, and frustrating, error codes is error 404, which means Page Not Found.

The layout for this command in the .htaccess file is as follows:

```
ErrorDocument errornumber /filename.html
```

If you create a page called 404.html and you want to use it as your 404 error page, the command is as follows:

```
ErrorDocument 404 /404.html
```

If you want to keep all the error pages in a separate directory, just include the directory name in the file path like this:

```
ErrorDocument 404 /errorpages/404.html
```

Table 11-1 lists the most commonly used error codes.

Table 11-1. *Common Web Site Error Codes*

Code	Name	Description
400	Bad Request	Typically a generic error.
401	Authorization Required	Invalid access to a protected area without authorization.
403	Forbidden	You do not have permissions to access the file.
404	Not Found	The page could not be found.
500	Internal Server Error	Internal server errors in any scripts you have running.

By customizing your error code pages, you will also be increasing the overall security of your server. Most servers use the same error codes that the server came with. This has led to people attempting to use Google to search for all the web pages that have a certain string of text in them in order to obtain a list of all the web servers running a certain version of software that has an exploit. Customizing error codes will help you stay away from these kinds of Internet searches and the exploits that the results target.

Using .htaccess to Control Access to a Directory

Password protection is one of the most commonly used features of .htaccess files. It is also a bit more difficult to set up than customized error codes, but it's far more versatile in its ability to control access to directories.

First, create a new file called .htpasswd in the directory you want protected. Create and save this file in the same fashion as the .htaccess file. The .htpasswd file will contain usernames and their passwords. Now, enter the username and password information into it. The information is stored in the following manner:

```
username:password
username:password
charles:mypassword
```

In the previous example, the username, a colon, and a password are on individual lines and do not have any spaces at the end of each line.

■**Note** The username fields remain in English, but the password fields need to be encrypted to keep them secure. Many scripts are available online that encrypt passwords for you. A quick Internet search should find plenty of scripts. We prefer to use sites such as http://www.coderz.com to find code for these types of tasks.

Once the file is created and the usernames and passwords are entered, the file must be uploaded in ASCII format and stored above your WWW or public_html folder, that is, in your online root (home) folder. (You might have to ask your host provider exactly what path this is and where it is located.) Remember that the .htaccess file will affect the current directory only, plus any subdirectories connected to it. Be sure you are placing this in the right folder. Sometimes one directory section needs protection; other times, the whole site needs it.

Next, you will need to add coding to the .htaccess file for the directory you want to protect:

```
AuthUserFile /home/pathto/.htpasswd
AuthType Basic
AuthName "THE Secret PlaceREALM"


<LIMIT GET POST>
require valid-user
</LIMIT>
```

Let's explore what this code means, starting with the first line:

- `AuthUserFile /home/pathto/.htpasswd` allows the browser to find the right path to your `.htpasswd` file. The rest of the command after `AuthUserFile` specifies the path leading to the actual file name.

- `AuthType Basic` defines the type of encryption to be used. There are multiple methods of encryption, but Basic is the most commonly used. However, it shouldn't be used for any systems that host high-traffic or high-security environments.

- `AuthName "Private Realm"` defines how your protected directory is referred to in the pop-up message box when the visitor hits the protected area. This name is yours to choose. The users see only what is inside the quotes.

This last part of the script tells the browser to check credentials that the visitor enters into the box against the information in your `.htpasswd` file:

```
<LIMIT GET POST>
require valid-user
</LIMIT>
```

When visitors try to access a page within a protected directory, they will get a dialog box asking for a username and password. If they enter bad information, they will be directed to an error page.

If you would rather password-protect a specific file than a folder, you can use this file name in your .htaccess file, where the `AuthUserFile` variable defines the specific file or web page for which you want to control access:

```
<files "filename.cgi">
AuthUserFile /home/pathto/.htpasswd
AuthType Basic
AuthName "Secret Place"
require valid-user
</files>
```

Finally, you can and should protect your `.htaccess` file from being viewed by visitors using this code in the `.htaccess` file:

```
<files ".htaccess">
order allow,deny
deny from all
</files>
```

Tightening Security with SSL

Secure Sockets Layer (SSL) began appearing on commerce servers on the Web in the mid-to-late 90s as a means to securely submit confidential financial data over the Web. This high-level open source security protocol is now an industry standard and has recently been expanded for use with various mail protocols, instant messaging protocols, and web sites. SSL is based on RSA Data Security's public-key cryptography algorithms and is denoted by the letter *S* in the https part of a web site's URL. By default, SSL operates over port 443, although this can be customized.

OpenSSL is the package that provides the SSL service for Mac OS X and Mac OS X Server. The current version of OpenSSL that is running on a system can be found by using the interactive command-line OpenSSL tool. To do this, use the following command:

```
openssl version
```

The openssl command then responds with an output equaling the following, showing the exact version of OpenSSL being run on the system:

```
OpenSSL 0.9.7l 28 Sep 2006
```

OpenSSL uses a shared key that is stored in the form of an X.509 certificate to encrypt communication between servers and clients.

Implementing Digital Certificates

Data that is transported back and forth from the web server to the web browser needs to be secured. All too often, this data is sent across the Internet unencrypted and exposed to anyone who has the ability to intercept it. Digital certificates such as SSL and TSL certificates were invented to cut down on this kind of information hijacking. When a digital certificate is used, an encrypted "handshake" is initiated with the server and browser. These certificates can be created using open source tools such as OpenSSL, or they can be purchased from companies such as VeriSign or Thawte, which offer many different configuration options for the certificate.

There are two ways to implement certificates. The first, and the least expensive route, is to use a self-assigned certificate. This option uses the built-in SSL feature of your server to create the certificate (more on this in Chapter 13). The second option is to purchase one from a trusted authority such as Thawte or VeriSign. The key difference to using the prebuilt SSL is whether the web site administrator will want to force the end user of a site to click the OK button when their traffic goes from HTTP-based traffic to HTTPS-based traffic. Implementing a third-party SSL certificate will enforce that procedure and make the acceptance of the certificate more streamlined for your visitors.

When considering whether to use SSL to protect your web site, it is important to consider whether you will have users interacting with web sites in such a way that they want their privacy to be protected. For example, if you have a very small web site that only provides data for users but does not have any forms or ways for users to actually enter data into your site, then you probably do not need SSL implemented on the web server. The certificate and infrastructure that is required for the use of SSL would simply not be worth the expense.

Protecting the Privacy of Your Information

It is important to protect your privacy. If you were interested in finding out who owns a site, you could perform a WHOIS lookup for the domain to find out more information about the site, including the name, phone number, physical address, e-mail address, and DNS servers of the domain, which could then be used for social engineering purposes. Many domain registrars, such as Network Solutions, even provide information about domain names by using a WHOIS button on their front pages. But it's not just Network Solutions that will provide this information; almost every domain registration web site will give the inquisitor access to a WHOIS database to look up information about a site. The WHOIS database is even accessible via the Network Utility in Mac OS X (see Figure 11-3).

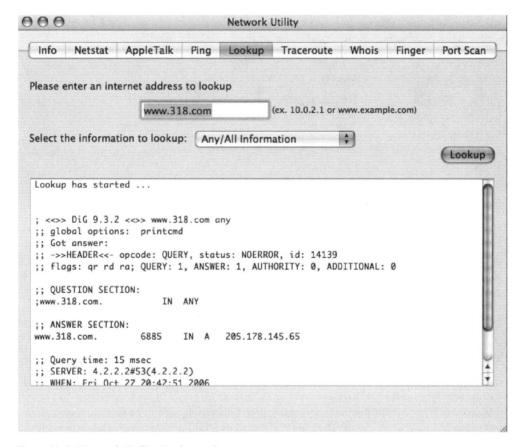

Figure 11-3. *Network Utility Lookup tab*

Once you know the IP address of a server, it is also possible to query ARIN within the Network Utility to discover more information about the owner of the web site (see Figure 11-4). Established in December 1997, ARIN is a nonprofit that allocates IP addresses and develops policies used to govern how they are used.

So, how can you protect your web site from displaying this information? To protect this sensitive information, many registrars offer an add-on service that allows you to hide your information from others, thus repelling a variety of spam and the discovery of other information.

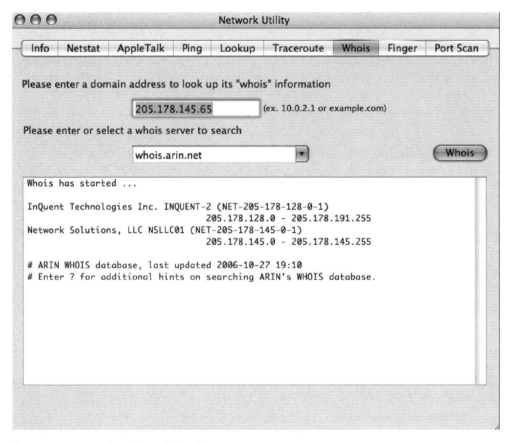

Figure 11-4. *Network Utility Whois tab*

Protecting from Google?

Google is one of the greatest hacking tools ever created, so it is important to understand what an attacker might use Google to do. Searching for servers with specific vulnerabilities has never been easier than it is with Google. An attacker might find a tool that can be run against a certain version of your web server, such as Apache 2.1. A search for web sites using Apache 2.1 is performed, and then the attacker isolates messages on error pages or default web sites that contain identifiers specific to that version of the software. Figure 11-5 shows an example of this.

Google also offers hackers the ability to find out information about a web site without leaving any traces. When you run a search, there are multiple ways for viewing a web site. One is to use the cached option on the site (see Figure 11-6). The Cached button loads the destination page by using a cached copy of your web site located on the Google web servers. This means you are not writing to the target web server's log files from your own computer. This gives savvy would-be attackers the ability to have Google show them information about a server without leaving a trace. An attacker would then gather as much information about a site as possible before launching the attack. To help prevent this, know what information Google has cached for your site, and if you want, disable the Googlebot from scanning your site at `https://google.com/webmasters/tools/siteoverview`.

Figure 11-5. *Version-specific web codes*

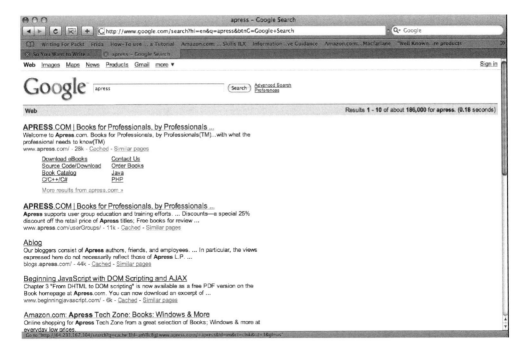

Figure 11-6. *Google cache*

Enumerating a Web Server

What other information is available about your web site? Apache communications occur by transferring text data over port 80. As is true with many ports, it is possible to use the text-based communications application Telnet to tap into port 80 and talk to the server without using a web browser. This is what the Terminal-based lynx web browser uses. For example, the command `telnet <IP Address> <port 80>` would result in a prompt that would enable you to send data to a web server and request a response. For example, the following command:

```
telnet www.318.com 80 <RET>
HEAD /HTTP/1.0 <RFT>
```

responds with the following lines:

```
<!DOCTYPE HTML PUBLIC "-//IETF//DTD HTML 2.0//EN">
<HTML><HEAD>
<TITLE>400 Bad Request</TITLE>
</HEAD><BODY>
<H1>Bad Request</H1>
Your browser sent a request that this server could not understand.<P>
client sent invalid HTTP/0.9 request: HEAD /HTTP/1.0<P>
<HR>
<ADDRESS>Apache/1.3.37 Server at 10.49.38.139 Port 80</ADDRESS>
</BODY></HTML>
```

As shown in the previous example, when using the Telnet command to get information about Apache, you are looking at the Apache banner to get information on the version number, local server IP address, and any information about the server that might not otherwise be available. Banners can be edited to reflect a different version number by changing the actual `httpd` banner, but this is risky and should probably not be done.

Securing Files on Your Web Server

File security plays an integral part in web security. If your server allows too much permission to files such as scripts, then you are opening yourself up to a wide range of attacks. This includes HTML files and CGI scripts.

Files located in standard web directories are typically assigned permissions of 751 (for more information on permissions, see Chapter 10), which gives the everyone user (unauthenticated web visitors are assigned to the everyone group) the read-only setting for HTML files. One exception to this includes `.html` pages that have to be rewritten and updated by a script. In that case, apply the 766 permission level to both the directory and the file. Permissions for files that are added to the server are controlled by the mask of the application that uploads the files. In some cases, these are the default permissions of FTP, Apache, a CMS package such as Post-Nuke, or maybe just the umask variable of your system.

CGI applications for different web sites that run on the same server all run with the same permissions, and in Mac OS X they all run as the same user account by default. CGI applications can be dangerous, especially when they have the wrong permissions applied to them, because they can possibly be edited and then run with arbitrary code. The proper permission for executable scripts is typically 755. However, it is common for certain developers to use 606, or other specific variants, according to what they are attempting to accomplish. If you do not have a specific reason to use something other than 755, it's a good idea to stick to the proper permission levels.

File permissions and how to change them are discussed in more depth in Chapter 3.

Securing Directory Listings

To make sharing files to the Web easy, Apache will, by default, serve all files that it can access to any user who tries to access it. Any files within a path to a web site or any files available using symbolic links within the web site code are accessible through Apache. This makes limiting access to files available to the Apache user an important aspect of web server security.

One way to mitigate this issue is to deny access to the file system and allow access only to the document root using the `httpd.conf` file. By adding the following code to the `httpd.conf` file, any access other than that granted by this line would be denied:

```
<Directory />
    Order Deny,Allow
    Deny from all
</Directory>
<Directory /Library/WebServer/Documents>
    Order Allow,Deny
    Allow from All
</Directory>
```

This uses the `Directory` option in Apache to limit access but still does not offer protection against following symbolic links located in directories that point to files within the directory structure. To do this, you would use what is known as an *options directive* to further limit access to files within the directory structure. Options directives are specified with a + sign or a – sign in front of the option to enable and disable access, respectively. `FollowSymLinks` is the option directive to control the ability to follow symbolic links. Use the following syntax to implement it:

```
<Directory /Library/WebServer/Documents>
    Order Allow,Deny
    Allow from All
    Options -FollowSymLinks
</Directory>
```

In many cases, symbolic links are required for code to properly execute. In this case, you can use the `SymLinksIfOwnerMatch` directive. This would allow symbolic links to function only if the owner of the link is the same as the owner of the file to which the symbolic link points. Here's an example of enabling `SymLinksIfOwnerMatch`:

```
<Directory /Library/WebServer/Documents>
    Order Allow,Deny
    Allow from All
    Options -FollowSymLinks  +FollowSymLinks

</Directory>
```

▓**Note** It is important to always provide the lowest level of permissions possible to users accessing the web server. The goal is to create the securest possible site while still allowing you to have a fully functional web site.

Uploading Files Securely

FTP is a protocol that is used by web developers to upload files to web servers. FTP is a very unsecure protocol that transmits usernames and passwords in plain text. Because it has been around just about as long as the Internet has, it's difficult to enforce that they use something else. So if they really must use FTP, configure Secure FTP (SFTP), in Apache. For more information on SSH, see Chapter 12.

■**Note** Never allow a database administrator to access a web site's database through a firewall. Database administrators should be accessing their code through a secure VPN tunnel and not by its IP address.

Cross-Site Scripting Attacks (XSS)

Cross-site scripting (XSS) attacks on popular web sites have been widely publicized recently. Cross-site scripting occurs when a web application is able to gather data from a user in a malicious manner. SSL and other methods of protecting sites do not help with XSS scripting attacks. Data can be gathered in the form of a link with malicious code that is embedded in the body of an e-mail or directly linked from another site. The attacker can then put the malicious portion of the link into the site in another encoding method to make the request less suspicious looking. Once the data is collected by a web application, it generates a page for the user that contains the malicious data originally sent to it. This data appears as valid content.

Many of the most popular content management systems and forums let users submit HTML and JavaScript-embedded posts. If an attacker logs into a site and reads a message posted by another user that contains malicious JavaScript, then it might be possible for the attacker to hijack the session using information from the bulletin board post. Attackers can also inject foreign code into a vulnerable application to steal data, which can lead to account hijacking, cookie theft, or false advertising. This kind of attack is called an XSS *hole*. If an XSS hole is found on a web site and the site uses cookies, then it might be possible to steal them. One example of a web application with XSS holes is PostNuke, a popular content management system. PostNuke has had a variety of XSS holes that have been exploited.

The easiest way to protect yourself, as a web site user, is to follow links only from the main web site you are visiting. If you visit one web site and it links to another one, visit their main site and use their search engine to find the page you would otherwise have been visiting. This eliminates the possibility of encountering most XSS attacks. Another way to protect yourself from XSS attacks is to turn off JavaScript in your browser settings, as explained in Chapter 5.

As a web site administrator, filtering input eliminates many XSS attacks. If your web site has forms, do not immediately trust the input as valid. Certain characters can allow unintended results. Convert < and > to < and >. You should also filter out (and) by translating them to (and). You should convert # and & to # (#) and & (&).

XSS vulnerabilities can allow malicious code insertion, which, in turn, might allow malicious code execution. If an attacker exploits a browser flaw, they might be able to execute commands on the client computer. Command execution is possible only on the client computer. And although command execution is not usually possible on a Mac, having a Windows system attacked by malicious code on your web server is definitely not a desirable result.

CHAPTER 12

■■■

Remote Connectivity

As a security expert, consider this: A passenger sits in the airport, working on his computer, waiting for the plane to start boarding. While sitting there, surfing on the wireless airport network, he notices that almost every laptop in sight is a Mac. On a hunch, he opens Bonjour Browser to discover that many of these laptops have Remote Management (the Apple Remote Desktop client, based on VNC), SSH, Telnet, or Timbuktu enabled. He also notices that many of these computers are not password protected, easily controllable by anyone with the gall to tap into the computer. Within about ten minutes, nearly all the laptop lids are closed with their owners suspiciously looking around, attempting to determine which passenger was entertaining them with the "joke of the day" on their display.

On a serious note, this is possibly the best-case scenario for these unsuspecting Mac owners in the airport. With Apple Remote Desktop (ARD), Timbuktu, and many of the other remote access options improperly secured on these machines, it would be possible to cause much more damage than simply sending a humorous message to their desktops. Deleting files, capturing passwords, reconfiguring operating system preferences, and issuing damaging commands from a shell are all possible. It would also be very easy to simply submit a program that would run in the background and provide access to anyone attempting to control it, using what is called a *root kit*. (Root kits are explained in further detail in Chapter 7.)

More often than not, communication over public networks is not properly secured. When sitting in an airport, coffee shop, hotel, or any other publicly available network, it is important not only to password protect the means of communicating but also to encrypt the traffic you are sending over the network. Sending information in an unprotected manner across a public network can be painfully embarrassing, not to mention expensive. This chapter will focus on securely configuring and using the most common remote management applications in the Mac community.

Built-in Remote Management Applications

ARD is a utility made by Apple that fills in many of the functionality gaps left in Mac OS X Server in regard to client management. It is a graphical interface that allows administrators to remotely administer systems either from within the company's network or from outside of it. ARD can be used to send shell commands to workstations, transfer files to client systems, and control and install software remotely on computers. ARD uses the VNC protocol, an open source and multiplatform remote connectivity protocol that allows you to remotely view and control Mac, Windows, or Linux systems.

Using a VNC client or VNC server on Linux or Windows, it is possible to establish connectivity between practically every operating system currently in use on networks; therefore, VNC is more widely adopted than ARD. And although it has a few more security features, the security controls of VNC are not as granular as ARD. For example, you cannot send Unix commands over VNC or set up tiered access to VNC.

ARD is easy to set up, and its customizable security features make the operating environment much more secure than VNC. Apple has expanded on VNC in its development of ARD and has added a lot of new features while maintaining backward compatibility with clients such as Chicken of the VNC and RealVNC. If you do not have the ARD client installed, then you can still use VNC to access another computer remotely. However, you will be limited by security settings such as lower-level encryption keys.

Screen Sharing

In Leopard there is a new feature called Screen Sharing that allows other Macs to connect to your computer over VNC simply by clicking an icon in the sidebar of a Finder window. This allows you to quickly tap into another computer and help someone with a project they're working on, make a quick change to the system, or grab a couple of files and transfer them to your computer. This is a dangerous aspect of computing if an attacker compromises the remote access to your system.

Other operating systems can connect using a standard VNC client. If you do not want to allow other systems to connect to yours, then disable this feature (it is not enabled by default). If you want other systems to be able to connect to yours, you can set this up securely. Let's walk through setting up Screen Sharing.

To enable Screen Sharing, open the Sharing preference pane. Then click the Screen Sharing check box (see Figure 12-1). Once you have started the ARD service, click the Allow Access For section, and set it to Only These Users.

One of the most critical aspects of configuring Screen Sharing is limiting which users are allowed to connect to your system remotely. The Allow Access For section is where you would configure which users (from the Accounts pane in System Preferences) have access to share any of these services by clicking the + button. Select the user from the list in the dialog box (see Figure 12-2) that you want to allow to access this preference, and then click the Select button.

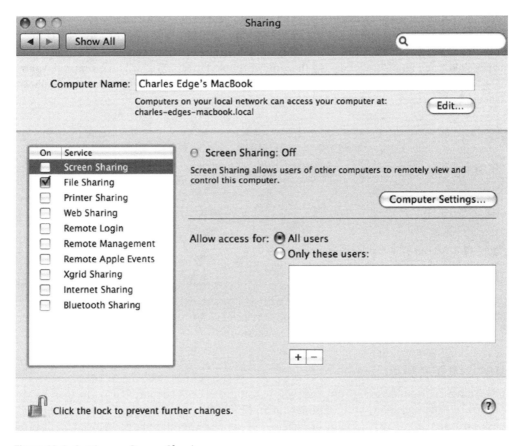

Figure 12-1. *Setting up Screen Sharing*

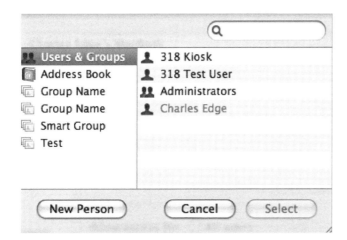

Figure 12-2. *Selecting users*

Once you have added the users and you want to enable the ability for a remote user to request access or to allow VNC clients access, click the Computer Settings button in the Sharing preference pane, and verify that the Anyone May Request Permission to Control Screen is unchecked (see Figure 12-3). Leaving this option enabled means you will be prompted when clients attempt to gain access. In many cases, it is preferable to be prompted because it allows users to be informed when a remote connection is being made.

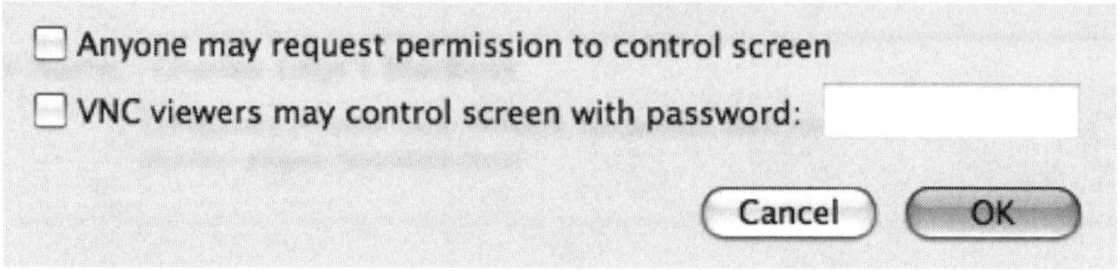

Figure 12-3. *Screen Sharing computer settings*

If you know that users without ARD (such as Windows workstations or those using Chicken of the VNC) will need to control the machine with a different VNC client, click the VNC Viewers May Control Screen with Password box. Otherwise, leave it unchecked because allowing any VNC access increases the susceptibility of a system.

Back to My Mac

If you have a current .Mac account and you are using Mac OS X Leopard (10.5), the Back to My Mac feature of .Mac allows you to connect to any computer that has your .Mac username and password entered in the .Mac pane of System Preferences. This eliminates the need to forward ports because it accesses the remote system using the .Mac system preference. Leopard's built-in Screen Sharing feature is used to allow both Back to My Mac and VNC to connect to your computer. You can stop or start Back to My Mac using the Back to My Mac tab in the .Mac preference pane (see Figure 12-4).

Back to My Mac is new and should be used with some reservation until the specific security implications are identified. If you trust .Mac to hold any information that you would place on your computer, then you can trust Back to My Mac equally.

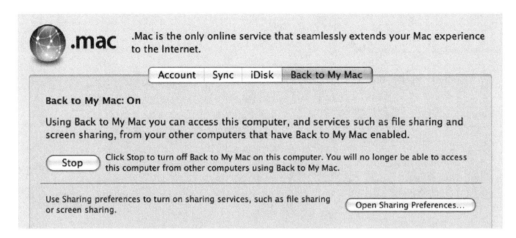

Figure 12-4. *Back to My Mac in the .Mac preference pane*

Remote Management

Now that you have specified the users who can remotely control the computer, you should specify the users who will be able to manage the system using the more advanced features of ARD, such as obtaining reports, sending commands, and restarting the system. In the Sharing preference pane, the management features are referred to as Remote Management and can be controlled granularly on a per-task basis. The Remote Desktop application, used to control Macs using ARD, is licensed separately. If you are using ARD Remote Management, then you will more than likely not need to use the free Screen Sharing feature built into Leopard.

Screen Sharing is great for home use, but ARD is far superior for larger environments with more requirements. If you are remotely controlling systems only, then Screen Sharing will typically suffice. If you have large numbers of systems to manage, then Remote Management is likely going to be of more use to you.

To enable Remote Management, click the Remote Management service in the Sharing preference pane (see Figure 12-5). From here, you should set the Allow Access For option to Only These Users and add the users who will have access privileges as you did for Screen Sharing in the previous section.

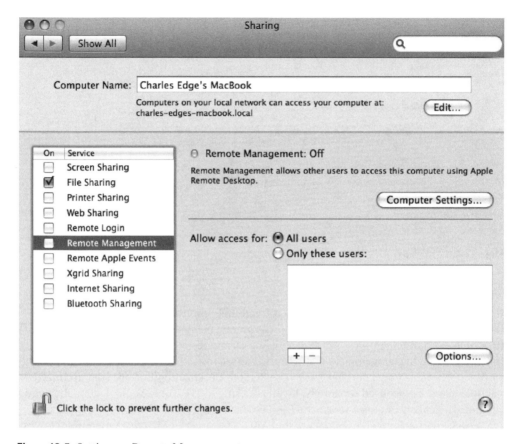

Figure 12-5. *Setting up Remote Management*

In the Sharing preference pane, you can also select what level of access other users have to your system. The Remote Management panel also lets you select what level of access a user should be given by clicking the Options button. Check the boxes (see Figure 12-6) for the appropriate level of access you want to grant. Remember that for every user, only the minimum required level of access should be given. For example, if you want ARD to be used to build reports on a machine only, then you would click the Generate Reports box and nothing else.

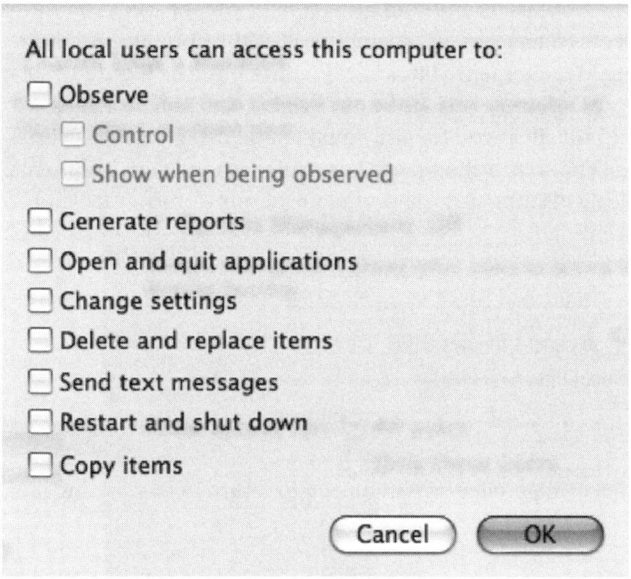

All local users can access this computer to:

☐ Observe
  ☐ Control
  ☐ Show when being observed
☐ Generate reports
☐ Open and quit applications
☐ Change settings
☐ Delete and replace items
☐ Send text messages
☐ Restart and shut down
☐ Copy items

(Cancel) (OK)

Figure 12-6. *Remote Management options*

Here are descriptions of the settings that can be enabled:

Observe: Remote users can see the activity on their computer but cannot take control of a session.

Control: Remote users can see the activity on their computer and can take control of the mouse and keyboard.

Show When Being Observed: Users being observed will see an icon in the toolbar indicating that their computer is being controlled.

Generate Reports: Remote users can view software, hardware, and other information about your system.

Open and Quit Applications: ARD can be used to open and quit applications without using the remote control function.

Change Settings: Application and System Preferences Settings can be changed without using menu options from within the Remote Desktop application.

Send Text Messages: The ARD text message feature can be used to send instant messages to the remote user.

Restart and Shut Down: ARD can be used to shut down the system and reboot it without controlling the screen.

Copy items: ARD can be used to copy data to the computer.

Once you have granted access to those users and configured management access for those who absolutely must have remote access management capabilities, click the Computer Settings button, and check the Show Remote Management Status in Menu Bar box (see Figure 12-7). This allows the user to see the Remote Desktop icon in the upper-right corner of the screen. For a smaller environment, this feature will allow you to easily enable and disable ARD access. However, the menu bar icon in the user's screen should not be enabled in larger environments. It is too easy for a user to inadvertently disable ARD, rendering the administrator unable to deploy software or manage the system.

Note You can also enable VNC clients to access the system in this screen, but keep in mind that VNC viewers will have a lower encryption protocol than ARD users.

Once you are satisfied with your settings, click the OK button to return to the Sharing preference pane.

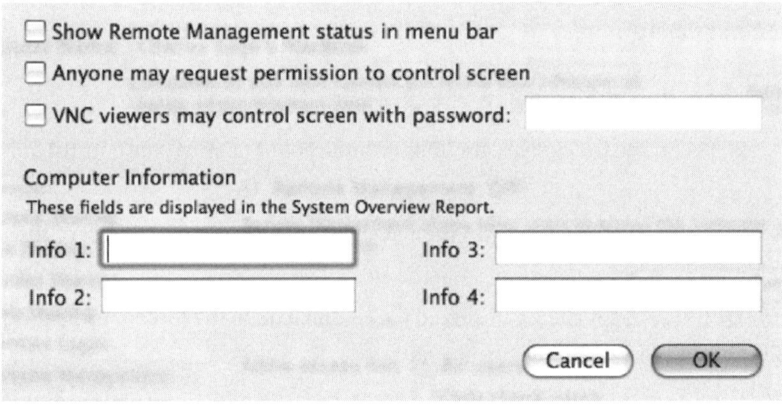

Figure 12-7. *Remote Management computer settings*

Timbuktu

Netopia's Timbuktu was the dominant remote administration application for a long time and is still widely used in many Mac and mixed platform environments. Although the utilization of this application has dropped drastically since the rise of VNC, Microsoft's RDC, and Apple's Remote Desktop, Timbuktu still has a strong following, and Netopia is still developing for it. The choice of whether to use Timbuktu over ARD is often a devout choice rather than one based on feature set and price comparisons. Timbuktu has been available to the Mac community for a long time, but many of the features that most administrators are looking for are mirrored in Screen Sharing or Apple Remote Desktop.

Setting up and establishing appropriate access for new users is the first and most important security step to take after installing Timbuktu. To set up a new user, click the Users button within Timbuktu, and click Add. From here, enter the name and password of the user you are adding. If the account is not connected to a directory service or set to use local OS X accounts, then set the Type menu to Timbuktu user. Enter a password, and then give the user the minimum permissions they need by checking the appropriate boxes for access (Figure 12-8). Unless you are using a modem to dial into the computer (which, in this day and age of high-speed Internet access is highly unlikely), uncheck the Let User Dial into Your Computer box, and click the Save button.

Figure 12-8. *Timbuktu User setup screen*

It is more secure to use accounts hosted in other directory service databases, which can be configured by changing the Type drop-down to Open Directory or Computer User. The Open Directory option type allows the administrator to set policies using the Open Directory services schema within OS X Server, essentially delegating security of the account to the directory services system. An added benefit to using an Open Directory–based user account is that all your computers will use the same username and password, which can help keep security management centralized and simple. It is far easier to routinely change the passwords on 100 computers by using an Open Directory account rather than trying to visit 100 desktops to push out a password change. This is more than likely not the case in smaller environments, however, so we will stick to the Timbuktu User type.

Once you have set your account up, test it by moving to another system and attempting to log in to the system that was just configured. At this point, you can use the Registered User or Registered User (Secure) option (see Figure 12-9). Clearly, we recommend using the secure version of login. We also recommend that you do not click Add to Keychain to save the password in the keychain. This can cause a security breach if the computer with stored passwords is compromised.

Figure 12-9. *Connecting to a Timbuktu client system*

Use the password rules built into Timbuktu to establish a minimum set of good password criteria (see Figure 12-10). These options include the following:

Allow Users to Save Passwords in Connection Documents: We typically disable this because it allows users to save passwords, which is a security concern.

New Passwords May Match User's 3 Previous Passwords: Disable this option because it allows the password to stay the same when it should routinely be changed as a best practice.

Allow Common Passwords: Disable this option because it allows users to use passwords that are routinely used in dictionary attacks.

Minimum Number of Characters in Password: Eight is fairly standard.

Number of Days until Password Expires: This should be enabled and set to the number of days before a password needs to be changed. We prefer 30, but 90 is good too.

The Server Password feature of Timbuktu allows administrators to set a password that locks users from changing any of the settings for Timbuktu's preferences. This feature should be enabled if you would rather not have remote users changing their Timbuktu settings on the computer. Use the Server Password preference pane (see Figure 12-11) to set the features that require entering the server password to enable; all of these options should be checked.

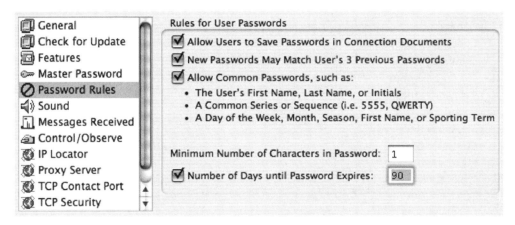

Figure 12-10. *Configuring the Timbuktu password rules*

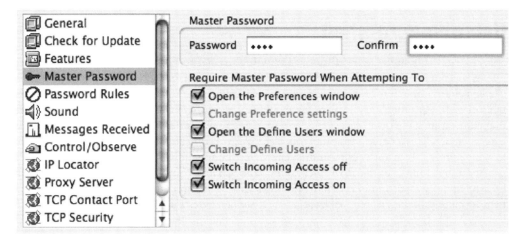

Figure 12-11. *Configuring the Timbuktu master password*

To configure maximum security options for Timbuktu, open the TCP Security preference (see Figure 12-12). Within this preference, you can select whether a system is browseable through Bonjour by unchecking the Register with Bonjour option. We highly suggest that you restrict all incoming connections to be SSH enabled by selecting the Only Accept Secure (SSH) Incoming Connections option. Also, Respond to TCP/IP Scanner should be disabled to help obfuscate your network traffic.

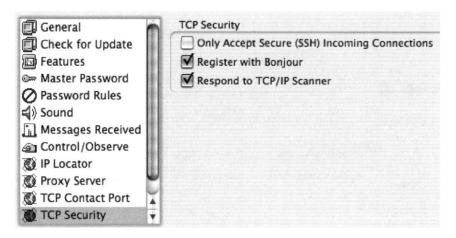

Figure 12-12. *Configuring Timbuktu services*

Using Secure Shell

SSH is a way of obtaining access through a remote shell or Terminal session to your computer. Telnet was once the primary method for remotely connecting to client systems over remote shells. Telnet connections are unencrypted and therefore insecure forms of transmitting information. As the Internet became more widespread, the security implications of having a service that allowed such low-level access to a system over a network became unacceptable, and SSH was created. SSH is a better version of this technology, giving an administrator a remote shell to send commands to a user computer over a secure connection. These commands can be used to transfer files, connect to other systems, and run any Terminal commands. SSH should be used in those environments where opening a variety of ports to allow remote ARD connectivity is undesirable and where GUI level access is not needed to remotely manage the computer.

To enable incoming SSH access to your system, click the Sharing preference pane, and click Remote Login Service (see Figure 12-13). From here, click Only These Users, and click the + button to add users who will be allowed to remotely access the computer using SSH. Checking the box turns the Remote Login indicator light green. You can now use SSH to access the system remotely.

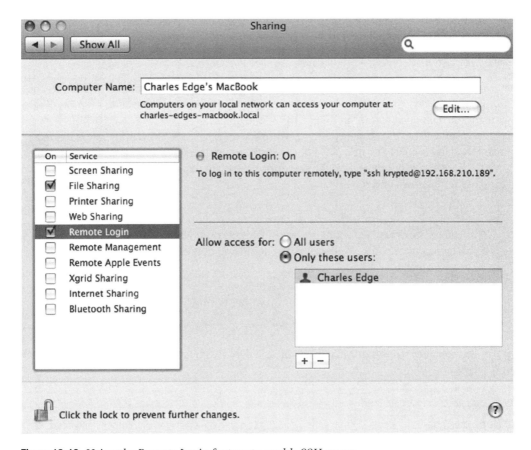

Figure 12-13. *Using the Remote Login feature to enable SSH access*

Further Securing SSH

SSH is a secure protocol, but you can make SSH even more secure by using public-private login keys, which prevent your password from ever going over the wire. The public-private keys can be saved into the keychain, so make sure that a passphrase is required to access them. You can also use the keys to allow access without the need for any passphrase at all. This can prove to be rather dangerous if someone were to obtain your private key and log in as you.

Connecting to an SSH host will request authentication from the client. If you have a key set, your SSH client will generate a temporary key based on your private key. It will then send this key to the server, and the server will compare it to the public keys that it has. If your public key there can unlock the temporary key, you are authenticated and allowed access. If the keys fail, then SSH drops back to password-based authentication and will prompt for a password.

In the following example, we will be connecting using a passphrase-free key. It's not as secure, but it is simple to do.

Note We assume you haven't generated an SSH key yet.

First you need to make a key pair. To do this, you will use DSA as the key type to ensure that you will be connecting via the more secure SSH2 protocol:

```
ssh-keygen -t dsa
```

You will be prompted for a filename; press Return to accept the default. You will then be prompted for a key passphrase. If you want it to prompt for a passphrase, enter it now; otherwise, for unchallenged logins, hit Return to set it to blank.

Now you will have your new public-private key set in `~/.ssh`. The private key is named `id_dsa`, and the public is `id_dsa.pub`. For the server to use the key, you must copy your public key to it. If keys have not been used for authentication up to this point, you can simply copy the key to the remote host and rename it:

```
scp ~/.ssh/id_dsa.pub user@host:~/.ssh/authorized_keys
```

This will create or replace your authorized keys file on the server.
If you have authorized keys already, you should add to the file like so:

```
cat ~/.ssh/id_dsa.pub | ssh user@host 'cat - >> ~/.ssh/authorized_keys'
```

Now try logging into the SSH server as you would normally:

```
ssh host.domain.com -l username
```

If you specified a passphrase, you will be asked for it; otherwise, it will automatically grant you access.

Note If you are using single sign-on with a Mac OS X Server, then passphrases can be handled by Kerberos instead.

When using keysets without passphrases, it is imperative that the key not fall into the wrong hands. If a compromised passphrase is suspected, it should be destroyed immediately and a new one should be generated right away.

Using a VPN

A virtual private network (VPN) is a private communications tunnel, established within a public network, between two points, one inside a network and one outside of it. Safe communication through this tunnel is possible through encrypted network traffic.

Connecting to Your Office VPN

Many companies will have a VPN in place that you can use to connect to the office. When you use the VPN to connect to your office, then you are using a public network (that is, the Internet) to establish a private network (the VPN tunnel). Once you have a private network, then you will likely be able to access many of the resources just as you would if you were in the office, only a little slower because you are working from the LAN.

If you are going to set up a VPN client, then you first need to obtain configuration settings from your office. First, you need to know what VPN protocol your network is using. The two main types of VPNs are PPTP and L2TP over IPSec. Once you know the type of VPN you are connecting to, then you will need to know the address of the VPN server. This is often an IP address or a DNS name.

To start, open the Network preference pane, and click the plus sign to open the Select the Interface screen. At the Select the Interface screen, choose VPN as the interface, and then choose appropriate VPN type (PPTP or L2TP) for your environment. Once you have entered this information, click the Create button (see Figure 12-14).

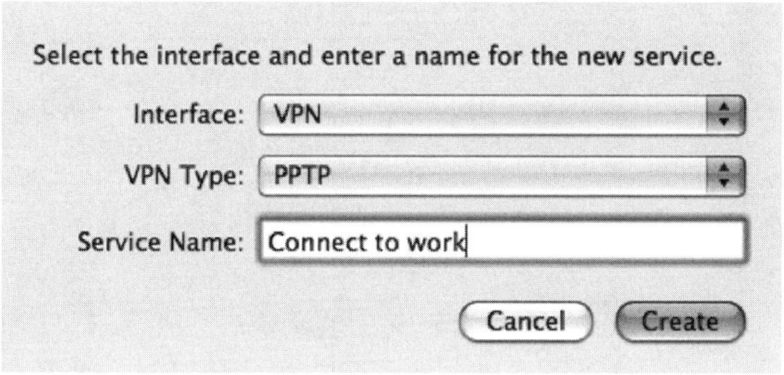

Figure 12-14. *Adding a VPN connection*

Setting Up PPTP

If you will be connecting to a PPTP-based VPN, then you will also need to know the username and password to connect with this connection. Once you have this information, you will be able to configure the VPN.

Once you have a connection created and you have obtained the correct address, account, and password, then you can complete the setup. To do so, open the Network preference pane, and click the PPTP connection you created earlier. Then enter the username in the Account Name field (see Figure 12-15) and the address of the VPN server in the Server Address field.

If you have another authentication method other than simple password authentication required to establish a connection, click the Advanced button. At the User Authentication screen (see Figure 12-16), select your authentication type, and click OK. Once you are finished configuring all the required settings, click Apply in the Network preference pane, and test your connection by clicking the Connect button.

■**Tip** To make connecting easier, select the Show VPN Status check box in Connection Settings. This will put an icon in the menu bar that allows you to quickly connect to any of the VPN connections you have set up.

Figure 12-15. *Configuring a VPN connection in System Preferences*

User Authentication:

○ Password: _____

○ RSA SecurID

○ Certificate [Select...]

● Kerberos

○ CryptoCard

[Cancel] [OK]

Figure 12-16. *PPTP user authentication types*

Setting Up L2TP

If you are given a choice of PPTP or L2TP, then you should use L2TP because it is more secure. If you will be connecting to an L2TP-based VPN, then you will have a few options available to you and will need to know more information about the technical nature of where you are connecting. In addition to some form of user authentication, L2TP also requires machine-based authentication, such as a shared secret or an SSL certificate (see Figure 12-17), which can be imported or manually added using the Keychain Utility.

Figure 12-17. *L2TP user and machine authentication types*

PPP + SSH = VPN

Whenever possible, you should use a VPN to tunnel all remote traffic. There is a PPTP VPN daemon available to Mac users running Mac OS X Server (which we cover more in Chapter 13), but unfortunately it is not available to standard Mac OS X client systems. However, there is a way around this by using an alternative solution: PPP and SSH can be combined to form a VPN link.

■**Note** If you have a VPN in your office or a Mac OS X Server, you do not need something this elaborate. This method is only for building a VPN between two Mac OS X client systems and not for connecting between a Mac OS X client and a Mac OS X Server.

This PPH + SSH method works by creating a PPP link between two systems over an SSH connection. The server machine initiates an SSH connection to the client. Once it has authenticated the connection, the client machine launches pppd, with output going to the inbound SSH session. On the server machine, pppd is launched to respond to the client's pppd. The two daemons sync up and begin passing packets, which are in turn encrypted by SSH. It is not the quickest connection possible, but it does the trick.

The client machine is the machine that is connected to the main network. This is the same box that would run the actual VPN server, but in this situation it is the client of the PPP link. This is also the easiest method of establishing a VPN connection because it allows the remote machine to build and tear down the VPN connection every time a connection is made.

To create this VPN, you'll first need to create an account in the Account pane of System Preferences on the client machine (for the purposes of discussion, we will refer to the client machine in this example as cedge.318.com) for our server machine to log into. The account being created should be a new account and should not be used for any other purpose than for the VPN, mainly because you'll be modifying some of the account settings that may break a normal user because of incompatibility issues. In this example, we will use the account named cedge.

The next step is to set up the VPN account with the ability to launch the PPP daemon. To do this, edit the sudoers file. Open the Terminal, and navigate to the file /etc/sudoers. You'll want to add the VPN Cmnd_Alias and VPN user privileges to make your sudoers file look like this one:

```
# Cmnd alias specification
Cmnd_Alias VPN=/usr/sbin/pppd, /sbin/route

# Defaults specification

# User privilege specification
root    ALL=(ALL) ALL
%admin  ALL=(ALL) ALL
vpn     ALL=NOPASSWD: VPN
```

Note For more information on the sudoers file, see Chapter 3.

The server machine is the machine you are using remotely. This machine will initialize the SSH connection and then respond to the PPP daemon launching on the client. In this example, the server machine is cedge.318.com. To log in to the client machine to launch pppd, you first need to generate a key, using SSH key authentication, and then copy the public portion of the key to the VPN account's home directory on the client machine. You don't need to use a password on the key.

First establish an SSH key. To do this, use the ssh-keygen command. The following iteration of this command will build a key using the RSA encryption method:

```
sudo ssh-keygen -t rsa
```

The command will result in the following lines. At each colon (:), type the password you will be using:

```
Generating public/private rsa key pair.
Enter passphrase (empty for no passphrase):
Enter same passphrase again:
Your identification has been saved in /var/root/.ssh/id_rsa.
Your public key has been saved in /var/root/.ssh/id_rsa.pub.
The key fingerprint is:
a2:3b:11:1d:dd:aa:bd:00:ff:aa:aa:ff:00:ab:ab:11 cedge@cedgetestcomputer
```

Now enter the following command to copy the key pairs to the second computer:

```
sudo scp /var/root/.ssh/id_rsa.pub vpn@cedgecomputer.com:~
RSA key fingerprint is a2:3b:11:1d:dd:aa:bd:00:ff:aa:aa:ff:00:ab:ab:11
cedge@cedgetestcomputer
```

Type yes at the verify prompt, and press the Enter key, as shown here. Once this is complete, type the password, and your preshared key setup will be complete.

```
Are you sure you want to continue connecting (yes/no)? yes
Warning: Permanently added cedge@66.4.4.2' (RSA) to the list of known hosts.
cedge@cedgetestcomputer password:
id_rsa.pub 100% |*************************************************************|
```

Once you've copied the public key to the client system, you'll want to connect to it and finish setting up the VPN account. First ssh into the client machine and then attempt to connect to the server machine from the client to exchange host keys, as shown here:

```
ssh cedge@cedgetestcomputer
cedge@cedgetestcomputer password:
```

Next, you'll want to confirm, adding the server to your client's known hosts:

```
ssh cedge@cedgetestcomputer
The authenticity of host 'cedge (66.4.4.2)' can't be established.
RSA key fingerprint is aa:aa:ff:11:11:11:aa:aa:aa:00:00:00:00:aa:aa:aa.
Are you sure you want to continue connecting (yes/no)? yes
```

Verify that there is a file in the VPN account's ~/.ssh folder called known_hosts. Next, move the generated public key to the file called authorized_keys in the ~/.ssh folder.

```
mv ~/apress.pub ~/.ssh/authorized_keys
```

Finally, configure the PPP daemon to launch passively upon login. The following commands will perform this task:

```
echo "sudo /usr/sbin/pppd passive; logout" > ~/.login
```

To verify that your client machine is set up properly, use the following command from the server machine:

```
sudo ssh cedge@cedgetestcomputer
```

At this point, your server machine should have connected to the client machine, authenticated via the SSH key, and begun to see the garbled output of the PPP daemon. If this is all working properly, then your client machine is ready to go. However, you're not completely out of the woods just yet. To finish configuring the server machine, you'll need to issue a few more commands.

As you saw earlier, when you ssh to the client machine, the PPP daemon will launch and start filling your screen with data garbage. To get the two machines to connect, you need to have the PPP daemon on the server machine launch to respond to the client's PPP daemon. The problem is that you can't launch pppd very well if there's a constant garbage stream that the client machine is outputting. You'll need to use a tool called pty-redir to get around this. This little program will execute a passed command on a separate TTY.

First download pty-redir (from http://www.shinythings.com/pty-redir/), and use the following set of commands to install it:

```
make
sudo mkdir /usr/local/bin
sudo cp pty-redir /usr/local/bin
```

These commands will put the pty-redir binary in your /usr/local/bin directory. To test it, use the following command:

```
sudo /usr/local/bin/pty-redir /usr/bin/ssh cedge@cedgetestcomputer.318.com.
```

You should see a result along the lines of /dev/ttyp4. This output tells you which TTY was allocated for your command and where its output is going. In this case, the client machine's PPP daemon is sending its connection information to the redirected TTY. To complete the link, launch pppd on the server machine and have it use the redirected port. This is accomplished with the following command:

```
sudo /usr/sbin/pppd /dev/ttyp4 local noauth proxyarp persist 192.168.10.1:10.0.0.55.
```

This will tell the server machine's PPP daemon to use the redirected TTY and use the IP address of 10.0.1.1 for the other end of the PPP link. The client machine's IP would be 10.0.0.55. If everything is working up to this point, you should be able to ping 10.0.0.55 and get a response from the client machine. This verifies that your connection is up and running.

Now that the tunnel is up, you can use a static route to point to the client machine's network. You will then be able to pass traffic to other hosts on the client's network through the encrypted PPP tunnel securely. If the network you are trying to access is 10.0.0.0/24, you would use the following command to create a route for traffic directed at specific IP addresses:

```
sudo /sbin/route add -net 10.0.0.0/24 10.0.0.55
```

Depending on the client machine's routing setup, you might be able to have the server machine pass all Internet traffic through the client machine. This is a good way to help secure traffic if you're using a wireless access point in a public place. You can bring up the VPN connection and then change your default route with the following command:

```
sudo /sbin/route add -net 0.0.0.0 10.0.0.55
```

This will route all of your Internet traffic through the VPN link, securing your wireless traffic. Remember, although it might likely take a hit in performance, slowing things down a bit, your traffic will be encrypted, passed through the tunnel, decrypted, passed out of the client machine, and then passed out onto the Internet. Performance slowdowns are an expected result.

The process to disconnect is fairly simple. Use `ps ax | grep pppd` to search for the PPP daemon's process ID. Then use the `sudo kill <Process ID>` command to stop the daemon. The server machine's PPP daemon will bring down the link. This allows the client machine's PPP daemon to quit. Upon quitting, the client machine will log the VPN user out of the connection. At this point, the PPP connection will have stopped, both daemons will have quit, and your SSH connection should be disconnected.

CHAPTER 13

■ ■ ■

Server Security

It may look similar, but Mac OS X Server has some very different functionality from OS X Client. So, it naturally follows that you will need to take additional precautions to secure Mac OS X Server. In this chapter, we'll primarily focus on the services that are specific to OS X Server and how to secure them, paying attention to where the best practices shift from Mac OS X Client.

A number of services are included with Mac OS X Server. We will focus on security as it pertains to the big ones: directory services, file sharing, web server services, wireless services, user account management, Internet security, and the iChat Server. Because many of the other services are dependent on directory services, we'll start by spending some time on security as it pertains to Open Directory, an innovation in Mac OS X Server that distinguishes it from Mac OS X Client.

Limiting Access to Services

A key aspect of Mac OS X Server is the ability to limit which users can access which services. The granularity of controls in Mac OS X Server is far greater than that in Mac OS X. When securing AFP, for example, you can control which share points each user can access. Or if you'd rather not make a configuration change that restricts a specific user from mounting a share point, you can also set a control that denies access to certain services for specific users.

■**Note** Web Objects, Tomcat, and other Java servers need to be configured within the service's security settings.

Service access control lists (SACLs) allow admins to limit access to services to certain users. To configure SACLs, open Server Admin, and click the name of the server. Then click Settings in the toolbar, and click the Access tab. Uncheck the Use Same Settings for All Services box. Next, click each service you want to limit access to, and then select Allow Only Users and Groups, as shown in Figure 13-1. Then, click the plus (+) sign, and drag the users to whom you would like to grant access to the list.

Figure 13-1. *Configuring SACLs*

■Tip This can be helpful with services such as VPN that do not have their own granular user controls within the service.

The Root User

Unlike Mac OS X Client, Max OS X Server enables the root user by virtue of a password at first boot. By default, the Server Assistant uses the local administrative user's password (such as *admin* or *mycompany admin*) that was entered during the setup screens for the password of the root user. Keep in mind that any subsequent password changes to that first administrative account are not replicated when you change its password. In practice, this often leads to a stale password for root if left enabled; in other words, the password does not have any policies applied to it. This is one strong argument for leaving the root user disabled on Mac OS X Server and enabling it only when it's needed. To disable the root user, use the following command:

```
dsenableroot -d
```

> ■**Note** If you disable the root user, then you will not be able to promote an Open Directory system to a replica. The root user does not need to be active during standard replication intervals but will need to be enabled during replica setup.

Foundations of a Directory Service

One of the most substantial aspects of Mac OS X Server and its impact on a Mac OS X–based network is the ability to run directory services. Open Directory, Apple's native directory service technology, is built on open standards such as OpenLDAP, SASL, and Kerberos. Open Directory gives administrators the ability to centralize usernames and passwords for an environment, increase security, and deploy policies to workstations across the network. For example, using directory services, it becomes possible to lock down client computers with the security settings you want, enforce password policies to keep users from having simple passwords, and limit the frequency passwords are required on the network, greatly increasing the overall security of your environment.

Defining LDAP

A *directory service* organizes hierarchical information such as users, groups, and computers. The directory service is the interface to the directory, and it provides access to the data that is contained in that directory. In addition to Open Directory, popular directory services include OpenLDAP, Active Directory, and eDirectory. The one item that nearly all directory service implementations share is Lightweight Directory Access Protocol (LDAP). LDAP is a centralized data structure that is commonly used to track information such as usernames, computers, printers, and other items on a network by performing fast queries of the database. LDAP is a popular protocol and allows for a wide variety of uses.

> ■**Note** When directory services are enabled on the first server of an organization, that server is considered the Open Directory *master*.

Apple's Open Directory technology runs LDAP on a Berkley Database accessible via OpenLDAP for storing user account information. Slapd is the process behind Apple's implementation of the OpenLDAP server. Slapd hosts access to the Berkeley Database where user account information, such as the user ID, is stored. These accounts are merely sets of attributes and values that, if you were to print them, the output would resemble a spreadsheet. Attributes constitute the makeup of a standard user, such as a username, a unique ID, a home directory path, and a password slot.

Defining Kerberos

Kerberos is a highly secure computer network authentication protocol developed at MIT that allows individuals, communicating over an insecure network, to prove their identity to one another in a secure manner.

Kerberos helps prevent eavesdropping to discover passwords or replay attacks (resending packets to obtain similar results from the original transmission) and ensures the integrity of the data. Its designers aimed primarily at a client-server model, and it provides mutual authentication—both the user and the service verify each other's identity.

Note In Greek mythology Kerberos was the hound guarding Hades—a monstrous three-headed dog with a snake for a tail and innumerable snake heads on his back.

Kerberos Deconstructed

Apple has modified Kerberos to handle communication with the Apple PasswordServer, which is responsible for building and replicating the user Kerberos database. PasswordServer keeps the passwords encrypted internally on the server, but Kerberos allows computers from the outside to communicate securely with the server. (You'll learn more about PasswordServer a bit later.)

Kerberos is divided into three components: the Kerberos key distribution server, the Kerberized service, and the Kerberos client. This trio communicates with a Kerberos network known as a *realm*. Kerberos guards your passwords and enables single sign-on to configured servers. Kerberos does this by using tickets known as *principals* to submit credentials over the network rather than sending passwords. Kerberos relies on a series of challenges and session keys that allow a user to be granted a time-sensitive principal known as a *ticket-granting ticket* (TGT). This TGT contains the time stamp used by the key distribution server to verify its authenticity.

Note Apple's implementation of the MIT Kerberos key distribution server (KDC) is krb5kdc.

The TGT is issued as an authentication token to gain access to additional service tickets during the TGT's lifetime. This can be illustrated by logging in as an Open Directory or Active Directory user, authenticating to the directory server, and then services such as the login window will obtain a TGT for the local KDC. This allows users to subsequently authenticate to Kerberized services such as the Apple File Protocol or Cyrus IMAP e-mail server.

■**Note** Clients who are using Open Directory for authentication (known as *binding*) will be automatically configured to use Kerberos using special entries provided and updated by the LDAP server. You can manually initialize the configuration by using the `kerberosautoconfig` command, but this is typically not required.

One of the most critical aspects of Kerberos configuration is time synchronization. If a client or server is more than five minutes apart from their Kerberos KDC server, then authentication will fail. This value is normally best synchronized using the Network Time Protocol (NTP). To enable the NTP service on the Mac OS X Server, configure the server as your Open Directory master (explained a bit later in the section "Configuring and Managing Open Directory"), and enable the NTP check box in the General settings of the Server Admin application. The NTP setting can then be pushed out to client machines using scripts or applications. The NTP client setting can also be configured manually in the Date & Time pane of System Preferences.

■**Note** Multiple time servers are supported when separated by a space.

■**Tip** You can also manually initiate time synchronization using the command line with the following command: `sudo ntd -q`.

Configuring and Managing Open Directory

Because directory services give such a boost to the security of larger environments, we will spend the first part of this section discussing how to set up and bind to Open Directory. Once you have a solid Open Directory environment, we will then show you how to secure Open Directory, more than it is secured in the stock implementation of Mac OS X Server, by disabling anonymous binding and implementing LDAP ACLs.

To start setting up Open Directory, open Server Admin, and click the name of the server. Then click Settings. In the toolbar, select the Services tab. On the Services tab (see Figure 13-2), check the Open Directory box, and click the Save button to see Open Directory added to the list of services available on the server.

Figure 13-2. *Adding the Open Directory service*

In the list of services, click Open Directory. You will now see that the Open Directory service is running as a stand-alone server. Click the Change button (see Figure 13-3).

At this point, the Service Configuration Assistant will open, and you will be stepped through a wizard asking you for some details in order to promote the server to an Open Directory master. Because this is the first system in the domain, click Open Directory Master, and click Continue (see Figure 13-4).

■**Note** As an Open Directory master, the system will run the LDAP database, run as a Kerberos KDC, run the PasswordServer, and be responsible for processing user and workstation policies.

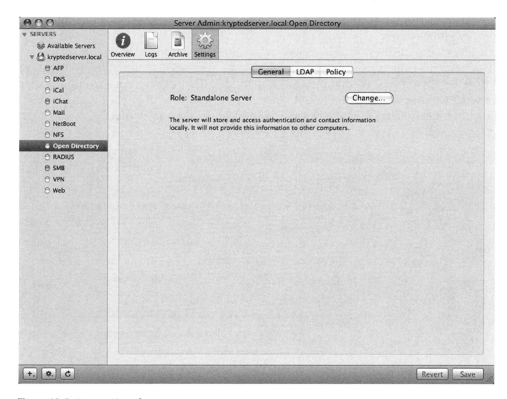

Figure 13-3. *Promoting the server*

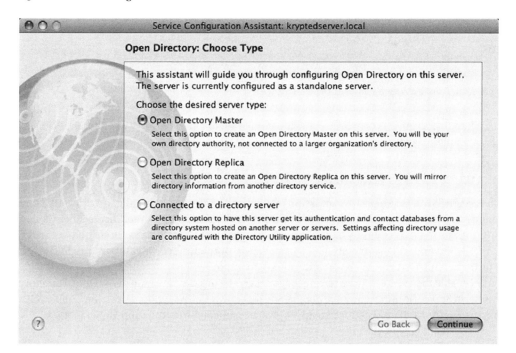

Figure 13-4. *Choosing a role*

Next, the Server Configuration Assistant will ask for a new set of credentials for the Open Directory administrative account (see Figure 13-5). The default value is *diradmin*, and since it is not advisable to use the default usernames, change this value to something else, such as *[company]admin* (where your company name replaces [company]). You will also enter a password for the Open Directory administrative account, and if you choose, you can customize the user ID of the administrative account. Once you are satisfied with your settings, click the Continue button to start promoting the system to an Open Directory master.

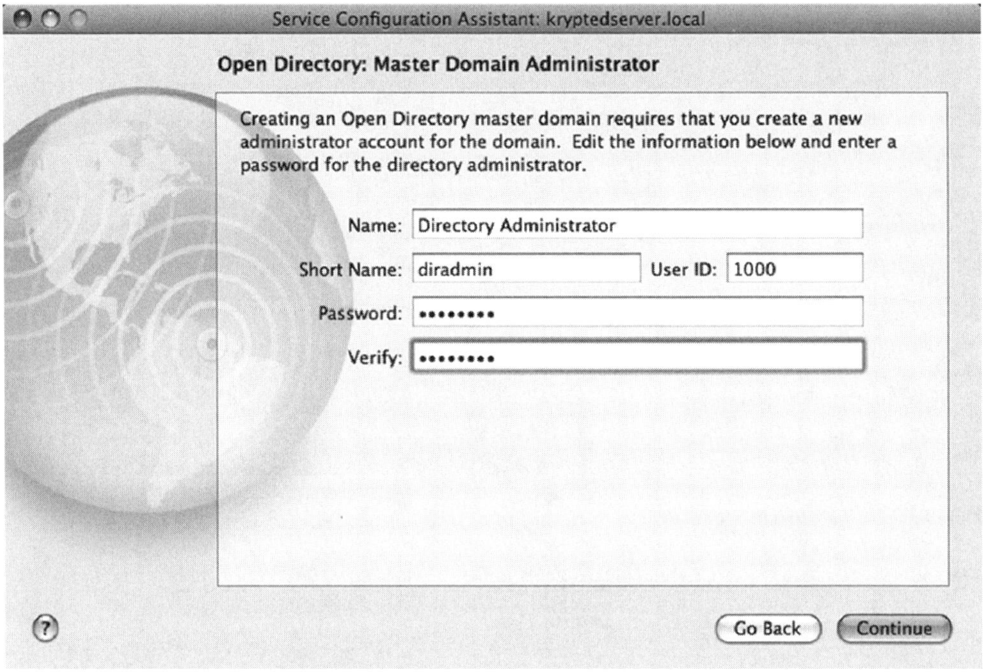

Figure 13-5. *Configuring the credentials*

When this wizard is complete, you will see Role set to Open Directory Master. It is time now to configure some basic security settings for LDAP.

Securing LDAP: Enabling SSL

You can use SSL to secure the transmission of passwords as users communicate with your Open Directory system. At this point, you may have already purchased an SSL certificate and installed it onto your server, or you may have chosen to use the default certificate Apple includes with Mac OS X Server during your testing. If you choose to purchase a certificate, you can follow the steps in the "SSL Certs for Web Servers" section to implement it.

To enable the SSL Certificate setting for your server, click the LDAP tab of the Open Directory settings in Server Admin. Using the Secure Sockets Layer (SSL) section, check the Enable SSL box (see Figure 13-6), and choose an appropriate certificate from the drop-down menu.

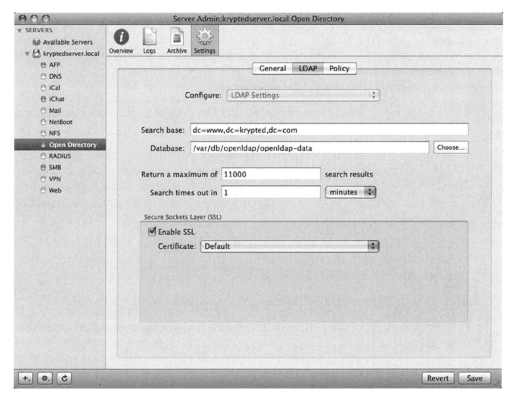

Figure 13-6. *Choosing an SSL certificate*

Once you have selected an SSL certificate, click the Save button to save the changes.

Securing Open Directory Accounts by Enabling Password Policies

Some password policies are available only globally (network-wide), while others are available on a per-user basis. To see global policies, open Server Admin, and click Open Directory. To edit password policies, click the Policy tab (see Figure 13-7), and then click the Passwords subtab.

▪**Note** Global password policies are overridden by user password policies and do not apply to administrative users.

Two types of global password policies exist. Disable Login controls when accounts are able to log in, and Passwords Must controls various requirements for a password to be allowed. We strongly recommend using as many of these as possible because they provide a substantial amount of security. We will briefly discuss each:

Disable Login Passwords: Allows logins to be disabled when the following criteria are met (per policy choice in Server Admin):

- *On specific date*: Disables the account on a date. Disabling accounts that could still be active can be an administrative burden, but it can be helpful for environments with a large number of temporary or freelance users.

- *After using it for*: Disables new accounts after they have been active for a determined number of days.

- *After inactive for*: Disables new accounts after they are dormant for a definable number of days. For most environments, a number between 7 and 30 is a suitable amount of inactivity for an account before it should be considered dead. This option helps for environments where the sheer number of accounts makes it difficult to keep track of account activity.

- *After user makes ___ failed attempts*: Disables accounts after a definable number of failed attempts have occurred. For most environments, a number between 3 and 10 is a suitable number of failed attempts.

Passwords Must: Allows password policies to be made, including the following:

- *Differ from account name*: This option keeps the password from being identical to the username.

- *Contain at least a letter*: This option forces an account to have at least one character from the alphabet (*a* to *z*) in the password. Passwords should not be a string of numbers such as 1234.

- *Contain both uppercase and lowercase letters*: This option requires at least one letter be uppercase and at least one letter be lowercase. An example of an acceptable password would be paSsworD. Passwords are case sensitive.

- *Contain at least a number*: This option forces a password to have a number in it. An example of an allowable password would be 1paSsworD1. Passwords should typically have at least one lowercase letter, at least one uppercase letter, and at least one numeric character.

- *Be reset on first login*: This is a good option for new accounts or accounts that have had their passwords reset. This will keep administrators from knowing their users' passwords (which administrators shouldn't know anyway). This will provide a certain level of comfort to users that the administrator is not snooping through their personal data. If you need access to an account, then you should be forced to reset a password to obtain it.

- *Contain at least*: This option allows you to define the minimum length of a password in characters. The minimum length of a password is something debatable in any environment. For many, 8 is a good number, but this is not as much a technical decision as it is a management decision.

- *Differ from last*: This option allows you to force users to change their passwords to something different every time for as many times as you deem necessary. Many administrators think 3 is enough, but others think 18 is better. This is a decision that should be made on a management level in many cases.

- *Be reset every*: This option allows you to force your users to change passwords at specific times and to define the number of days, weeks, or months that can transpire before a new password must be set. Passwords should also be changed as often as management will allow.

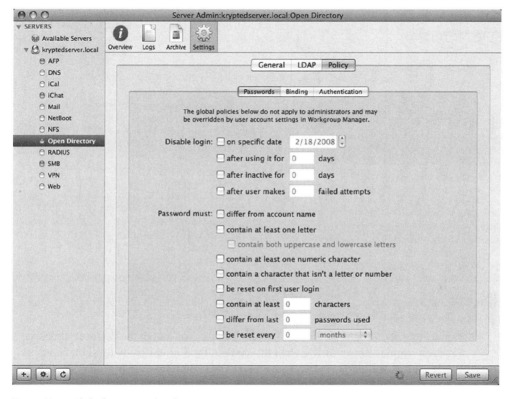

Figure 13-7. *Global password policies*

Securing Open Directory Using Binding Policies

Once you have set up Open Directory to effectively secure client systems and communications between clients and the server, you'll want to secure the actual Open Directory services. The next step after using SSL to secure transport communications is to move on to securing the communications between clients and the server by using binding policies.

On the Binding subtab of the Open Directory Policy tab (see Figure 13-8), you will find the option Enable Authenticated Directory Binding. This option is used to have Mac OS X clients provide a domain directory administrator's username and password to create a computer record in the Open Directory database with the specified name. This standard computer record is then associated with a Kerberos principal, though you won't see a difference in the graphical interface. With the Kerberos principal, the client and server can verify the integrity of their communication with one another.

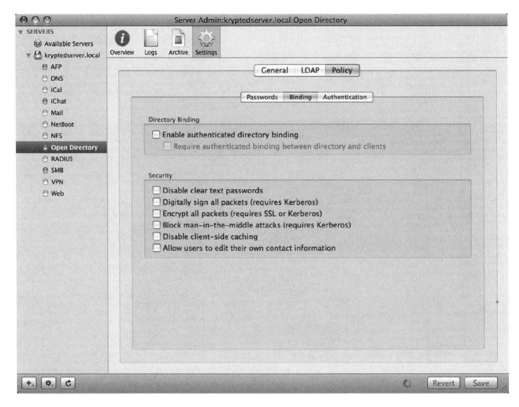

Figure 13-8. *Binding policies*

Once you have enabled authenticated directory binding, you can go the next step and force Mac workstations into the binding by selecting the Require Authenticated Binding Between Directory and Clients option. This will require a Mac OS X client to actually bind to the domain rather than just query it for login settings.

Binding to Open Directory increases the security of the network by forcing all clients who log into the server to be bound to the server. Binding options can also enforce more stringent security requirements by forcing client systems to follow certain rules in how they communicate with the server, whether they are Mac OS X clients or another LDAP client. The options listed in the Security field enforce communication policies and include the following:

Disable clear text passwords: This forces clients to encrypt data communications to the server.

Digitally sign all packets: This places checksums on digital communications.

Encrypt all packets: This forces clients to use SSL or Kerberos.

Block man-in-the-middle attacks: This option checks to see whether the signatures match the session keys.

Disable client-side caching: By default, OS X clients cache LDAP information. This option disables this caching in the event that you suspect a client system has been compromised.

Allow users to edit their own contact information: If you are not using the Address Book integration with the server, then disable this option because users should typically be allowed to edit only their own information in a self-updating address book environment. When disabled, this option will edit the LDAP-based ACLs, which we will discuss later in this chapter.

■**Tip** Once you have enforced the appropriate binding policies, keep a detailed account of what has been enforced, because the client setup will require the policies you are using to be mirrored in the configuration there.

Securing Authentication with PasswordServer

In Open Directory on Leopard, the password is stored, by default, in the password database. This is a very secure approach to handling passwords. In previous versions of Open Directory, the password could be stored in an encrypted form in the LDAP database. This had a potential of allowing any user to cache a password offline and attempt to crack it with various password-cracking tools. But in Leopard, the location of the password in the password database is referenced in the LDAP database so that passwords cannot be cached and then decrypted at a later date. The password slot is a location in the database of the PasswordServer. By listing the password slot rather than having the password itself, the password is never exposed to end users.

The PasswordServer is then used for standard authentication for many services such as the Apple File Protocol. It is based on the Simple Authentication and Security Layer (SASL) standard originally created for the Cyrus e-mail system but ported into Open Directory. It allows various protocols within Open Directory to communicate with one another while still keeping passwords well encrypted.

In addition to handling standard password requirements, the PasswordServer can also limit the types of passwords that can be used and has the ability to enforce rules on passwords. These rules include enforcing the quality of passwords that can be used, the frequency of required password resets, and how passwords can be used by various services in Mac OS X.

PasswordServer handles password exchanges of the following authentication types:

LAN Manager, NTLMv1, and NTLMv2: Mostly used for the Windows File Sharing engine known as SMB. Apple added SASL support for the more modern NTLMv2 password format in version 10.4 of Mac OS X.

DHX: Diffe-Hellman exchange, used extensively for communications of proprietary protocols, such as the Apple File Protocol, and services such as the directory service clients (that is, the Workgroup Manager application).

MS-CHAPv2: Microsoft Challenge Access Protocol, typically used for the Apple Point-to-Point Tunneling Protocol (PPTP) Virtual Private Network (VPN) server.

WEBDAV-Digest: Used for authenticating user sections of a web site, known as *realms*, when connecting with a standard web browser or Web Distributed Authoring and Versioning (WebDAV) client such as the Mac OS X Finder's Connect to Server dialog box.

APOP: Authenticated Post Office Protocol, a legacy option held over from the standard.

Cyrus SASL libraries: Used for IMAP.

You can enable and disable authentication methods via the Server Admin's Open Directory service on the Authentication subtab of the Policy tab, as shown in Figure 13-9.

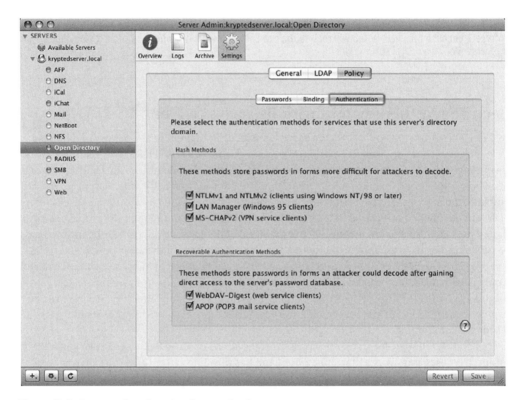

Figure 13-9. *Password authentication methods*

Disable any authentication methods you do not require. For example, in the likely event that you do not support Windows 95 clients in your environment, you can prudently disable the option for LAN Manager. If you do not have VPN enabled, then disable the option for MS-CHAP. If you are not using POP3, then disable the option for APOP. By disabling the authentication methods that are not being used, you will increase the security of your environment.

Many other methods are not listed in the GUI, and it is a good idea to go through them and disable the ones you do not need. To configure authentication methods with the command line, use the slapconfig command:

```
slapconfig -getauthmechanisms
```

```
"SMB-LAN-MANAGER" Enabled Hash
"CRAM-MD5" Enabled Hash
"NTLM" Disabled Hash
"APOP" Disabled Plain
"TWOWAYRANDOM" Disabled Plain
"MS-CHAPv2" Enabled Hash
"PPS" Enabled Hash
"DHX" Enabled Hash
"OTP" Enabled Hash
"SMB-NTLMv2" Enabled Hash
"WEBDAV-DIGEST" Disabled Plain
"SMB-NT" Enabled Hash
"DIGEST-MD5" Enabled Hash
"GSSAPI" Enabled Hash
"KERBEROS_V4" Disabled Hash
"CRYPT" Disabled Hash
```

Note The command `slapconfig` is useful for server setup scripts and can also be used with scripts that run on a schedule such as `crontab` or `launchd`.

To disable authentication methods you do not need, you can use the `-setauthenticationmethods` argument on the `slapconfig` command. This will allow you to turn off each method you are not using.

```
slapconfig -setauthmechanisms APOP off
slapconfig -setauthmechanisms WEBDAV-DIGEST off
```

Note In previous versions of Mac OS X Server, this functionality was covered by the `NeST` command rather than `slapconfig`.

Securing LDAP by Preventing Anonymous Binding

In the previous section, we discussed the Require Clients to Bind to Directory option, but it is important to note that it affects only automatically configured clients. When this option is enabled, no changes are made to the running LDAP process (slapd). This option enables a preference key in the Open Directory client configuration container cn=config. This preference key will be enforced on Mac OS X clients that read this record. You can view this client configuration record using `dscl`:

```
dscl /LDAPv3/127.0.0.1/ -read Config/macosxodpolicy
```

When the setting is enabled, you will see the Binding Required key set to `true` when you review the output of `dscl`. However, because only Mac OS X clients read this configuration, they are the only LDAP clients that are actually "required" to bind. In other words, you are not restricting access to your LDAP server; you are in fact requiring binding only for clients that use the Apple LDAP plug-in. A standard LDAP browser from a rogue machine would still be able to anonymously bind with this option enabled. If you want to restrict access to only authenticated users, you must add the `bind_anon` option to the top of the OpenLDAP configuration file stored at `/private/etc/openldap/slapd.conf`.

Note Be aware that configuring slapd to refuse anonymous connections means all clients will be required to bind. This includes the Open Directory master, which is automatically configured with the local host value 127.0.0.1 upon its promotion to be an Open Directory master. You will need to update this and all other entries before clients will be able to access the database.

Once connected, test that your binding is working by running the following command:

```
dscl localhost list /LDAPv3/127.0.0.1/Users
```

Note This command should print a list of all the users in your Open Directory domain. If it does not, go back to Directory Access, and recheck your binding username and password.

Once you have verified that your server can access your authenticated LDAP server, you are ready to disallow anonymous binding. Edit the slapd configuration tool using your favorite text editor:

```
sudo nano /private/etc/openldap/slapd.conf
```

Add the following `disallow bind_anon` near the top of the file:

```
#
# See slapd.conf(5) for details on configuration options.
#
# This file should NOT be world readable.
#
disallow bind_anon
```

Next, save the configuration file, and restart the LDAP service by sending it a HUP signal using the following command:

```
sudo killall -HUP slapd
```

Securely Binding Clients to Open Directory

Once you have set up Open Directory on the server, you can now bind the individual client workstations to the directory service. At this point, all the password policies are enforced, and many of the services' communications will be Kerberized. So, why move forward with binding clients? If client workstations are not bound, then workstation policies will not be enforced. This includes pushing out Software Update Server settings, mobility and network home folder settings, and any of the managed preferences you may have defined. Also, usernames and passwords for workstations would not be centralized, which is a key to effectively managing and securing larger numbers of systems.

To implement the managed preferences settings by binding the client workstations, use the open Directory Utility (Directory Access Utility for Tiger Users) from the client workstation, and click the lock to authenticate as an administrative user. Once you have authenticated, click the plus sign, and choose Open Directory from the Add a New Directory of Type drop-down menu (see Figure 13-10). (In Tiger, you will need to click LDAPv3 on the Services tab, and click the Configure button.) Next, type in the IP address of the Open Directory server, and click OK.

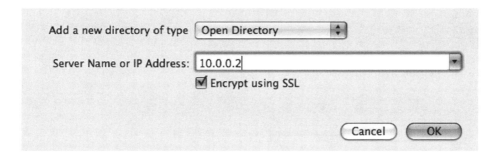

Figure 13-10. *Binding to Open Directory*

If you are implementing an SSL certificate, check the Encrypt Using SSL box here. We will explain setting up SSL certificates later in this chapter.

Once you have added the server, you will want to apply the same security settings that you applied when securing the Open Directory master under the binding policies. To do this, click the Services icon in the Directory Utility toolbar, and click the Open Directory Master server (named ODM in Figure 13-11). Once you click the appropriate server, click Edit to change the settings.

Here you can choose the items that correspond with the setup of your Open Directory master where appropriate using the Security Policy section of the screen (see Figure 13-12). When connected, the title of the window should reflect the hostname of the connected server. If it does not obtain direct access to the server using the local Directory Access application, then the title will not be displayed properly.

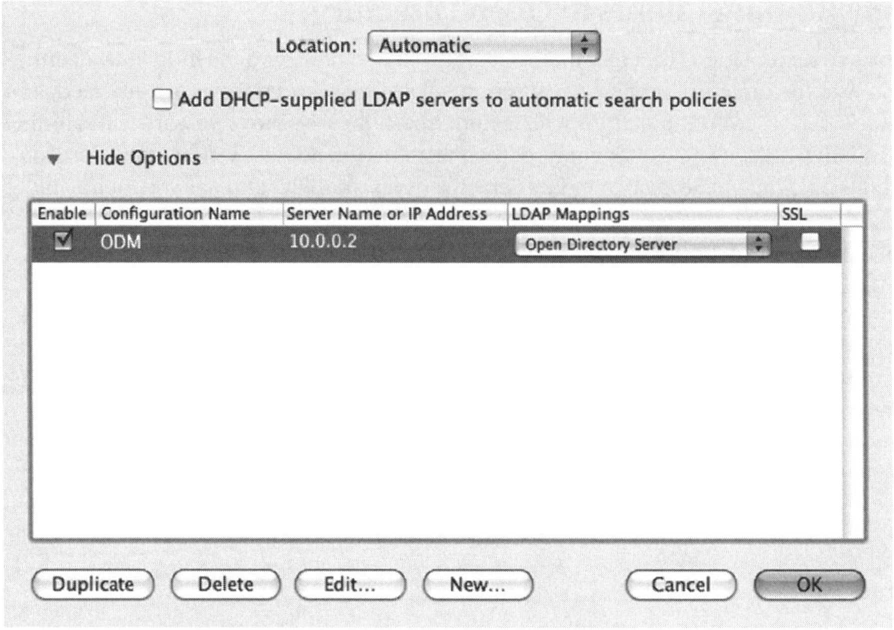

Figure 13-11. *Choosing a directory service to configure*

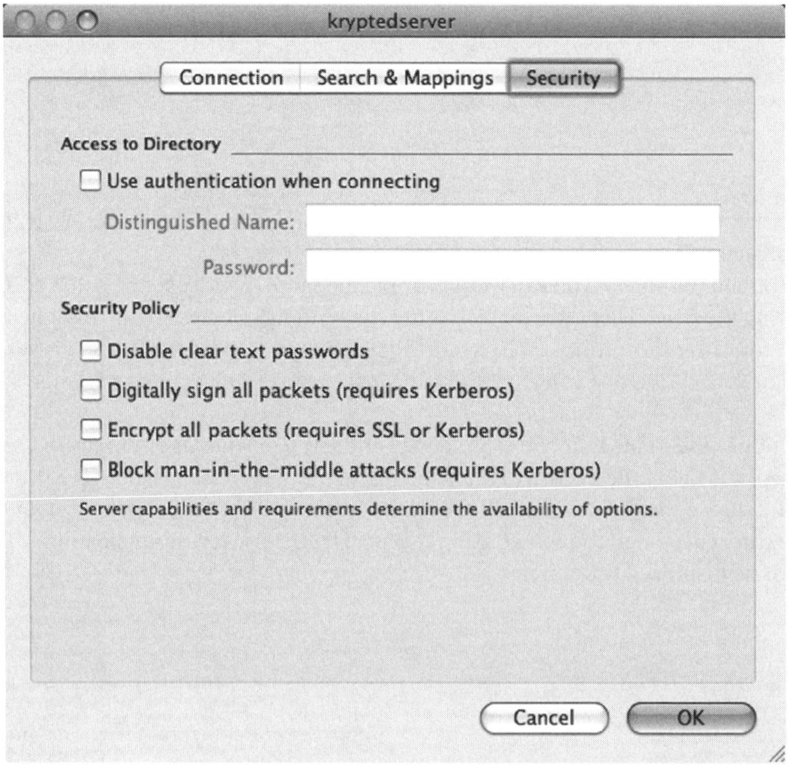

Figure 13-12. *Configure service security*

Further Securing LDAP: Implementing Custom LDAP ACLs

An access control list for LDAP is a way to push out security for the OpenLDAP database. This is secure, because it enforces who can access and change things in the LDAP database. ACL policies are enforced at the server level. If ACLs are not configured, you can use LDAP data to access information about network layouts, users, and other information without authentication. One form of this kind of policy is to use the Force Clients to Bind option in the Open Directory policy settings in Server Admin. But beyond this, you will need to jump into the command line to create these ACLs.

■**Note** You can use `ldapsearch` from the command line to search LDAP databases without authenticating.

To restrict bound users from viewing attributes of other users, use this series of commands:

```
Access to dn=".*,dc=your dcname,dc=.com" attr=userPassword
    by self write
    by * auth
Access to dn=".*,dc=your dcname,dc=.com"
    by * read
```

To fully disable anonymous reads, use this series of commands:

```
Access to dn=".*,dc=your dcname,dc=.com"
    by dn"uid=nssldap,ou=people,dc=dcname,dc=com" read
    by * none
```

To restrict access to an LDAP database and allow users to change their own LDAP information in the shared address book, you would add an LDAP ACL to your `slapd.conf` file. To add an ACL to your `slapd.conf`, add a series of lines that look similar to the following (we will go into further detail on LDAP ACLs later in this chapter):

```
access to
attrs=mail,sn,givenName,telephoneNumber,mobile,facsimileTelephoneNumber,street,
    postalAddress,postOfficeBox,postalCode,password
by self write
```

Creating Open Directory Users and Groups

Now that you have Open Directory set up securely, you might want to start building out the users and groups for your server. Later you can log into client systems using these accounts, but for now you'll need to set up accounts securely so they can log into the server and run services. You can create users and groups in the LDAP database in Mac OS X Server by using the Workgroup Manager application in /Applications/Server.

To create your first user, open Workgroup Manager from the Open Directory master, and select the LDAPv3/127.0.0.1 directory (see Figure 13-13). Now click the New User button in the toolbar, and give the user a name and password.

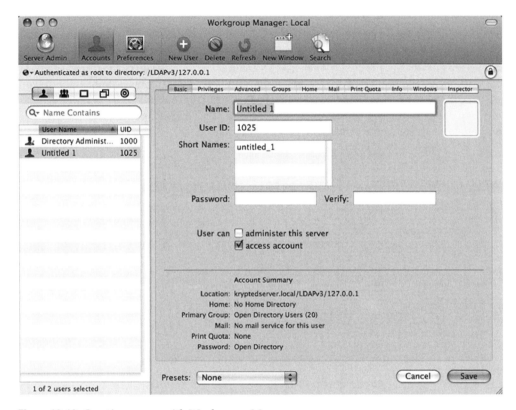

Figure 13-13. *Creating a user with Workgroup Manager*

Next, click the Privileges tab (see Figure 13-14), set Login Shell to None (which removes the new user's ability to open Terminal on the server), and uncheck the Allow Simultaneous Login on Managed Computers box (which will allow each user to log into only one machine concurrently). Once you are satisfied with the user settings, click the Save button to create the user account.

To create a new group, click the Groups tab in Workgroup Manager, and then click the New Group button in the Workgroup Manager toolbar. Enter the name of the group and any comments you have about the group. Click the Members tab, and drag any users who should be in the group into the list of users. Next, click the Options button to configure user policies. At the Policies screen, you will be able to configure a limited set of policies similar to those available in the global policies (see Figure 13-15).

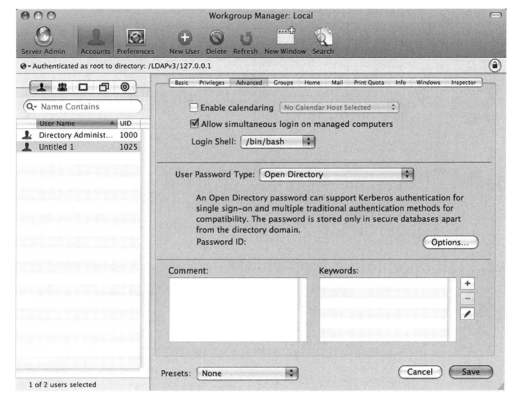

Figure 13-14. *Setting user privileges*

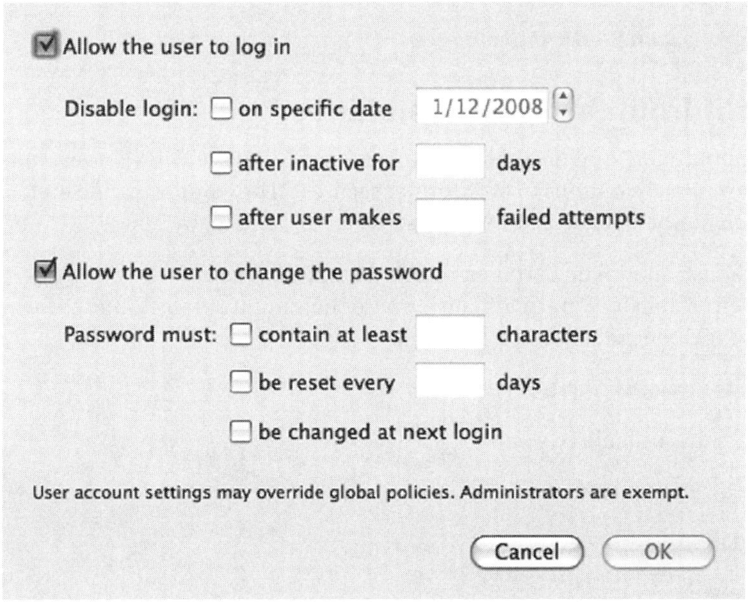

Figure 13-15. *User policies*

Click OK when you are satisfied with your password policies, and then click Save (see Figure 13-16) when you are satisfied with the other settings for the account you have just created.

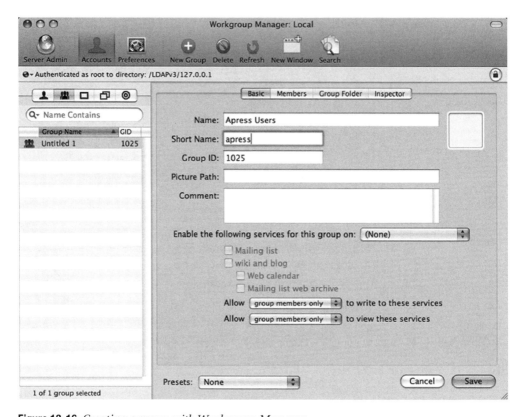

Figure 13-16. *Creating a group with Workgroup Manager*

Securing Kerberos from the Command Line

Kerberos is a powerful application, and the options you have in the GUI are fairly limited, but the command line gives you more options to help further secure it. The command-line tools available to further secure Kerberos include `kinit`, `klist`, `kdestroy`, and many others.

`kinit` is used to establish and cache Kerberos connections. This is useful when troubleshooting Kerberos errors and looking to initiate Kerberos communications. Options for the `kinit` command include the following:

- `-F`: Makes tickets nonforwardable
- `-f`: Makes tickets forwardable
- `-P`: Makes tickets nonproxyable
- `-v`: Forces validation
- `-R`: Renews tickets

`klist` lists tickets. This is useful when looking to list all of the Kerberos service principals that a user is authorized to access. Options for `klist` include the following:

- `-4`: Lists only Kerberos 4 tickets

- `-5`: Lists only Kerberos 5 tickets

- `-A`: Lists all tickets

- `-s`: Runs silently

`kdestroy`: Removes tickets from the cache. This is useful in troubleshooting Kerberos/KDC issues. The following is the option:

- `-a`: Destroys all tickets

■**Note** As is true with Windows, a RAM-based ticket cache is used instead of a file-based ticket cache as with most versions of Kerberos for Unix and Linux variants.

Some command-line applications available for the Kerberos server include the following:

- `kdcsetup` creates the first admin account.

- `kerberosautoconfig` creates the keytab files.

Managed Preferences

The ability to manage preferences is one of the most powerful aspects of directory services. In previous sections, we showed how to set up Open Directory to have a centralized repository of usernames and passwords. You can further secure the server itself (and any other servers in our environment) using Kerberos and password policies. We have also showed how to secure Open Directory accounts by enabling password policies and restricting the types of communications with the server. Now, we'll cover enforcing policies, known as *managed preferences*, on client systems.

To access and configure policies in Tiger systems (which we will use as an example because it is the dominant operating system in the wild today), open Workgroup Manager, click Preferences, and change to the directory service for Open Directory. Then click a computer, user, or group on the left column, and click the type of policy in the right column (see Figure 13-17).

Each policy has options for First or Always. The First option pushes managed preferences out to end users the first time they log in. The Always option pushes managed preferences out to end users every time they log in.

These policies include the following:

Applications: Chooses the applications that users can access or denies access to specified applications.

Classic: Controls users' ability to use Classic applications and controls how they are handled.

Dock: Controls what icons are in the Dock, where the Dock is located, and whether auto-hide can be configured.

Finder: Controls whether Simple Finder is used and what settings for the Finder are used. Simple Finder disables items on the finder such as keystrokes. Other more granular settings include the ability to configure whether the computer shows mounted disks on the desktop, where new Finder windows place users in directory trees, and whether to confirm when emptying the trash.

Internet: Controls mail server, mail account type, and home page settings.

Login: Sets login items, adds share points to login items, installs scripts to run for computers, controls login items preference pane settings for computers, and controls Fast User Switching settings.

Media: Controls whether users can access CDs, DVDs, and removable storage.

Mobility: Sets up roaming profile settings for OS X clients and selects which folders sync with the server during intervals specified by the administrator. This is useful when configuring backup systems (backing up is covered further in Chapter 15).

Network: Configures the proxy settings for all client machine network interface cards (NICs).

Printers: Pushes out printers to client machines as well as controls which printers the users can view.

Software Update: Pushes out software update server settings to client machines.

System Preferences: Controls which System Preferences users can access.

Universal Access: Controls settings for users with special needs.

Managed preferences are stored in MCX files. An MCX file is an XML file that will enforce managed settings by caching the file on the local workstation. If you are using a third-party LDAP structure, then you can use MCX files to push out managed settings, even if you do not use Open Directory (although Open Directory makes it easier by providing administrators with an easy-to-use GUI for controlling policies). You can also use custom MCX files to build managed settings for applications or settings that are not provided in the GUI for Server Admin.

The features available in an MCX include access to removable hard drives, how the drives appear to users, login items, and Finder settings. They are standard configuration files that are mostly configured by the GUI in the Computer Policies section under Settings in Workgroup Manager. However, administrators can go far deeper into granular control by creating custom MCX files. A custom MCX can be pushed to client systems and will enforce custom policies for third-party software or settings that Apple didn't include in the default policies (such as items available to the `defaults` command).

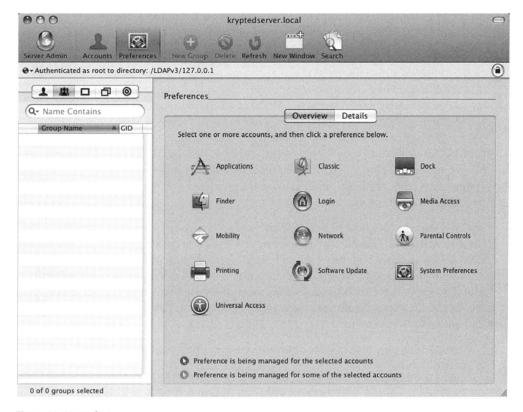

Figure 13-17. *Policies*

Enhanced Security for Managed Preferences in Leopard

In the upgrade from Tiger to Leopard Server, there were some new policies added, and features for some of the existing policies were expanded upon. These include the following:

Applications: There are now more features in managed features for applications. The most important one is a more advanced limiting of user access to applications. You can now allow or disallow user access to applications by selecting the user individually or by selecting a folder full of applications. This means you can allow access to applications located in the /Applications folder but disallow all applications located in the /Applications/Utilities folder. There are also controls now for allowing specific widgets as well as the ability to disable the Front Row application, an unnecessary application in most corporate environments. This limiting of user access functionality is a fix that has been overdue for a while. The original application launch restrictions were based solely on a bundle identifier key within applications. A would-be attacker could easily change this key. In fact, because of the launch restrictions configurable only at the application level and not in the kernel of the operating system, even Apple's own software would allow you to bypass these limitations by configuring an application to launch when clicking an assigned mouse button. This is no longer the case in Leopard.

Finder: There are new options to limit users from performing tasks when in the Finder such as ejecting a disk, connecting to servers, rebooting, and burning optical media such as CDs or DVDs.

Login: There is a more fine-tuned control of the login process. You can now control the list of users displayed to a user at the login screen, including mobile accounts and network users. You can also show/hide the Restart button, disable automatic logon, enable Fast User Switching, set the local computer record name to the name of the computer on the server, enable guest access, control the inactive time to log out users, and configure computer-based ACLs. In previous operating systems, when you disabled the Restart, Shutdown, and Sleep buttons at the login window, users could still access this functionality using special commands at the username prompt such as >shutdown or >restart. This workaround has been deprecated in Leopard.

Mobility: Mobility now allows administrators to set an expiry for a user's home folder on the system they are logging into. This allows administrators to keep local desktop systems from getting polluted with hundreds of home folders without using custom scripts to do so. Administrators can also now force accounts on local systems to use FileVault with Mobility accounts to keep data on local systems as secure as possible and set quotas for user home directories. Finally, it is also now possible to control the path that the user home folder points to on local desktops.

Network: Administrators can now disable Internet Sharing, AirPort, and Bluetooth for client computers.

Parental Controls: Administrators can hide profanity in the dictionary, control access to web sites, set the amount of time per day that a computer is allowed to be used, and set times when login is not allowed in this new managed preference.

Printing: Users can be forced to put their username, date, and/or MAC address in a page that is sent with each print job.

System Preferences: Users can be allowed or denied access to each system preference.

You can enforce these managed preferences on systems that use Active Directory by modifying the LDAP schema in Active Directory. Third-party applications, such as Thursby's ADmitMac, will store this MCX data outside the Active Directory system, allowing you to manage your Macintosh clients without modifying your Active Directory infrastructure. Other third-party directory clients such as Centrify's DirectControl software rely primarily on custom code for preference management.

Note Most Active Directory administrators will not want to modify the LDAP schema since schema extensions cannot be undone in Active Directory.

Providing Directory Services for Windows Clients

In Microsoft Windows, a primary domain controller (PDC) can be configured to enforce client systems to authenticate based on usernames and passwords stored in Open Directory databases. This PDC feature is available only in Mac OS X Server when it is running as an Open Directory master. A backup domain controller (BDC) should be used in this environment, because without a live PDC or BDC, clients will not be able to authenticate using their Open Directory–based credentials. The BDC must be run on a replica. It also provides some form of high availability for the Windows domain structure.

Although Windows systems can authenticate through the PDC, they cannot have Windows-based policies enforced in this Open Directory–based environment. However, you can push out home folders for roaming profiles and login scripts using LDAP attributes that are built into Workgroup Manager using the Windows tab.

To enable an Open Directory server as a PDC, open Server Admin, and click Windows. Then click Settings, and choose Primary Domain Controller under the role (see Figure 13-18). Once the role has been set, enter a computer name and a workgroup name. Optionally, you can enable WINS registration on the Advanced tab. Legacy Windows systems need legacy authentication methods such as LAN Manager authentication. Therefore, you will need to determine whether your server will be supporting older clients such as Windows 95 or third-party appliances requiring this authentication type. Disable WINS registration if legacy clients will not be accessing the server.

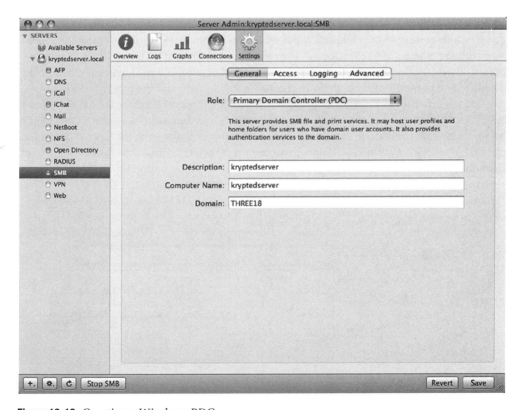

Figure 13-18. *Creating a Windows PDC*

Active Directory Integration

The Apple Active Directory service plug-in (AD-Plugin) is an extension that Apple added to its DirectoryService API. It can be configured using the Directory Access application. The AD-Plugin allows users of Mac OS X Client or Mac OS X Server to bind to Active Directory easily. It was developed by Apple to provide interconnectivity with Microsoft's Active Directory, and it supports Kerberos autoconfiguration for clients bound into Active Directory using DNS entries known as *service* (SRV) records.

When you use the Active Directory plug-in to bind to Active Directory, you can set up Open Directory to connect to an Active Directory domain controller and have items accessible to Open Directory from Active Directory. Because you are connecting to an existing directory service, you will more than likely have all the policies for binding and passwords in place in your Active Directory environment.

■**Note** Much of the Active Directory integration configuration is available in the GUI for 10.5 and 10.4 and in the command line for 10.3.

Using the AD-Plugin

When attempting to bind to Active Directory, you will need to know the forest (top-level directory structure) and domain name to which you are trying to bind. All Windows Active Directory setups include at least one domain and one forest. A *forest* is the top level of any Active Directory infrastructure, and a *domain* is a logical segmentation of a forest. In a basic Active Directory setup (and most Active Directory environments are a basic setup), you will have only one domain in a forest and therefore will use the same name for the domain and the forest.

To configure the OS X machine to use Active Directory, open Directory Utility, click the lock to authenticate, and enter the local administrator's username and password. Then click the + button, enter the domain name of the Active Directory domain, enter the desired computer name (see Figure 13-19), and click Bind. Provided that the Active Directory environment is set up properly, you will now have a Mac OS X Client or Server that is bound into Active Directory.

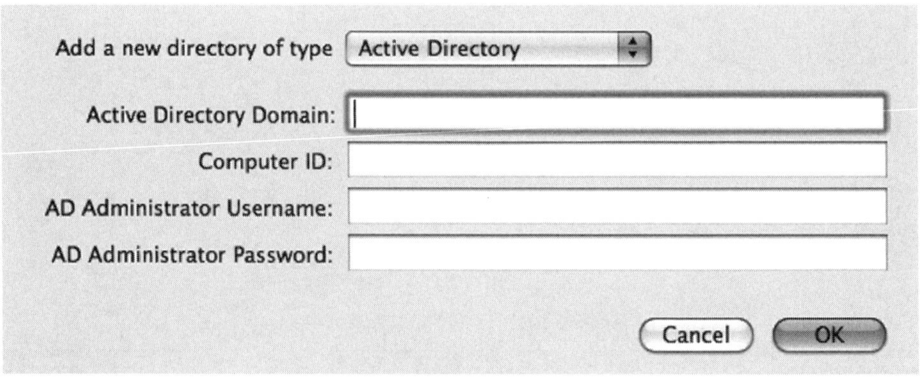

Figure 13-19. *Binding to Active Directory*

■**Note** If you need to do an advanced setup, the name of the domain will match the name of the forest because the domain is a member of that forest. With a Windows server, when you create the first domain controller and give that domain a name, the forest will also take on that same name. Now, that is not to say you cannot have different domains in the same forest; you can, in which case you would leave the forest the same but change the name of the domain. Remember that all domains belong to a forest, and multiple domains can belong to a single forest.

Setting Up Network Homes with Active Directory Clients

A universal naming convention (UNC) is used for mapping drives within the Windows operating system. The Use UNC Path from Active Directory to Derive Network Home Location option in Directory Access will allow you to use the Active Directory home directory to map drives—the directory specified under Active Directory Users and Computers that is mapped for any user. An example of this is \servershare. By default, a home directory is not created; however, in a Windows environment, it is best practice to enable this home directory in order to ensure that the users' data is stored on the server for the centralization of sharing, permissions, and auditing. The option offered here will allow you to keep that structure in the Apple environment as well, allowing for Active Directory–planned structures to be preserved (including mapped home directories that have been established in Active Directory).

For the option Network Protocol to be Used, you can choose one of two protocols from the drop-down menu: SMB or AFP. This determines how a home directory is mounted on the desktop. (By default, SMB is used, and in most cases when dealing with a Windows network, this is preferable.) Server Message Block (SMB) is the application-level protocol used by Windows to communicate with other Windows computers when accessing shares (this includes printers, files, and serial ports). The SMB option here will allow Apple workstations to communicate with the Windows server using the native protocol that Windows uses to communicate with its files and directories. Unix variants can communicate with SMB using their version of the protocol called Samba.

Using the AD-Plugin from the Command Line

It may become necessary to bind a Mac to Active Directory using the Active Directory plug-in from the command line. Perhaps you need to force the binding, you want to use a setting not available in the GUI, or you want to use the Active Directory plug-in in a server script. For times like these, you will find the command dsconfigad to be handy. dsconfigad does not require root privileges to run and can be used from the command line to force certain aspects of directory services to work even when the GUI will not bind clients as needed. These include the following:

- -enableSSO enables Kerberos authentication for services, such as AFP, by generating Kerberos principals (commonly used with the magic triangle, described in the next section).

- -ggid maps group ID information.

- -mobile automates the enabling of mobile accounts.

- -preferred enables the use of a preferred server.

- `-localhome` places the home folder on the local system rather than using a server shared home.

- `-f` forces the command to run (which is useful when forcing an unbind).

These become very helpful with scripting. A script can be told to run on the first access of an imaged system. This allows for easy mass deployment and for the scripting of specific options to be pushed out to clients for binding.

Integrating Open Directory with Active Directory: The Magic Triangle

Setting up the *magic triangle* involves the administrator building an Open Directory infrastructure, binding it to an Active Directory infrastructure, and then binding the clients to both Active Directory and Open Directory. It is a common way in the Mac OS X Server community to get Mac management policies and still use centralized Active Directory–based directory services. This seemingly awkward setup results in Active Directory handling password authentication and Open Directory handling policy management, giving administrators a fairly simplistic way to manage their Mac systems, even if within the confines of Active Directory. It is also possible to extend the Active Directory schema (which Windows administrators are generally resistant to) to include MCX attributes that can be used to manage Mac workstations or use augmented records (a new feature in Leopard Server).

To set up a magic triangle, promote your first server to an Open Directory master. Next you will need to strip the KDC functionality out of Open Directory since Kerberos functionality will be hosted by Active Directory. To do this, remove Kerberos from `sso_util` using the `sso_util` command as follows:

```
sudo sso_util remove -k a <diradmin> -p <pass>
```

Next you will need to delete any stale Kerberos configuration data if there is any. If there isn't any, you will receive an error that the data could not be found, which is fairly common with newer installations. To remove the stale Kerberos data, use the following two commands:

```
dscl -u <diradmin> /LDAPv3/127.0.0.1 -delete /Config/KerberosKDC
dscl -u <diradmin> /LDAPv3/127.0.0.1 -delete /Config/KerberosClient
```

Then, bind the server into Active Directory as described in previous sections. Once the Open Directory server is bound into Active Directory, it is possible to reenable single sign-on functionality. To do so, run the following command:

```
dsconfigad -EnableSSO
```

Now, bind Mac clients into both directory structures (using the same steps for both Open Directory and Active Directory that were mentioned previously). Active Directory will now process user credentials, and Open Directory will now process system policies for the Mac clients.

Note We have stepped through this in a very simplistic manner. In reality, you might have a variety of problems with DNS, Active Directory, Open Directory, or server communications. If this is the case, check the forums at http://www.AFP548.com to see whether others have experienced the same issues and published fixes for them.

Web Server Security in OS X Server

Chapter 11 discusses web server security for Mac OS X Client. Apache is the same in Mac OS X Server as it is in Mac OS X Client for the most part. But there are differences in how the web server operates in OS X Client versus OS X Server. We will cover the differences between the two and discuss how to configure secure settings for the web server in OS X Server.

Using Realms

As we discussed in Chapter 11, using htaccess files is the traditional way to password protect a folder in Apache. However, htaccess can get rather complicated and, if not configured correctly, could cause more security headaches than solved. Instead, try using realms. In Mac OS X Server, when discussing the web server, a *realm* is a password-protected folder that uses the Open Directory username and password in OS X to share files. Realms use WebDAV, a special protocol designed with this purpose in mind that Apple has integrated with Kerberos. With WebDAV you will be using a password from your directory service rather than one stored in an htaccess file (this is more secure because it is often easy to find a password in unencrypted text rather than in the highly encrypted PasswordServer).

To use realms, create a site that has a subdirectory that you want password protected. Create the users who will need to access the directory in Workgroup Manager. Next, open Server Admin, and click Web. Then click Sites in the Server Admin toolbar, click the appropriate site that the realm will be built for, and click the Realms tab. If you have not used realms before, the list of realms will likely be empty (as shown in Figure 13-20).

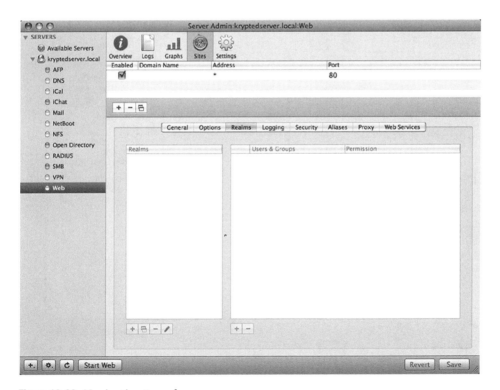

Figure 13-20. *Navigating to realms*

Click the + sign, and enter the name of the realm at the new screen (see Figure 13-21). Also enter the folder to access, and choose an authentication type (we suggest Kerberos). When you are satisfied with your settings, click OK.

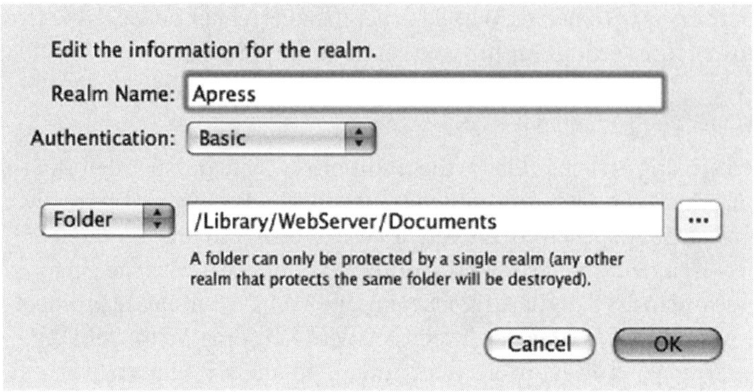

Figure 13-21. *Creating a realm*

Now, click the plus sign (see Figure 13-22) to open the Users & Groups list, and drag the users or groups that require access to the realm to the Users & Groups panel. Under Groups, drag the groups, and set the value in the Permission column for each of the objects in the Users & Groups list.

Figure 13-22. *Assigning permissions to a realm*

Once you are satisfied that the users and groups have the appropriate permissions, you will now be able to log into the site using Kerberos (or the protocol you set earlier).

SSL Certs on Web Servers

If you are doing any form of e-commerce, you should be using an SSL certificate. Many would argue that if you are trading any information with a client computer, such as a web form for submitting a support request, you should also be using SSL to encrypt the traffic. To enable HTTPS Access (SSL) on the web server, you will first need to create and install an SSL certificate (we discuss setting up SSL on OS X Server later in the chapter). Then from Server Admin, you will click the web service and click the + icon to add a new site.

On the General tab (see Figure 13-23), enter the appropriate domain name in the Domain Name field, and enter **443** in the Port field.

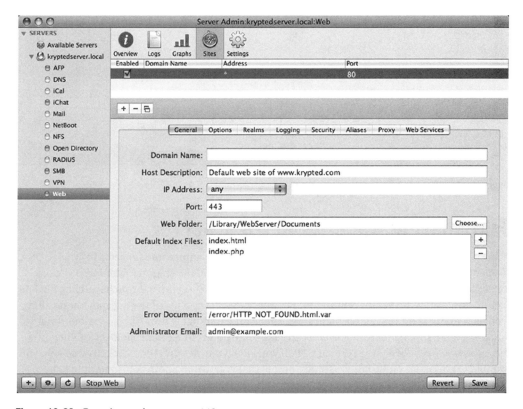

Figure 13-23. *Creating a site on port 443*

To assign the appropriate certificate, click the Security tab (see Figure 13-24), and check the box to enable SSL. Next, select the appropriate SSL certificate, and click Save to complete the setup.

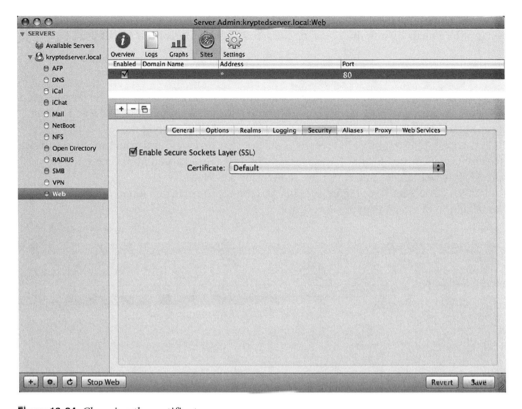

Figure 13-24. *Choosing the certificate*

File Sharing Security in OS X Server

File Sharing is more unified and able to be more granularly configured for security in Mac OS X Server than it is in Mac OS X Client. For example, to view all the shared folders on a system, open Server Admin, and click the name of the server in the Servers list. From here, click the File Sharing button in the Server Admin toolbar, and you will see a list of the logical volumes that your server can see along with a handy disk space image showing how full the various volumes are (see Figure 13-25). At this point, you can click share points to see which folders are currently being shared over SMB, AFP, NFS, or FTP. If you click Volumes and then click Browse, you will be able to configure new folders as share points that you would like others to be able to access. To do this, browse to the folder to be shared, and then click the Share button in the upper-right corner below the toolbar.

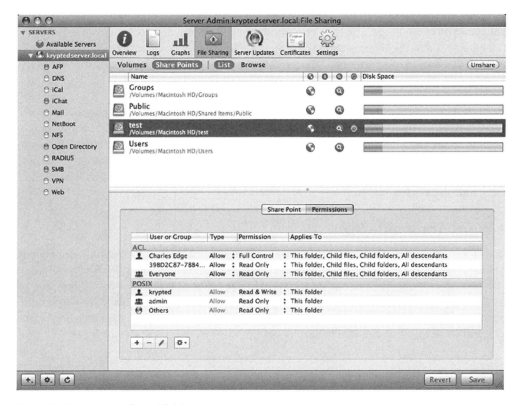

Figure 13-25. *Viewing shared folders*

In the File Sharing admin screen, you will see three tabs along the bottom: Share Point, Permissions, and Quotas (if quotas are enabled). From here, click Share Point, and review the options:

- Enable AutoMount provides options to set up an Open Directory link to the volume.

- Enable Spotlight Searching allows the volume to be searchable using Spotlight.

- Enable as TimeMachine Backup Destination means client computers can back up using Time Machine.

- Protocol Options opens the screen that allows SMB, AFP, NFS, and FTP settings to be configured (and looks similar to the old screen in Workgroup Manager).

■**Note** From a security perspective, you should enable only the file sharing protocols that are necessary on a per-share basis.

Once you have configured the options for your share point, click the Permissions tab. This will allow you to configure who has access to shared data. From here, the main change from Tiger Server is that the Users & Groups window is a floating window, with a new look and feel, but with the same overall feature set. The next major change is that ACLs are listed above POSIX permissions, and when you drag a user or group into the window, a blue line will appear indicating that dropping the object into the screen will cause it to stay.

Server security also includes not allowing users to fill up the hard drive space on a server. This often means implementing quotas on volumes. To implement quotas, click the Quotas tab, and notice that when you enable quotas, you cannot drag users and groups into this window. Only users with home folders on the volume can be configured for quotas using Server Admin. Make sure to issue warnings to your users. They might not be used to quotas and it may take some time to get used to them.

A Word About File Size

One of the challenging aspects of being a Mac admin is that Mac users (artists and designers) typically work with large files. In some cases, single files can be in the hundreds of gigabytes. Mac users accustomed to files normally 100MB in size are less likely to notice that they are sending files to each other that are too big for emailing. So, limit files, but make sure to communicate what's appropriate with the users in order to reduce support calls. Explain when to use FTP or file sharing and when not to use it. Also, limit the overall size of the mailboxes.

NFS

NFS is less secure than AFP. It has limitations on how it can granularly handle permissions for shared data, and there is no encryption built into it. The settings for NFS in Server Admin are minimal at best. NFS trusts the client, which is one reason that it has such a high number of security flaws. However, Leopard NFS on OS X Server is now Kerberized, making it a bit more appealing. One great feature of NFS is that it provides home folders to large numbers of computers by using the automount feature combined with the NFSHomeDirectory attribute in LDAP.

NFS has two global service options in Server Admin: the number of server daemons and the option to use TCP or UDP (or both) for serving up your data, neither of which is very security policy–friendly. But, notice that you cannot stop or start the NFS daemon from Server Admin. There are only two services like this: Open Directory and NFS. If you have NFS enabled for any share point, then you're stuck running the NFS daemon; if not, the daemon will not start. If you don't have an export on any share points, then you can't run it, so in order to stop the NFS daemon, verify that no shares are using NFS.

Workgroup Manager settings give the administrator per-export (share point) configuration capability. This is where you can secure each export independently. This is very different from securing AFP shares, for example. When you set up an export, you will have the option to export the directory listing to Client (certain IPs), World (everyone), or Subnet (all IPs in the specified subnet). These options are included to mitigate the risks associated with running NFS (such as man-in-the-middle attacks). Once you have chosen who can access this data, you can determine how to handle data access. Each export has the ability to map the root user to nobody (the root user receives permission as guest), map all users to nobody (all users act as the guest permission set), and can be set to read-only (useful for backups or remote sync operations).

The NFSD settings mirror the server admin settings. NFSD is the remote NFS server and is mostly used to initiate the NFS daemon and forward any requests to mount a directory to `mountd`. The `mountd` processes mount requests based on the `exportsfile`, which contains a list of shares to export and the attributes (permissions, and so on) for them. Options for `mountd` include the following:

- `-n` allows nonroot mount requests to be served.

- `-r` allows requests for regular files.

- `-D` enables the debug log.

- `-d` means `mountd` does not daemonize and sends logs to stderr rather than syslog (which is helpful with troubleshooting).

You can use the exports file (`/etc/exports`) for getting a little more granular with the security of your share points. The options (taken from a `man` command on `export`) are as follows:

- `-maproot - user` means the credential of the specified user is used for remote access.

- `-maproot - user:group1:group2:...` means the colon-separated list is used to specify the precise credential to be used for remote access by root.

- `-mapall - user or -mapall=user:group1:group2:...` specifies a mapping for all client UIDs.

- `-alldirs` allows clients to mount at any point within the file system.

- `-ro` specifies that the file system should be exported read-only (the default is read/write).

- `-32bitclients` guarantees directory cookies will fit within 32 bits even though directory cookies are 64, which is required with some versions of Windows.

AFP

The AFP service in Mac OS X Server is similar to that in Mac OS X Client. However, it has a myriad of other features that can be used to further secure the box or increase performance for the AFP service. As we covered AFP in Chapter 10, we will be picking up where Chapter 10 left off here and investigating unique aspects of the AFP service in OS X Server.

Disabling AFP Masquerading

One feature that is unique to the Apple File Protocol engine in Mac OS X Server is its ability to authenticate any user account with the password for any administrative account. This is called *AFP masquerading*. AFP masquerading will allow any administrative account on a system to potentially compromise all users' AFP access. Password policies don't apply to administrative accounts. If an administrative password is compromised, then the administrator can access all files as though they were any user. If one admin user had the password *Charles*, then all accounts on the system would authenticate with *<username>:password "Charles"* such as *afp://user:password@server/*.

Although this may be helpful in verifying a host operating system's interpretation of access permissions, it should always be disabled when not in use. It does not require a restart of the service or server for the setting to be disabled.

To define access methods for AFP in Mac OS X Server, open Server Admin, and click AFP. Then click the Access tab, and uncheck the Enable Administrator to Masquerade As Any User box (see Figure 13-26). You will also want to limit the number of users to AFP to something that is reasonable in order to keep the AFP server from crashing (AFP can typically handle only approximately 350 clients mounting from the volume). To do so, change the Client Connections in the Access screen.

■**Note** Guest access is disabled by default for AFP but can be enabled by new administrators. To verify that it is disabled, use the Access screen to verify that the box Enable Guest Access is unchecked.

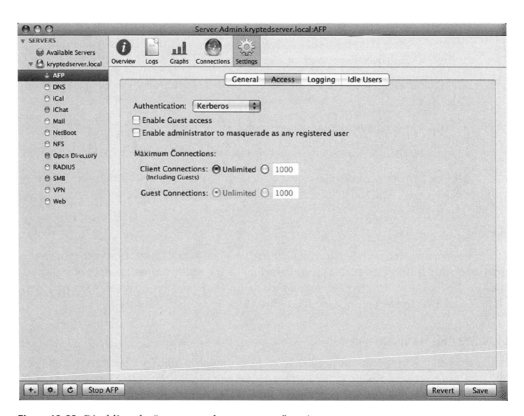

Figure 13-26. *Disabling the "masquerade as any user" option*

Kerberized AFP

Kerberos authentication, as mentioned earlier, is a superior authentication method to the standard Diffe-Hellman exchange (DHX) authentication scheme. Kerberos authentication can be required for the AFP server, but it is worth noting a few gotchas with this configuration:

- When Kerberos authentication is required, only clients with a properly configured `edu.mit.Kerberos` file can authenticate with the service. This may disable access for any client that is not bound into the Open Directory network.

- Clients must not have a time skew longer than five minutes. This should be configured on the client by using a network time server.

- Users within the local authentication database will not be able to authenticate to the AFP server because their passwords are not *Open Directory*. This may prevent the first user created on the system from being able to authenticate because they are created in the local authentication database.

Forcing Kerberos authentication requires AFP clients to use Kerberos to connect to the server. This is a good way to increase the security of your AFP environment. To force Kerberos authentication, set the authentication type to Kerberos on the Access tab of the AFP Service in Server Admin (see Figure 13-26).

■**Note** Users that are not in the Open Directory database will not be able to authenticate via Kerberos. This means that those clients with local accounts that do not have proper Kerberos configurations files in `/Library/Preferences/edu.mit.kerberos` will not be able to authenticate to the AFP server once this setting is turned on.

In Tiger Server, there was a feature in the Access screen called Enabling Secure Connections, which allowed administrators to connect to AFP over SSH. This gave AFP the same level of security that they would have with SSH. Administrators could then click Go in the Finder and select Connect to Server from the menu of the client system. Then at the password dialog box, they could click the picture of a cogwheel and check the Secure Connection box. This feature is no longer available in Leopard.

AFP Logging

By default Mac OS X Server does not log all events. From a security perspective, if there is a compromised server, then you will want as many logs as possible to pull data from in order to reconstruct the events that transpired on your server.

To maximize logging, open Server Admin, and click the AFP service. Then click the Logging tab, and choose what you want the AFP service to log. We recommend checking all the boxes, but if you have a large quantity of AFP traffic, then this could prove cumbersome to your log files. If so, reduce the scope by lowering the logging level incrementally until you have a workable solution.

■**Note** You will not see the path to files and folders in the logs. Even if logging is maximized, these seemingly important elements will still not appear.

SMB

Mac OS X Server and Windows integration often go hand in hand. Let's look at some of the areas of Windows integration that are important.

First, SMB signing is an integral part of file sharing security for Windows Server 2003 and Windows Server 2008 when using the Windows Server Lockdown tool (distributed by Microsoft), as is LDAP signing. Neither of these is supported in Mac OS X 10.4 without using DAVE. DAVE is a third-party tool for integrating Macs into Windows environments and is bundled with Thursby software's Active Directory client software ADmitMac (more on DAVE in Chapter 10).

■Note LDAP signing is still not supported in Mac OS X 10.5 without using a third-party tool such as ADmitMac.

Samba also has the capability of authenticating via Kerberos when used with an Active Directory domain controller. This is accomplished by the following additions to the /etc/ smb.conf file:

```
security = ads
realm = apress.com
use spnego = yes
```

The Simple and Protected GSSAPI Negotiation Mechanism (SPNEGO) allows for the Samba engine to negotiate a Kerberos connection with an Active Directory server. This means a Windows client can use a principal from a Windows Active Directory Kerberos realm to authenticate to the Samba file share point on Mac OS X Server.

The Samba process also runs the NetBIOS server in Mac OS X Server. Often overlooked is the NetBIOS name command option, which should match the hostname of the server, to support correctly formatted Kerberos tickets. This is analogous to the name chosen when binding to Active Directory via the Directory Utility.

```
netbios name = iduro
```

These additions can be facilitated by using the dsconfigad command to enable single sign-on using the command:

```
dsconfig -enableSSO
```

Once completed, you can verify that the Kerberos principals were created in the local keytab by using the ktlist command and searching for the key name of cifs:

```
klist -kt | grep cifs
```

```
2 01/14/08 14:41:56 cifs/iduro.wallcity.org@WALLCITY.ORG
2 01/14/08 14:41:56 cifs/iduro.wallcity.org@WALLCITY.ORG
2 01/14/08 14:41:56 cifs/iduro.wallcity.org@WALLCITY.ORG
```

> **■Note** Three keys are listed because of the variations of encryption used when creating Kerberos principals: these keys are stored in /etc/krb.keytab and must be kept secure (by default they are readable only by root). An attacker could use them to authenticate to the service without knowing the password of a given user.

FTP

Apple's built-in FTP server supports Kerberos authentication and can be used with third-party software to allow for better authentication security. By default, FTP transmits the session username and password via clear text. When using the Apple FTP server with a third-party client such as Fetch.app, the FTP client software can negotiate a GSSAPI connection using Kerberos. This allows the client to authenticate with a Kerberos ticket rather than a password. Although this does allow for better security during the authentication exchange, it does not prevent an attacker from watching the session data. Apple's current built-in FTP server does not support transport layer security such as SSL, while the OpenSSH suite does have a more secure protocol known as SFTP, which supports both Kerberos authentication and session layer security. Unfortunately, it cannot be easily configured via the graphic interface, and as a result, users effectively are not jailed (or trapped) within a specific directory such as their home folder or linked share points.

> **■Note** A chroot command is a technique under *nix whereby a process is permanently restricted to an isolated subset of the filesystem. Because there are insecurities within FTP and use in Mac OS X, chroot can be used to further secure FTP. One easy way to obtain this functionality without a lot of command-line configuration is to use Rumpus, a web-enabled FTP application.

Wireless Security on OS X Server Using RADIUS

Remote Authentication Dial In User Service (RADIUS) can help take the security of your wireless network to the next level, beyond standard WPA authentication. With RADIUS, password policies for users can be applied to wireless encryption as well. Prior to Leopard, RADIUS communications could be obtained using Elektron or OpenRADIUS running on OS X, but in Leopard, no third-party software is required beyond Leopard Server.

Before you begin this walk-through of implementing RADIUS on your server, make sure the server is running Open Directory and that the forward and reverse DNS information for the server is correct.

The first step to using RADIUS is to enable it. To do this, open Server Admin, click the name of the server in the Servers list, and click the Services tab. Find RADIUS in the list of services below each server, and place a check mark in the box to the left of it. Click Save, and you should see RADIUS in the Servers list.

Now that RADIUS has been enabled, let's select a certificate. For the purpose of this walk-through, we're going to use the default certificate that comes with OS X Server. Click RADIUS under the Servers list, and then click the Settings button. Click the RADIUS Certificate drop-down menu, and select the Default certificate. Click the Edit Allowed Users button.

By default all users of OS X Server will have access to authenticate to the wireless network setup, so we are going to get granular on which services they can access by clicking the For Selected Services Below radio button. Then click RADIUS in the Service list. Now click Allow Only Users and Groups Below, and then click the + sign. Drag the users and groups into the Name list from the Users & Groups window. Once all users that should have access to your new wireless environment have been enabled, click the Save button.

From here, click RADIUS, and click the Start RADIUS button in the bottom-left corner of the screen. RADIUS is now ready to accept authentication. The next step is to configure an AirPort device to work with RADIUS. To do this, click the Base Stations button in the toolbar at the top of the screen. Now click Browse, and select the first base station of your wireless envi-ronment from the list of found base stations. Enter the password for the AirPort device, and click Save. Wait for the AirPort device to complete its restart.

To log in from a client, select the name of the wireless network from the wireless networks list, and enter the username and password to the environment. The first time you do so, you will get a second dialog box asking you to enter the 802.1x username and password. Enter the same username and password, and click OK. If you click the Use this Password Once check box, then this password will not be saved for future use.

■**Note** Chapter 7 covers 802.1x in more depth.

That's all there is to it. This setup may be a little more complicated than WPA personal or WEP 128, but it's far more secure and should be considered for any AirPort environment that has an OS X Server. Although the default certificate will work for clients, things are often easier from a deployment and interoperability perspective if you purchase a certificate from a certif-icate authority (CA) such as Thawte.

DNS Best Practices

Over the years DNS has had a variety of weaknesses that have come to the attention of the Mac administrator community. These vulnerabilities are often there because DNS servers are improperly configured DNS servers. But most recently there have been attacks against even the best-defended servers. Some of these attacks seem fairly innocuous, such as the act of gaining too much information about an environment, while other attacks will actually forward data through the DNS responder to arbitrarily execute commands. We suggest keeping public-facing DNS on a server outside your environment (with your registrar perhaps) so that other servers can find your domain for mail and web services while not exposing your environment to hacks.

A good number of other services require DNS to function properly, such as Open Directory, Mail Server, and some Apache modules. If the DNS service is overloaded, other services on other servers that use that DNS service will have problems and also potentially crash. There-fore, we suggest you maintain a separate internal DNS infrastructure that is not accessible from outside your network. It is also strongly suggested that you customize the resources that the DNS service has available to it using `sandbox`.

▪**Note** Apple and Microsoft both suggest naming your internal domain something other than what you use for your public presence. Although this may ease the burden of administration, maintaining separate domain names does not generally ease the burden on the DNS servers.

▪**Tip** As with all services, you should maximize logging for DNS. To do so, open Server Admin, and click DNS. Then click Settings, and click Logging. Then change Log Level to Debug.

SSL

To install an SSL certificate in OS X Server, open Server Admin, and click the server name. Then click the Settings tab and the Certificates subtab. Next, click the plus sign, and enter the appropriate information into the boxes (location, name, and so on). If you want to purchase a certificate rather than a self-signed certificate, click Request Signed Certificate from a Certificate Authority (CA). This will give you a text blob that you can paste into a CGI form with Thawte or the CA that you choose.

Once your certificate has been approved, paste the code obtained from the certificate authority into Server Admin on this screen, and your certificate will be active. Keep in mind that most certificates are based on server names, so make sure that it's spelled correctly.

Once your certificate is active, you will be able to use SSL when connecting to Open Directory. To do this, click Open Directory from Server Admin, and click the Protocols tab. From here, check the Enable SSL Certificates box, and choose the appropriate certificate. Once complete, click Save. Now you are ready to authenticate from an SSL-enabled client.

To use SSL on the client, follow these steps:

1. Import the certificate using Keychain Access (not required if the certificate is from a CA).

2. Open Directory Access from the `/Applications/Utilities` folder.

3. Click LDAPv3, and select your Open Directory environment.

4. Check the Encrypt Using SSL box.

5. Use DSCL to test whether you can query the Open Directory database.

To generate a self-signed certificate, you can use the Certificate Assistant or the command-line CA utilities that ship with Mac OS X's OpenSSL implementation. An easy-to-launch link to the Certificate Assistant is available from the Keychain Access application in the `Utilities` folder. However, you may choose to purchase and implement a third-party certificate, which can be far easier to distribute across your environment.

To create a self-signed certificate, follow these steps:

1. First create a new keychain to hold the new certificates and public and private key data.

2. From the File menu, choose New Keychain.

3. Highlight the new keychain in the list.

4. From the Application menu of Keychain Access, choose Certificate Assistant.

5. From the submenu, choose Create a Certificate Authority.

6. For the name, choose your domain.

7. Check the Let Me Override Defaults box, and leave the serial number as the default value.

8. Set the validity period to days (change this only if you want to change the default one-year value).

■**Note** Choosing a short life span for your CA will mean increased security in case the file ever falls into the wrong hands; however, a smaller value will increase administrative burden because of the need for routine reinstallation of your certificate on all your clients.

---

9. Set User Certificate Type to SSL Server.

10. For Key Usage Extension for Users of This CA, choose Data Encipherment.

11. For Extended Key Usage Extension for This CA, verify that the Any option is selected.

12. For Email Address, choose an administrative e-mail address.

13. Name (Common Name) is important for your signed certificates and must match the fully qualified hostname of the service in question. For the CA, you may choose the domain itself.

14. Key Usage Extension for the CA should be selected as well.

15. Verify the Signature and Certificate Signing options are enabled.

16. Specify a location for the certificate.

17. For Keychain, choose the keychain you created earlier.

18. Check the On This Machine, Trust Certificates Signed by This CA box.

19. In Server Admin, create a new certificate.

20. From the Action or Gear menu, choose Generate Certificate Signing Request (CSR).

21. If you do not want to mail the CSR, you can drag the certificate icon out of the window on the desktop and manually copy the file to your certificate server.

22. From the Keychain Access menu, select the option Create a Certificate for Someone Else As a Certificate Authority.

23. Drag the CSR test from the previous steps, and drop it on the new window.

24. Now you can drag and drop the resulting certificate.

You have created a self-signed digital certificate that you can now use with other applications on the system.

Reimporting Certificates

If you need to reimport this certificate, you will need to convert it to a PEM certificate by running the command:

```
openssl x509 -in your.domain.com.cer -inform DER -out
    malkin.wallcity.org.crt -outform PEM
```

Open the resulting `.crt` file in a text editor and copy the contents. Then, from Server Admin, choose Add Signed or Renewed Certificate from Certificate Authority, and paste the contents in from the previous step. Next your certificate should show that it has been signed by your CA (if you are using `serveradmin` on the same machine as your certificate server, then the certificate should be trusted as well).

SSHD

Mac OS X Leopard Server ships with the SSH service automatically enabled. This service, by default, will allow connections on port 22 by any authenticated user known to the server. This has many security implications, such as the ability for standard accounts to run services on ports 1024 and higher. This means that by default any user of your server has the ability to start a proxy or traffic redirector (such as the Internet relay chat client Bouncer) without admin authorization.

Firewall safeguards should prevent remote access to those services, but even in a full firewall lock down, if port 22 is open, there are still many vectors that an attacker with user credentials could use to cause mischief and mayhem, so disable SSH unless you will use it. If you use it, make sure to secure it as described in Chapter 12. An example of this type of exploit of SSH would be the ability for users to send large quantities of spam e-mail through the default mail (postfix) system. Spammers who have compromised systems often use this technique to send large quantities of unsolicited e-mail.

If you are not using SSH to manage servers, disable SSH in Server Admin by clicking the server name, then clicking Settings, and then clicking General. In this screen, uncheck the SSH box, and click Save.

▦**Note** As mentioned in the SACLs section earlier in this chapter, you cannot create an Open Directory replica when SSH is disabled. Once the replica is created, then SSH can be disabled, but for the replica creation process, it will need to be enabled.

You can also increase security of the SSH daemon by limiting older encryption protocol versions that have known exploits and by restricting access to certain groups. You can do this by editing /etc/sshd_config to include the following lines:

```
Protocol 2
PermitRootLogin no
```

Then type the following:

```
sudo dseditgroup -o edit -a <USERNAME> -t user com.apple.access_ssh sudo
    killall -HUP sshd
```

Server Admin from the Command Line

Mac OS X Server is a strange beast. It can make you think it's the greatest gift known to sysadmins giving you the ability to perform all kinds of complicated configurations quickly through a nice GUI. It can also dismay many of us who know where Unix-specifics live in the operating system and would prefer to configure things there. So, where are all those settings that override so many of the default Unix configuration files? serveradmin is the command that gives access to much of what you see in Server Admin and much of what you don't.

To see all the services you can configure and view, use the command serveradmin list. Or use the serveradmin settings vpn command and see the settings applied to the firewall service. serveradmin use starts out with viewing data on a specific service. For example, type sudo serveradmin fullstatus vpn to see a full status on the settings and use of the VPN service. Then use the command serveradmin start vpn, followed by a serveradmin stop vpn. Suddenly you are stopping and starting services on a server using the command line, meaning you can actually issue these over an SSH session rather than having to use a remote management utility such as ARD to connect. This can become invaluable when a bad firewall rule locks you, the admin, out of the Server Admin tool. Just issue a serveradmin stop ipfilter command, and you're right back in!

You can also configure settings that aren't available in the GUI. For example, we'll use VPN to customize where we put our logs.

First, type sudo serveradmin settings vpn. Now, look for the following entry:

```
vpn:Servers:com.apple.ppp.pptp:PPP:Logfile = "/var/log/ppp/vpnd.log"
```

To change this setting, type the following:

```
Serveradmin settings vpn:Servers:com.apple.ppp.pptp:PPP:Logfile =
"/var/log/ppp/pptpvpnd.log"
```

Now the PPTP logs will be stored in a separate location than the logs for the rest of the VPN service. This can be done only using the serveradmin command and not with a configuration file. Nifty, huh?

To see all of the useful things that can be done with the serveradmin command, we suggest running a man command on serveradmin.

iChat Server

Instant messaging is very quickly becoming one of the cornerstones of modern communication, or at the very least, it is making great strides and doesn't show any signs of slowing down.

With its heavy presence in the modern workplace, it has become common for business-related communications to be sent over IM. Because of its humble consumer upbringings, these communications are often not encrypted at all. Many modern packet sniffers have plug-ins or filters specifically designed for tracking session data such as connection passwords and chat transcripts. Because of IM's prevalence and its potential for eavesdropping, securing your IM communication by way of an encrypted chat server should be a top priority.

The Leopard iChat Server uses the XMPP protocol with an available option to enable SSL. You can use the default SSL certificate created when your Mac OS X Server was first configured, or you can choose to import your own. If you opt not to purchase a SSL certificate from one of the public CAs, make sure to generate your own certificates for distribution to your clients, as covered in the previous section on SSL.

Customizing the welcome message to new users of your iChat Server is a fairly simple task, and from a security context it allows an administrator to push out an acceptable use policy for their iChat environment. For this, we'll cover the Jabber configuration because Jabber is the open source package on which iChat Server is built.

When you first set up Jabber, the `/etc/jabber` directory will be created. Inside this folder is a file called `jabber.xml`. Open the `jabber.xml` file, and look for the `welcome` tag. Then, any data between `"welcome"` and `"/welcome"` will be the information that is shown in a welcome screen when a new user signs onto the iChat Server.

■**Tip** Before you edit the `/etc/jaber/jabber.xml` file, make sure to back it up.

For this example, we will have all new users receive a message that says "Welcome to the 318 iChat Server."

To do this, delete or comment out the information between the existing `welcome` tags, and add the following information:

```
"welcome" "subject"to our iChat Server"/subject" "body "Welcome to the 318
    iChat Server"/body" "/welcome"
```

Save the `jabber.xml` file, and you've now customized the welcome message for your iChat Server.

■**Note** For the purpose of this chapter, the < and > have been replaced with quotes ("). However, you will need to use the < and > in your environment while using the `jabber.xml` file.

Securing the Mail Server

The mail server in Mac OS X Server has a few settings designed specifically for security. In Chapter 5 we discussed using the SpamAssassin and ClamAV features to limit mail that SpamAssassin and ClamAV identify as potentially sent from a spammer or system that has been infected with viruses. But what if your server is hijacked and set up as an open relay used to send spam? An *open relay* is a server that allows any user to relay mail through it. To verify your system isn't being used as an open relay, follow these steps:

1. Open Server Admin.

2. Click Mail.

3. Click Settings.

4. Click the Relay tab.

5. Remove servers not in your local network from the Accept SMTP Relays from These Hosts and Networks box.

Limiting the Protocols on Your Server

To reduce the footprint of mail services, you should also limit the number of protocols in use on your server. To do so, click the Settings tab for the Mail service in Server Admin, and verify you are using only the services you need (see Figure 13-27). For example, many environments will use only POP or IMAP. If you aren't using one of the two protocols, then disable the other (for a more in-depth discussion of POP, IMAP, or SMTP, see Chapter 5).

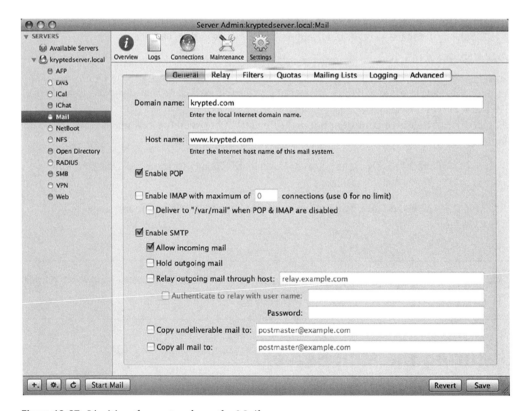

Figure 13-27. *Limiting the protocols on the Mail server*

PART 5

Workplace Security

■■■

## CHAPTER 14

Network Scanning, Intrusion Detection, and Intrusion Prevention Tools

Would your network withstand the attack? How easy would it be for someone to break into your network, find anything they want on your Mac, and steal enough information to masquerade with your identity on the Internet? To answer this question, you'd need to take a good hard look at your network and audit for intrusion vulnerabilities. Now imagine having to catalog all the programs, files, and services that run on your Mac, cross-referencing each program and file extension on the Internet, one at a time, against all the known exploits. This auditing procedure could take a considerable amount of time. Unfortunately, hackers have access to these auditing tools as well and already have a good idea of which exploits to look for. Thankfully, auditing techniques and auditing software are available to help expedite this process.

That's not to say you shouldn't be mindful of open ports, listening services, and the daily activities of a computer when analyzing security on a machine. You should be. Keep in mind, however, that each item that represents a security risk will need to be handled separately. The more time you can save in the actual audit of a computer, the quicker you will be able to secure the items that are flagged as a security threat. In this chapter, we'll cover the types of scans that hackers and auditors are likely to employ and how to use auditing software to counteract them.

Scanning Techniques

White-box testing is a methodology used when the auditor has full knowledge of the target environment. If you know all the relevant network information about the environment, such as the IP address of each system and what types of computers and network appliances exist, then you do not have to perform any discovery and can move straight into attempting to exploit systems or document threats.

Black-box testing assumes that the person scanning the network knows nothing about the environment. Because security information about an environment can be difficult to obtain, black-box testing should be conducted to assess security threats in the environment. If you're new to the environment, the first step in black-box testing is to understand what kind of information an attacker might be able to obtain. Once you have a full understanding of an environment, the techniques then become similar to those used in white-box testing. For the discovery portion of black-box testing, you can use a variety of techniques, which generally fall into either active or passive scanning techniques.

Active scanning is the act of using a system's network resources to scan itself, leaving traces of scanning on the system. Many attackers will not perform active scans because they can create a trail in a system's logs, making their activities easier to trace. Active scanning methods include sending web links to users of an environment so they will visit a web site that will track their IP address and operating system information from logs, reviewing a server's web site(s) for insecure code or passwords, and performing port scans against servers.

Passive techniques use nontraditional means of observation to scan a system so as not to leave traces of their scanning. Passive scanning requires much more patience, because the techniques are rather investigative in nature. Searching newspapers and job boards for specific technologies used in an environment or for support requests on a web site's support page and hunting for clues as to what technology is supported on the network are all ways to determine more information about an environment. When looking for information that could be used against an organization, the search will be rather comprehensive, often including chat rooms, the WhoIs database, news groups, web sites, search engines, and the target user or company's web site. A company web site can even give an attacker usernames, e-mail addresses, and the location of CGI scripts on web servers. Sometimes there will even be passwords discovered (or at least hints as to the current password to log into the web site). To help reduce the amount of information about your organization that is on the Web, consider routinely using Google to search for pertinent information that is broadcast about your organization.

Fingerprinting

Fingerprinting is often the first and most convenient way for hackers to obtain information about your systems. Fingerprinting is meant to get as much information as possible about a system's security, including its remote access capabilities, vulnerable services, and open ports. Successfully attacking a system depends on having this information. Tools that can be used in fingerprinting include Sam Spade, NSLookup, Traceroute, and Neotrace.

Open source fingerprinting is the easiest and safest way to go about finding information about a company. This includes researching and collecting any information available to the public, including phone numbers, addresses, and other seemingly innocuous information. Company blogs are wonderful mediums to discuss technology, but they can also be the greatest resource to extract information about a company's infrastructure. Most companies post information about themselves on their web site but beware of publishing information such as the systems you have deployed, the revisions of services running on these systems, and the security solutions used to protect these services. A lot of this information can be very useful to hackers.

Let's fingerprint the site `wallcity.org` to find out as much as we can about Zack Smith, a contributor to this book. Reviewing the web site, we know he plans on putting up an Apple wiki in the future (see Figure 14-1).

Here, click the Mail icon, and you get a login to a Kerio MailServer (see Figure 14-2), so you can see that he is running a Kerio MailServer on his domain. Running a registrar scan using the WhoIs feature on NetSol shows his main e-mail contact is `spamme@wallcity.org`, which is obviously a spam-trapping e-mail address.

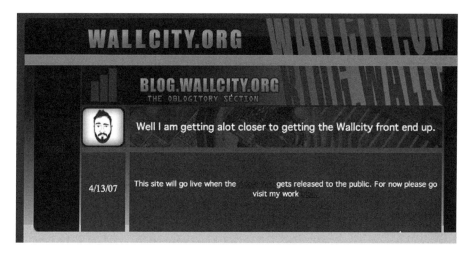

Figure 14-1. wallcity.org *front page*

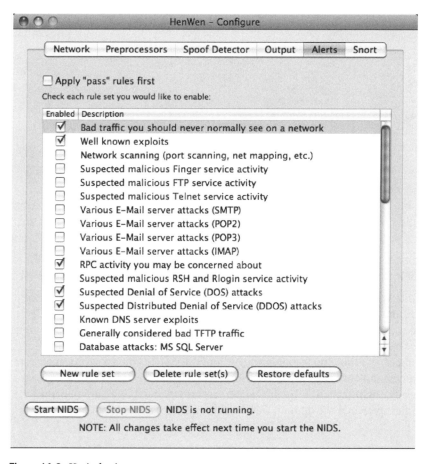

Figure 14-2. *Kerio login screen*

Next, let's find the IP address of wallcity.org. Ping it, and you will come up with 208.113.244.156. Next, if you perform a DNS lookup of the name for wallcity.org, you will find that the DNS is hosted by DreamHost. If you perform a WhoIS for this IP, you will see that it is managed by DreamHost, so you now know that both the IP address and the DNS information are hosted by DreamHost. Next, ping again, and set the interval between packets to 1 millisecond. Set the number of seconds to wait until a ping times out to 5 and the ping size to 500 bytes, and then send ten pings. The result? Ten packets sent and ten packets received. So wallcity.org returned a message within an average of 0.35 seconds for every packet sent. Later, the intervals can help tell you the amount of traffic on a system, the type of connection a system is behind, and even the version of the operating system or specific services running on the system using OS fingerprinting techniques.

A cornerstone of fingerprinting is port scanning. In the following example, we will show how to use the built-in port scanner for OS X, using the Port Scan tab of the Network Utility application (located in the /Applications/Utilities folder), but later in this chapter we will review nmap, a more robust port-scanning utility. Open Network Utility, and click the Port Scan tab. Then, type **wallcity.org**, and see what kind of services are running on that computer by clicking the Scan button. To look at some of the more important ports, we'll truncate our port scan to scan only from 1 to 125. Our results are as follows:

```
21    TCP    ftp
22    TCP    ssh     SSH 1.99-OpenSSH_2.30
25    TCP    smtp
53    TCP    domain
80    TCP    www
110   TCP    pop3
111   TCP    sunrpc
113   TCP    ident
```

From this scan, you can see that wallcity.org has HTML and e-mail ports open, so it is running a mail server and a web server. It's also running FTP, and it's using Post Office Protocol version 3 (POP3), Sun Remote Procedure Call (SUNRPC), and ident. All these services are services that someone could use hacking tools to exploit, provided there are exploits available for the implementation of the services.

Enumeration

Network enumeration is the process of identifying domain names and their associated networks. It entails performing queries on the many WhoIs databases found on the Internet. What is then gathered from this technique is information needed to attack a system from a social engineering standpoint. *Social engineering* is the act of convincing network users to release private information (information they should not be giving out) about the systems on a network such as IP addresses, usernames, and even passwords. Company domain names are listed with registrars. Often listed alongside this information are the people involved in managing a domain, the DNS servers for a domain, and when the domain was purchased. There are four types of enumeration queries:

Registrar query: Provides information on potential target domains.

Organizational query: Provides all instances of the target's name.

Domain query: Locates the address, domain name, administrator, contact information, and domain servers. Most information for a given domain can be hidden for an extra fee to the registrar.

Network query: Discovers network blocks owned by a company based on its American Registry for Internet Numbers information.

■**Note** DNS zone transfers are used to pass DNS information between DNS servers. Many environments are mistakenly configured to allow untrusted hosts to perform a DNS zone transfer, which means that any machine masquerading as a DNS server performing a DNS zone transfer can obtain DNS server information by using a DNS interrogation. You can find a wide variety of tools on the Internet that can be used to perform DNS interrogation. For more information on DNS security, see Chapter 13.

Firewalk

Firewalk is a tool that can be used to determine the rules in place for a firewall without actually communicating with the target computers behind the firewall. It is an active reconnaissance tool that has the ability to determine the protocols a given IP forwarding device will allow to pass. Firewalk works by sending TCP or UDP packets with a TTL one number higher than the targeted gateway. If the gateway allows the traffic, it will forward the packets to the next hop. Here, packets expire and elicit an ICMP_TIME_EXCEEDED message. If the gateway does not allow the traffic, it will drop the packets, or there will be no responses from the target.

Vulnerability and Port Scanning

Scanning occurs on two levels: network and host. Scanning with a vulnerability scanner allows you to rapidly review your computer and the computers running on your network for known security holes such as outdated software. You can then move it into penetration testing, which typically starts by going a step beyond scanning and into running automated tools that attempt to exploit vulnerabilities.

Be careful, especially when trying to access any open ports you may find. Brute-forcing an FTP or a web server can also land you in a pile of trouble. As a rule of thumb, if attempting to access a service on a port requires a password, you probably shouldn't be there. On the flip side, if you access something important and the system does not ask you for a password, then this should be resolved immediately.

nmap

nmap is a network exploration tool that can be installed on Mac OS X from `nmap.org`. nmap is one of the most essential tools to a security engineer or penetration tester (someone who attempts to break into a system in order to test its security). It is used, as its name suggests, as a network-mapping tool. With nmap you can probe an entire network and discover which services are listening on each specific port on every workstation, server, and router accessible. nmap also incorporates a certain degree of fingerprinting. By comparing different fingerprints, nmap gives users an educated guess as to the operating system a target machine is running.

nmap has a good number of options or flags that let you manipulate how it scans. For example, you can perform a `tcp()connect` scan (which makes a full connection to the host) or a SYN scan (also known as a *half connection*). You can test firewall rules and distinguish whether they are firewalls or packet filters. You can idle scan and spoof your IP through another machine. You can also throw out decoys to make your presence less traceable. Table 14-1 describes the nmap options for the actual binary command. The proper 4.53 usage of nmap includes the following:

```
nmap [Scan Type(s)] [Options] <host or net list>
```

Table 14-1. *Common Scanning Options*

Option	Description
`-sO`	Use raw packets.
`-sS`	TCP SYN stealth port scan (default if running as root).
`-sT`	TCP `connect()` port scan (default for nonroot users).
`-sU`	UDP port scan.
`-sP`	Ping scan (find any reachable machines).
`--interactive`	Interactive mode (then press H for help).
`-sR/-I`	RPC/Identd scan (use with other scan types).
`-O`	Use TCP/IP fingerprinting to guess remote operating system.
`-p <range>`	Define ports to scan. Example range: `1-80`, `8010`, `8080`, `10000`.
`-F`	Scans only ports listed in `nmap-services` to speed up scans.
`-v`	Verbose. Its use is recommended. Use twice for greater effect.
`-PN`	Don't ping hosts (needed to scan `www.microsoft.com` and others).
`-D decoy_host1,decoy2[,...]`	Hide scan using many decoys.
`-6`	Scans via IPv6 rather than IPv4.
`-T <timing>`	General timing policy. Settings are Paranoid, Sneaky, Polite, Normal, Aggressive, Insane.
`-n/-R`	Do not use DNS resolution/always resolve (the default is to sometimes resolve).
`-oN/-oX/-oG <logfile>`	Output normal/XML/greppable scan logs to `<logfile>`.
`-iL<inputfile>`	Get targets from file; use - for stdin.
`-S <your_IP>/-e <devicename>`	Specify source address or network interface.

Here's an example:

```
nmap -v -sS -O www.318.com 10.0.0.0/16 '10.0.*.*'
```

The stealthiest and most widely used nmap-scanning method is SYN scanning, also known as *half open* or *stealth scanning*. There are a couple of downsides to using this method. Unfortunately, most intrusion detection systems (described more later in this chapter) can detect these packets, and some firewalls and packet filtration mechanisms will drop SYN packets, which make it harder to get a fingerprint of what ports the host is running.

With a SYN/stealth scan, you do not actually make a full connection with the host. It will send a SYN packet and request a connection. The host being scanned then responds with a SYN/ACK packet informing you about whether the port is open and responding. As soon as you receive the SYN/ACK packet from the remote host, nmap sends one RST packet terminating the connection. It does not make a full connection or three-way handshake (full connection), which is why SYN/stealth scanning is called a *half scan*.

Running a SYN/Stealth Scan

Here is what an nmap SYN/stealth scan would typically look like. First we initialize the scan with the following Terminal command, assuming we are scanning a system with the IP address of 10.0.04:

```
nmap -sS 10.0.0.4
```

This command results in the following output:

```
Starting nmap 3.30 ( http://www.insecure.org/nmap/ ) at 2003-07-17 05:07 EST
Interesting ports on 10.0.0.4:
(The 1637 ports scanned but not shown below are in state: closed)
Port State Service
21/tcp filtered ftp
22/tcp open ssh
23/tcp open telnet
111/tcp open sunrpc
139/tcp open netbios-ssn
1024/tcp open kdm
6000/tcp open X11

nmap run completed -- 1 IP address (1 host up) scanned in 3.194 seconds
```

■**Note** A filtered port, such as the filtered FTP port 21, as it appears in the previous scan, usually indicates the machine is running a firewall.

Here is a log of a stealth SYN scan from an intrusion detection system called snort (we will discuss snort later in this chapter):

```
[**] [111:13:1] spp_stream4: STEALTH ACTIVITY (SYN FIN scan) detection [**]
09/21-19:18:03 10.0.0.4:80 -> 10.0.0.8:88
TCP TTL:255 TOS:0x0 ID:2304 IpLen:20 DgmLen:42
******SF Seq: 0x90AB763  Ack: 0x0  Win: 0x1000  TcpLen: 20
9-21 19:18:04 10.0.0.4:80 -> 192.168.0.8:88 SYN ******S*
```

As you can see by the warning message, snort has built a rule set that is able to identify nmap's SYN/stealth scanning sequence.

Other nmap Scans

nmap scans can be limited to specific criteria. For example, if you wanted to scan only UDP ports 1 through 80 on a server using the IP address 10.0.0.4, you would use the following command:

```
nmap -sU -p 1-80 10.0.0.4
```

nmap -I Ident lists the owners of each process scanned. This scan is useful because the individual scanning of the system can determine what services are running as root and target them. Services running as root, if hacked, will give an attacker more capabilities than otherwise. Not every service needs to run as root, so make sure that services run with the least privileges required. To get this information, you must make a full TCP connection to the machine, which we will do by using the following command that produces the output after the command:

```
nmap -sT -I 10.0.0.4
```

```
Starting nmap 3.30 ( http://www.insecure.org/nmap/ ) at 2003-09-22 15:11 EST
Interesting ports on 10.0.0.4:
(The 1629 ports scanned but not shown below are in state: closed)
Port State Service                      Owner
21/tcp open ftp                          root
22/tcp open ssh                         root
25/tcp open smtp                       root
80/tcp open http                          www-data
113/tcp open auth                         identd
139/tcp open netbios-ssn         root
443/tcp open https                       root
548/tcp open afp                       root
993/tcp open imaps                     root
995/tcp open pop3s                     root

nmap run completed -- 1 IP address (1 host up) scanned in 9.202 seconds
```

Other Scanning Techniques

The following are other scanning techniques you can use:

Ping sweep: Pings a range of IP addresses to find out which machines are awake.

TCP scan: Scans ports on machines to see which services are offered. TCP scans can be performed by scanning a single port on a range of IP addresses or by scanning a range of ports on a single IP.

UDP scan: Sends garbage UDP packets to a desired port. Generally, this is an ineffective technique because most machines respond with an ICMP "port unreachable" message, which means that no service is available, which may or may not be true.

OS identification: This involves sending illegal ICMP or TCP packets to a machine. The machine responds with unique invalid inputs and allows the hacker to find out what the target machine is running.

Scanning a network for intrusion is only one piece of the network intrusion pie. We must now make steps to secure the vulnerabilities that can be perpetrated that we've scanned for. So that we aren't overlooking anything, we should first look for intrusion instances that may have already been attempted and then implement measures to prevent future attempts.

Intrusion Detection and Prevention

In information security, *intrusion detection* is the act of detecting actions that have attempted to compromise (or succeeded in compromising) a network resource. Intrusion detection does not typically include the prevention of intrusions; however, we will discuss some preventive measures that can work in tandem with network intrusion detection. With any intrusion detection solution, what is important is determining whether an intrusion was perpetrated on the system, examining what exactly was attempted, investigating whether it was done maliciously, and then taking preventative measures based on this information.

Host Intrusion Detection System

The purpose of a host intrusion detection system is to monitor and analyze a system in such a way that an administrator can determine whether a change has occurred on a system. Most host-based intrusion detection systems focus on checking for changes to configuration files or folders containing binary files (applications).

Tripwire

Tripwire is an intrusion detection system that is used to track changes to the files on a computer. Tripwire can scan for files on computers by creating a checksum of the files and folders on a system, creating a different checksum, and then comparing the two. This enables a fast scan of a variety of files and folders on a computer. Regular Tripwire scans will alert system administrators of changes to the file system for folders that should be scanned regularly.

Some folders we recommend scanning regularly include the following:

```
/dev
/opt
/usr
/usr/sbin
/bin
/mach.kern
/Library/Preferences
/Library/FileSystems
/etc
/System/Library/extensions
/System/Library/core services
```

Tripwire Installation

To install Tripwire, first download Tripwire from `tripwire.darwinports.com`. Then extract the Tripwire files to a folder, and run the following command in that folder:

```
sudo ./install.sh
```

When prompted, enter the appropriate passphrases/passwords. Then enter the short name of the primary user of Tripwire (in other words, root, admin, or your username). Next, allow Tripwire to define the baseline state of the computer.

To update your Tripwire database after making system changes, run this command:

```
./tripwire m u -r ../report/day-month-year-initials.twr
```

To update your Tripwire config, change the `/usr/local/etc/twcfg.txt` file, and run this command:

```
./twadmin -m F -S ../key/site.key ../../etc/twcfg.txt
```

To enforce a new policy, edit the `/usr/local/tripwire/policy/twpol.txt` file, and run this command:

```
./twadmin -m p > ../policy/twpol.txt
```

To view Tripwire reports, run this command:

```
./twprint -m r -r ../report/*.twr
```

■**Note** A `.twr` file is a Tripwire report file.

To scan what changes have been made to the system, `cd` into `/usr/local/tripwire/bin`, and run this:

```
./tripwire -m c
```

To e-mail these changes to the e-mail address listed in the config file (if you have identified an e-mail address), run this:

```
./tripwire -m c -M
```

Using Checkmate

Checkmate is a GUI tool based on Tripwire available for older versions of Mac OS X. When installed, it creates a preference pane for System Preferences that allows you to generate and compare secure MD5 checksums of critical files. This can be used to detect whether these files have been altered by viruses, root kits, Trojan horses, or other possibly malicious programs.

Checksum validation can be run manually from inside the preference pane and scheduled to run hourly, daily, weekly, monthly, or each time you restart.

If the validation process finds any files whose checksums don't match the values stored, several notification options can be triggered, including a pop-up dialog box and e-mail. In addition to the default list of files that are included for validation, you can easily add and remove additional files that you want to validate.

You can also export the list of file checksums to a file to be stored somewhere other than the computer it was made on (such as on your iDisk). You can later load this externally stored file into the preference panel to verify that the checksums themselves haven't been altered.

Network Intrusion Detection

Host-based intrusion detection scans the system for changes. But it is also possible to use a network intrusion detection system (NIDS), which can scan the network interface of systems to identify traffic patterns based on signatures from known exploits. One example of a popular NIDS application is snort.

snort from the Command Line

snort is an open source network intrusion detection and prevention system that is capable of packet logging and real-time traffic analysis. Proprietary versions with integrated hardware and support services are sold by Sourcefire, and there are hundreds of additional rule sets and downloads available to extend the snort platform.

snort can perform protocol analysis along with content matching, and it is often used to help detect attacks and probes. But it's mainly used as a means to finding existing threats to your network infrastructure. Some of the attacks that are detected include buffer overflows, Back Orifice, and stealthy port scans (such as those stemming from nmap). snort also has the ability to detect specific CGI attacks, SMB probes, and OS fingerprinting techniques. snort can also be used for intrusion prevention purposes by dropping attacks as they are taking place or permanently augmenting your firewall to block future attempts from flagged IP addresses. snort-Snarf, sguil, OSSIM, and the Basic Analysis and Security Engine (BASE) help administrators wade through the mountains of data generated by snort by providing visual representations of SNORT's logs.

▪Note snort patches are available from Bleeding Edge Threats (`http://www.bleedingthreats.net`) that can be configured to work with antivirus scanning within ClamAV. Any potential threats are isolated into signatures. These signatures are network traffic patterns that are then recorded. When future traffic comes through the network interface that matches these signatures, snort will perform the action that it is configured to perform (more on configuring these later in this section).

To obtain snort, go to `http://www.sourcefire.com/products/snort`. Once you have snort, you can install it using MacPorts. First have MySQL 5 (`http://www.mysql.org`) and PHP 5 installed (in Leopard PHP 5 is installed by default). Next, install BASE, the front end to snort. To install, perform this command to install BASE and its dependency, the adodb library, via MacPorts:

```
sudo port install base
```

Make symbolic links to the Apache document root:

```
cd <Apache-docroot> (often /Library/WebServer/
sudo ln -s /opt/local/share/adodb  adodb
sudo ln -s /opt/local/share/base  base
```

Make a copy of the BASE sample file without the `dist` in the name:

```
cd /opt/local/share/base
sudo cp base_conf.php.dist base_conf.php
```

Edit the following variables in the file `/opt/local/share/base/base_conf.php`:

```
$BASE_urlpath  = '/base';
$DBlib_path    = '/<Apache-docroot>/adodb';
$alert_dbname      = 'snort';
$alert_host        = 'localhost';
$alert_user        = 'snort';
$alert_password    = '<mysql-snort-password>';
$archive_dbname    = 'snort';
$archive_user      = 'snort';
$archive_password = '<mysql-snort-password>';
$archive_host      = 'localhost';
```

Now for the actual snort configuration:

```
sudo port install snort +mysql5 +server
```

Install snort rules, and make a place for snort settings files, rules, and logs:

```
sudo mkdir -p /opt/local/etc/snort/rules
sudo mkdir /var/log/snort
```

Go to the snort rules page at `http://www.snort.org/vrt/`, download the snort rules package, and unzip it:

```
cd <snort-rules-download-dir>/rules
sudo cp * /opt/local/etc/snort/rules
sudo cp *.config /opt/local/etc/snort
```

Rename the `snort.conf` sample file to `snort.conf`:

```
cd /opt/local/etc/snort
sudo mv snort.conf.dist snort.conf
```

Then open `snort.conf` in a text editor, and enter the following:

```
sudo pico /opt/local/etc/snort/snort.conf
```

Modify the `RULE_PATH` and database variables exactly as shown and the `HOME_NET` as appropriate:

```
# Path to your rules files
var RULE_PATH /opt/local/etc/snort/rules
# database: log to a variety of databases
output database: alert, mysql, user=snort password=<mysql-snort-password>
    dbname=snort host=localhost
var HOME_NET [10.1.1.0/24,192.168.1.0/24]
```

The defaults for the other variables in `snort.conf` should be OK for most purposes. Next, import the snort database schema into the snort MySQL database using the following commands:

```
cd /opt/local/share/snort/schemas
cat create_mysql | mysql5 -u root -p snort
```

Add the tables that BASE needs to the snort database with these commands:

```
cd /opt/local/share/base/sql
cat create_base_tbls_mysql.sql | mysql5 -u root -p snort
```

Now it's time to fire up snort and test it. If you have installed snort, then the first thing you will want to do is run the following command to initialize snort:

```
sudo snort -c /opt/local/etc/snort/snort.conf
```

After the initialization information is displayed, you will see live packet capture information on the Terminal screen if you are connected to a network. Now kill the snort foreground process by pressing Ctrl+C to take a look at the summary information. You should be ready to go if you see packet captures that resemble Figure 14-3.

To test whether BASE is working, go to the URL `http://localhost/base/index.php` from the host running the BASE server.

■**Note** For official snort training, see `http://www.sourcefire.com/services/education/`.

```
22:16:54.128008 192.168.1.5.1700 > 192.168.1.3.1700:
udp 53 (ttl 255, id 3, len 81)
0x0000   4500 0051 0003 0000 ff11 3840 c0a8 0105
0x0010   c0a8 0103 06a4 06a4 003d 4d16 2b01 0035
0x0020   dbe6 8ec4 cf70 8d5f fc78 954a e441 b5c2
0x0030   1a11 0000 0009 fa0b 5331 302e 302e 322e
0x0040   311a 1000 0000 09fc 0a0b 7365 7276 6963
0x0050   65
22:16:55.407865 192.168.1.3.1700 > 192.168.1.5.1700:
udp 53 (ttl 255, id 5, len 81)
0x0000   4500 0051 0005 0000 ff11 383e c0a8 0103
0x0010   c0a8 0105 06a4 06a4 003d 4b5c 2c01 0035
0x0020   5e2f 0460 3093 716c c683 f672 0586 a47a
0x0030   1a10 0000 0009 fc0a 0b73 6572 7669 6365
0x0040   1a11 0000 0009 fa0b 5331 302e 302e 322e
0x0050   31
```

Figure 14-3. *Packet capture*

■**Note** snort has no mechanism to update rules automatically. To keep snort updated, every few weeks you should make a habit of downloading the latest rules and then restarting snort to make sure it is running with the latest attack profiles.

HenWen, snort with a GUI

HenWen is a network security package for Mac OS X that makes it easy to configure and run snort by using a GUI tool rather than the command line. You can also use HenWen to access more advanced features of snort from the command line by going into the /Applications/ HenWen.app/Contents/Resources file, where you will find the actual binary files for the snort application. This is also where you will find the Guardian Perl script (which will be discussed later in the chapter), the snort rules, and the snort.conf file.

HenWen does have its weaknesses. Not all options available from the command line are available from the GUI. And customizing the application from the command line can render the GUI tool useless (as is true with many different applications that can be controlled via the command line).

You can download HenWen from http://seiryu.home.comcast.net/henwen.html. Once downloaded, run the installer and allow it to complete. Once you have completed the installer, you will have two new applications installed. The first is HenWen, and the second is LetterStick. When you open HenWen, it is preconfigured for the most basic rule set.

Under Alerts, select the rules you want to add. Be careful here. Although it is good to integrate as many rules as possible, unless you know what these rules are doing, try to be conservative with the experimental rules. You can also add rules by downloading them, placing them into a folder, and then using the New Rule Set button in HenWen to access them. Custom rules to consider adding on the Mac are Mac-specific rules or protocol-specific rules such as those capable of looking for brute-force attacks against SSH.

The Preprocessors tab (shown in Figure 14-4) in HenWen flags port scanning, involves Back Orifice detection, detects stealth port scans, and enables stream reassembly. Using the Preprocessors tab, you can also choose to not scan packets with either a source or a destination of a specified known IP address.

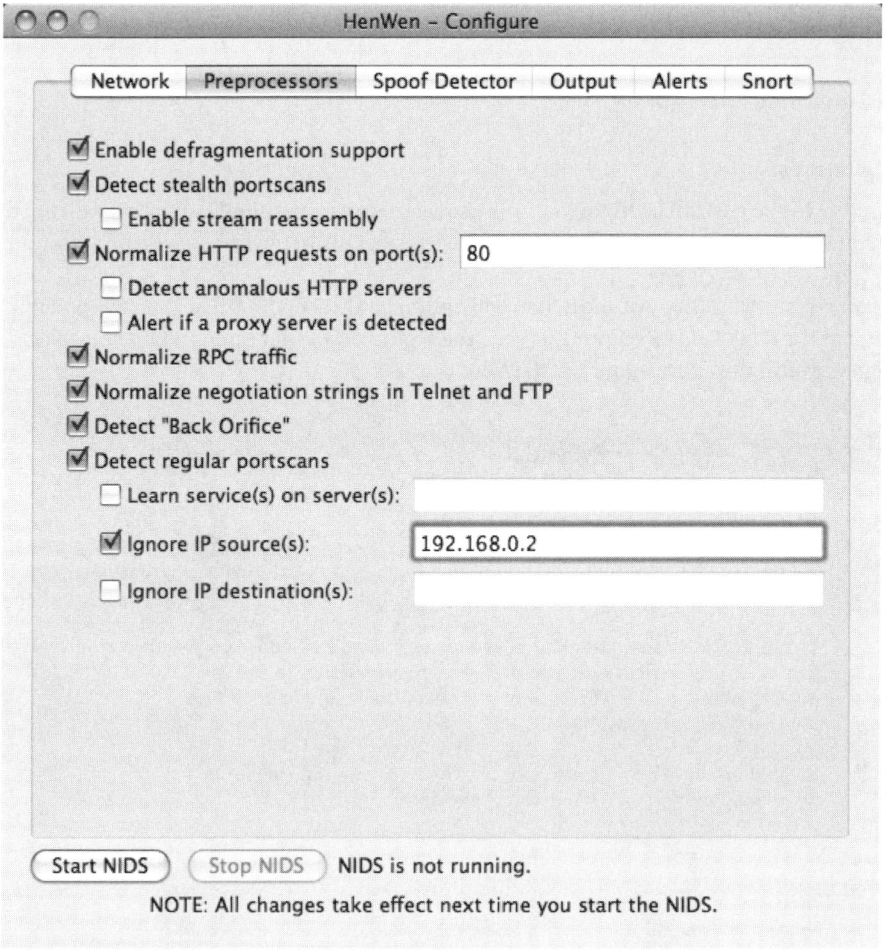

Figure 14-4. *Configuring HenWen*

Using the Network tab, you can define on which interface (en0, en1, and so on) to run snort. You can also set environment variables for snort if needed. An environment variable is a global variable that can be set for a system.

Once you are satisfied that your settings for HenWen are set, click the Start Network Intrusion Detection System (NIDS) button.

Intrusion Prevention with Guardian

Guardian is a Perl script that plugs into snort. Guardian updates the Mac OS X Firewall when HenWen flags traffic. This is helpful by providing an automated action alert based on the information snort is able to find on suspicious traffic. To use Guardian, select the Launch Guardian option from the Script menu of HenWen (see Figure 14-5).

Figure 14-5. *Launching Guardian*

Custom Signatures

It is not possible to use custom traffic signatures with HenWen from the GUI. For this, you need to use the command-line snort and invoke each custom signature in your snort configuration file.

Once you register your copy of snort, you will obtain an Oink code. Once you have an Oink code, enter it at the Oink Code Required screen (see Figure 14-6) that opens when you select Custom Signatures in the snort menu of HenWen.

Figure 14-6. *Oink code required for custom signatures*

Alerting with LetterStick

LetterStick is a bundled application that works with HenWen to send security alerts via e-mail or desktop pop-up windows. Before you can use LetterStick, you will need to check the Log Alerts to a Unix Socket box in HenWen on the Output tab and restart the NIDS engine. The first time you run LetterStick, it will create a menu icon in your menu bar. From here, open LetterStick from the menu bar, and click Preferences. This will allow you to configure the e-mail address to which you want to send alerts. Enter the e-mail address in the E-Mail the Alert To field. If you want to see a prompt on the screen, check the Put Up an Alert Panel box. To hear a sound effect when the alert is sent, check the Play a Sound Effect box (see Figure 14-7).

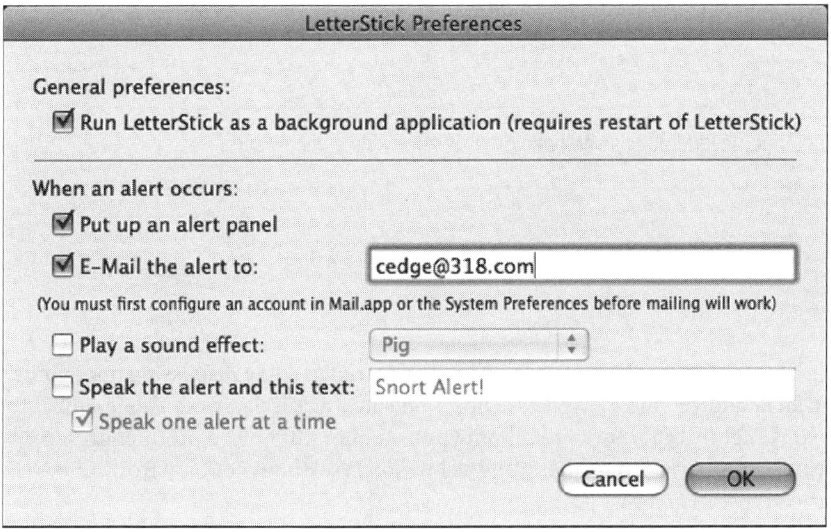

Figure 14-7. *LetterStick preferences*

If you require finer-grained control of LetterStick, you can go into the application from the Terminal command line and edit the settings there. To do this, browse to the `/Applications/LetterStick.app/Contents/Resources` folder. From here, edit the `classifications.config` file, and comment out (typing a # in front of the line) any items for which you do not need to receive alerts. For example, common tasks such as regular network port scans are not needed (you might still want to receive alerts about stealth port scans when they happen).

Honeypots

A *honeypot* is a trap set by a network administrator to detect, deflect, or in some manner counteract attempts at unauthorized use of the network. Generally, it consists of a computer, data repository, or network resource that appears to be part of a network, containing information valuable to attackers, but is actually isolated and monitored by the network admins.

Honeypots are valuable surveillance and early-warning tools. Honeypots should have no production value and hence should not see any legitimate traffic or activity. Whatever they capture can then be surmised as malicious or unauthorized. For example, honeypots designed to thwart spam by masquerading as zombie systems can categorize the material they trap 100 percent accurately: it is all illicit. A honeypot needs no spam-recognition capability and no filter to separate ordinary e-mail from spam. Ordinary e-mail never comes to a honeypot. This script can be found in Chapter 11, Web Site Security.

Also, web traffic can be reviewed in the same manner. We recently wrote a script to put a file in a web directory that tells bots not to search the folder. If a bot then searches the folder, we update the firewall logs on that server to block future traffic from the IP address of the originating bot. This is a rudimentary form of a honeypot.

Honeypots can take on other forms, such as files or data records or even unused IP address space (for example, a file that is watched with verbose logging called payroll.xls).

■**Note** A honeypot that masquerades as an open proxy is known as a *sugarcane*.

A collection of honeypots is known as a *honeynet*.

HoneyPotX

HoneyPotX is the open source project most commonly referred to when discussing honeypots. *Honeyd* listens on an IP address and then takes action when an attack is detected. This is similar to snort, but Honeyd is slightly different in that honeypots are not put on live production server computers but run virtual servers masquerading as live servers. HoneyPotX is a front-end GUI application for the Mac for *Honeyd*.

To get HoneyPotX up and running, download it from www.versiontracker.com. Then, open HoneyPotX, and click Fake Server System. Go through the tabs to configure HoneyPotX for the specific server features that you want to spoof. Once configured, click Listen to start HoneyPotX listening for attacks (see Figure 14-8).

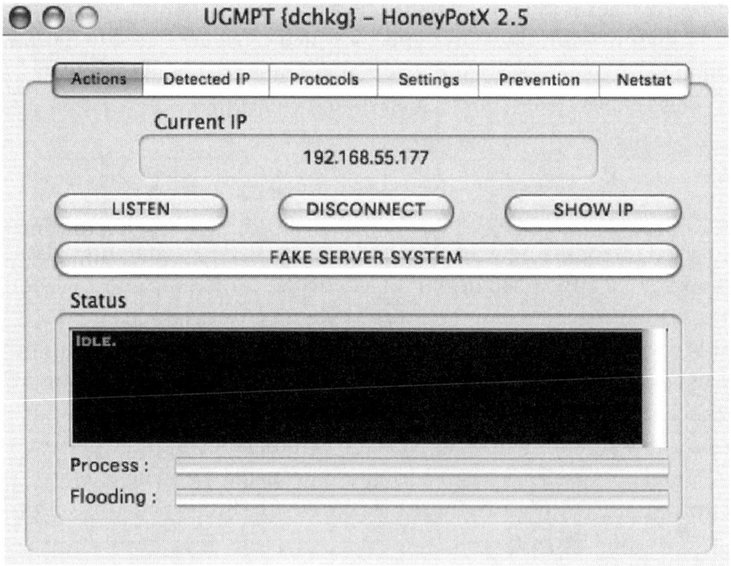

Figure 14-8. *HoneyPotX*

In the Detected IP section, you will find all the IPs of the systems that have been caught sending traffic to the server. On the Protocols tab, you can configure the following:

- Connection keep-alive settings

- Floods to send back to attackers

- E-mail alerts to the attacker's ISP

- Alternate port checking

- Specific additional ports to listen on

■**Note** On the Netstat tab, you can view the raw packet data used by Honeyd.

Security Auditing on the Mac

Several products on the market allow for vulnerability scanning and security auditing on the Mac. Some of them are freeware, and some of them are not. SAINT, Nessus, and Metasploit are our favorites for this critical piece of the security puzzle. Only Nessus and Metasploit are free products.

SAINT

SAINT, or Security Administrator's Integrated Network Tool, is a vulnerability scanner that scans local area networks for security flaws. SAINT then prepares reports detailing the extent and seriousness of these weaknesses and providing links to fixes and recommended security procedures for these vulnerabilities. Although SAINT was originally developed for Unix-based systems, it has recently been ported to the Mac OS X command line.

Installation

You must install and configure SAINT via the Terminal. To install SAINT, download it to your desktop from `www.saintcorporation.com`, and then open Terminal. The following commands will start the installer:

```
cd ~/Desktop
sudo./saint-install-5.0.1
```

To start SAINT, type the following:

```
cd ~/Desktop/saint-5.01
sudo ./saint
```

To remove SAINT, use the following:

```
sudo rm -rf ~/Desktop/saint-5.01
```

Once SAINT is running, however, things become much easier. The tab-based interface is fairly familiar, and the documentation is easily accessible. To use SAINT, the user needs to know only the IP ranges of the machines to scan. SAINT provides six levels of scanning intensity, allowing for long and involved scans or quick checks. Scan results can be viewed in real time, and all scan data is conveniently saved into an internal database that is stored between sessions. Scans can even be scheduled to be performed on a specific date or at regular intervals, and through the use of OS X's cron daemon, the scans will run in the background with no user interaction required.

SAINT's scan covers a staggering number of vulnerabilities, ranging from warnings about open shares or writable directories, to more critical problems such as services with known buffer overflows. SAINT's comprehensive scan uses the Common Vulnerabilities and Exposures (`http://cve.mitre.org/`) database to provide detailed information and updates on each vulnerability. SAINT releases updates regularly to keep SAINT's scanning abilities up to speed.

SAINT's reports are professional and comprehensive. SAINT supports six types of reports with varying detail, allowing for everything from a quick overview to detailed technical summaries. For more information on vulnerabilities, SAINT provides automated links to Common Vulnerabilities and Exposures (CVE) bulletins. CVE is a standardized list of vulnerabilities that many different security vendors reference.

Nessus

Nessus is a comprehensive vulnerability scanner and analyzer, which is estimated to be used by more than 75,000 organizations. Nessus consists of two parts. *nessusd*, the Nessus daemon, performs the scanning, and *nessus*, the client, generates the scan's results to the user.

Nessus begins by performing a port scan with its own internal port scanner (or it can optionally use nmap) to determine which ports are open on the target and then tries various exploits on the open ports. The vulnerability tests, available as a large body of plug-ins, are written in Nessus Attack Scripting Language (NSAL), a scripting language optimized for custom network interaction.

Optionally, the results of the scan can be reported in various formats, such as plain text, XML, HTML, and LaTeX. The results can also be saved in a knowledge base for reference against future vulnerability scans. Scanning can be automated through the use of a command-line client by using the `nessus` command located in the `/Library/Nessus/i386/bin` folder.

If the user chooses to do so (by disabling the option `safe checks`), some of Nessus's vulnerability tests may try to cause vulnerable services or operating systems to crash. This lets a user test the resistance of a device before putting it in production.

Nessus provides additional functionality beyond testing for known network vulnerabilities. For instance, it can use Windows credentials to examine patch levels on computers running the Windows operating system and can perform password auditing.

Installing Nessus

To install Nessus, you'll need two components. The Nessus server is the system that actually runs a scan. The Nessus client is the system that compiles and prepares a scan. Both can live on the same system, or they can live separately. To install, go to the Tenable Network Security web site at `http://www.nessus.org`, download the Nessus installer, and run it. During the install, it gives you the option to choose whether you want the server to start when the system boots or whether you want to start it manually. If the system is a dedicated Nessus station, then you will want the Nessus daemon to fire at start-up. Otherwise, it's unnecessary if the machine is not a dedicated station (especially if this is installed on a laptop, mainly because it can be a resource hog).

To use the Nessus client, you will first need to start the Nessus server. To start the server (unless you have set the server to automatically start up), open the Nessus Server Manager application, and click Start Nessus Server (see Figure 14-9).

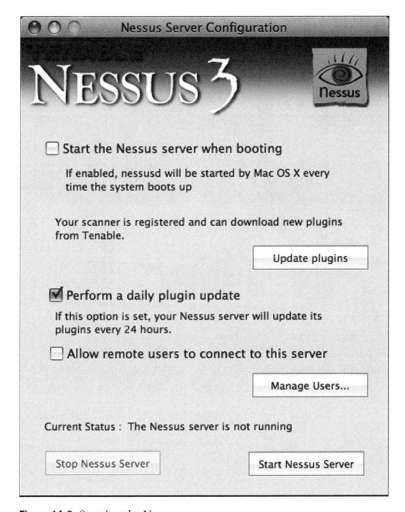

Figure 14-9. *Starting the Nessus server*

Once Nessus has been installed and the server has been started, launch the Nessus client, and select the IP address of the server. Once you have selected the client, you will see a window to begin a new scan (the window will be titled Untitled). When you compile all the settings for a scan in this window, it can save the scan settings for future quick scans of your systems. Configure the server to scan by clicking the + sign in the Networks to Scan section of the Scan window (see Figure 14-10).

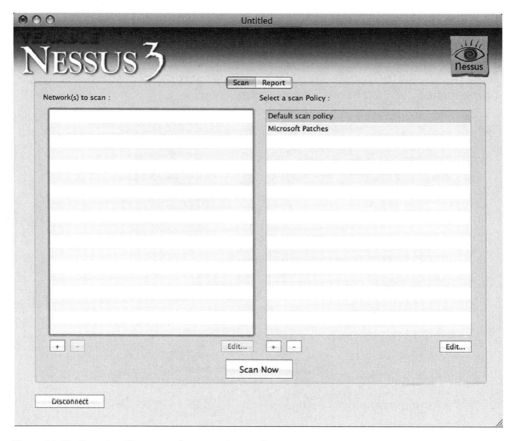

Figure 14-10. *Opening Nessus and connecting to the server*

There are multiple options for defining a target (see Figure 14-11). These options can further expedite the scanning process and give security auditors a more granular approach to scanning. They are as follows:

- Single host

- IP range

- Subnet

- Hosts in file

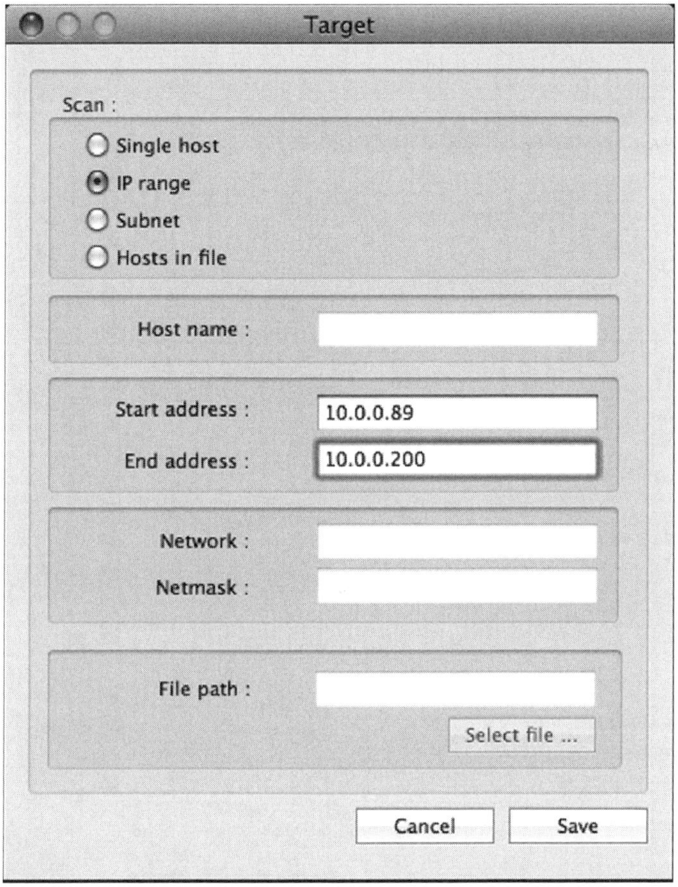

Figure 14-11. *Defining the target*

Next, we'll explore how to create a new scanning policy. To create a new policy, click the plus sign under Select a Policy (see Figure 14-10). From here set the plug-ins that will be used for the scan (see Figure 14-12). Each plug-in typically corresponds to a specific vulnerability. Reducing the number of plug-ins that are selected will speed up scans. For example, if you disable the ColdFusion Debug Mode scan, then the full scan can run more quickly than it would otherwise. This is one place where knowing which vulnerabilities are available for each OS will allow you to scan large numbers of systems quicker. Take caution with disabling plug-ins because disabling a scan on a vulnerability that is known (but not known by you) could be disastrous if the vulnerability is exploited.

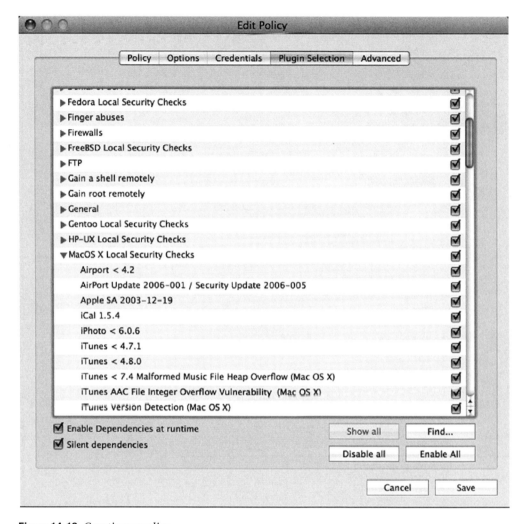

Figure 14-12. *Creating a policy*

Running a Scan

Once you have selected the appropriate plug-ins and options, it is time to scan your systems. Save your policy (name it if you will be using it again in the future) by clicking the Save button, and then click Scan. Now you can click the Report tab to view each vulnerability available for your system (see Figure 14-13).

Note Until the scan finds a vulnerability, you will not see the left column populated with any data.

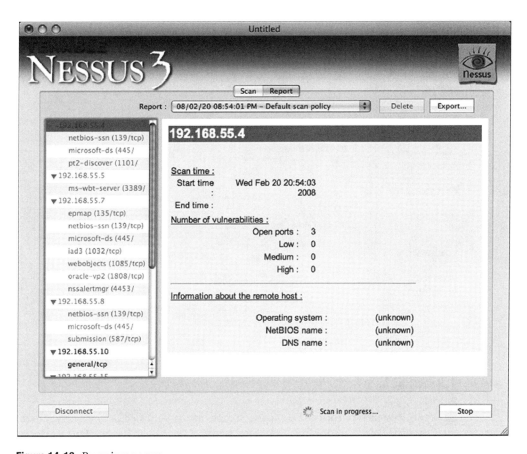

Figure 14-13. *Running a scan*

Once the scan is complete, any vulnerability warnings Nessus finds will appear under the left column of the report screen (see Figure 14-14). If you click each item, you will see an overview of the exploit that is available for it, if any.

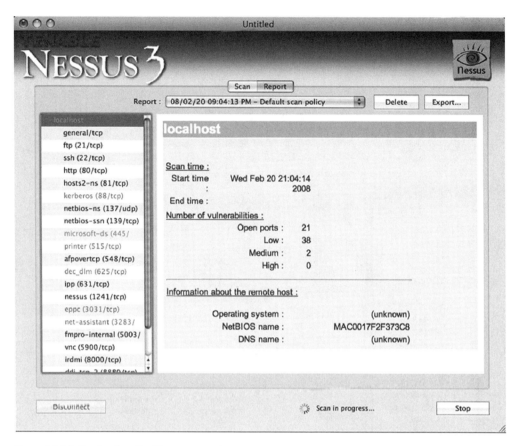

Figure 14-14. *Reviewing the Nessus report*

You can export Nessus reports into HTML to make reviewing and saving them easy. There are companies that specialize in running automated scans of servers on behalf of institutions such as credit card processors and insurance companies. Such companies often simply rebrand a Nessus scan by replacing the images in the HTML exports. To export a scan, click the Export button in your report. Scans resemble the scan report displayed in Figure 14-15.

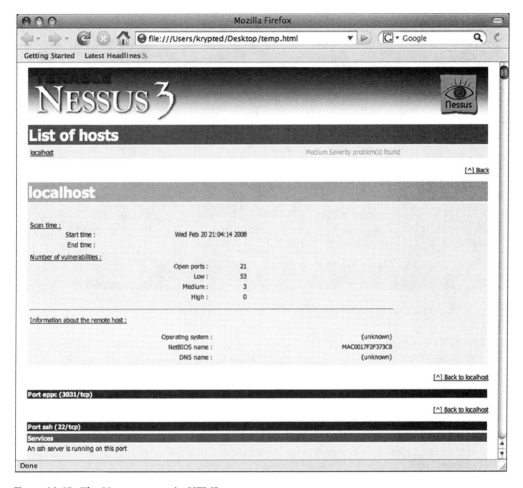

Figure 14-15. *The Nessus report in HTML*

Metasploit

Metasploit is a free, open source framework that can be used to launch automated exploits (already developed) to target known vulnerabilities in networks. Using the Metasploit framework, it is possible to test and use these exploits to discover how vulnerable a network is.

You can download the latest version of Metasploit at `http://www.metasploit.com`. Once you have downloaded the application, copy the files to where you want them to live on your hard drive. For this example, we are copying the Metasploit to the `/Applications` folder and renaming the folder to `Metasploit`. Next, we'll show how to use the Terminal and `cd` into the `/Applications/Metasploit` folder. From within the `Metasploit` folder, we run the command `./msfconsole`, which results in the screen shown in Figure 14-16.

Figure 14-16. *Metasploit opening screen*

This will put you at an msf> prompt. At the msf> prompt, you have a variety of commands that can be run. To access more detailed information for each command, see the help section of Metasploit. Commands include the following:

cd: Changes the working directory (exactly like standard terminal commands)

exit and auit: Exits the msf console

info: Obtains detailed information about the exploit or payload that you are running

reload: Reloads the exploits and payloads you have chosen

save: Saves your configuration into ~/.msf3/config

setg: Sets the global variables of Metasploit, including logging, nops, debug level, and alternate exit

show: Shows the exploits, payloads, encoders, and nops available to the msfconsole (for example, show exploits or show payloads)

unsetg: Clears the environmental variables set using the setg command

version: Shows the version of the msfconsole being used

use: Sets the exploit to be used (a list of exploits is included later in the chapter)

Once you have set an exploit, you can type show payloads to see the available payloads for the exploit you will be running. You will also need to set an rhost and an lhost before launching an exploit. The rhost is the target, and the lhost is the IP address that Metasploit will tell packets used in the exploit to return to. To set an rhost, you use the set rhost command followed by the IP address of the target system, as shown here with a target of 10.10.10.2:

`set rhost 10.10.10.2`

To set an lhost of 10.10.10.203, you would use the following command:

`set lhost 10.10.10.203`

Once you have set your IP addresses, it is time to set the *payload*, or action that will be taken. Available payloads for Mac OS X include the following:

`mac_osx_ppc_bind`: Listens on a TCP port for connections and then executes `/bin/sh` redirected from the command line.

`osx_ppc_bind_stg`: Listens for a TCP connection and then executes a second payload.

`osx_ppc_reverse`: Connects to target and redirects to `/bin/sh`.

`osx_ppc_reverse_stg`: Connects to a host and provides the ability to run a second payload.

`osx_ppc_reverse_nf_stg`: Establishes a TCP connection to a target and then sends a null-free payload.

`osx_ppc_findrecv_stg`: Searches open files for a 4-byte tag sent by the attacker. Once the tag is found, it executes `/bin/sh`.

`osx_ppc_findrecv_peak_stg`: The same payload as `osx_ppc_findrecv_stg` except it is null-free and uses the `MSG_PEEK` flag.

In addition to setting a payload, you should set an exploit. Common exploits for Mac OS X include the following:

`osx_ia32_bind`: Listens for a TCP connection and then executes

`arkeia_type77_macos`: Executes a stack overflow against the Arkeia backup software

`firefox_queryinterface_osx`: Exploits a vulnerability in Firefox 1.5

`samba_trans2open_osx`: Runs a buffer overflow against Samba 2.2.0 to 2.2.8

`afp_loginext`: Runs a stack overflow against the AppleFileServer

`webstar_ftp_user`: Executes a stack overflow against the WebStar FTP server

`smb_sniffer`: Attempts to capture LanMan and NTLM passwords

`phpnuke_search_module`: Runs a SQL injection attack against PHP Nuke 7.5 to 7.8

Next, you will need to set the target. Each payload has a specific set of targets. To see which targets are available for the payload that you have chosen, type `show targets`. This will open a screen of targets that can be used to exploit a system. Next, type `set` followed by the target number you select, for example, `set target 0`.

Once the payload, exploit, target, and hosts have been set, it is time to launch your first exploit. Enter the command `show options` to review your settings, and make sure everything is set as intended. If it is, enter the exploit command to run your first exploit.

CHAPTER 15

■ ■ ■

Backup and Fault Tolerance

"**S**top hackers dead in their tracks by securing your systems and network." That has been our mantra up to this point. However, there is another piece in the network security pie that often goes unexamined. Any conversation about security on a system or network must go beyond discussing the prevention of unauthorized access. Securing the data on these systems with a reliable data backup scheme is a crucial element in any security framework. As digital assets become increasingly valuable, organizations are becoming more and more reliant on their data. In fact, many companies have invested large amounts of labor in building their company data, and if they were to suffer a catastrophic loss of data (for some this could mean as little as 30 percent), the hours it would take to re-create that data would prove impossible to rebuild and would simply cause them to go out of business. Therefore, backing up data is very important in any security footprint and critical in any organization.

When developing a backup schematic, you should answer some important questions:

- What is the source to be backed up?

- What is the destination device for the data to be backed up to?

- How far back in time will the backups need to go?

As we go through this chapter, we will examine how backups are performed for a variety of software packages. We will start by discussing the most simplistic backup topology and work our way up to more complicated backup schemas, including fault-tolerant solutions. This will allow you to see the increasing complexity and weigh it against your needs to eventually choose which is best for you. Once you have a backup solution that you trust, you should continue to refer to this chapter, because as your needs increase, so will the complexity of your backup topology.

Time Machine

Time Machine is an application introduced in Mac OS X Leopard that allows you to back up your computer to a second hard drive at set regular intervals for the backups. Time Machine is a straightforward application that is simple to configure. However, it is a new feature of OS X and is fairly limited in its scope. The good thing is that Time Machine is installed by default on every new Mac, so you don't need to purchase any additional software. To set up disk-based backups using Time Machine, open the Time Machine preference pane (see Figure 15-1).

Figure 15-1. *Time Machine preference pane*

Next, select the target device for your backups. This is where the data that is backed up on your computers is stored. Click the Choose Backup Disk button to select the device you want to backup to (see Figure 15-2).

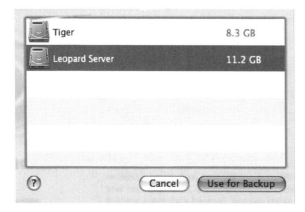

Figure 15-2. *Choosing the backup device*

Once you have selected the target disk, the screen will change to reflect the critical statistics of your backup operations (see Figure 15-3). Here you will see the volume you are backing up to, how much available free space is on that volume, the date and time of both the oldest and most recent backups, and when the next backup is scheduled. For many smaller backup environments, this information is the most crucial to track.

Figure 15-3. *Time Machine configured*

On this screen, you can also click the Change Disk button at any time to change the destination of your backups. This will allow you to fill up a disk and then move on to the next disk in your backup scheme. Multiple disks can give you a deep historical backup set of your data, which is crucial if collecting multiple versions of files is important to your backup strategy.

You can also set what data on your computer will not be backed up. By default, Time Machine will back up all the data on your computer's hard drive. To limit what is backed up, click the Options button, and you will be presented with the Do Not Back Up window (Figure 15-4). Here you can specify which items are to be excluded from the backup sets.

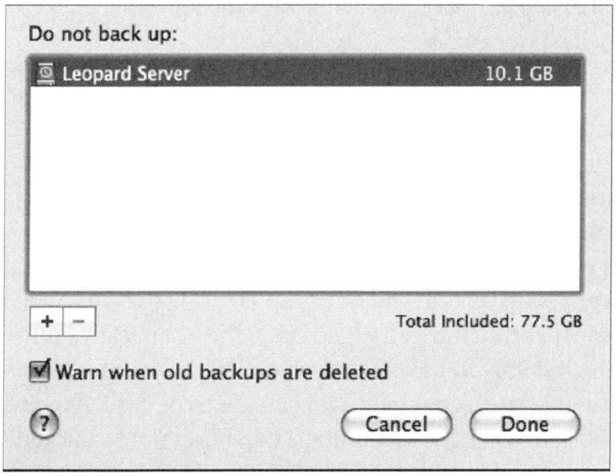

Figure 15-4. *Time Machine device exclusions*

Next, if you click the + button, you will be able to browse to folders that are not worth the space to back up. For example, most users do not need to back up the following directories unless they plan to do a "bare-metal" restore (a restore from a hard drive crash without reinstalling the operating system):

- /Applications

- /Library

- /System

- Invisible items (which are accessible by unchecking the Show Invisible Items check box) include the following:

  - /.TemporaryItems

  - /.Spotlight-V100

  - /.Trashes

  - /bin

  - /opt

  - /private

  - /sbin

  - /var

  - /Network

Note To view the files that are not backed up by default, check the information listed in the file /System/ Library/CoreServices/backupd.bundle/Resources/StdExclusions.plist.

The data that is backed up is really dictated by your personal backup strategy. Some feel comfortable backing up the whole machine. For others, just backing up the /Users folder is sufficient because that is where the bulk of the irreplaceable data is stored.

Once you have selected all the items you are going to exclude, click the Exclude button (Figure 15-5), and the initial setup of your backup system will be complete. The backups will run an incremental backup (backups of any files that have changed since the last backup) once an hour, every hour. According to how much data you have, the data can fill up your backup drive rather quickly, because every change to a file, big or small, will cause it to be copied to the Time Machine destination again. For this reason, we suggest Entourage databases not be backed up in Windows Exchange or IMAP environments where a database is backed up elsewhere, as is the case with many corporate environments. We also suggest reviewing the larger files on your systems and deciding whether you need to back them up. If they are changed often, then you will more than likely want to back them up, but educating yourself about the files that you are backing up can often be an eye-opener for you. Also, you should strongly consider investing in a rather large hard drive, 500GB at the minimum, but we often see 2TB drives as a good size for backups if you want historical backups of your data.

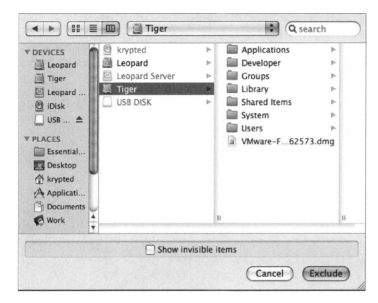

Figure 15-5. *Time Machine file exclusions*

You can disable Time Machine backups altogether. To do so, click the Time Machine preference pane, and use the slider to move the backup status to the Off position (see Figure 15-6).

Figure 15-6. *Turning Time Machine on or off*

Restoring Files from Time Machine

To restore files from Time Machine backups, open Time Machine from the /Applications folder. When the Time Machine restoration utility opens, use the timeline on the left side of the screen to select the restore point you are going to restore to (see Figure 15-7). Next, browse to the file or folder you want to restore, and click the Restore button.

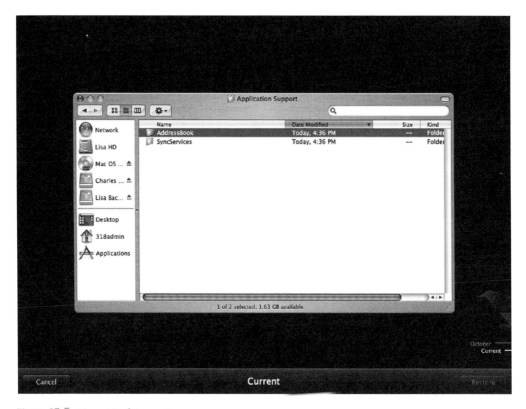

Figure 15-7. *Time Machine restore screen*

You can also see the files that were backed up and restore files by browsing to the Backups.backupdb directory located on your target drive. Inside this directory you will see a folder containing your computer's name. If you are backing up multiple computers to a single device, you will see multiple computer names in this directory. If you open these folders you will see the date that a backup was run and the files that were backed up during this backup.

Using a Network Volume for Time Machine

Time Machine is capable of performing backups over the network. These backups can be saved to a disk attached to an AirPort device using AirPort disk sharing, an AFP volume hosted by a Mac OS X Server, or any other volumes to which your computer has access. To allow backups over a network volume, make sure the network volume is mounted, and simply select the network volume from the Change Disk menu option in the Time Machine configuration page, as mentioned earlier.

Apple officially supports using Time Capsule and Mac OS X Server share points with the Time Machine check box enabled for network backups only. However, if you want to use an unsupported network disk type for your Time Machine archives, such as a different type of server or a NAS appliance, running the following command on workstations will allow you to do so:

```
defaults write com.apple.systempreferences TMShowUnsupportedNetworkVolumes 1
```

SuperDuper

One of the easiest-to-use and most versatile third-party backup programs available for the Mac platform is SuperDuper, a free app developed by David Nanian and available from `http://www.shirt-pocket.com/SuperDuper`. SuperDuper is more flexible than Time Machine and has more features. If you're willing to plunk down $30 for the software, you'll be given the extra ability to write custom backup scripts, schedule backups, and use sandboxing (a highly useful utility that backs the system up to a separate volume that can be used to boot the machine if it crashes).

After you've downloaded and installed SuperDuper, a configuration window opens that allows you to configure what data should be backed up and where it should be backed up to (see Figure 15-8).

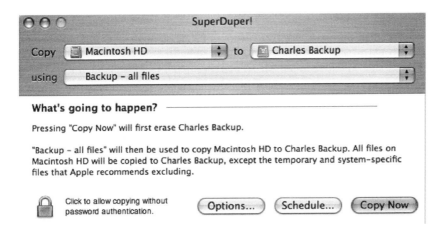

Figure 15-8. *SuperDuper configuration window*

Using the default options will back up the entire hard drive. However, you may choose to back up only the `/Users` folder if you're not concerned with having to rebuild the operating system if the machine crashes (see Figure 15-9).

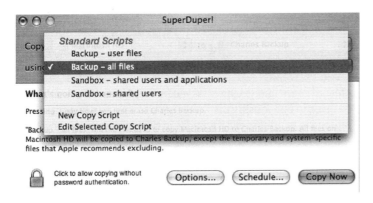

Figure 15-9. *Backing up all files with SuperDuper*

You can use SuperDuper to back your computer up to an image file. You can also store multiple image files on one hard drive for historical backups or back up multiple computers to one drive. To make this organized and clean, you can also back up multiple computers to one drive by partitioning the drive that the backups will reside on and dedicating a partition to each user's backup.

Backing Up to .Mac

Another easy way to back up your Mac is by using a .Mac account. Because .Mac has become an integral part of the Mac operating system, it's highly likely that if you own a Mac, you either own a .Mac account or at a minimum know what a .Mac account is. Apple sells .Mac accounts to give Mac users space on Apple servers to access their files, web sites, and e-mail from remote locations. The .Mac accounts can also be a great way to back up and store a small amount of critical data in an offsite location.

If you haven't set your computer to log into .Mac, then you will need to do that before you can back up, or *sync*, any of your data to Apple's servers. To configure your computer to work with a .Mac account, go to the sign-in screen in the .Mac preference pane, as shown in Figure 15-10. At this screen, enter your .Mac username and password, and click the Sign In button. If you don't yet have a .Mac account, you can click the Learn More button to obtain one.

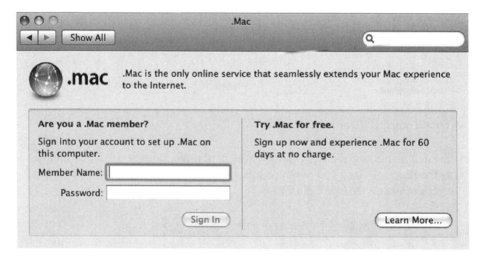

Figure 15-10. *.Mac sign-in screen*

If you are using an existing .Mac account and you have logged into it from another computer previously, you will be prompted to log in either using the same name or using a different name. Select Use Same Name if you want to log in. This is all that needs to be done to configure your computer to communicate with the .Mac account. Legacy data is always important to consider with destination for any media, so keep in mind that any data you sync from this new system will overwrite any data that is currently being hosted by your .Mac account (see Figure 15-11) if you select Use the Same Name. If you have data that you want to review before removing it, then select Enter another name, which will give you the chance to manually browse .Mac to see what's up there before you overwrite it.

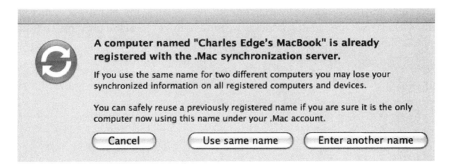

Figure 15-11. *File overwrite warning*

Once you have configured your computer to talk to the .Mac account, you can then configure it to sync information with the account. Using the Sync tab of the .Mac preference pane, you will be given a list of preconfigured locations where your Mac thinks you may have pertinent data to sync, as shown in Figure 15-12. Items such as Dashboard Widgets Dock Items and Preferences are probably not necessary to back up because they are easily re-created (additional drive space on a .Mac account is pricey, so discretion is necessary).

Figure 15-12. *.Mac sync preferences*

Once you are satisfied with what you are going to sync, you will need to instruct the system as to when this information should be synchronized. Click the Synchronize with .Mac dropdown box next to Manually to display the various options for scheduling (see Figure 15-13).

Here you will be able to tell the system to sync Automatically (when changes are made), Every Hour, Every Day, or Every Week. As faulty humans, we tend to forget to manually sync data, so we recommend that you have it sync automatically.

Automatically
Every Hour
Every Day
Every Week
✓ Manually

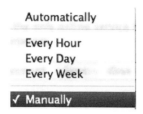

Figure 15-13. *Manually syncing the .Mac account*

Once you have set the time interval to sync, click the Advanced button. This will show you the computers that you have authenticated to synchronize with your .Mac. You can remove a system from the list using the Unregister button, clear out what is currently stored on the .Mac servers by using the Reset Sync Data button, or just check the last time that any systems were synchronized (see Figure 15-14).

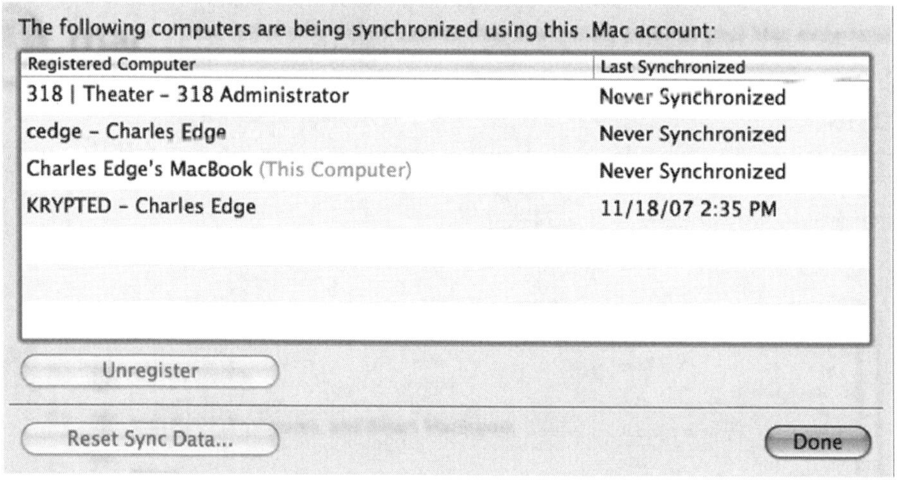

The following computers are being synchronized using this .Mac account:
Registered Computer
Last Synchronized
318 | Theater - 318 Administrator
Never Synchronized
cedge - Charles Edge
Never Synchronized
Charles Edge's MacBook (This Computer)
Never Synchronized
KRYPTED - Charles Edge
11/18/07 2:35 PM
Unregister
Reset Sync Data...
Done

Figure 15-14. *Computers synchronized with .Mac*

Conversely, backing up your iDisk data to your computer allows you to access your iDisk data locally. This can be useful if the .Mac data is lost and you're finding that it takes an unusually long amount of time for Apple to restore it. This can also be useful if you want to work on data that is stored on your iDisk while your computer is offline. To set iDisk up to synchronize with your computer, click the .Mac preference pane, and click the iDisk tab (as shown in Figure 15-15). Then click the Start button in the iDisk Sync Sharing section of the screen. You can (and probably should) set the Update option to Automatically.

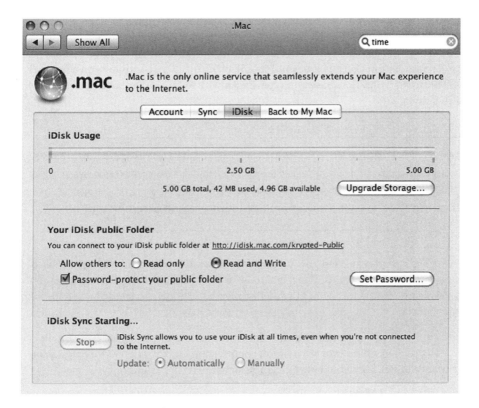

Figure 15-15. *Backing up with iDisk*

Unless you are looking to distribute files from it, it would be wise to change the permissions that others have to access your iDisk public folder. You don't want this information falling into the hands of random intruders. To restrict access to your public folder, select the check box to password-protect your public folder, click the Set Password button, and then enter the password you want users to use to access your data if you do plan on sharing files. You should also select the Read Only option to let other users only read your iDisk content, and not edit it, from the iDisk.

Note You may want to obtain more storage with your .Mac account. The Upgrade Storage feature on the iDisk tab (shown in Figure 15-15) will allow you to do so. Apple routinely increases the levels of disk space provided, and your disk quota will automatically be upgraded to the level you purchased.

Retrospect

We initially discussed Time Machine to explain how to simply back up your Mac. Then, for those who require a slightly more capable solution (albeit slightly different), we reviewed how to use SuperDuper. Then we explored using the .Mac Sync feature to create an offsite copy of your most critical data. Now we'll move on to covering how to use a more powerful application altogether, called Retrospect. At its most basic usage, Retrospect can perform any of the features that SuperDuper or Time Machine can perform. However, the power of a more advanced application such as Retrospect can also go far beyond this, backing up client computers on a network, moving data between computers based on type, backing up to tape drives, and performing many other features.

▪Note There was a time when backing up a system meant writing data to a tape using a Unix `tar` command. Backups needed to be scripted from the ground up using shell scripts. Assigning different values to blocks and troubleshooting `tar` issues were standard daily routines. Many of these tasks have been automated with current software. (That's not to say that backups don't still require troubleshooting, mind you.)

Since we have already explored how to duplicate data and perform backups in a disk-to-disk capacity with other applications, let's spend some time discussing how to perform backups to tape using Retrospect. Before we begin, let's describe a few basic principles that go into performing a disk to tape backup:

Compression: Compression can slim your data sets down, tremendously saving on disk space. However, most hardware will perform compression for you. Therefore, compression typically should not be enabled in your scripts because it is not required.

Encryption: Encrypting your data with passwords will make it difficult for those who obtain your data without authorization to actually view the backups. You should always encrypt your backup tapes and other targets.

Configuring Retrospect to Backup to Tape

To set Retrospect to back up to tape automatically, you must first build a script (all automated backups in Retrospect require a script). In Retrospect, a *script* is a set of rules involving sources, targets, and schedules relating to a backup. Each script will have a source or collection of sources, which can be a file or folder on a disk either connected locally or to a remote computer.

To create that first backup script, open Retrospect, and click the Automate tab. Then click the Scripts button. This will take you to the Retrospect Scripts menu (see Figure 15-16).

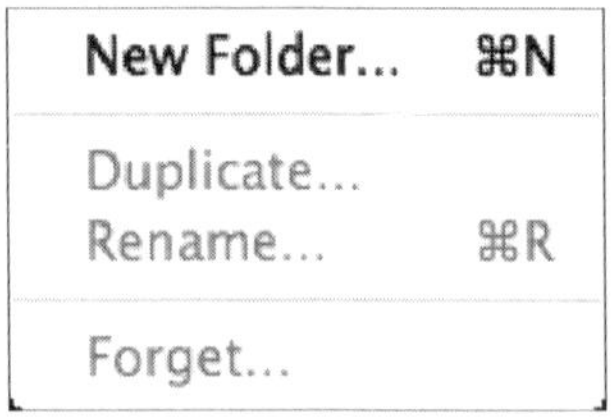

Figure 15-16. *Retrospect Scripts menu*

Create the script by clicking the New button, which will allow you to configure the script in the Retrospect Script Options menu (see Figure 15-17).

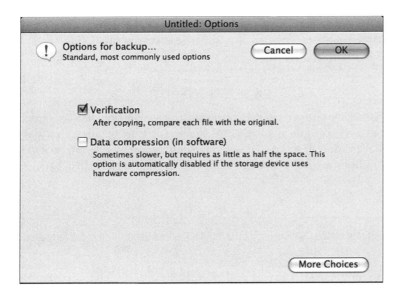

Figure 15-17. *Retrospect Script Options menu*

Click OK and then click in the Sources field, and select the source you want to back up. For the purpose of this example, we're going to back up the /Users folder. To select the Source, click the Sources button, browse to the desired location, and then click Define to set the location for the source (see Figure 15-18).

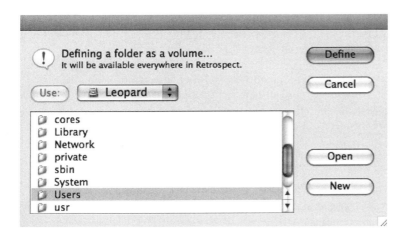

Figure 15-18. *Setting up a source*

Once you have selected that folder, click the Destinations button of the Scripts screen. A Retrospect script must have a destination. The destination is where the redundant copy of the source data will be stored. Retrospect destinations include the following:

Disk: A whole disk is allocated to Retrospect, which then creates a collection of compressed files on the disk that store your data. This can be any disk your system can access.

Tape: A magnetic tape, typically DLT, DDS, AIT, or LTO.

File: A single file that contains all the files meant to be backed up.

To allow the destinations to be virtualized, Retrospect looks at a collection of disks, tapes, or files as a set. Each set can have multiple members (this can be a mixture of tapes, files, and disks) and can back up from a variety of scripts. To set up the destination for a script, click the button beside destinations, click the Add button, and then select the first backup set to back up to (see Figure 15-19).

■**Note**   Tape drives are configured on the Configure tab by using the Devices button. Tapes are formatted here as well.

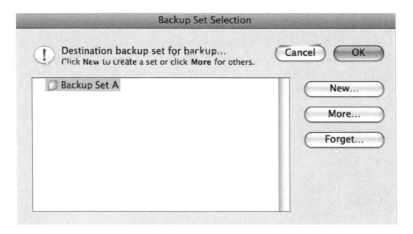

Figure 15-19. *Configuring a set*

■**Note**   Verification is the process whereby Retrospect reviews the source and destination to ensure the integrity of the data. You can also configure selectors. Selectors allow you to limit what will be backed up based on file type, labels, and other attributes.

Once you are satisfied with your configuration, then you can proceed with scheduling the backup job. To do so, click the Schedule button from the script, and then click the Add button.

Here, you will see a screen similar to Figure 15-20, where you can select the type of schedule that you will be deploying. If you will be running the script daily, then click Day of Week, and then click OK.

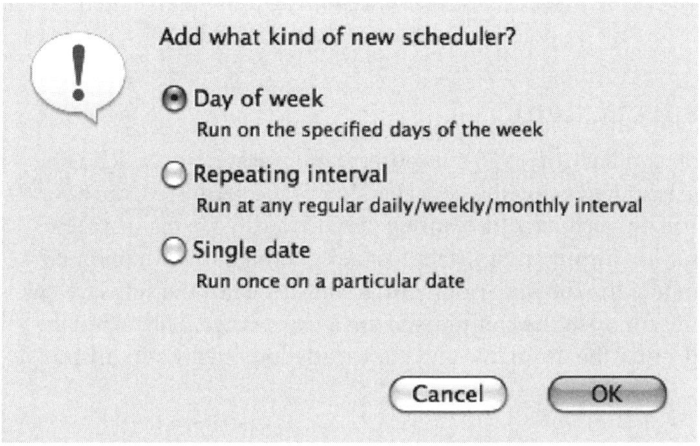

Figure 15-20. *Schedule intervals*

Now that you have selected the type of schedule to implement, click the days of the week and the time that you want your scheduled execution to run. If you want to perform a task once every other week, you can click the Weeks field and set it to 2. Select each day you want the scheduled backup to run, and then select the action you want it to run. If you want each run of a script to add its data to the set without recycling, then you can use Normal Backup. If you want the run of the script to reformat the tapes and perform a new backup, then you can select the Recycle Backup option (shown in Figure 15-21).

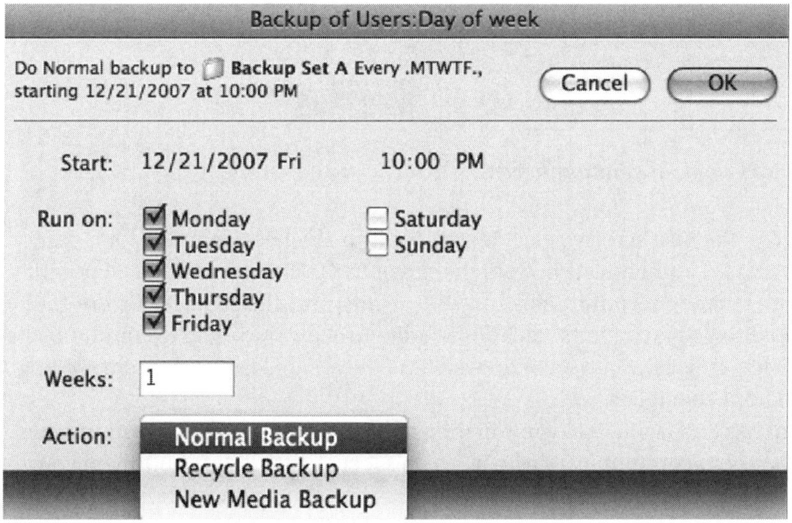

Figure 15-21. *Setting up the frequency of a schedule*

Once you have completed setting the first of your schedules, you can set further schedules. It is a good idea to set up a week of normal backups and then perform a recycle backup on Saturday. This allows you to continually append to the backups for a week and then start the backups over on the weekend.

Once you have set up all your schedules, then save the script. The Run menu in Retrospect will allow you to immediately run any scripted action that you have created.

Installing the Retrospect Client

Retrospect Workgroup Edition can back up to 25 computers before it requires a licensing upgrade. These clients can be installed using the latest version of the software from http:// www.emcinsignia.com/supportupdates/updates/ (or by using the copy located in the Installers directory on the Retrospect server, if your environment is lucky enough to have one).

Download the latest version of the software from EMC's website. Once the software has been downloaded, unzip the file, or open the compressed installer package. Then open the installer, and when prompted, enter the username and password required for administrative access (see Figure 15-22).

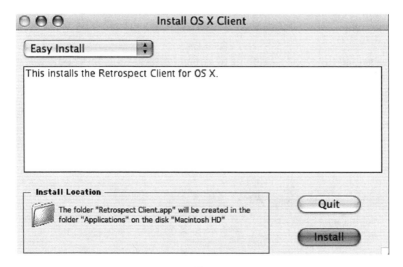

Figure 15-22. *Retrospect Client installation screen*

When prompted at the next screen, select Install. Next you will be prompted for a password that allows encrypted authentication from the server to the client computers. Enter the password you will use to encrypt communication with clients, and click OK (see Figure 15-23)

At the prompt for firewall exceptions, click Yes in order to allow the server to communicate with the client (see Figure 15-24), even if the firewall has been enabled (and if you're reading this book, we would hope that it has been).

Once your client has been installed, you will then need to set up the system running the full version of Retrospect to communicate with it. To do so, click the Clients button on your main Retrospect system, and select the client from the list that opens. From here, you can enter the password assigned earlier in this section. Once completed, the client drives will show up in the Sources listing in your script setup.

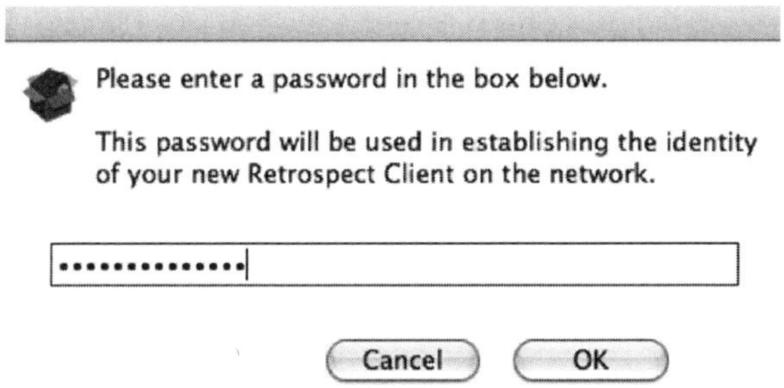

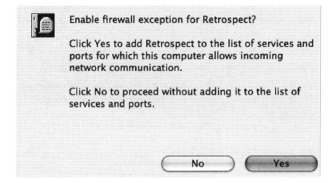

Figure 15-23. *Retrospect Client password screen*

Figure 15-24. *Enabling the firewall exception for Retrospect*

Checking Your Retrospect Backups

Once you have configured and started your backups, then it is critical to review their performance. There are typically too many moving pieces to blindly trust that the backups are running as they should and actually backing up all your data in a restorable format.

Many organizations perform checks on their backups daily, weekly, or biweekly. Often, they will also perform a test restore monthly or quarterly. To keep staff (or yourself) from missing critical steps in the backup checking process, it is wise to use a checklist to make sure you don't miss a step in the process. A quick and easy checklist should include the following:

All backups executed successfully:

[ ] Yes

[ ] No

If not, please identify cause(s):

[ ] Destination full

[ ] Source unavailable

[ ] Error with backup software

[ ] Operating system error

[ ] Other: _____

Corrective action(s): _____

Free space for future backup(s): _____

Every environment will require a different level of needs for how often to check backups. Some organizations choose to check their backups on a daily basis, while others will check weekly. No matter what, it is important to check the logs and make sure your systems are being backed up rather than trust that the software has you covered.

In addition to checking that the backups are occurring on schedule, it is also important to occasionally perform a restore just to make sure that the backups are not corrupt or incomplete. Some people choose to restore a folder or a randomly selected file, while others choose to restore an entire volume and check the contents to see whether all the required data has in fact been backed up as it should be. This is strongly suggested, especially if you are backing up to tape or to compressed disk images.

In Retrospect, you can check your backups by opening Retrospect, clicking the Reports tab, and then clicking the Log button. You will see the options to view the report, which is a quick rundown of what was backed up and how many errors were encountered. You will also see the logs, which show you a detailed description of each event performed with Retrospect (see Figure 15-25).

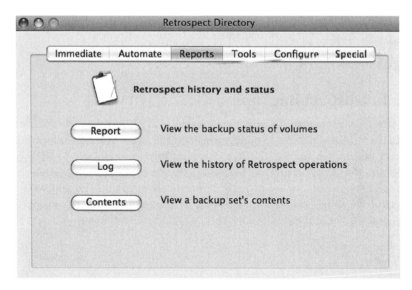

Figure 15-25. *Retrospect reports options*

Using Tape Libraries

Retrospect is a great application and fairly simple to use when backing up to a single tape drive with only a few tapes involved in your sets. There are other products that are designed from the ground up with tape libraries in mind. BRU by the Tolis Group, NetVault by Bakbone, PresStor by Archiware, and Time Navigator by Atempo are the primary applications currently used to provide more industrial-strength backups. They are used primarily to back up Xserve RAIDs and other larger volumes ranging from 2TB to 150TB.

A tape library will typically consist of one or more tape drives and a *hand* (also referred to as a *robot*) that is used to move tapes within the library, placing them in the tape drives. Many libraries will also come outfitted with a bar-code scanner in order to quickly find assets within the library. Many tape libraries come with a dedicated slot that is meant to be used for housing a cleaning tape. Routinely cleaning your drives when they get dirty is critical to ensure that the drives will perform as needed.

Many of these applications will also allow you to "stage" your data onto disk. By staging data to a disk, it is possible to restore data more quickly. Your backups are also compartmentalized because they are being written to a much more efficient storage medium. For example, this could be a FireWire disk or a RAID. The name that many of these programs call this compartmentalization is different, and many vendors will consider it an add-on that requires an additional charge to use it, but when you begin backing up a large amount of data, you will find it to be a lifesaver and well worth the extra money.

Backup vs. Fault Tolerance

Data backup frameworks don't need to stop at redundant copies of data. Backup and downtime discussions go hand in hand. How long would it take to get a system back online if a primary server with important data went down? How crucial would this be to the organization's operation?

Fault tolerance goes a step beyond the conversation of backing up your data and into the conversation of what you would do if any component of the whole network environment failed. For example, if you are running a mail server and your primary Internet connection goes down, then what is the contingency plan? What if you were to lose the hard drive on the server because of hardware failure? What if the logic board on the server dies? Some organizations go so far as to have a duplicate of every device in their environment. For most, though, it is a matter of analyzing what you can live without in the event of a failure because some fault-tolerant solutions do not have an appropriately high return on investment in case of a failure.

If downtime is a critical factor in keeping a data structure alive, you should consider implementing a failover or *fault-tolerant* solution. In fact, the cost of providing fault tolerance could actually mitigate the cost of downtime in cases where downtime can cause loss of productivity. When configuring Mac OS X Server (or Mac OS X Client as a server) hosting various services, you may choose to provide a fault-tolerant solution when high availability is required.

Fault-Tolerant Scenarios

Fault tolerance comes in two types. The first is *active-passive*. In an active-passive topology, you would maintain a host spare of the service you are load balancing, which is passive (or dormant) until the primary server crashes. The OS X service that maintains this fault-tolerant scenario is *failoverd*.

As with most failover services, once the primary server comes back online, you must manually tell the backup server to stop processing requests (backups) and reactivate the primary host. Failoverd is not meant to be a load balancer. You do not receive any additional benefits other than maintaining a backup server that you would flip to if the primary were to go down. Typically, the backup server will be a less expensive version of the primary server. For example, a cluster node might be a backup to an Xserve.

The second type of fault-tolerant solution is called *active-active*. In an active active topology, multiple active servers are used. In this scenario, you will often also engage in load balancing those servers. This gives you the ability to provide increased bandwidth to mission-critical services. The complexity introduced in this scenario is that the data store must be either synchronized with the primary server or shared between the servers, as is the case with using multiple servers as bridgehead servers using an Xsan to reshare data. Data in an active-passive topology must be synchronized between the servers, but not as frequently as in active-active environments.

Round-Robin DNS

While active-passive topology traffic reroutes data using the failover daemon (failoverd), in an active-active topology traffic must be routed between multiple servers on a constant basis. There are two predominant methods for doing this. The first is using *round-robin DNS*. Round-robin DNS controls the order in which a load-balanced service forwards traffic across multiple servers. The administrator fills the domain records with multiple address records using the same host name but points to one or more IP addresses that serve the same service. As the DNS request is looking for your DNS server, the web server responds to the client with the next address from the list.

The most basic round-robin DNS setup shapes traffic based on the assumption that each server can handle the same load, which is considered an *equal cost path*. A typical list of A addresses in your zone file might look like the following if you have three servers:

```
afp  IN  A       10.0.0.7
afp  IN  A       10.0.0.8
afp  IN  A       10.0.0.9
```

You can tell one server to handle more traffic than the others, as is the case with *unequal cost paths*, or paths that send more traffic to one server than the others. You can do this by listing the same server multiple times in the listing of A records for a given address. For example, if you have one server at 10.0.0.4 that is much faster than the others in a six-node cluster of web servers, you might direct traffic using the following entries in a zone file:

```
afp  IN  A       10.0.0.4
afp  IN  A        10.0.0.4
afp  IN  A       10.0.0.5
afp  IN  A       10.0.0.6
afp  IN  A        10.0.0.7
afp  IN  A       10.0.0.8
```

You can use the `rrset-order` command to define how round-robin requests are forwarded. The default `rrset` order is cyclic. There are three different options for record handling:

- Cyclic records are returned in numerical order.

- Fixed records are returned in the same order that they are listed in the file.

- Random records are returned in a random order.

When using round-robin DNS, the traffic is shaped in a static manner and cannot adapt to changes in the servers, such as performance counters and current user load.

Load-Balancing Devices

A *load balancer* can provide many features. Among them is the ability to shape traffic based on multiple factors (IP addresses, port, amount of traffic), automatically failover to another server when one server becomes unresponsive, and provide a single address for systems to use when requesting a service. The load balancer will probably not handle synchronizing data but will perform almost everything else that will be required when architecting this type of solution. Load balancers include Coyote Point Equalizers, F5s/Dell BigIPs, Barracuda Load Balancers, and Cisco Load Directors.

The cost of deploying a solution using round-robin DNS is typically very low compared to the cost of purchasing a load balancer. However, the load balancer will become a more scalable solution over the long run. In cluster environments, the load balancer can become a single point of failure. To build a completely fault-tolerant environment, implement a backup load balancer to automatically go live if there is a problem with the main load balancer. It may seem redundant, but even load balancers can and will fail.

Cold Sites

When discussing redundancy, it is important to explore the physical redundancy of the actual location where your equipment resides. Secondary locations are important for situations where there is a need to be back up and running quickly in the event of a communications error with your primary location. The secondary location, or *cold site*, often consists of a set of servers that are slightly below the speed of your primary site, that are shut down (or offline), and that contain a fairly recent copy of the data stored in your hot site.

Planning is everything when dealing with a secondary location. Much like an evacuation procedure at an office, in the event of a failure at your primary site a procedure should be written and followed to activate the cold site. These processes often resemble a series of steps that enable you to be online providing the assets that you need quickly and efficiently. An example of this might include a complex flowchart, or it might be as easy as a simple checklist outlining what steps to take.

We cannot stress enough the importance of documenting and testing these mission-critical business processes before you begin to rely on them.

Hot Sites

For locations that require even more redundancy and cannot suffer a performance loss should the primary site go down, a redundant site, or *hot site*, should be implemented. With a hot redundant site, practically a one-to-one ratio of your equipment in the primary location would be available in the secondary site. A hot site is critical for large web sites, such as Amazon.com, that would lose millions of dollars an hour if users were unable to check the status of accounts, book travel, or purchase MP3s because of an outage.

The goal of any hot site is not to quickly be up and running with a subpar system, as it is with a cold site, but instead to be instantly up and running with an equally powerful system. Many hot sites begin as a redundant location used only in an emergency and often end up running in tandem with various systems in the primary site, allowing any of the systems in the primary site to fail over to the secondary. This can lead to increased throughput capacity for server farms, which might otherwise be sitting idle.

CHAPTER 16

■■■

Forensics

You never can be completely prepared. Even if you take every precaution and follow every security measure, you're never really prepared when it happens. Thievery is one of the unpleasant realities of our world today. And data theft as a result of a break-in or security breach is one of the hardest hurdles to overcome. Some companies don't survive it. Others take years to recover from the damage. Fortunately, a field has developed over the years in which investigations of computer crimes are conducted to find the perpetrators of these crimes and bring them to justice. And a conversation about security would not be complete without a discussion surrounding the field of *computer forensics*.

Computer forensics is the scientific investigation and review of digital assets in order to provide evidence of a crime to a court of law. A variety of forensic tools can be used to sleuth out the scene of a computer crime. In this chapter, we'll discuss key elements of computer forensics and explore some of the tools used to perform these investigations. This chapter is by no means meant to be a comprehensive discussion of the computer forensics field. There are many books and courses dedicated to this field, and you can find a number of resources on the Web for guidance. If forensics fascinates you, we encourage you to join online computer forensics groups such as Computer Forensics World (http://www.computerforensicsworld.com) or the Yahoo Mac Forensics group (http://tech.groups.yahoo.com/group/macos_forensics/) to learn more about computer crime investigation.

Incident Response

The first part of any discussion about forensics involves *incident response*. Incident response involves answering these basic questions: How will I as a home user or IT administrator deal with a break-in involving data theft? If someone broke into our file server tomorrow, copied all the data, and then reformatted our data drive, what would we do immediately following the break-in?

It is important to create a step-by-step plan to handle these types of situations. What immediate action is taken after the break-in is considered the incident response. The incident response plan is your blueprint to how you are going to handle a breach in data security. Much like keeping the phone numbers of the various medical and law enforcement agencies near the phone in case of emergency, the incident response plan should be developed and communicated to all persons involved in your IT security policies. Incident response time should also go hand in hand with any service-level agreements you may have with an IT support company (if you outsource your IT resources) to make sure there is an adequate response to the crime. The impact of the incident response depends on how quickly and efficiently steps are made to remedy the situation.

We've all seen crime dramas on television where the investigator wears gloves when handling evidence at the scene of a crime. Their bare fingerprints can damage the evidence. The same is true when mounting a drive. Any data that is written to it is like taking the gloves off; it can damage the evidence. You should always disable *disk arbitration*, or the ability of your system to automatically mount a drive, unless you are using a write blocker.

Disk arbitration is a background process, or daemon, that handles mounting drives as they are attached to the system. You can also disable the disk arbitration daemon to tell the system not to mount drives as they're attached to the system. To do so, move the file /System/Library/ LaunchDaemons/com.apple.diskarbitrationd.plist to another directory such as the desktop. Once the file is renamed, reboot the system. When the system comes back online, then it will no longer automatically mount volumes. To mount a drive, you will be required to use the mount command, a forensic software tool, or Disk Utility.

Write blocking, or the halting of writing data to a drive, is key to establishing a chain of custody. In fact, you can purchase a write-blocking device known as a *write blocker* to stop data from being written to the drive. These devices allow the system to communicate to a drive but will stop any data from actually being written to it. Write blockers are built by a variety of vendors, including BlackBag Technologies, Wiebetech, and UltraBlock.

MacForensicsLab

AccessData's Forensics Toolkit (FTK) and Guidance Software's EnCase are two of the predominantly used packages for digital forensics in law enforcement today. However, they are not natively installable on the Mac platform; therefore, we will concentrate on SubRosaSoft's MacForensicsLab, which is native to the Mac platform and has many of the same features as other non-Mac native apps. It is the best Mac-native solution for forensics on the market today.

■Note MacForensicsLab can run on Windows and Linux as well.

MacForensicsLab automates many aspects of the acquisition, analysis, auditing and reporting of digital forensics. The techniques we will be describing here should lay the framework for any forensics software you may choose to use, because these techniques are standard techniques used in the digital forensics field.

Installing MacForensicsLab

In this section, we'll show how to set up and use MacForensicsLab to write block your system. When you first run the MacForensicsLab software, you will be asked to set up the case database. This is where all the information on each of your cases will reside. A *case* is each investigation that you will perform. This could be each system that you take in, or this could be a number of systems that have related information. The database for this example will reside in a local file; however, if there are multiple users, we would likely choose to use a MySQL or REAL SQL database server to store our data. To set up the local file during the initial install process, click the Local File option below the Database toolbar item (see Figure 16-1).

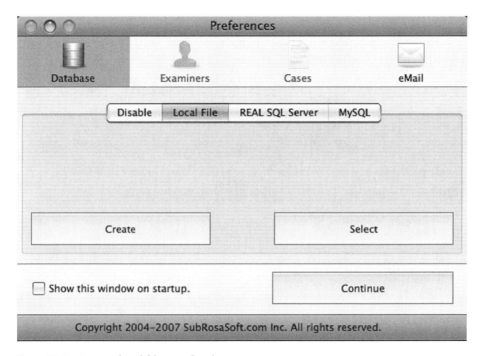

Figure 16-1. *Using a local file as a database*

■ **Note** You can use MacForensicsLab without using a database, but it will not track your actions, which is important to protect your chain of evidence.

Next, click Create, and indicate where the file should be located. Once you have browsed to the appropriate location (see Figure 16-2), then click the Save button. This will take you back to the Preferences screen.

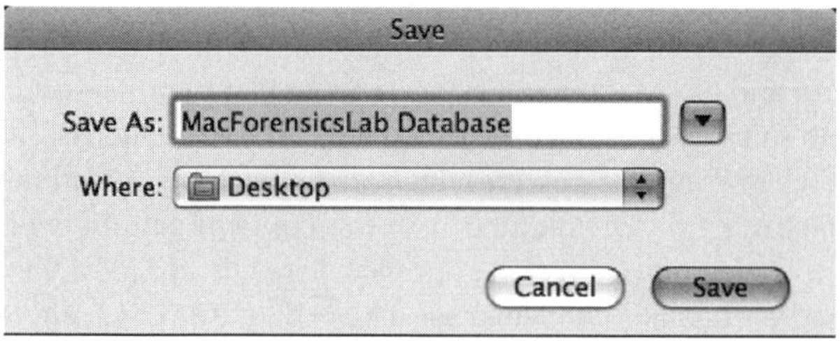

Figure 16-2. *Creating a database*

Once you have created your database, you will want to set up the *examiners*, which are the users who will be investigating the case. To add an examiner, click the Examiners icon in the menu bar and then click the + sign (see Figure 16-3).

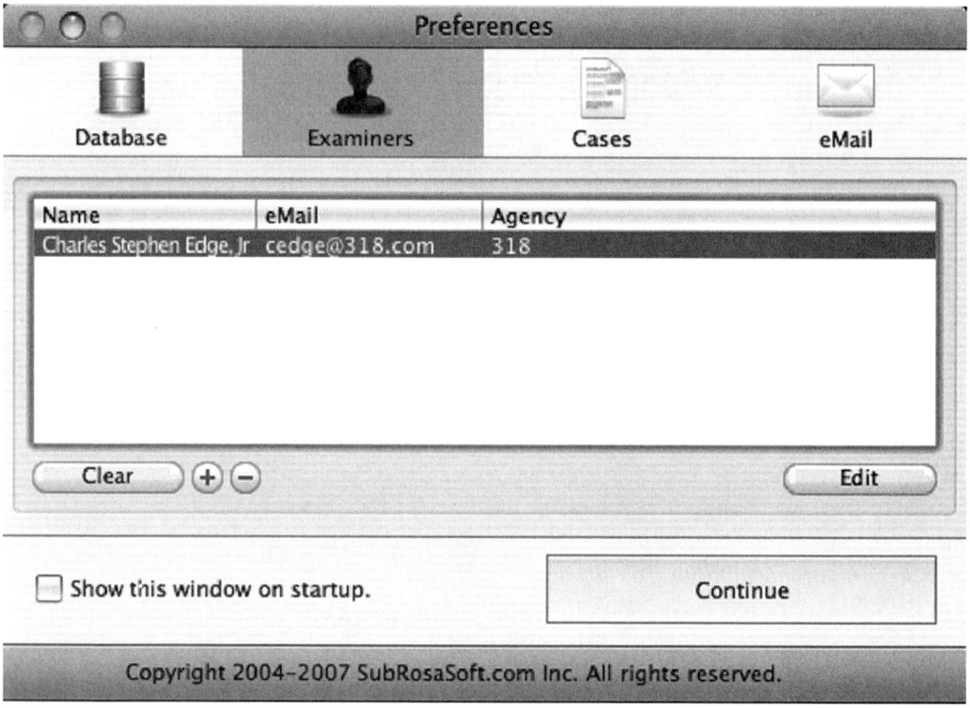

Figure 16-3. *The Examiners screen*

From here, a default user will be added (see Figure 16-4). If it is just one person, you can simply edit the default user. Add their user's name, e-mail address, phone number, and agency. You can also add an image to the user, which can later be used by reports from this screen. When you are satisfied with the information for the user, click the Save button.

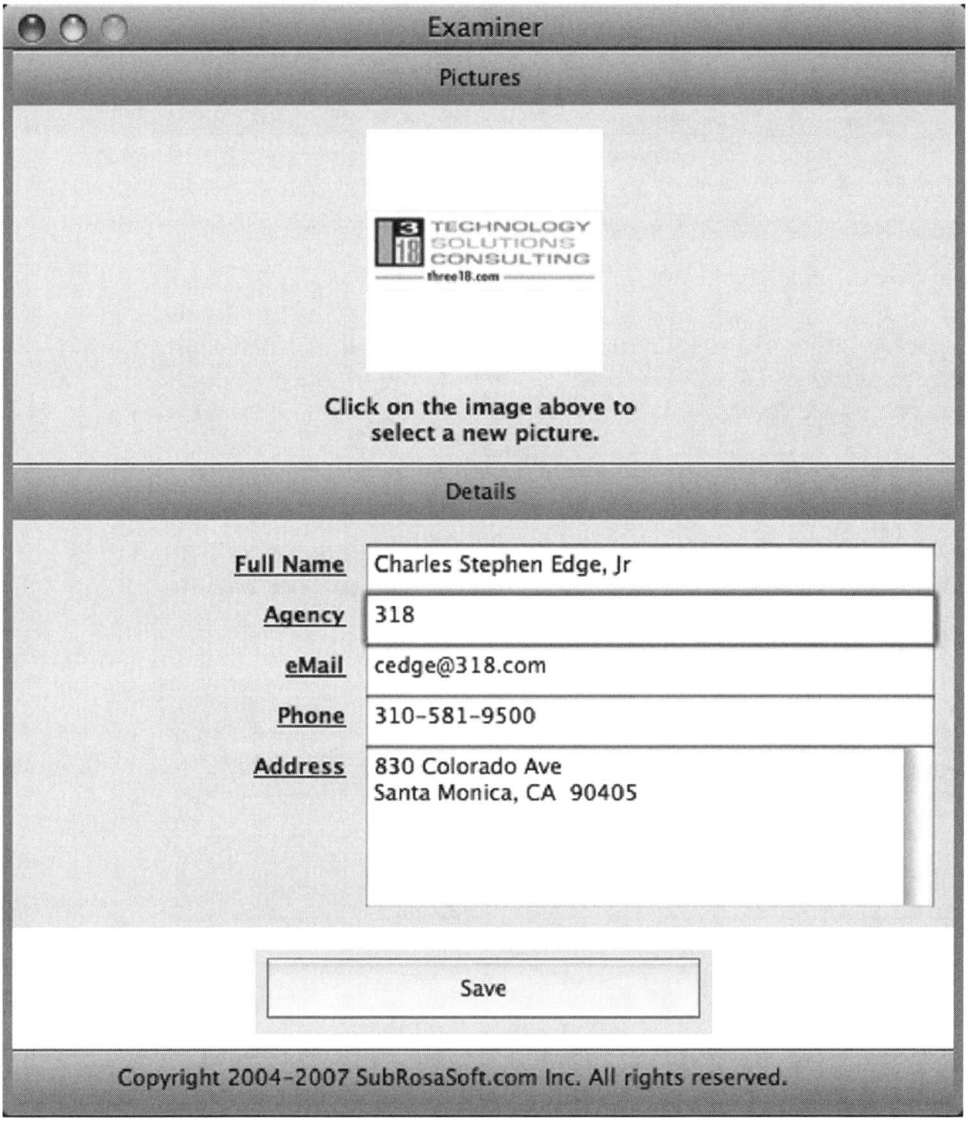

Figure 16-4. *Creating an examiner*

Once you are satisfied with the examiners you have created, you will want to set up your first case. Click the Cases button in the toolbar, and click the + sign to create a case for the investigation you will be conducting (see Figure 16-5).

For this test case, we'll call the investigation "whereswaldo." At the new screen, enter **whereswaldo** and any pertinent description of what is involved with this case (see Figure 16-6).

Figure 16-5. *The Cases screen*

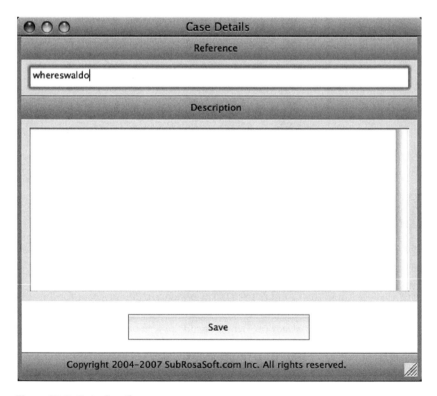

Figure 16-6. *Case details*

Once you have completed setting up the case, then click the eMail button in the toolbar. This is where you will set up e-mail updates to alert you as to the progress of the software. E-mail updates can be extremely helpful, especially because large hard drives can take hours to examine during the acquisition process. Here, enter the required information needed to send e-mail updates through your mail server, and click the Continue button (see Figure 16-7).

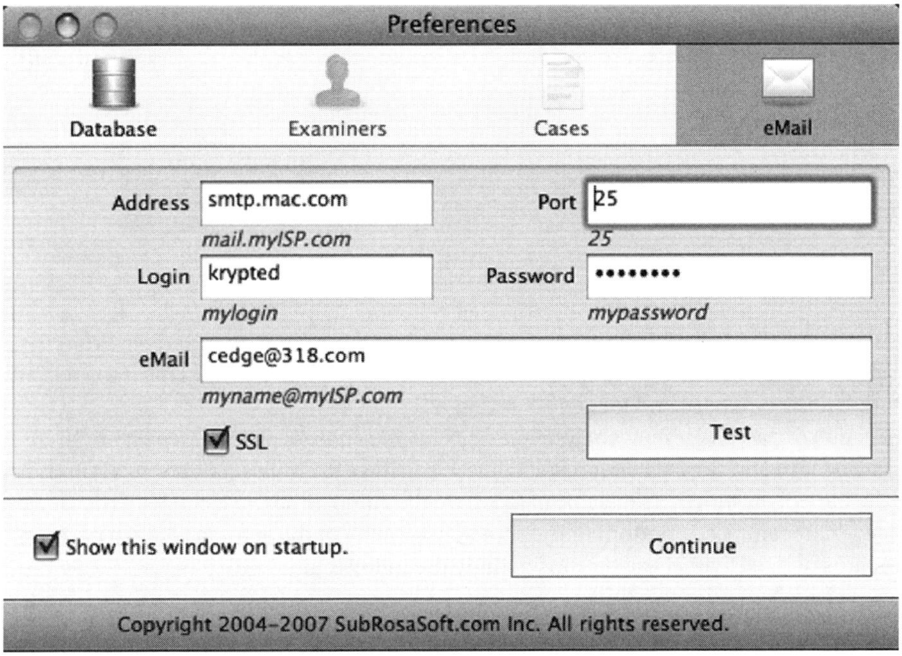

Figure 16-7. *E-mail setup*

Using MacForensicsLab

Once you have completed the setup process, it is time to start investigating the evidence. Before you can investigate the workstation, you need to create an image of the unaltered evidence in order to keep it from appearing that it was tampered with and that evidence was possibly planted. When you open the software for the first time, you will be prompted to disable disk arbitration. For imaging workstations, always disable disk arbitration (see Figure 16-8) unless you are using a hardware write blocker, as described in the "Incident Response" section of this chapter.

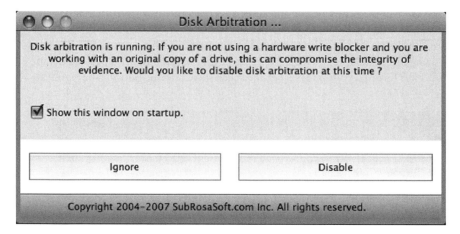

Figure 16-8. *Disk arbitration setup*

After setting up the disk arbitration status, you will be taken to the main screen. From here you can select a drive and see the statistics for the volume (see Figure 16-9). This information will be stored in the database and tagged accordingly.

Each section of the screen shows a different aspect of the analysis process (see Figure 16-9). Devices are displayed on the Device screen. A device can have multiple volumes, or at times no volume. The file screen shows critical information on the volume that is selected on the Device screen. The toolbar along the bottom of the screen lists many of the actions you can perform, given the status of the drive. These options include the following:

Acquire: Creates a forensic image of the system

Search: Searches a volume for a narrow selection of data

Analyze: Analyzes files in their raw format, sector by sector or byte by byte

Salvage: Retrieves deleted files

Browse: Browses a file system

Audit: Performs an automated review of assets

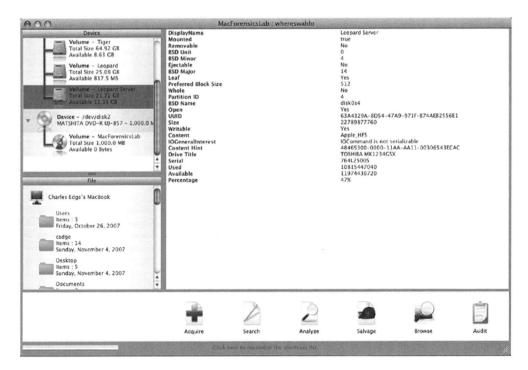

Figure 16-9. *The main MacForensicsLab screen*

Image Acquisition

At this point, you can move forward with acquiring your first drive image. When acquiring an image, it is important to keep in mind what type of image you will be acquiring. If you are building an image of a live system, as is often the case with a server or a system that has not been turned off yet and is running MacForensicsLab from the DVD, you will typically want to perform what is known as a *smeared image*. Images that are created from live media and not frozen in time are referred to as a *smear*. If you were to use a smeared image and the case were to go to court, then you would need to defend the choice in court.

A different option is to create a *golden master*, or a second unaltered copy of the data in case the original physical media the data is captured from becomes compromised. Most forensics investigators today will maintain a golden master at all times; however, if you are imaging a system solely for the purpose of sending it to someone else for analyzing, then you probably will keep only the original media.

MacForensicsLab also has the ability to split an image into segments. This is a nice option if you plan on providing a copy of your image on optical media such as CD or DVD to another party.

A checksum is a computed value based on the contents of a packet at the packet's destination. The receiving system computes a new checksum based on the data and compares it with the one sent with the packet. The Packet Size feature of MacForensicsLab allows you to assign a size for each block of data that will be checksummed.

To acquire an image, click the volume or disk you want to acquire, and set the options for the imaging process (see Figure 16-10). Once you are satisfied with all your choices, click the Acquire button to move to the next screen.

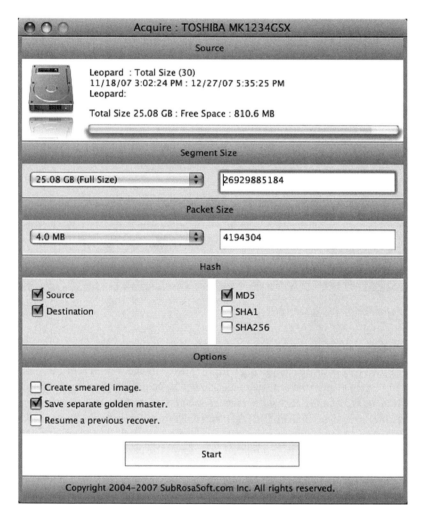

Figure 16-10. *Acquire screen*

Once you click the Start button, the system will ask you where you want to save your image. At the Save dialog box (see Figure 16-11), browse to the location to store the image, and click the Acquire button.

Note Before you start imaging, verify that there is enough hard drive space on the target volume.

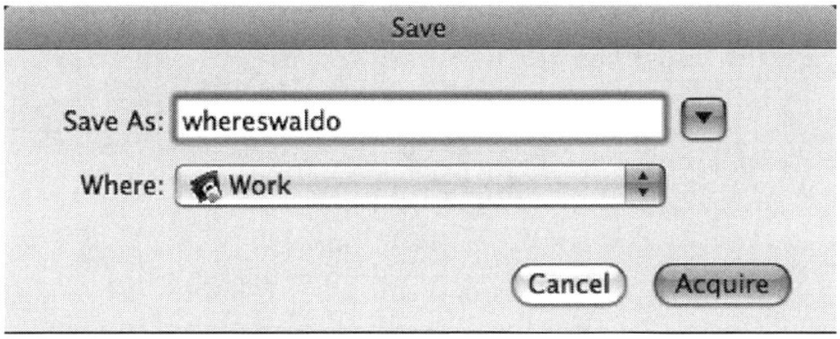

Figure 16-11. *Saving the database*

Analysis

Once you have acquired the image, you will be ready to begin analysis of the data. Many forensics professionals will analyze data manually, looking for files throughout the system that they know will contain crucial information. To browse the file system manually, click the disk in the Device portion of the MacForensicsLab screen, and double-click the folder you want to browse through in the File portion of the screen (see Figure 16-12).

Figure 16-12. *Browsing drive contents*

You can now simply browse to a file and double-click it. This will open the Analyze screen for that file (see Figure 16-13). The Hex Content tab of this screen will show you the raw data that makes up the file. The Native tab will show you how the file should look to the system (for example an image file will appear on the Native tab as the image).

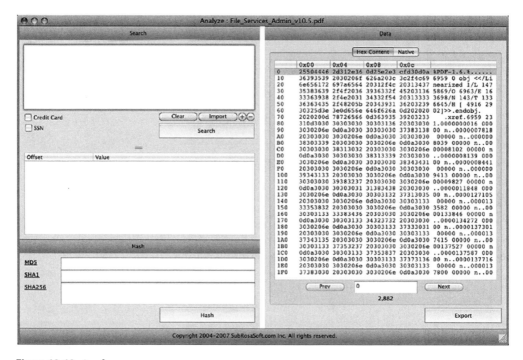

Figure 16-13. *Analyze*

Another way to conduct analysis is to search for files and then view them. This can be espe-
cially helpful if you are looking for all the files on a disk that are of a certain type, such as images.
For example, if you wanted to search a drive for all the Adobe EPS or PSD files, you would click
Search on the MacForensicsLab toolbar. This opens the Search window (see Figure 16-14).
From the Search window you can use the Filters section to add the file extensions for the appli-
cation file types you are looking for. In this case, you would enter **.eps** and **.psd** to look for these
Adobe files.

In addition to finding files with certain names, you can search for files by content. This will
search the contents of all files and display any with the contents that are indicated. You can
also use the Credit Card and SSN check boxes to have the system search for credit card numbers
and Social Security numbers.

The options on the right side of the Search window deal with how you want to manage the
search results. The Browse Results check box will allow you to see a listing of all files found that
match your search criteria. The Bookmark check box will bookmark all files discovered by
the search in the Active Cases bookmarks. The Hash option allows you to establish a chain of
custody on all files discovered by calculating a hash value for them and adding them into the
case database.

Once you are satisfied with your search criteria, click the Search button toward the bottom
of the screen, and wait for the search to complete.

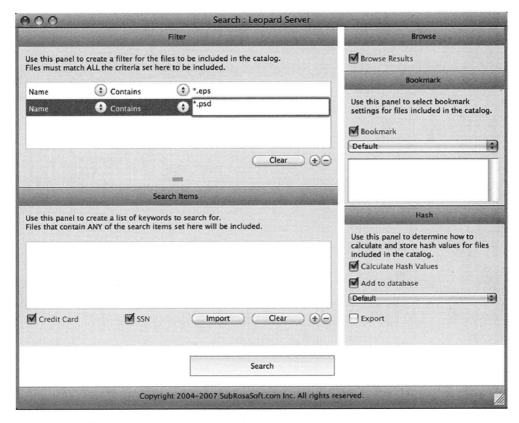

Figure 16-14. *The Search window*

Salvage

If you do not find the file you are looking for using the Search feature, the Salvage feature of MacForensicsLab can be another place to find what you want. The Salvage feature will look through free space and attempt to find any files that have been deleted, even if the trash has been emptied. This feature is not very effective if a Secure Empty Trash operation has been performed, but it can be quite effective for finding files not emptied from a Secure Trash Empty command. From the main MacForensicsLab screen, click a drive, and select the Salvage button. This opens the Salvage screen (see Figure 16-15).

You can select two options in the Salvage window: Free Space Only and Search for Embedded Files. The Free Space Only check box will limit the search to free space on the hard drive or to space that was possibly marked as free when a Secure Empty Trash operation has occurred but has not yet been overwritten by files. The Search for Embedded Files check box will attempt to search within other files for files matching your search criteria.

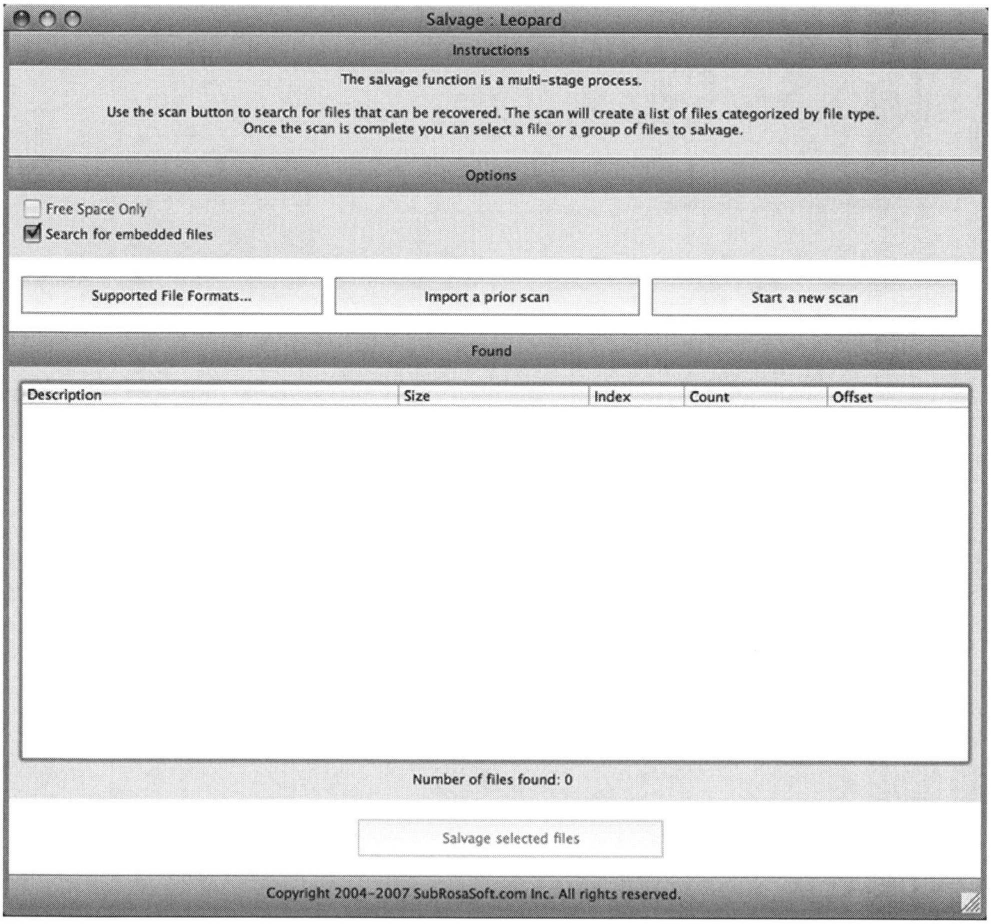

Figure 16-15. *The Salvage window*

To define the types of files you want the Salvage operation to find, click the Supported File Formats button. This opens the File Types to Include window (see Figure 16-16). From here, hold down the Command key and select all the file types you want to find. To continue with the example from the Search section, we'll look for all Adobe files. Next, click Continue and then click the Salvage selected files button from the Salvage window.

Figure 16-16. *The File Types to Include screen*

Once the Salvage operation is complete, you will see a listing of all salvaged files in the Found screen (see Figure 16-17). Salvaged files will lose their names but not their contents in this process.

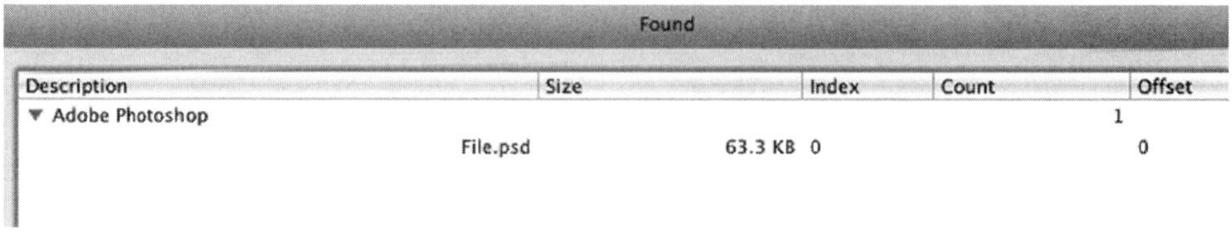

Figure 16-17. *The Found screen with the results*

Other applications can perform salvage operations, such as FileSalvage (also by SubRosaSoft), MacDataRecovery, and, our favorite, Data Rescue II from ProSoft. Although these tools are helpful, it is important to keep as much information logged about the case in the MacForensicsLab case notes as possible. Whenever possible, it is preferable to use a forensics tool before using any nonforensics tools to keep all the actions logged, preventing future allegations of evidence tampering.

Performing an Audit

Another aspect of reviewing a drive, and one of the most powerful and timesaving features of MacForensicsLab, is the Audit feature. Clicking the Audit button on the MacForensicsLab screen opens a listing of all the users who have home folders on the drive you are auditing. When you click the Audit button (see Figure 16-18), you will see information that the system has found on that particular user. The information includes folders, preferences, Address Book entries, cookies, Safari bookmarks, Safari history, iChat sessions, e-mails, and e-mail attachments.

Figure 16-18. *Audit screen: cookies*

The audit feature is not foolproof, but it does provide a quick review of some of the most critical aspects of an investigation without having to know details of the structure of user folders and where old copies of information can be stored.

Reviewing the Case

Once you have found the information you are looking for and think you have compiled the evidence you are looking to compile, then it is a good idea to have someone else review the case for any omissions or errors. One effective way to review a case is to use the chronology of events as recorded on the drive to verify that all the actions taken have the correct checksums. These time records are crucial for the case to stand up in a court of law, and they can rule out any possibility that evidence was contaminated by foreign files or overwrites.

To view the chronology of a case, click Window and then click Database. At the database screen you will see a Chronology tab. If you click the Chronology tab, you will be able to trace each step an auditor took on a case, click by click (see Figure 16-19).

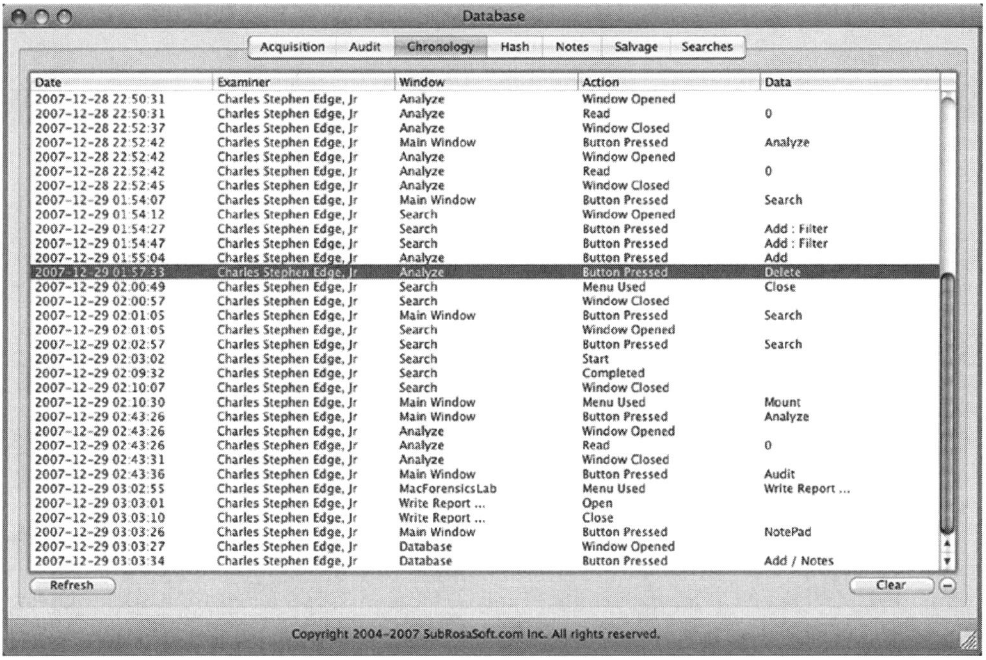

Figure 16-19. *Reviewing chronology*

Reporting

Once you are comfortable that the work will stand up under scrutiny, then you can move on to building a report. You can use the report to give an overview of the case details to another person within your organization for review. You can access the reporting mechanism of MacForensicsLab using the Write Report option under the File menu. When the Report screen opens, you can select which type of information to include in the report (see Figure 16-20) by clicking the appropriate check boxes. Once you are satisfied with the report contents, click the Start button to run the report.

Figure 16-20. *Report settings*

When the report is finished running, you will be provided with content that can be used to present evidence to another party and eventually, if need be, to be used in a trial.

Other GUI Tools for Forensic Analysis

MacLockPick is a tool from SubRosaSoft that allows an investigator to grab contacts, logs, and other data from a sleeping system in a covert manner. MacLockPick takes advantage of the fact that the default state of the Apple Keychain is open, and it uses the settings files of commonly used programs to keep track of contacts, Internet histories, passwords, and logs.

A database of the tracked information is placed on the MacLockPick flash drive. This database can then be read by the log readers in Microsoft Windows, Linux, or Apple Mac OS X computers. MacLockPick also includes a log reader for accessing the data from other platforms. MacLockPick functions in a forensically safe manner and will never write to the disk or device being investigated.

MacQuisition is a tool also developed by BlackBag Technologies. MacQuisition was designed to make the process of acquiring a forensic image simple. MacQuisition is a bootable Mac OS X DVD used to boot a suspect computer and acquire a forensic image, saving it either to a locally mounted external drive or to a network storage location.

MacQuisition doesn't provide tools for analyzing an image. It does, however, provide a simple method for acquiring that image. This can be a far better fit than a more complicated package such as MacForensicsLab for first responders who simply need to acquire the image and do not need to perform any further processing of those images.

Command-Line Tools for Forensic Analysis

A wide variety of command-line tools are included with Leopard that can be used with forensic investigations and primarily the acquisition of forensic images.

You can use the mount command to mount connected disks to a forensic system. To mount a system as read-only for inspection, you can use the mount -r command. Once the disk is mounted, you will typically want to use dd on the drive.

The dd command is a method for creating disk images that can be used for acquiring a forensic disk image. The dd command is preferred over Disk Utility because it can create a disk image without being required to actually mount a drive, which, as discussed, can potentially contaminate the drive for future use as evidence. The dd command can also split disk images into segments, allowing you to burn the image to optical media or place it onto hard drives to present evidence to another party for their own forensic investigation.

Once the disk has been imaged, you can move on to building a hash of the drive using the openssl command. Be aware, though, that unless you know exactly what you are doing with the command-line tools, you run the risk of contaminating your evidence. This is one instance where the danger of breaking your chain of custody may outweigh the cost of purchasing a package like MacForensicsLab.

APPENDIX A

∎∎∎

Xsan Security

Xsan is Apple software that allows you to virtualize your hard drive environment. Using Xsan, you can take any Fibre Channel storage device (often referred to as a *target*) and connect Mac systems to it in a highly configurable manner. This allows multiple users to access data striped across a large amount of data (let's just say five Xserve RAIDs' worth) as though they're one volume. Each user can then access data at speeds of up to 4Gbps. The Xsan software then ties the environment together.

Uses for Xsan include web farms, file-sharing farms, high-definition video environments, and multiuser/high-bandwidth creative environments.

The Xsan software is actually based on software from ADIC (now Quantum) called StorNext. The StorNext software is similar to Xsan, and most Xsan code is taken from StorNext. Because it isn't Apple-only, StorNext can be used to support Macs, Windows, and *nix communications over a fast Fibre Channel environment. Not all commands and features have been ported by Apple. But when looking to secure Xsan, you may find that there are specific features of StorNext that you want to use. Because Xsan is based on StorNext, many of the features are built into the Xsan software but might not be accessible through Xsan Admin. To begin unlocking some of the hidden features of Xsan, you will need to dip into the command line to access the StorNext features.

Xsan configuration files are stored in the `/Library/Filesystems/Xsan/Config` directory. The binaries are in the `bin` directory at the same place in the tree as the `Config` directory. The `Config` directory contains information about the structure of the SAN and any volumes on the SAN. The `Config` directory should not be world accessible, because it could be used to delete the entire SAN volume if all the copies were lost. One problem with this is that users who are admins of their local system can do things they shouldn't be able to do, by nature of being local and because Xsan appears to the local workstation as a local file system.

Commands to control Xsan are `cvlabel`, `cvadmin`, `cvfsck`, and `cvcp`. These commands are similar commands to some Unix commands, but they are specific to Xsan. Be wary of using any similar Unix commands that are not Xsan-specific (for example, you should never `fsck` the volume of Xsan).

Metadata

The metadata in an Xsan environment is like the master boot record of a hard drive. Metadata is stored on a dedicated Fibre Channel storage logical unit number (LUN). This metadata is a table containing the location to look on each LUN for various parts of files. Since the metadata contains the locations of all the files, it is important that it live on mirrored drives, without any risk of being lost.

Xsan storage is broken down into three parts:

LUNs: Logical segmentations of targets. LUNs are destinations for data. These are essentially RAIDs or parts of RAIDs.

Storage pools: A group of LUNs. Each client can write to multiple LUNs through a single storage pool.

Volumes: The actual logical data seen by clients.

Each SAN client requires full access to all LUNs in order to write data. The metadata is simply a pointer that tells the SAN where to write data and not a redirector of the data itself. If any of the LUNs that make up a storage pool cannot be seen through Fibre Channel by a metadata controller or a client, the storage pool reports "STRIPE GROUP DOWN," and Xsan will go down. For example, if you were to unplug the cable for one target, you would likely bring an entire Xsan environment down. Therefore, physical security becomes very important with Xsan environments.

The root user of any workstation that is connected through Fibre Channel to an Xsan environment can write directly to any LUN by writing data into /dev/<the location of the LUN in devs>. A common path might be /dev/rdisk4, which can be found in the Xsan labels for each LUN. If you write enough arbitrary data into the metadata LUN, then you will cause a volume to no longer become accessible. This can be dangerous, because once the Xsan environment is restarted, it will read an invalid amount of data on itself and, therefore, be unable to mount the volume. This is essentially a denial of service to the SAN that can be initiated by any client system that has a valid admin/root account. This is very dangerous, and there is no workaround for it, other than restricting access to administrative or root accounts on SAN clients.

Fibre Channel

Fibre Channel switching is like Ethernet switching. With Ethernet switching, you can *stack* two switches by using a special stacking cable. With Fibre Channel, the terminology is different, but the concept is the same. You can *cascade* two switches by *bonding* (sometimes referred to as *stacking*) their backplanes with a 10GB to 20GB connection. From a security perspective, one nice feature of a stacked environment is that you can perform access controls across multiple switches. But most environments use bonding in order to achieve very fast speeds between switches.

Affinities

Storage pools can be assigned an *affinity*. When data is moved to the affinity, space is allocated from a specific storage pool rather than in a round-robin fashion across all the storage pools. Affinity data can be restricted to specific LUNs. Access to affinities can be limited to certain groups.

You can use Xsan Admin to assign an affinity to a folder at the top level of a volume. However, to assign an affinity to a nested folder, use the cvmkdir command. For example:

```
cd /Library/Filesystems/Xsan/bin
```

```
sudo ./cvmkdir -k <affinity-name> <path-to-folder>
```

Protocol Issues

Windows clients can have different permissions. This gives the ACL more value. Each protocol is configured differently, so new files added to the SAN volume will have the same permissions, no matter how the specific services are configured.

Access control lists on Xsan can be very useful. To enable one, open Server Admin, and browse to the root of a volume. Click Sharing, and then click the All button. Next, click the root of an Xsan volume, and then click Enable Access Control Lists on This Volume. Next, configure the permissions that should be in the ACL box, and then click the Save button.

Data that is written to the Xsan volume will now have the permissions of the folder above it. ACL entries can easily be added using Workgroup Manager. This can be far easier than using the default, umask. Umask isn't implemented with file copies, so ACLs can help force permissions.

Quotas

Quotas are also part of Xsan: you can set hard and soft quotas for every user on the Xsan. A *quota* is the amount of space a user can take up on the SAN. A *soft quota* lets the user continue to save files but warns them that they are over their limit. When they reach the *hard quota*, they will not be able to save any more data until the SAN administrator gives them more space or they delete some files. When users near their quotas, they will be alerted.

Other SAN Solutions

Xsan is a fast and fairly straightforward SAN product. It does not come with backup/snapshots, it is not as fault tolerant as it should be, and it is a little too latent for certain applications (such as Pro Tools by Digidesign).

Other SAN providers include EMC, Network Appliance, Inc (NetApp), and LeftHand Networks. These can be made to work on the Mac OS X platform, although many do not work without using special software. For example, the Studio Network Solutions software is used to mount LUNs from EMC targets. However, most of these do not offer a clustered file system for the Mac. In fact, most are filers (NAS heads) when they mount on a Mac. EMC CX (Clarrion) can be used as LUNs for Xsan or can be used to mount an HFS+ volume as read for many but only write for one, meaning it is not a true clustered file system in that case.

Vmirror by Vicom Systems gives you the ability to mirror LUNs. This gives redundancy to losing a RAID. If a RAID is lost in an Xsan environment, the whole SAN will be lost. Vmirror can stop this from happening.

Cloverleaf by Cloverleaf Communications gives the ability to snapshot Xsan and has some other benefits such as more granular control over virtualization and the ability to combine the presentation of various forms of storage to a wide variety of devices.

APPENDIX B

■ ■ ■

InfoSec Acceptable Use Policy

■**Note** Created by or for the SANS Institute. Feel free to modify or use for your organization. If you have a policy to contribute, please send e-mail to stephen@sans.edu.

1.0 Overview

InfoSec's intentions for publishing an Acceptable Use Policy are not to impose restrictions that are contrary to <Company Name>'s established culture of openness, trust and integrity. InfoSec is committed to protecting <Company Name>'s employees, partners and the company from illegal or damaging actions by individuals, either knowingly or unknowingly.

Internet/Intranet/Extranet-related systems, including but not limited to computer equipment, software, operating systems, storage media, network accounts providing electronic mail, WWW browsing, and FTP, are the property of <Company Name>. These systems are to be used for business purposes in serving the interests of the company, and of our clients and customers in the course of normal operations. Please review Human Resources policies for further details.

Effective security is a team effort involving the participation and support of every <Company Name> employee and affiliate who deals with information and/or information systems. It is the responsibility of every computer user to know these guidelines, and to conduct their activities accordingly.

2.0 Purpose

The purpose of this policy is to outline the acceptable use of computer equipment at <Company Name>.

These rules are in place to protect the employee and <Company Name>. Inappropriate use exposes <Company Name> to risks including virus attacks, compromise of network systems and services, and legal issues.

3.0 Scope

This policy applies to employees, contractors, consultants, temporaries, and other workers at <Company Name>, including all personnel affiliated with third parties. This policy applies to all equipment that is owned or leased by <Company Name>.

4.0 Policy

4.1 General Use and Ownership

1. While <Company Name>'s network administration desires to provide a reasonable level of privacy, users should be aware that the data they create on the corporate systems remains the property of <Company Name>. Because of the need to protect <Company Name>'s network, management cannot guarantee the confidentiality of information stored on any network device belonging to <Company Name>.

2. Employees are responsible for exercising good judgment regarding the reasonableness of personal use. Individual departments are responsible for creating guidelines concerning personal use of Internet/Intranet/Extranet systems. In the absence of such policies, employees should be guided by departmental policies on personal use, and if there is any uncertainty, employees should consult their supervisor or manager.

3. InfoSec recommends that any information that users consider sensitive or vulnerable be encrypted. For guidelines on information classification, see InfoSec's Information Sensitivity Policy. For guidelines on encrypting email and documents, go to InfoSec's Awareness Initiative.

4. For security and network maintenance purposes, authorized individuals within <Company Name> may monitor equipment, systems and network traffic at any time, per InfoSec's Audit Policy.

5. <Company Name> reserves the right to audit networks and systems on a periodic basis to ensure compliance with this policy.

4.2 Security and Proprietary Information

1. The user interface for information contained on Internet/Intranet/Extranet-related systems should be classified as either confidential or not confidential, as defined by corporate confidentiality guidelines, details of which can be found in Human Resources policies. Examples of confidential information include but are not limited to: company private, corporate strategies, competitor sensitive, trade secrets, specifications, customer lists, and research data. Employees should take all necessary steps to prevent unauthorized access to this information.

2. Keep passwords secure and do not share accounts. Authorized users are responsible for the security of their passwords and accounts. System level passwords should be changed quarterly, user level passwords should be changed every six months.

3. All PCs, laptops and workstations should be secured with a password-protected screensaver with the automatic activation feature set at 10 minutes or less, or by logging-off (control-alt-delete for Win2K users) when the host will be unattended.

4. Use encryption of information in compliance with InfoSec's Acceptable Encryption Use policy.

5. Because information contained on portable computers is especially vulnerable, special care should be exercised. Protect laptops in accordance with the "Laptop Security Tips".

6. Postings by employees from a <Company Name> email address to newsgroups should contain a disclaimer stating that the opinions expressed are strictly their own and not necessarily those of <Company Name>, unless posting is in the course of business duties.

7. All hosts used by the employee that are connected to the <Company Name> Internet/Intranet/Extranet, whether owned by the employee or <Company Name>, shall be continually executing approved virus-scanning software with a current virus database, unless overridden by departmental or group policy.

8. Employees must use extreme caution when opening e-mail attachments received from unknown senders, which may contain viruses, e-mail bombs, or Trojan horse code.

4.3 Unacceptable Use

The following activities are, in general, prohibited. Employees may be exempted from these restrictions during the course of their legitimate job responsibilities (e.g., systems administration staff may have a need to disable the network access of a host if that host is disrupting production services). Under no circumstances is an employee of <Company Name> authorized to engage in any activity that is illegal under local, state, federal or international law while utilizing <Company Name>-owned resources.

The lists below are by no means exhaustive, but attempt to provide a framework for activities, which fall into the category of unacceptable use.

System and Network Activities

The following activities are strictly prohibited, with no exceptions:

1. Violations of the rights of any person or company protected by copyright, trade secret, patent or other intellectual property, or similar laws or regulations, including, but not limited to, the installation or distribution of "pirated" or other software products that are not appropriately licensed for use by <Company Name>.

2. Unauthorized copying of copyrighted material including, but not limited to, digitization and distribution of photographs from magazines, books or other copyrighted sources, copyrighted music, and the installation of any copyrighted software for which <Company Name> or the end user does not have an active license is strictly prohibited.

3. Exporting software, technical information, encryption software or technology, in violation of international or regional export control laws, is illegal. The appropriate management should be consulted prior to export of any material that is in question.

4. Introduction of malicious programs into the network or server (e.g., viruses, worms, Trojan horses, email bombs, etc.).

5. Revealing your account password to others or allowing use of your account by others. This includes family and other household members when work is being done at home.

6. Using a <Company Name> computing asset to actively engage in procuring or trans-mitting material that is in violation of sexual harassment or hostile workplace laws in the user's local jurisdiction.

7. Making fraudulent offers of products, items, or services originating from any <Company Name> account.

8. Making statements about warranty, expressly or implied, unless it is a part of normal job duties.

9. Effecting security breaches or disruptions of network communication. Security breaches include, but are not limited to, accessing data of which the employee is not an intended recipient or logging into a server or account that the employee is not expressly authorized to access, unless these duties are within the scope of regular duties. For purposes of this section, "disruption" includes, but is not limited to, network sniffing, pinged floods, packet spoofing, denial of service, and forged routing information for malicious purposes.

10. Port scanning or security scanning is expressly prohibited unless prior notification to InfoSec is made.

11. Executing any form of network monitoring which will intercept data not intended for the employee's host, unless this activity is a part of the employee's normal job/duty.

12. Circumventing user authentication or security of any host, network or account.

13. Interfering with or denying service to any user other than the employee's host (for example, a denial of service attack).

14. Using any program/script/command, or sending messages of any kind, with the intent to interfere with, or disable, a user's terminal session, via any means, locally or via the Internet/Intranet/Extranet.

15. Providing information about, or lists of, <Company Name> employees to parties outside <Company Name>.

Email and Communications Activities

1. Sending unsolicited email messages, including the sending of "junk mail" or other advertising material to individuals who did not specifically request such material (email spam).

2. Any form of harassment via email, telephone or paging, whether through language, frequency, or size of messages.

3. Unauthorized use, or forging, of email header information.

4. Solicitation of email for any other email address, other than that of the poster's account, with the intent to harass or to collect replies.

5. Creating or forwarding "chain letters", "Ponzi" or other "pyramid" schemes of any type.

6. Use of unsolicited email originating from within <Company Name>'s networks of other Internet/Intranet/Extranet service providers on behalf of, or to advertise, any service hosted by <Company Name> or connected via <Company Name>'s network.

7. Posting the same or similar non-business-related messages to large numbers of Usenet newsgroups (newsgroup spam).

4.4 Blogging

1. Blogging by employees, whether using <Company Name>'s property and systems or personal computer systems, is also subject to the terms and restrictions set forth in this Policy. Limited and occasional use of <Company Name>'s systems to engage in blogging is acceptable, provided that it is done in a professional and responsible manner, does not otherwise violate <Company Name>'s policy, is not detrimental to <Company Name>'s best interests, and does not interfere with an employee's regular work duties. Blogging from <Company Name>'s systems is also subject to monitoring.

2. <Company Name>'s Confidential Information policy also applies to blogging. As such, Employees are prohibited from revealing any <Company> confidential or proprietary information, trade secrets or any other material covered by <Company>'s Confidential Information policy when engaged in blogging.

3. Employees shall not engage in any blogging that may harm or tarnish the image, reputation and/or goodwill of <Company Name> and/or any of its employees. Employees are also prohibited from making any discriminatory, disparaging, defamatory or harassing comments when blogging or otherwise engaging in any conduct prohibited by <Company Name>'s Non-Discrimination and Anti-Harassment policy.

4. Employees may also not attribute personal statements, opinions or beliefs to <Company Name> when engaged in blogging. If an employee is expressing his or her beliefs and/or opinions in blogs, the employee may not, expressly or implicitly, represent themselves as an employee or representative of <Company Name>. Employees assume any and all risk associated with blogging.

5. Apart from following all laws pertaining to the handling and disclosure of copyrighted or export controlled materials, <Company Name>'s trademarks, logos and any other <Company Name> intellectual property may also not be used in connection with any blogging activity

5.0 Enforcement

Any employee found to have violated this policy may be subject to disciplinary action, up to and including termination of employment.

6.0 Definitions

Term Definition

Blogging Writing a blog. A blog (short for weblog) is a personal online journal that is frequently updated and intended for general public consumption.

Spam Unauthorized and/or unsolicited electronic mass mailings.

7.0 Revision History

APPENDIX C

■ ■ ■

Secure Development

Apple has designed its security around the Common Data Security Architecture (CDSA) model, developed by Intel. CDSA is a set of layered security services and a cryptographic framework that provide an interoperable, cross-platform infrastructure for creating security-enabled applications for client-server environments. CDSA covers the essential components to equip applications with security services that provide cryptography, certificate management, trust policy management, and key recovery.

CDSA defines a horizontal, four-layer architecture:

- It includes applications such as Mail, Safari, iChat, Disk Utility, Keychain Access, and other applications developed by Apple.

- It includes layered services and middleware including the APIs used by the applications listed in the previous bullet. An *application programming interface* (API) is a set of definitions of the ways one piece of computer software communicates with another. It is a method of achieving abstraction, usually (but not necessarily) between lower-level and higher-level software. These APIs include interfaces for keychains, file signing, SSL, and certificate management.

- The Common Security Services Manager (CSSM) infrastructure's Cryptographic Services Manager has functions to create and verify digital signatures, generate cryptographic keys, and create cryptographic hashes.

- Security service provider modules, also known as *add-in modules*, are third-party and nonapplication items built using the APIs in the second layer of the CDSA. This allows for extensibility to the framework.

The CDSA is an open source framework, allowing it to closely parallel many of Apple's other initiatives for security and development and receive peer review from a larger audience than just Apple users. CDSA allows Apple and the community of third-party developers to architect software in a secure manner while still supporting the network features required for the modern applications of today and tomorrow. For more information on the CDSA model, see the Intel CDSA site at `http://www.intel.com/ial/security`.

APPENDIX D

■■■

Introduction to Cryptography

Cryptology is derived from the Greek words *kryptos*, which means "hidden," and *grafein*, which means "to write." Through history, *cryptography* has meant the process of concealing the contents of a message from all except those who know the key. Cryptography is used to protect e-mail messages, credit card information, and corporate data. Cryptography has been used for centuries to hide messages sent through means where they might be intercepted, such as the Internet.

A wide variety of cryptographic techniques are in use with computers. They are typically provided for one of two reasons: to protect data on the computer or to protect data as it is being transferred.

Most cryptographic techniques for submitting data over the Internet rely heavily on the exchange of keys.

Symmetric-key cryptography refers to encryption methods where both senders and receivers of data share the same key and data is encrypted and decrypted with algorithms based on those keys. The modern study of symmetric-key ciphers revolves around block ciphers and stream ciphers and how these ciphers are applied.

Block ciphers take a block of plain text and a key and then output a block of cipher text of the same size. DES and AES are block ciphers. AES, also called Rijndael, is a designated cryptographic standard by the U.S. government. AES usually uses a key size of 128, 192, or 256 bits. DES is no longer an approved method of encryption. Triple-DES, its variant, remains popular. Triple-DES uses three 56-bit DES keys and is used across a wide range of applications from ATM encryption to e-mail privacy and secure remote access. Many other block ciphers have been designed and released, with considerable variation in quality.

Stream ciphers create an arbitrarily long stream of key material, which is combined with plain text bit by bit or character by character, somewhat like the one-time pad encryption technique. In a stream cipher, the output stream is based on an internal state, which changes as the cipher operates. That state's change is controlled by the key and, in some stream ciphers, by the plain-text stream as well. RC4 is an example of a well-known stream cipher.

Cryptographic hash functions do not use keys but take data and output a short, fixed-length hash in a one-way function. For good hashing algorithms, collisions (two plain texts that produce the same hash) are extremely difficult to find, although they do occur.

Symmetric-key cryptosystems typically use the same key for encryption and decryption. A disadvantage of symmetric ciphers is that a complicated key management system is necessary to use them securely. Each distinct pair of communicating parties must share a different key. The number of keys required increases with the number of network members. This requires very complex key management schemes in large networks. It is also difficult to establish a secret key exchange between two communicating parties when a secure channel doesn't already exist between them.

Whitfield Diffie and Martin Hellman are considered to be the inventors of *public-key cryptography*. They proposed the notion of public-key (also called *asymmetric-key*) cryptography in which two different but mathematically related keys are used: a public key and a private key. A public key system is constructed so that calculation of the private key is computationally infeasible from knowledge of the public key, even though they are necessarily related. Instead, both keys are generated secretly, as an interrelated pair.

In public-key cryptosystems, the public key may be freely distributed, while its paired private key must remain secret. The public key is typically used for encryption, while the private or secret key is used for decryption. Diffie and Hellman showed that public-key cryptography was possible by presenting the Diffie-Hellman key exchange protocol. Ronald Rivest, Adi Shamir, and Len Adleman invented RSA, another public-key system. Later, it became publicly known that asymmetric cryptography had been invented by James H. Ellis at GCHQ, a British intelligence organization, and that both the Diffie-Hellman and RSA algorithms had been previously developed. However, the truth is difficult to decipher in this regard.

Diffie-Hellman and RSA, in addition to being the first public examples of high quality public-key cryptosystems, are among the most widely used.

In addition to encryption, public-key cryptography can be used to implement digital signature schemes. *Digital signatures* are somewhat like ordinary signatures; they are easy for a user to produce but difficult for anyone else to forge. Digital signatures can also be permanently tied to the content of the message being signed because they cannot be "moved" from one document to another; any attempt would be detectable. In digital signature schemes, there are two algorithms: one for signing, in which a secret key is used to process the message (or a hash of the message or both), and one for verification, in which the matching public key is used with the message to check the validity of the signature. RSA and DSA are two of the most popular digital signature schemes. Digital signatures are central to the operation of public-key infrastructures and to many network security schemes (SSL/TLS, many VPNs, and so on). Digital signatures provide users with the ability to verify the integrity of the message, thus allowing for nonrepudiation of the communication.

Public-key algorithms are most often based on the computational complexity of "hard" problems, often from number theory. The hardness of RSA is related to the integer factorization problem, while Diffie-Hellman and DSA are related to the discrete logarithm problem. More recently, *elliptic-curve cryptography* has developed in which security is based on number theoretic problems involving elliptic curves. Because of the complexity of the underlying problems, most public-key algorithms involve operations such as modular multiplication and exponentiation, which are much more computationally expensive than the techniques used in most block ciphers, especially with typical key sizes. As a result, public-key cryptosystems are commonly "hybrid" systems, in which a fast symmetric-key encryption algorithm is used for the message itself, while the relevant symmetric key is sent with the message, but encrypted using a public-key algorithm. Hybrid signature schemes are often used, in which a cryptographic hash function is computed, and only the resulting hash is digitally signed.

Cryptography continues to move forward in an almost exponential manner. Although much of the cryptographic data in use today stems from the research done in the 1970s and earlier, new advances and refinements occur all the time. New techniques are emerging today that will change the shape of cryptography 10 to 20 years from now, making the keys, hashes, and algorithms we use today look like child's play. As data grows and computers get faster, though, it is important to have a basic understanding of some of the cryptographic standards you will run into on a regular basis.

Index

■Y

■Z

You Need the Companion eBook

We believe this Apress title will prove so indispensable that you'll want to carry it with you everywhere, which is why we are offering the companion eBook (in PDF format) for $10 to customers who purchase this book now. Convenient and fully searchable, the PDF version of any content-rich, page-heavy Apress book makes a valuable addition to your programming library. You can easily find and copy code—or perform examples by quickly toggling between instructions and the application. Even simultaneously tackling a donut, diet soda, and complex code becomes simplified with hands-free eBooks!

Once you purchase your book, getting the $10 companion eBook is simple:

❶ Visit **www.apress.com/promo/tendollars/**.

❷ Complete a basic registration form to receive a randomly generated question about this title.

❸ Answer the question correctly in 60 seconds, and you will receive a promotional code to redeem for the $10.00 eBook.

eBookshop

Apress®
THE EXPERT'S VOICE™

2855 TELEGRAPH AVENUE | SUITE 600 | BERKELEY, CA 94705

Offer valid through 10/08.